The History of Human Society

Edited and with introductions by
J. H. PLUMB
Fellow of Christ's College, Cambridge

This series will provide a picture of man's social life—accurate, vivid, readable, free from cosmic theories, concerned with the diversity of human experience, analytic yet evocative, and charged with that sense of reality which only the finest scholarship can create. Its aim will be twofold—to bring a full understanding of the societies described and to illustrate the growth of man's control over the physical universe.

PIONEER AMERICA

The History of Human Society

Edited and with an introduction by
J. H. PLUMB

Prehistoric Societies by Grahame Clark and Stuart Piggott (1965)
The Dutch Seaborne Empire: 1600–1800 by C. R. Boxer (1965)
The Spanish Seaborne Empire by J. H. Parry (1966)
Pioneer America by John R. Alden (1966)

Other volumes to be announced.

PIONEER AMERICA

by

JOHN R. ALDEN

James B. Duke Professor of History
Duke University

Alfred · A · Knopf

NEW YORK

1966

L. C. catalog card number: 66–12396

THIS IS A BORZOI BOOK,
PUBLISHED BY ALFRED A. KNOPF, INC.

FIRST EDITION

TO THE MEMORY OF

Washington Duke

There is a history in all men's lives,
Figuring the nature of the times deceased;
The which observed, a man may prophesy,
With a near aim, of the main chance of things
As yet not come to life, which in their seeds
And weak beginnings lie intreasured.
Such things become the hatch and brood of time;

Shakespeare: *Henry IV*, Part II

Preface

When Dr. John H. Plumb asked me to do this book, I gladly accepted his invitation, not only because he offered me a splendid opportunity to write about a large and fascinating part of the history of American society but also because he gave me a chance to address readers outside academic halls. Having been fortunate enough to spend several decades with professors, teachers, students, deans, and university presidents in such chambers, I retain respect and affection for the community of scholars. It is absurd to condemn that able historian who writes, with copious footnotes, for other historians. Such scholars, instructing their fellows, are often the most influential of all teachers, ultimately or even immediately. I hope sincerely that this volume will not be found seriously wanting in the academic world because of lack of citations, learning, or judgment. But I also hope that it will not drive away readers, whether academic or lay, because of gross deficiencies in style. I have tried to put the content of this book in such fashion and form that no special information or extraordinary zeal for knowledge is required in order to read it. If, to a degree, I have succeeded, I shall be much pleased.

Portraying American society as it developed up to the close of the Civil War, this volume may properly be entitled *Pioneer America*. To name it so is not to suggest that American society became stagnant or utterly different after the middle of the nineteenth century. But it did then alter, in some ways remarkably. Its progress during the past century will be described appropriately in another book in the *History of Human Society Series*.

Few will deny that the society of earlier America pioneered in fundamental and diverse ways. No historian can be expected to say that I have depicted all of its facets in their true proportions and brilliances. Nor will my judgments of common and uncommon people who appear in these pages be acceptable to all scholars. It will be apparent, I hope, to the reader that I have striven to set aside prejudices, which afflict all of us; that I have found no universal law or laws governing the course of American society; that, alas, I know of no simple and swift remedy for the shortcomings of that society or any other.

I must express my gratitude to several persons associated with Duke University who gave me encouragement and assistance. Among them are: Dr. Benjamin Powell, Librarian; Clarence Gohdes, James B. Duke Professor of English; John Tate Lanning, James B. Duke Professor of History; Dr. Mattie Russell, Curator of Manuscripts; Mrs. Martha C. Love, secretary of the Department of History; and James Broussard, my research assistant. The Duke University Research Council generously provided funds for secretarial and other services. My daughter, Anne M. Alden, typed the final draft of the manuscript without pay or complaint. I must, of course, also thank Dr. John H. Plumb for his helpful planning and criticism. I hardly dare to hope that my achievement is commensurate with the generous assistance I have been given.

J. R. A.

Contents

1	The American Indians	3
2	The English Plantings	16
3	Jewels of Empire	32
4	The Colonial Americans	47
5	The Onset of the Revolution	62
6	The Revolutionary Climax	80
7	A New Order	96
8	A Stronger Union	111
9	The Federalists in the Saddle	126
10	The Jeffersonian Republic	141
11	Over the Appalachians	157
12	Gentlemen and Democrats in Washington	174
13	The Peculiar South	189
14	The American Renaissance	202
15	The Offensive against Slavery	218
16	To the Pacific	231
17	Toward Tragedy	247
18	The Union against the Confederacy	262
19	The Overthrow of the Confederacy	277
20	Changing America	289
	Essay upon Authorities	299
	Index	FOLLOWS PAGE 309

Illustrations

The following illustrations appear in a group after page 162

1a William Pitt, First Earl of Chatham
    Courtesy, The North Carolina Museum of Art

1b Washington and His Family
    Courtesy of Jeremy North

2   Andrew Jackson
    Courtesy, Yale University Art Gallery, Mabel Brady Garvan
    Collection

3   A Pennsylvania Farm Scene
    Courtesy of the Abby Aldrich Rockefeller Folk Art Collection,
    Williamsburg, Virginia

4   Kitchen Ball at White Sulphur Springs
    Courtesy, The North Carolina Museum of Art

5a Edgar Allan Poe
    Courtesy of the Harris Collection of American Poetry and Plays,
    Brown University Library

5b The Bloomer Girl
    Courtesy of The Library of Congress

6   Camp Meeting
    Courtesy of the New-York Historical Society, New York City

7   Kindred Spirits
    Courtesy of the New York Public Library

8   The Banjo Player
    Courtesy, The Detroit Institute of Arts

Maps

1. American Regions   22
2. British North America After the Seven Years' War   69
3. Expansion of the United States, 1783–1819   148
4. American Settlements, 1830   167
5. American Settlements, 1850   206
6. The Texan Revolution   233
7. Division of the Oregon Country   242
8. Expansion of the United States, 1845–1853   244
9. The Confederacy   271

Introduction

BY J. H. PLUMB

1

OVER THE LAST FIFTY to a hundred years, man's belief that the historical process proved that he was acquiring a greater mastery over nature has received a brutal buffeting. In his early youth H. G. Wells, a man of vast creative energy, of rich delight in the human spirit, and of all-pervading optimism, viewed the future with confidence; science, born of reason, was to be humanity's panacea. When, in the years of his maturity, he came to write his *Outline of History*, his vision was darker, although still sustained with hope. World War I, with its senseless and stupid slaughter of millions of men, brought the sickening realization that man was capable of provoking human catastrophes on a global scale. The loss of human liberty, the degradations and brutalities imposed by fascism and communism during the 20s and 30s, followed in 1939 by the renewed world struggle, these events finally shattered Wells's eupeptic vision, and in sad and disillusioned old-age he wrote *The Mind at the End of its Tether*. His hope of mankind had almost vanished. Almost, but not quite: for Wells's lifetime witnessed what, as a young writer, he had prophesied—technical invention not only on a prodigious scale but also in those realms of human activity that affected the very core of society. And this extraordinary capacity of man to probe the complexities of nature and to invent machinery capable of exploiting his knowledge remained for Wells the only basis for hope, no matter how slender that might be.

If the belief of a man of Wells's passionate and intelligent humanism could be so battered and undermined, it is not surprising that lesser men were unable to withstand the climate of despair that engulfed the Western World, between the two World Wars. The disillusion of these years is apparent in painting, in music, in literature—everywhere in the Western World we are brought up sharply by an expression of anguish, by the flight from social and historical reality into a frightened, self-absorbed world of personal feeling and expression. Intellectual life, outside science, has pursued much the same course as artistic life, although it has shown greater ingenuity and a tougher-minded quality. Theology, philosophy and sociology have tended to reduce themselves to technical problems of exceptional professional complexity, but of small social importance. Their practitioners have largely ceased to instruct and enliven, let alone sustain the confidence of ordinary men and women.

In this atmosphere of cultural decay and of professional retreat, history and its philosophy have suffered. As in so many intellectual disciplines, its professional workers have resolutely narrowed the focus of their interests to even more specialized fields of inquiry. They majority of historians have withdrawn from general culture in order to maintain, at a high intellectual level, an academic discipline. They have left the meaning and purpose of history to trained philosophers and spent their leisure hours tearing to shreds the scholarship of anyone foolish enough to attempt to give the story of mankind a meaning and a purpose: writers, as diverse as H. G. Wells and Arnold Toynbee, have been butchered with consummate skill. The blunders of scholarship and the errors of interpretation have counted everything; intention nothing. Few academic historians, secure in the cultivation of their minute gardens, have felt any humility towards those who would tame the wilderness. In consequence, an atmosphere of anarchic confusion pervades the attitude of Western man to his past.

A hundred years ago, in the first flood of archaeological discovery, scholars possessed greater confidence: the history of mankind seemed to most to point to an obvious law of human progress. The past was but a stepping-stone to the future. First adumbrated by the philosophers of the late Renaissance—Bodin in France and Bacon in England—the idea of progress became an article of common faith during the Enlightenment. And prog-

ress came to mean not only the technical progress that had pre-
occupied Bacon but also moral progress. By the 19th century the
history of man demonstrated for many an improvement in the
very nature of man himself as well as in his tools and weapons.
Such optimism, such faith in man's capacity for rational behaviour, was shaken both by discoveries in science and in history as
well as by events. By the middle of the 20th century man's
irrational drives appeared to be stronger than his intellectual
capacities. Freud and Marx laid bare the hollow hypocrisy of so-
called rational behaviour either in individuals or in society. Also,
the rise and fall of civilizations, laid bare by the spade, seemed to
point to a cyclical pattern in human destiny which made nonsense of any idea of continuous progress; and this naturally attracted the prophets of Western doom. Yet more persuasive still,
and, perhaps, more destructive of confidence in human destiny,
was the utter loss of all sense of human control brought about
by global wars and violent revolutions. Only those men or societies who felt life was going their way, the revolutionaries and,
above all, the Marxists, believed any longer in the laws of historical progress. For the rest, retrogression seemed as tenable a
thesis as progress.

This disillusion in the West suited academic historians. It relieved them of their most difficult problems. If they happened to
be religious they were content to leave the ultimate meaning of
history to God; if they were rationalists they took refuge either
in the need for more historical knowledge or in the philosophic
difficulties of a subject that by its very nature was devoid of the
same objective treatment that gave such authority to scientific
inquiry. In the main they concentrated upon their professional
work. And this was an exceptionally important and necessary
task. What the common reader rarely recognizes is the inade-
quacy of the factual material that was at the command of an
historian one hundred years ago or even fifty years ago. Scarcely
any archives were open to him; most repositories of records
were unsorted and uncatalogued; almost every generalization
about a man or an event or an historical process was three-
quarters guesswork, if not more. Laboriously, millions of facts
have been brought to light, ordered and rendered coherent
within their own context. Specialization has proliferated like a

cancer, making detail livid, but blurring the outlines of the story
of mankind, and rendering it almost impossible for a professional
historian to venture with confidence beyond his immediate province. And that can be very tiny—the Arkansas and Missouri
Railway Strike of 1921; the place-names of Rutland; 12th-
century Rouen; the oral history of the Barotse; the philosophy
of Hincmar of Rheims. And so it becomes ever more difficult
for the professional historian to reach across to ordinary intelligent men and women or make his subject a part of human
culture. The historical landscape is blurred by the ceaseless activity of its millions of professional ants. Of course, attempts at
synthesis have to be made. The need to train young professional
historians, or the need to impart some knowledge of history to
students of other disciplines, has brought about competent di-
gests of lengthy periods that summarize both facts and analysis.
Occasionally such books have been written with such skill and
wisdom that they have become a part of the West's cultural
heritage. A few historians, driven by money or fame or creative
need, have tried to share their knowledge and understanding of
the past with the public at large.

But the gap between professional knowledge and history for
the masses gets steadily wider: professional history becomes
more accurate, more profound whilst public history remains
tentative and shallow.

This series is an attempt to reverse this process. Each volume
will be written by a professional historian of the highest technical competence; but these books will not exist *in vacuo*, for
the series is designed to have a unity and a purpose. But,
perhaps, first it is best to say what it is not.

It is not a work of reference: there are no potted biographies
of the Pharaohs, the Emperors of China or the Popes; no date
lists of battles; no brief histories of painting, literature, music.
Nor is this series a Universal History. All events that were critical in the history of mankind may not necessarily find a place.
Some will; some will not. Works of reference, more or less
factually accurate, exist in plenty and need not be repeated. It is
not my intention to add yet another large compilation to what
exists. Nor is this a 'philosophic' history. It does not pretend
to reveal a recurring pattern in history that will unveil its pur-

pose. Fundamentally philosophy, except in the use of language, is as irrelevant to history as it is to science. And lastly this series will not cover all human societies. There will be two volumes devoted to Russia, none to Germany. There will be histories of China and Japan but not of Indonesia. The Jews have a volume to themseves, the Parsees do not. And so on. Yet the series is called *The History of Human Society* for very good reasons. This history has a theme and a position in time.

The theme is the most obvious and the most neglected; obvious because everyone is aware of it from the solitary villagers of Easter Island to the teeming cities of the Western World; neglected because it has been fashionable for professional and Western historians to concern themselves either with detailed professional history that cannot have a broad theme or with the spiritual and metaphysical aspects of man's destiny that are not his proper province. What, therefore, is the theme of *The History of Human Society*? It is this: that the condition of man now is superior to what it was. That two great revolutions—the neolithic and the industrial—have enabled men to establish vast societies of exceptional complexity in which the material well-being of generations of mankind has made remarkable advances; that the second, and most important, revolution has been achieved by the Western World; that we are witnessing its most intensive phase now, one in which ancient patterns of living are crumbling before the demands of industrial society; that life in the suburbs of London, Lagos, Djakarta, Rio de Janeiro and Vladivostock will soon have more in common than they have in difference: that this, therefore, is a moment to take stock, to unfold how this came about, to evoke the societies of the past whilst we are still close enough to many of them to feel intuitively the compulsion and needs of their patterns of living. I, however, hope, in these introductions, which it is my intention to write for each book, to provide a sense of unity. The authors themselves will not be so concerned with the over-riding theme. Their aim will be to reconstruct the societies on which they are experts. They will lay bare the structure of their societies—their economic basis, their social organizations, their aspirations, their cultures, their religions and their conflicts. At the same time they will give a sense of what it was like to have lived in them.

Each book will be an authoritative statement in its own right, and independent of the rest of the series. Yet each, set alongside the rest, will give a sense of how human society has changed and grown from the time man hunted and gathered his food to this nuclear and electronic age. This could only have been achieved by the most careful selection of authors. They needed, of course, to be established scholars of distinction, possessing the ability to write attractively for the general reader. They needed also to be wise, to possess steady, unflickering compassion for the strange necessities of men; to be quick in understanding, slow in judgement and to have in them some of that relish for life, as fierce and as instinctive as an animal's, that has upheld ordinary men and women in the worst of times. The authors of these books are heart-wise historians with sensible, level heads.

The range and variety of human societies is almost as great as the range and variety of human temperaments, and the selection for this series is in some ways as personal as an anthology. A Chinaman, a Russian, an Indian or an African would select a different series; but we are Western men writing for Western men. The westernization of the world by industrial technology is one of the main themes of the series. Each society selected has been in the main stream of this development or belongs to that vast primitive ocean from whence all history is derived. Some societies are neglected because they would only illustrate in a duller way societies which appear in the series; some because their history is not well enough known to a sufficient depth of scholarship to be synthesized in this way; some because they are too insignificant.

There are, of course, very important social forces—feudalism, technological change or religion, for example—which have moulded a variety of human societies at the same time. Much can be learnt from the comparative study of their influence. I have, however, rejected this approach, once recorded history is reached. My reason for rejecting this method is because human beings experience these forces in communities, and it is the experience of men in society with which this series is primarily concerned.

Lastly, it need hardly be said that society is not always synonymous with the state. At times, as with the Jews, it lacks even territorial stability; yet the Jews provide a fascinating study of symbiotic social groupings, and to have left them out would be unthinkable, for they represent, in its best known form, a wide human experience—a social group embedded in an alien society.

As well as a theme, which is the growth of man's control over his environment, this series may also fulfil a need. That is to restore a little confidence in man's capacity not only to endure the frequent catastrophes of human existence but also in his intellectual abilities. That many of his habits, both of mind and heart, are bestial, needs scarcely to be said. His continuing capacity for evil need not be stressed. His greed remains almost as strong as it was when he first shuffled on the ground. And yet the miracles created by his cunning are so much a part of our daily lives that we take their wonder for granted. Man's ingenuity—based securely on his capacity to reason—has won astonishing victories over the physical world—and in an amazingly brief span of time. Such triumphs, so frequently overlooked and even more frequently belittled, should breed a cautious optimism. Sooner or later, painfully perhaps and slowly, the same intellectual skill may be directed to the more difficult and intransigent problems of human living—man's social and personal relations—not only directed, but perhaps accepted, as the proper way of ordering human life. The story of man's progress over the centuries, studded with pitfalls and streaked with disaster as it is, ought to strengthen both hope and will.

Yet a note of warning must be sounded. The history of human society, when viewed in detail, is far more often darkened with tragedy than it is lightened with hope. As these books will show, life for the nameless millions of mankind who have already lived and died has been wretched, short, hungry and brutal. Few societies have secured peace; none stability for more than a few centuries; prosperity, until very recent times, was the lucky chance of a small minority. Consolations of gratified desire, the soothing narcotic of ritual and the hope of future blessedness have often eased but rarely obliterated the misery which has been the lot of all but a handful of men since the beginning of history. At long last that handful is growing to a significant proportion in a few favoured societies. But throughout human

history most men have derived pitifully little from their existence. A belief in human progress is not incompatible with a
sharp realization of the tragedy not only of the lives of individual men but also of epochs, cultures and societies. Loss and
defeat, too, are themes of this series, as well as progress and
hope.

2

Most human societies exist in clusters with marked similarities
in economic activity, political institutions and social structures:
the striking likenesses between Imperial Rome and Classical
China or Mediaeval Europe and Japan of the Samurai are immediately apparent even to the general reader. North America,
however, has no fellow: only, perhaps, a second cousin in Australia. Apart from these countries, no other areas of large European settlement have totally dislodged the indigenous peoples
and rendered them socially insignificant. In Central and South
America, in New Zealand or South Africa the native peoples
have remained numerous and effective both economically and
socially, thereby creating political problems of formidable inten-
sity. Whatever social problems face Australia and America, they
do not arise from their indigeneous peoples. The redskin and the
aborigine are remnants, preserved like flies in amber. But there is
one overwhelming difference in ethnic matters between Australia and America—the problem of the Negro. This, perhaps, is
the oddest and most terrible of all aspects of America seen in the
light of the history of human society. Primitive men and women
of entirely differing cultures and tribal experiences were deprived, by acts of violence, of the setting usual to all human
life—the family. They were shipped in conditions of exceptional
brutality to a nightmare land, where work, habits, customs and
morality were utterly alien to what they had ever known. Often
unable to communicate not only with their masters but also with
their fellow slaves, they were temporarily condemned to a
world of silence as well as suffering. And worse was to follow.
American slavery was the harshest form of slavery known to
man; not only was manumission rare, but the slaves were prevented from forming even the most basic of human structures—

their own family life. Marriage was discouraged: children could be sold separately from their parents, just as husband and wife would be sold as the owner pleased.

Yet as an economic system slavery flourished and it became the basis of a rich, quasi-aristocratic social structure which contrasted markedly with the rest of America—more feudal, more hierarchical, and one, perhaps, in which social attitudes, ideology and even literary expression were more tightly intertwined. So, within the womb of the South, there grew the most monstrous of human problems for which the Civil War provided the bloodiest of births. In this volume, the problems which slavery was to produce develop within the confines of the South, but lack that full and terrible impact that now lies like an ugly jagged wound across the gracious affluence of Industrial America. To heal it will require compassion on the part of the Negro, let alone the white, as vast as God's.

In Pioneer America slavery and the South give a unique twist to its social history. And against the background of the Western Plains, the covered wagon, the log cabin, the canny, tough quickshooting pioneer of legend and fiction should be superimposed the chain gang, the slave market, and the harrowing laments of a lost people. These deep human problems are as old as American society, wounding the conscience of the sensitive and callousing the spirit of the possessors.

Unique and grievous as the commitment to slavery proved to be, it was nevertheless not the only singular feature of North American life when it is viewed in relation to human experience elsewhere. North America is the most conscious and deliberate creation of any human society: for Australia, and to a lesser extent New Zealand, followed the American pattern and did not initiate one of their own. Migrations of human groups to fresh territories is as old as human society itself; indeed humanity has always been in movement, seeking food, seeking empty spaces, seeking to fulfill the deep biological urge to spread and multiply, an urge that will soon take men to the planets and the stars. But the colonization of America was a more conscious endeavour, and the basic structure of this new social group more deliberately conceived than ever before in history. The Spanish involvement with Aztecs and Incas had forced them to think

deeply about the nature and morality of Empire, but their context had been the context of Europe with its hierarchical society
and Church. New England, if not Virginia, broke this pattern.
The early societies of New England were a deliberate conscious
act to create societies *de novo* on agreed principles. And so both
tradition and the sheer inertia of historical inheritance, that is to
be found in all societies, was given a check, although, of course,
not obliterated. This did not last long: men can bend principles to their immediate purpose: tradition and history are too
emotive in human terms not to be exploited. But principles, if
bent, retain something of their original nature, and the exploitation of history had to pay lip-service to the early settlers' stern
disapproval of inherited social status. And this was fortified by
two situations—one by the empty immensity of America and
the other by the failure of Balkanization. The latter danger was
probably greater than historians have realised. With Dutch and
Swedes as well as English and Spaniards along the Eastern seaboard, with Spaniards on the West Coast and, together with the
French, deep in the South, and with the French also in the
North, to say nothing of the Russians seeping down from Alaska
in the eighteenth century, Balkanization remained a potential
threat to the unity of America. Before the Revolution, it was
saved from disunity by the naval strength and commercial im-
perialism of Britain: her avarice and greed preserved American
unity. After the Revolution, it was not only the superior financial and industrial strength of the North-East but also the technological developments—steam power, railways, telegraph—that
made the economic and social unity of so vast a territory prac-
tically possible. Progress and time proved to be just in balance.
And unity was also aided by emptiness, for by the time
peoples were sufficiently dense in the Far West, in the Plains and
in the South to form separate societies, the economic structure
and political institutions of Eastern America, no matter how
loosely applied, were both too useful and too strong to be rejected. By 1840, the value of Federal government for expansion
and exploitation became increasingly apparent, and the bloody
struggle of the Confederate States to break the unity of America
was a forlorn cause from its beginning. The preservation of
America's geographical unity from coast to coast and from the

Great Lakes to the Caribbean is, perhaps, the greatest achievement of Pioneer America, for it resulted in conscious acquisition by a non-indigenous people of a land mass far greater than any previously absorbed. Russia, it is true, during the same period, was acquiring huge territories in Southern and Eastern Asia but in these regions indigenous peoples with complex institutions and a sophisticated culture were already deeply entrenched. And Siberia, emptier far of people than the Western Plains of America, precluded, like Canada, by reason of the ferocity of its climate, the same experiments in human society which the vast lands of Western America, teeming with natural resources, were bound to induce. Yet there remained many similarities with Russia, particularly in Russia's first great expansion to the Urals and her absorption of the Black Sea regions along the Lower Volga.

In the late seventeenth and early eighteenth centuries Russia with abundant, fertile and empty lands, with its ever growing need for a professional class, with its miragelike inducements for a quick fortune in furs or gold, possessed some of the seductions of the nineteenth-century American West; like America it attracted English, Scots, Frenchmen, Jews and above all Germans. But with an elaborate, authoritarian state system, the flow of immigration was always controlled and limited to the technical and professional classes, and the new regions were populated largely by the Russian peoples themselves. And the divergencies of Russian and American growth remained far more important than their similarities. Russia never had the difficult problem of ethnic assimilation which America faced. Also America avoided the direct problems of colonial rule—the alien cultures, religions, economic systems that faced Russia during her period of rapid growth. This situation strengthened Russian despotism, as its absence in America made the concepts of human freedom easier to adopt. And again owing both to their geographical contiguity with the mother state as well as to the constitutional absolutism of the Russian monarchy, the new lands of Russia were never able to develop new forms of social and political organisation, except through revolution in the core of the old state. Again, in marked contrast to America, where revolution directed against Britain proved easy.

The American Revolution, unlike the French or Russian or

Chinese, did not create a new society. It possessed elements of
social protest, but economic structure, even primary political
and constitutional structures, were mainly the same *after* as *before* the Revolution. Oddly enough, the British institutions of
local government, largely mediaeval in origin, sometimes acquired a renewed strength in the American context—the sher-
riff, his posse, the powers of the Justice of the Peace, as well as
trial by jury, and much common law, remained as firmly rooted
in America after the Revolution as before. The Revolution was a
revolution of authority, not of society, and the failure during
the revolutionary period to reconstruct American institutions,
law or social relationships in their most fundamental forms in
township and village meant that America remained tied more
deeply perhaps than men realised to her European roots. Indeed,
it can be argued that America has remained an expatriate society
with a multiplicity of homelands. Its institutions, like its language, are all American grafts on European roots. Even the Constitution itself, with its careful separation of powers, is, ironically enough, based on a misconception of eighteenth-century
political philosophers such as Montesquieu and Bolingbroke.
The Founding Fathers accepted their view of what the pure
form of the English constitution, uncorrupted by the Hanover-
ians, was.

   Awareness of expatriation, of roots and ancestors in the tradi-
tion-bound countries of Europe, has long haunted the American
people. Indeed, America and Europe exchanged dreams, and the
Atlantic became a dual-track highway, one swollen with the
poor immigrant, eyes greedy with hope, willing to accept conditions of poverty and labour that were driving their European
cousins into rebellion and anarchism; the other, less crowded at
first, but the numbers of newly affluent constantly swelling, as
they came back to search for the roots they had lost or for that
veneer of culture which they felt could never be theirs so long
as they stayed at home. Hence the long, at times seemingly
hopeless, struggle of the American people to achieve a cultural tradition of their own which they could respect. And
this, therefore, as well as the initial smallness of communities and
the distance between them, added to that sense of loneliness, of
rootlessness, of not belonging, which has haunted so many

Americans and driven others into an ostentatious gregariousness in which neighbourliness has become a cult and clubs and societies a way of life.

The size of the country, slavery, the assimilation problems of vast multi-national immigration, the absence of strong historical traditions in local institutions, the failure to achieve, except in the Eastern seaboard, both North and South, an intellectual elite conscious of its past as well as its destiny, were all potentially disruptive of American society. And the miracle of America lies not so much in its fabulous affluence but in its maintenance of unity of government, local and national, together with a common identity of language and communication over so vast a landmass: and this government, too, was rarely authoritarian and permitted a freedom of expression without parallel in the history of mankind. It was the result of America's economic momentum. The government in Washington was needed not only to deprive the Indians of their territories, to check the Canadians and force back the Spaniards, but also to give legal sanction to the trusts and combines that wrested the exploitation of America's wealth from small-scale efforts to national structures capable of developing America's economy on a continental scale. Both the Texas rancher and the railway baron, much as they might detest the concept of Federal government, ultimately required its sanction. The dialectic of American history is to be found in the interaction between economic development and the growth of Federal power, a dialectic which still holds a profound and developing meaning for America and one still far from achieving its ultimate synthesis. Cutting across this, interrupting its development and constantly confusing the issues, lies one of the greatest obstacles to America's moral and social development—the *state*. The state system, so necessary in times of primitive communications for the agrarian exploitation of a great landmass, had, even by the end of the period of American history described in this book, become a handicap to social development as well as to full exploitation of America's fabulous strength in national resources. And yet, ironically enough, the state as an ideological concept has acquired a greater weight of historical tradition and emotive force than almost any other American political institution. Indeed, this is another unique feature of American life. In no other society, as complex and as industrialized as America, has local government been allowed to maintain such vast legal, political and economic powers. Although the state had a great function in the colonization of America, using colonization in its widest sense, the reason for the power and inertia it acquired in a more complex society lies in the murky worlds of patronage, economic interests, or small-town but professional politics, the world of wheeling and dealing which is usually safer and more effective on the local level. Naturally it grew as the state developed in economic and social complexity. And behind the passionate defence of state rights in the name of individual liberty are the sharp-eyed men of power and profit. And so the long-term momentum of American economic growth has often collided with the immediate gratifications of short-term economic exploitation. And the strains inherent in this duality of authority had reached the breaking point by the time this book ends. The question was then being asked in the blood and guts of men as to who possessed the ultimate moral authority in American life, a question which has hung over the American people for this last hundred years and still awaits a plain answer. No other society has entangled moral and political problems in subordinate constitutional institutions to the degree that America has. At times it seems to an outsider that the freedom, so vaunted, has been bought at the expense of morality.

And yet in spite of these forces of disintegration, strong as they are, the preservation of a geographical and, ultimately, a constitutional and economic unity has been America's greatest triumph. But beneath this superstructure intractable problems as old as American society remain: assimilation of people of different colour has proved impossible; the creation of a society in accordance with the human rights avowed in its Constitution has always failed. Yet the great achievement of Pioneer America remains in the control under one economic and political structure of the most complete exploitation of national resources as yet witnessed by man. The achievements of Americans prior to the Civil War made this possible; by then the pattern of living, diverse, conflicting, subject to strain though it may be, was not only established but was contained within a physical entity so large that the growth of a human society vaster in resources, more complex in social relations, more affluent, for the many as well as for the few, than the World has ever known before in its history, had become inevitable. How this developed will be the subject of *Industrial America*. In this present volume, John Alden brilliantly analyses how that dynamic situation arose. He underlines, as one must always underline, the uniqueness of the American experience.

PIONEER AMERICA

CHAPTER 1

The American Indians

※※※

THE AMERICANS WHOSE HISTORY and gifts to civilization form the burden of this book are, in more than one sense, gone. For in these pages will be narrated and considered the saga of the Americans before they began to profit very heavily and to suffer very seriously from the rise of industry. Herein briefly appear the first inhabitants of the New World, the Indians; and at much greater length the Americans who flourished from the founding of Jamestown into the later decades of the nineteenth century.

Those Americans were Anglo-American, the principal element in their blood stock being English. Their culture was founded upon an almost overwhelmingly English legacy. The English commonly looked upon them as cousins; often, from the viewpoint of London, they were "poor relations," or, more accurately, social and cultural inferiors. To be sure, those Americans became, with the passage of time, less and less like the English. They altered remarkably in a New World environment. They were never hopelessly poor; they became a "people of plenty." Their chief occupations were agricultural and commercial rather than industrial. Humble folk in America were prosperous in comparison with their English and European contemporaries. Most of them were not constantly threatened with loss of home or bread. The natural resources at the command of the Americans were immense, nearly untouched by the Indians, seemed almost inexhaustible. They enjoyed wide and free horizons, for their lands were not crowded and their cities were not metropolitan. Indeed, the Americans did not fully occupy the vast spaces between the Atlantic and the Pacific that came under their flag until the nineteenth century was drawing to its end.

Not severely cramped by Nature, much less trammeled by heritage than Europeans and Asians, long free, thanks to the oceans, of formidable military menace, the Americans went far toward political and social equality. They were inventive in mechanics as well as in statecraft. In optimistic spirit they laid the groundwork for mass education, and at length began to exhibit distinguished figures in the domain of letters. They were profoundly convinced that America had a special mission, that she was to lead the nations and peoples of the world toward a just, better, and happier order. Their opportunity was unique; their history is fascinating. They survived an exhausting Civil War. Their America then altered remarkably. Massive infusions of immigrants from Europe came, tens of thousands of factories, giant cities, fabulous wealth, and military danger. Even so, what the older Americans did and what they thought continued to affect deeply the course of things human everywhere. Which is not to say that the America and the world of which they dreamed have appeared, or will come about. The pessimist may cogently contend that they lived in a unique paradise that has vanished, and that the notions they developed within it will not and cannot endure. Their institutions have persisted, have even been improved; their aspirations have been inherited. We may continue to indulge in a hope for a noble and free society upon this globe; we must fear even that man will wreck himself and all his splendid works.

The future, perhaps fortunately, is veiled. A mist, growing ever thicker as time becomes more remote, covers the past. History, based upon written records and other physical remains, is sufficiently uncertain. When one attempts to penetrate into ages before human beings learned to write, information about them becomes thinner and less reliable. Myth, containing elements of fact, tends to replace history, and fancy to supersede myth, for man is wondrously credulous as well as perceptive and imaginative. Upon the classical legend of the "lost world" of Atlantis, a continent beyond the Pillars of Hercules that sank beneath the waves, has been erected the fancy that Atlantis supplied the first Americans, the red Indians. An almost equally fascinating tale would have it that the first inhabitants of the Western Hemisphere came to it from a long-vanished continent in the Pacific

Ocean, Mu, of which only sun-drenched islands now remain. Many are the extraordinary theories about the origins of man in the Americas. Once and again it has been announced that remains have been found in the Western Hemisphere of very early man and even of his progenitors, but the "evidence" offered has been no more solid than that for settlement from Atlantis or Mu. The broad landscapes of the New World were at one time naked of those creatures who have looked upon themselves as masters of the Earth, who begin to traverse their solar system, and who sanguinely propose to venture into the universe beyond. Informed and unromantic opinion asserts that the first inhabitants of the New World were hunting folk who wandered from Siberia to Alaska over the Bering Sea or the Bering Strait, or over a land bridge that has since been covered by the ocean. It is plausibly guessed that they left the Orient in successive small bands over a long period of hundreds, perhaps thousands of years. Their unheralded and unrecorded passage probably began about 20,000 years ago, although it is possible that the first wave of settlers arrived earlier, perhaps 30,000 years ago, possibly at an even more ancient time. In any event, these folk were the principal, if not the only, ancestors of the American Indians. They and their descendants moved southward and eastward, occupying the continents and adjacent islands of the Western Hemisphere. The Indians lived in the Americas in isolation for ages, their progress, even their existence, remaining almost unknown to contemporary Asians, Africans, and Europeans until Columbus made his way across the "Ocean Sea" in the autumn of 1492.

Of what race or races were the forefathers of the Indians? Ancestors have been supplied them, not only from Atlantis and Mu, but, entirely or partly, from Egypt, Phoenicia, Israel, Carthage, and other European and African regions. Here again, there is more fervor and fancy than fact. All, or almost all, of the forebears of the redmen entered the Western Hemisphere long before there was an Egypt. There is no good reason to believe that they were joined by men from the states of the Near East, or from Africa, before the birth of Christ. Moreover, it may be asserted that any infusion of new blood, beyond the trifling, between the opening of the Christian era and the first voyage of

Columbus, is most unlikely. After his journey across the Atlantic, of course, there was extensive intermarriage almost everywhere in the New World, between the Indians and whites,
between the Indians and Negroes. Neither Columbus nor any
other European explorer following behind him, although they
saw many wonders, found a blue-eyed redman in any area not
recently visited by whites; and the dark eyes of the Indians, we
may be quite sure, were inherited from ancestors who came to
the New World long before the birth of Christ. The close kin-
ship of the Indians and the Asians remains obvious. The Indians
physically resemble the Japanese and the Chinese.

Geography and geology prosaically tell us that man's entrance
into the Western Hemisphere was the Bering passageway, and
they warn us against belief in voyages across the broader parts
of the Pacific and the Atlantic to the New World before that of
Columbus. Remarkable as were the journeys of the Polynesians
in their outrigger canoes, it is unlikely that they reached South
America; it is improbable that Chinese craft crossed the North
Pacific; similarly, one must doubt that Carthaginian vessels un-
furled their sails in harbors of the West Indies or at the mouth
of the Amazon. One may enjoy the many accounts of the "discovery" of the western continents before Columbus opened them to
the view of Europe, but one may not accept them, except for
one, as factual. It is altogether likely that the Norse briefly in-
truded into the New World at the beginning of the eleventh
century A.D. If so, they were hardly "discoverers." It is said that
St. Brendan and other Irishmen, who went to sea and found a
"Promised Land of the Saints," sailed to the Americas in the sixth
century. A playful hoax which has been seriously accepted by
the unwary, and even expanded, tells of a voyage and a settlement in that part of North America which became the United
States by Prince Madoc and other Welshmen in and after the
year 1170. It has been suggested, upon the basis of the Zeno
narratives published in Venice in the sixteenth century, that adventurers from the Faroe Islands debarked upon the western
shores of the Atlantic in the last quarter of the fourteenth. Some
would have it that fishermen from European ports were quietly
catching cod on the Grand Banks of Newfoundland before 1492.
It has been contended that Danish, French, English, and Portu-

guese expeditions arrived in the coastal waters of the American
continents immediately before the Genoese explorer set foot on
the Bahama Islands. Such "discoveries" may be ascribed largely
to national vanity, wishful thinking, ignorance, the wiles of
humorists taking advantage of the credulous, and the lure of the
romantic.

Nevertheless, it may not be said that Columbus was the first to
sail across the Atlantic. Although it is unlikely that journeys
were made across the wide expanses of the central Atlantic and
the central Pacific, during centuries when ships were small and
not easily maneuvered, it is to be believed that the Northmen did
enter the Western Hemisphere. Steppingstones across the North
Atlantic lay before them—the islands north of Scotland, and
Iceland, and Greenland; from Greenland it was but a short passage to regions assuredly part of the New World. It is beyond
question, even well known, that the Norse in their open ships
reached and colonized Iceland, and that they put themselves
down on the southern tip of Greenland about the year 985.
Physical evidence of their settlements in Greenland still survives.
Their historical sagas say that they made their way westward
beyond Greenland to Vinland and other regions at the opening
of the eleventh century. They tell us that Leif Ericson was the
first to reach Vinland, that he was followed by other adventurers. It is probable that Ericson and those who sailed in his wake
did indeed reach the continent of North America. What parts of
it they visited, how long they sojourned upon it, no one can say
with assurance. The "Kensington Stone," which relates the
melancholy fortunes of a band of Norse in Minnesota in the year
1362, is a forgery. Scandinavians put down in that state in the
nineteenth century. Vinland has hopefully and enthusiastically
been located at various spots between Labrador and Chesapeake
Bay. Remains of a settlement found in northern Newfoundland
have quite positively been identified as those of the Norse. Their
adventures stimulate curiosity, but they did not "discover" the
New World. To the best of our knowledge, they were intruders,
rather than permanent settlers, in North America. They retreated from the Western Hemisphere without leaving descendants behind them, so far as is known; and they were remembered
neither by the Eskimos nor by the Indians. In fact, they aban-

doned their footholds on Greenland in the fifteenth century, and
they did not return to it for generations. If Northmen did indeed
reach the North American continent, they were quite unaware
that they had penetrated into a New World. They merely reported that they had found Vinland and other regions beyond
Greenland; and it is most unlikely that their narratives gave inspiration to Columbus or any other explorer, except for the
searchers who have found too many wonders in the sagas. As
yet, one may not proclaim the Norse to be more than sojourners
in the New World, who left behind them no important trace,
who bequeathed no knowledge of their voyages or findings, directly or indirectly, to Columbus.

The massive and imposing pyramids that white invaders saw
in Mexico after the death of Columbus, which still awe the observer, were neither built by nor inspired by Egyptians, and the
amazingly accurate calendars of the Maya found by their Spanish conquerors were not derived from watchings of the skies by
Babylonian priests. Those pyramids and those calendars testify
to the splendid achievements of the Indians during a long separation from the rest of mankind. The Indians were not merely
savages who made it somewhat awkward to spread the benefits
of European civilization in the New World. Their progress in
isolation provides proof, if any be needed, of the astounding ingenuity, the creative abilities of all men. It will never be known
what further advances they would have made, had they been
able to pursue their own course indefinitely without interference
from other people; they and their works, especially in the regions which became the United States and Canada, withered
under the physical and cultural onslaughts of the whites.

Let it not be thought that all the Indians took equally long
steps upon the road of civilization, or even that they all moved
along the same highway. Hardly homogeneous when they
pushed into the Western Hemisphere, they afterward had
diverse histories. Scattering over the capacious Americas and
their offshore islands, they grew further apart from each other.
Establishing themselves on varied terrains in many climates, they
responded in relative isolation to different and compelling forces
of Nature. They came to speak in hundreds of tongues, and
often could exchange ideas only through their famous "sign language." Cherokee and Choctaw warriors were hardly more able

to communicate with each other than Magyars and Celts, Mongols and Persians. To be sure, in time, intellectual notions, religious beliefs, knowledge of tools, skills of agriculture and architecture, and produce of land, sea, and hands, passed about among their villages, tribes, and confederacies. They learned from each other as the barbarous Germans did from their cruel Roman enemies, as the ancient Japanese did from their Chinese antagonists. A religious cult found among the Indians of Florida may have its origins in the Valley of Mexico. Tobacco smoke was exhaled by redmen who did not grow the weed, and wampum beads and belts made of seashells on the shores of Connecticut and Long Island were worn and exchanged by Indians who lived far from the Atlantic Ocean.

There were Indians who lived the simplest of existences. Beset by an unkind Nature, some wandered naked over the cold, windswept, forbidding landscapes of Patagonia and wrested sustenance from a most unpromising land. In the sandy wastes of the Great Basin centering upon the state of Nevada dwelled a people who led equally difficult lives. Whites who encountered them gave them the name Diggers because they delved into the ground for roots that occasionally survived a harsh environment. Now and then the Diggers caught small stray game. Some of them fed principally upon acorns. On the shores of British Columbia, Indians lived meagerly upon easily caught fish. Such simple folk, in the eyes of the whites, were dirty and brutish, in no way "noble savages."

But in happier habitats, and in some not much favored by Nature, the Indians did not remain mere hunters, or artless tillers of the soil, or unsophisticated fishermen. During the millennium before the birth of Christ, Indians from Mexico to the northern border of Chile learned to cultivate effectively corn, beans, squash, and other plants, and so to create a reliable food supply. They also grew in numbers, beginning to congregate in villages and towns. They learned to irrigate and to make finer pottery. On the slopes and in the valleys of the mountainous Andes they domesticated the llama, worked with copper, gold, and other metals. Almost strangely, they began to flourish, not only in mountain valleys of Mexico and Peru, but in the hot jungles of southeastern Mexico and Central America.

In the course of the fifteen centuries before the advent of

Columbus came several flowering times among those Indians.
Massive cities, a complex society, and a dominant priesthood
appeared in the Andean highlands, then the stable Incan empire,
spreading over Peru, Bolivia, and Ecuador. The advance of the
peoples who came under the sway of the Incan emperors was
long led by priests; they lost power to warriors before both were
subjugated by the Spanish. Priests were also in the forefront in
the rise of the Maya of Mexico and Central America, whose
achievements in building, sculpture, and mathematics continue to
startle. Their pyramids, constructed or faced with stone, have
been uncovered in thick jungle. They learned to use the zero, to
make two strikingly accurate calendars, and to write in picto-
graph. Blooming twice, the Mayan culture was in decay when
the conquistadors forced their way into the country of that remarkable people. Meanwhile, to the west of the Maya, other
Indians erected huge pyramids of adobe brick, painted impressive murals, manufactured beautiful pottery, and devised a society both stable and colorful. The ruins of their works in the
Valley of Mexico, in Oaxaca, and elsewhere, impressively testify
to their accomplishments. In those regions, too, the priests were
peculiarly the creators and were at length replaced by military
men. Within the two hundred years before Hernando Cortes the
conqueror landed on the eastern coast of Mexico, the Aztec
confederacy rose to a zenith. The Aztec were inheritors rather
than creators of civilization, but a remarkable people. Addicted
to warfare and to human sacrifice, they were also fond of flow-
ers. Although they fought desperately, they only briefly withstood the assaults of Cortes, who was helped by thousands of
Indian warriors avenging wrongs heaped upon them by the
Aztec.

When the whites came to stay, the Indians who lived in the
regions that became part of the United States were generally
much more advanced than the Diggers but did not match their
Incan and Mayan brethren in cultural progress. They numbered
perhaps 400,000, or about a twentieth of all the redmen. Few of
them were still mere hunters, although most did seek game or
fish for part of their sustenance. Those who lived east of the
Mississippi River and near the shores of the Pacific commonly
had fixed residences and engaged more than casually in agricul-

ture; on the Great Plains hunting was the primary pursuit of the Indians. Whether they were more devoted to hunting or to tillage, they had not learned to write, and they knew no mathematics. Like the Inca and the Maya, they made no use of the wheel. They did not excel in sculpture. Their tools were of stone and copper, not iron. Some of them were cannibals on special occasions. Their only domesticated animal was the dog. They believed in good and evil spirits, in magic, and in magicians. Some of them worshiped the sun. Belief in a vague ruling spirit, belief in an equally vague future life, were not uncommon.

There was among the Indians who lived north of the Rio Grande and the Gulf of Mexico no empire so impressive politically or militarily as those of the Inca and the Aztec. However, confederacies that could send several thousand warriors to battle did exist. Quite often the head chief of such a combination acquired his authority by hereditary right rather than by wisdom in council or valor in war. Assemblies of delegates from many villages could and did reach decisions binding upon a whole confederacy. In consequence, some of the Indians were comparatively well organized politically and were formidable in the field. Such were the Six Nations, or Iroquois, long the masters of extensive domains in New York, Pennsylvania, and Ohio; the Cherokee, whose lands lay on both sides of the southern Appalachians; and the Creek, possessors of a wide region in Georgia, Florida, and Alabama. Even so, it ought not to be assumed that large numbers of those Indians habitually thought and acted in union. The head chiefs, who seemed to the English and French to be "kings" or "emperors," persuaded rather than governed. Decisions taken in formal conclave did not invariably lead to common action by all the members of a confederacy. Often villages, and occasionally even individuals, flouted the will of the majority and moved independently. Chiefs and warriors were capricious, and allegiances were local. The Iroquois, Cherokee, and Creek were riven by factions, and their quarrels produced weakness. Clashes within could be used by enemies without. While the Iroquois as a whole pursued a pro-English policy, French agents were usually able to maintain among them a party favoring France. Although the Choctaw, who lived east of the lower Mississippi River, were long allied to France, the English at times obtained support from some of the Choctaw. The whites constantly fomented and encouraged divisions among the red-men, to their own advantage. In this way they sapped Indian resistance.

The feuds and warfare among the many nations and confeder-acies of Indians even more gravely weakened the Indians in their struggles to defend their lands and their independence against the whites. Most of the redmen engaged in chronic warfare, the Iroquois against their northern neighbors, the Huron; the Chero-kee against the Creek; the Choctaw against the Chickasaw. Skill and bravery in war were highly valued, and an Indian male commonly had to prove his manhood by slaying an enemy tribesman. Every such killing called for revenge, and Indian braves therefore went frequently upon the warpath. Although the Indians usually engaged in raiding rather than massive on-slaughts against one another, their enduring feuds weakened all of them vis-à-vis their European assailants. Moreover, the whites, to their own benefit, not only stimulated antagonism and fighting between the Cherokee and the Creek, but turned Chero-kee against Cherokee. The Indians were usually unable to unite in defense of their homes, their way of life, and their lives. Worse yet, their quarrels and vendettas on occasion led them to take the field as allies of the whites against men of their own color. Cher-okee warriors helped the English against the Yamassee, and Catawba tribesmen joined them against the Cherokee.

Had the Indians been able to band together, the white con-quest and occupation of the Western Hemisphere must have been delayed. That the invasion from Europe could have been halted is most unlikely. The aggressors were physically vigorous as well as intellectually advanced. Their weapons were far supe-rior, and their military discipline gave them a great advantage. In the first clashes between whites and reds, the Europeans, pro-tected against clubs, arrows, and lances by armor, often slaugh-tered the Indians with guns as well as pikes and swords. The Spanish so swiftly overran a large part of the Western Hemi-sphere that most of their Indian enemies did not have time to acquire and to learn to use the better weapons of the invaders. Only the Araucanian nation of Chile was long able to withstand the assaults of the Spanish. The English, the French, and the

Dutch did not try to sweep rapidly across North America; at least they did not pour across it with the celerity displayed by the Spanish in their conquests of the Aztec and the Inca. Accordingly, the Indians of North America generally had the opportunity to acquire and to employ some of the arms of their white assailants against them. Sometimes the Indians were given muskets and tomahawks by whites to be used against other Indians and other whites; often they obtained such weapons through trade with the whites, receiving them in return for furs and deerskins. Thus they became better equipped for warfare and were able to offer stiffer resistance. However, the most powerful and the most efficient weapons of the whites were withheld from the Indians. Armed with musket and hatchet, they had to face enemies using cannon, rifles, and pistols. Also embarrassing to their military efforts was their inability to make ammunition for their guns or to repair them. Hence, unless they were assisted by whites, they could not fight indefinitely. Their ultimate defeat was inevitable.

Nevertheless, the Indians in North America, it is well known, were formidable enough. They were brave and had great powers of endurance; their swift attacks and sudden raids were difficult to check; and they were not easily caught in flight. Many generations passed before they were entirely deprived of support by whites. The English offered them arms to be used against the French; the French gave them weapons to be employed against the English; the English and the Spanish supplied them with guns and hatchets to be wielded against the Americans. Not until well into the nineteenth century were the Indians deprived of European allies and support. But the help they received merely served to put off the day of subjugation. They became increasingly dependent upon the whites, not only for arms, but for clothing, alcohol, cosmetics, jewelry, and even for sustenance. Taught to use the gun instead of the bow and arrow in the hunt, they came to need the gun in order to get game, animal skins, and furs. They could not go back to the bow and arrow, especially because the animals they pursued became less abundant as time went on. Becoming accustomed to the white man's coat, they did not find out how to make it. Becoming addicted to the white man's liquor—much too fond of it in fact

—they did not master his methods of manufacturing it. They ceased to fashion the trinkets with which they adorned themselves. They wanted the mirrors they could obtain only from white traders. More and more they copied the whites, abandoning their own way of life and with it a measure of their freedom. The whites learned that they could force the Indians to yield by refusing them guns, clothing, and liquor. They also learned that the best way both to defend against and to subdue the Indians was to invade their country, burn their villages, destroy their crops, and kill their game. Thus the Indians were made to suffer from want, their morale was destroyed, and so the Iroquois, the Cherokee, and the Creek were at last brought down.

Submerged or washed aside by waves of advancing whites, the redmen, when they were no longer dangerous, won the general sympathy of those who displaced them. So long as the Indian was able to fight and to kill, the prevailing opinion among the whites was, in the well-known phrase, "A good Indian is a dead one." That statement was not utterly unjustified. The warrior often slew men, women, and children without distinction; and his wife joyfully tortured prisoners. The whites also committed atrocities. Both the conquered and the conquerors were perfidious on occasion. However, from the time the two races first met, there were whites who felt for the redmen, wished to Christianize and to educate them, desired to live in peace with them, and sought to prevent the seizure of their hunting grounds and the destruction of their villages. Whites with such views often used, and even more often sought to use, governmental power to protect and defend the Indians. Their efforts availed little and only temporarily. Clashes between the races continued until the Indians could resist no longer, until they had lost all of their lands coveted by the whites. Only then did the white man's conscience come to dominate his policy toward the redman. In the twentieth century the "great white fathers" in Washington sought to make the Indians full and prosperous citizens in the country which had once been theirs. A few of the Indians in isolated areas were encouraged to continue in or to resume their own patterns of life. After World War II many Indian nations that had been forced or persuaded to sell their lands too cheaply received added sums for them.

The Indians who benefited from the tardy generosity of the whites were not the Indians of yore. It is often said that they became more numerous in the twentieth century than they had been before they were molested by the whites. But it is doubtful that pure-blooded Indians had actually increased in number. Many who were counted as Indians in 1920 or 1940 were of mixed stock; and a few were entirely white. Intermarriage between reds and whites and between reds and Negroes began early and did not cease. The American "melting pot" contains Indian ingredients. Some Americans are proud to possess an ancestor or ancestors who crossed the Atlantic in the seventeenth or eighteenth century. Others, boasting of Indian progenitors, may remind us with pride that they are descendants of the very first comers.

Although the Indians of the United States were ultimately and largely remolded in the patterns of the whites, they in turn exerted an influence upon the whites. Warfare between the two peoples was usually local and always sporadic. The enemies were frequently friends. The English language, at least the American variety of it, was enriched by Indian words, such as "squaw," "succotash," "papoose," "wampum," and "wigwam." The whites derived pleasure from Indian legends and oratory. The redmen taught them how to grow tobacco, corn, and vegetables unknown in Europe; corn became and remained of the first importance in the white man's agriculture and economy. The races exchanged diseases along with more pleasing gifts. Smallpox and tuberculosis, which the Indians acquired from the whites, did them possibly greater injury than the ravages of war. It would nevertheless seem that the whites were hurt even more by the exchange. It appears that the sailors of Columbus contracted syphilis from the red women of the West Indies. A mild disorder among the Indians, it raged among Europeans, enfeebling, maddening, and killing peasant, prince, and prelate, Castilian, Bavarian, and Russian. It may be that syphilis balanced all the wrongs inflicted by all the whites upon all the Indians of the Americas. We cannot match two immense incommensurables. Nor is it possible to make an easy and simple moral judgment about a complex relationship between the two colliding and embracing races.

CHAPTER 2

The English Plantings

✻✻✻

As the year 1606 drew to a close, three small sailing ships weighed anchor and slipped down the estuary of the Thames from London. Leaving behind the chill of winter in the Bay of Biscay, they made their way southward toward the sunny Azores. Off those islands they caught the trade winds in the bellies of their sails. Then, following the route taken by Columbus 114 years earlier, they crossed the Atlantic. They stopped briefly in the West Indies so that the men aboard could secure water and refreshment, turned northward, entered Chesapeake Bay in the spring of 1607, and deposited 105 male settlers on the banks of the James River. There, at Jamestown, that small band of men founded the first permanent English settlement in that part of the New World which became the United States of America. From it developed Virginia, the Old Dominion. That it would survive was for some years doubtful—Jamestown was momentarily abandoned three years later. Even so, the drama of settlement and westward expansion which began there was preceded by a lengthy prologue. Behind that shaky beginning were a slow awakening of interest in the New World, schemes for colonization that were abandoned, and plantings that failed.

The English have been admired, respected, and assailed as the makers of a magnificent empire. The territorial possessions over which their flag once flew have been compared to those of the Romans, and they have even been assigned a remarkable, a unique genius for imperial enterprise. If the English had special qualities which made them peculiarly fitted for adventures on and beyond the seas, these were not quickly displayed in the contest among the European nations for colonies in the Americas. The English, like the French and Dutch, did not secure a firm foothold in the New World until the first voyage of Columbus was more than a century in the past; the Swedes and Russians even more slowly fastened upon parts of the Western Hemisphere. The Portuguese were firmly established in Brazil generations before the English put down at Jamestown. By that time, except for Brazil, all of South America belonged to Castile, as did the islands of the Caribbean, Central America, Mexico, the Florida peninsula, and parts of the present-day American states of New Mexico, Arizona, and California.

Although John Cabot plowed his way across the North Atlantic in English service in 1497 and made it possible for England to claim the northeastern part of North America by right of discovery, England did not even become a principal contender in the struggle for empire beyond the ocean before the reign of Elizabeth I. England did not hold back because a Spanish claim to all of the New World except Brazil was accepted in London. Her entrance into the conflict was delayed by fruitless expenditure of energy in behalf of Henry VIII, who wanted to play a great part on the European continent; by religious and civil strife at home; by the marriage of Queen Mary I to Philip II of Spain. However, before Elizabeth ascended the throne, Henry VIII founded the English navy, and the English people turned toward external commerce as a source of wealth. Immediately before her death Mary ceded Calais to France, putting an end to English aspirations across the Channel. Elizabeth, firmly establishing the Anglican Church, was increasingly threatened upon her throne by Roman Catholic claimants to it, Mary, Queen of Scots, and especially Philip II of Spain. An Anglican and Protestant England under her sway gradually moved to challenge Spain in both the New World and the Old. The clash opened with a voyage in 1562 to the West Indies by John Hawkins.

Four years after Elizabeth ascended the throne, two years before the birth of Shakespeare, John Hawkins, engaging in a business that was afterward looked upon as vile, sailed to Africa, secured Negro slaves, carried them to the West Indies, and sold them to Spanish planters. In the Englishmen of the Elizabethan

Age lust for gain at any cost was mingled with literary majesty,
crudity with nobility of character, duplicity with extraordinary
courage. Hawkins made a profit on that voyage. Forbidden by
the Spanish crown to traffic with its subjects in the New World,
he went there a second time to sell Negroes, and a third. Then
he was attacked by a Spanish squadron at Tampico, Mexico, and
many of his men were led off to prison. Hawkins and other
English sailors and adventurers, believing that he was a victim of
treachery, resolved to seek revenge and to plunder the possessions of Philip II. With the tacit consent, then with the open
approval, then with the support of Elizabeth, they raided the
Spanish settlements in and along the shores of the Caribbean.
Thus commenced an undeclared war in the New World. To
wage it more vigorously Englishmen sought to establish bases
across the ocean; they also were stimulated to think of founding
colonies there. Might they not find silver and gold in vast quantities as the Spanish had in Mexico and Peru? Might not England
have a great commerce with her own territories in the New
World? Other forces drove the English on toward empire in the
Americas; these included the search for a western passageway to
Asia, the lure of the teeming fish on the Grand Banks off Newfoundland, even the desire to Christianize the heathen redmen.

Sixteen years after the first voyage of Hawkins, Elizabeth
herself formally announced that England was a contestant for
territory beyond the Atlantic. In 1578, still avoiding a general
war with Spain, she nevertheless gave to Sir Humphrey Gilbert
the right to colonize in those parts of North America not actually occupied by the Spanish—this despite their claim to all of
that continent. The charter in which she authorized Gilbert to
proceed is therefore a pregnant document. It is perhaps even
more important because it required that laws enacted by Gilbert
be as like those of England as possible and also that trial by jury
and property rights be established as in England. These safeguards, repeated in later charters, declared that English settlers
and their descendants were not to be subjected to capricious
exploitation.

In a sense Gilbert actually did found the first colony in North
America, for he went out to Newfoundland in 1583 and officially took possession of St. John's, already a haunt and refuge

for fishermen of several nations. Otherwise Gilbert's efforts came to nought; returning from North America, he was lost at sea off the Azores. Sir Walter Raleigh, who inherited the hopes and resumed the labors of Gilbert, also failed to found a true colony in North America. That many-sided man was somewhat more successful as a courtier than as a constructor of empire. He was a half-brother of Gilbert. Elizabeth gave him a charter much like the one she had granted to Gilbert. During the years 1584–87 expeditions sent out by Raleigh made no fewer than four landings in North Carolina. In the last one, men, women, and children were put ashore at Roanoke Island to build a "City of Raleigh." But the venture failed. For various reasons, including a massive attack launched against England by Philip II and his Great Armada in 1588, Raleigh was unable to send reinforcements. A hasty visit to Roanoke two years later by an English ship revealed that the colonists had abandoned their "city." Their fate remains a mystery; it is likely that they were attacked and killed by neighboring Indians.

Although he was not rich enough to continue alone with his venture, Raleigh not only named Virginia but had something to do with the ultimately successful effort to build a colony within it. The sailing of the Great Armada contributed largely to the failure of his Roanoke venture, but the crushing defeat of that fleet, announcing the wane of Spanish power on the sea, encouraged the English to make further efforts to establish themselves in the New World. Moreover, a device which would make possible larger and more sustained endeavors had made its appearance—the company. Raleigh had taken partners into his enterprise; and these and other men eventually formed companies that carried on the work done by Gilbert and Raleigh.

In 1606, six years after the formation of the East India Company that brought so much wealth to England from the East, James I chartered two companies that sought to reap profits from territories to the west and to fill them with Englishmen. One of these, the London Company, was to exploit the region around Chesapeake Bay; the other, the Plymouth Company, was assigned New England. Neither made money. The Plymouth Company immediately but vainly tried to establish a settlement

on the coast of Maine. Indeed, all its efforts to plant men were
unsuccessful. Nevertheless, the Plymouth Company, led by Sir
Ferdinando Gorges, was a useful machine that encouraged the
occupation of New England. Those who invested in the London
Company lost rather than gained money but could take pride in
the fact that they had founded the colony of Virginia—if they
lived long enough to learn that it was to survive. For it was they
who sent out the three ships that went to Jamestown in 1607.
They had dreamed that they would become rich, that precious
metals would be found near the Chesapeake. They received
from Virginia a shipment of "fool's gold," iron pyrites. The
leaders of the company, noblemen, public personages, and
wealthy merchants, could not report to the stockholders about
handsome returns; instead, they frequently asked for additional
capital. It was given, but more and more grudgingly. A decade
after the first comers threw up their huts at Jamestown, hopes of
profit revived. Might not tobacco-growing bring great rewards?
Might not fields of the soothing weed be vegetable equivalents
of the mines of Mexico and Peru? But tobacco-raising did not
bring quick and vast revenue. It did assure the permanence of
the colony of Virginia less than a generation after its founding.
Ultimately the proceeds from tobacco would far surpass the
value of the precious metals.

Most of the first settlers at Jamestown died of hardship or
disease, or were killed by the neighboring Indians. The few who
escaped early death underwent prolonged miseries. The human
stock of the colonies was replenished more than once, and
women were added to it. Supplies of food, clothing, and tools
were sent out from England. Sporadic attacks by the Indians
threatened the very existence of the colony until 1622, when an
assault upon Jamestown, leading to the destruction of many of
its huts, failed. But the Indians were friendly more often than
they were hostile, and they taught the settlers how to grow
corn, how to catch fish, how to bring down deer in the forest.
Servants at first of the company, the colonists were soon permitted to acquire land for themselves. Scattering out from
Jamestown, they established themselves on the banks of the Virginia rivers and pushed steadily westward and inland. A half-
century after the first planting, both the permanence and the

prosperity of the Old Dominion were as assured as might be.

Before that half-century had passed, the political and social institutions of Virginia had acquired shape and solidity. The Anglican Church was legally established in the colony as early as 1609. Ten years later Negro "servants" were brought to the Chesapeake by a Dutch sea captain. The legal status of these and of other blacks put ashore later remained uncertain until the seventeenth century was well advanced. At length the Negroes were definitely and legally made slaves. Gradually their number increased; the tobacco plantation made its appearance; and a Cavalier gentry owning both slaves and plantations began to emerge. The year in which the Negro made his entrance upon the scene was remarkable also for the first meeting of a representative assembly in English America. During the first twelve years of its existence the colony was ill managed by a council and then arbitrarily ruled by a governor with almost unlimited authority. Pushed on by Sir Edwin Sandys, the London Company authorized the first election of the House of Burgesses. That body was originally devised to place burdens upon the Virginians rather than to secure their rights. Containing men chosen by voters in their several settlements, it met not only in the year 1619 but quite regularly in the years that followed. With the governor and a council it made laws. Not at first confined to lawmaking, the House of Burgesses at length became a true legislative body. It survived the London Company. Failing as an economic venture, riven by internal discord, not sufficiently responsive to the will of James I, the London Company lost its political authority by the decree of an English court in 1624. Thereafter, the governor and council of Virginia were appointed by the Crown. First in so many ways, Virginia was also the first royal colony in America. Its system of government was the model for many other English colonies.

The settlement of Virginia did not expand northward across the Potomac River, but the new English empire did, and quickly. Maryland, in several basic ways another Virginia, was created by royal charter in 1632. Like Virginia, Maryland was named after an English queen, but a Roman Catholic one, Henrietta Maria, wife of Charles I. It is well known that this first neighbor of Virginia was intended to serve as a haven for

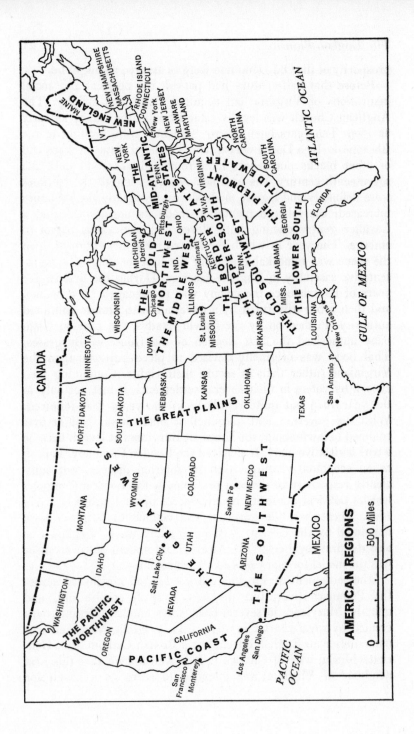

AMERICAN REGIONS

0   500 Miles

Roman Catholics persecuted in England. But that was not the first purpose of the Calverts, the Lords Baltimore, who were given Maryland and the right to establish a hereditary, proprietary, and almost feudal regime within its boundaries. The Calverts above all sought profit, and they obtained it, from the sale of land. Themselves Roman Catholic, the Calverts were too well entrenched socially and too much respected to be seriously punished in England because of their faith. They felt for their fellow believers who were subject to oppression, and they did what they could for them. They encouraged Roman Catholics to seek refuge in Maryland, and they granted manors there to the richer ones. The first settlement upon the domain of the Calverts was made at St. Mary's in 1634. About half of the colonists who made the first voyage to that place were Catholics. But the Calverts did not bar Protestants, and the Protestants became an ever larger majority with the passing years. Many of them entered Maryland from Virginia. The funds that the Calverts could command were commensurate with those of Raleigh, not with those of the London Company. Moreover, Maryland was long the scene of harsh and harassing internal strife, both religious and political. However, the colony expanded and prospered; it spread along both the eastern and western shores of the Chesapeake. In the main, Maryland flourished, her people profiting from the experience and following the example of the Virginians. Like their neighbors to the south, they found economic salvation in tobacco. Indeed, the Potomac was neither an economic nor a social boundary. The fortunes of the Marylanders, like those of the Virginians, rose—and sometimes sank— in accordance with tobacco yields and prices. Negro slaves and plantations and their aristocratic owners did not fail to appear in Maryland.

Clash between the Calverts and dwellers in Maryland was almost unavoidable, since the proprietors sought both to make money from and to rule over their domain. Just as understandably, many of the settlers preferred their own economic interests to those of the Calverts, and tried to confine the authority of the proprietors. Required by their charter to secure the assent of the freemen in the colony to all laws, the Calverts permitted them to elect a legislative body similar to the House of Bur-

gesses. With little delay, it sought to increase its own powers at
the expense of the Calverts and the governor and council appointed by the head of the family. It also spoke for the
Protestant majority in the colony. Gradually it took authority from the proprietors, their agents, and their allies in
Maryland. Religious discord added bitterness to almost
every public question. The Calverts tried to mollify contentious Christians upon their "estate," without quick success.
They even had to exert themselves to prevent the formation
of a Jesuit subcolony in Maryland. Roman Catholic landlord
and Protestant tenant disliked each other for more than
economic reasons. Men who migrated to Maryland from
Virginia brought with them loyalty to the Anglican Church.
In 1649, at the urging of the Calverts, the Maryland
Assembly enacted a famous "Toleration Act." It assured
freedom of worship, so far as a law might do it, to all
believers in Christ and the Trinity. It also, at the instance of the
Protestants, subjected those who denied Father, Son, and Holy
Spirit to a death penalty. The law alleviated rather than cured.
Within the next forty years there were no fewer than three
revolts in Maryland against the Calverts. They were ultimately
unable to prevent the establishment of the Anglican Church in
their colony. When, in 1715, its proprietor announced his conversion to Christianity in the Anglican mode, the charter rights
of the Calverts were firmly established. The family clung to
Maryland until the War of Independence.

If the first foundations of the British empire in North America were laid beside the Chesapeake, others were almost as
quickly sunk in New England. Much less active than the London Company, the Plymouth Company did not found and frame
a great colony. It did encourage exploration of its domain. Re-
modeled as the Council for New England, it granted lands to
individuals who sent settlers to New Hampshire and Maine. It
also at times hindered the efforts of English Puritans to plant
themselves in New England. But they would not be held back,
and they flooded over the whole region, making it their own.
They also put down on New York's Long Island.

The empire of England grew because of her distresses as well
as her successes. If the Church of England became finally Prot-

estant in the early years of the reign of Elizabeth I, its doctrines, machinery, and ceremonies remained too much like those of Rome to please many Englishmen. They—called Puritans— sought to reform it; some of them, radical Protestants, came to believe that the national church was beyond repair, that it was not sanctioned by the Scriptures. These so-called Separatists formed congregations outside the Church of England. Both they and more moderate Puritans who tried to change the official church were persecuted by Elizabeth and her Stuart successors. To the Puritans, James I and Charles I were political and religious enemies. They lost hope of remolding English institutions to their hearts' desire. Economic troubles added to their discontent. They sought refuge, religious freedom, and prosperity— worldly goods at least for their descendants—beyond the Atlantic. Swarming out of England, they went, not only to New England, but to Virginia, Bermuda, and islands in the Caribbean. Their "Great Migration" dictated much of the later history of the English in North America and of the American republic.

The first of the Puritans to strike big roots in New England were the Pilgrims who went ashore at Plymouth, Massachusetts, late in the year 1620. The nucleus of the Pilgrims came from the village of Scrooby in eastern England. There, under the leadership of men educated at Cambridge University, some scores of plain folk, farmers, mechanics, and workmen, turned toward Separatism. Fearing persecution, they fled across the North Sea, in 1607 and 1608, to Holland, where they were permitted to worship as they would. They spent more than a decade at the Dutch town of Leyden. But they were hard pressed to make a living in a foreign country; they saw that, if they remained in Holland, they must lose their religious identity; and they realized that they could not permanently remain English among their friendly Dutch neighbors. For the Dutch, "the English of the Continent," were not English. Moreover, Spanish attacks upon Holland threatened. The bulk of the exiles resolved to move again, to go to North America, where they might live under the English flag and lay the groundwork for the true church. Even though they expected that most of them would perish in the attempt, they determined to cross the ocean. A syndicate of English merchants agreed to help them emigrate; the merchants were to be repaid by the settlers in services and in trade. There followed the famous voyage of the *Mayflower* with 101 passengers, men, women, and children. With the Pilgrims from Holland went other Separatists from England, some employees of the merchants, and some "strangers" who were allies but not members of the band of "saints." Not quite sure where they wished to go, the bold voyagers arrived off Cape Cod in November. Beset by storms, worried because winter was at hand, they searched about for a new home and so landed at Plymouth. More Separatists came on from Holland and England the next year and afterward.

Weak from their ocean voyage, the *Mayflower* passengers suffered from lack of food and from the cold at Plymouth. More than half of them died within a few months. Gradually the survivors, and those who came after, moved toward a moderate prosperity. They extorted crops from thin and sandy soil, pulled codfish from the ocean, engaged in lumbering, and traded with neighboring Indians. Moving out from Plymouth, they built several other villages. Establishing Congregational churches, they—at least the majority, the "saints"—worshiped as they pleased. They secured title to the lands they occupied from the Council for New England. Before landing, the first settlers had agreed, in the Mayflower Compact, to erect, respect, and sustain a system of government. It was given a corporate form. Only church members were permitted to vote, but most of the males were, or could be, such. Not utterly democratic, Plymouth Colony was truly republican. After seven decades it became a part of Massachusetts.

Plymouth was colonized by hundreds, Massachusetts Bay by thousands, by Puritans of a somewhat more moderate religious stripe than the Pilgrims. Some of them settled in small numbers during the 1620s at several places along the coast north of Plymouth. Then, others secured control of the Massachusetts Bay Company, chartered by the Crown in 1629 and authorized to form a colony upon that coast. The Puritans thronged across the North Atlantic in 1630 and during the decade that followed. Villages sprang up rapidly about Boston, which became their capital. Their origins were not so humble as those of the Pilgrims; generally of the middle class in England, they were led by educated gentlemen and learned clergymen. They fled England to escape the wrath of orthodox Anglicans and of Charles I. They sought to create a new Israel in the wilderness; many of them also hoped that they and their progeny would profit economically by leaving England.

The hardships encountered by those who went to the Bay Colony were not prolonged, and it soon achieved economic success and political stability. The Englishmen who made new homes in it, perhaps 20,000 of them during the 1630s, were of sturdy stuff. Industrious and thrifty, they brought with them skills, tools, livestock, and a passionate desire to succeed. Like the Pilgrims, they drew all possible riches from the forests, from thin lands, and from fertile waters. Under the guidance of John Winthrop and other able men, they used—and misused—the Massachusetts Bay Company charter as a constitution. They elected their lawmakers and their executive officials. Had Winthrop and other gentlemen and divines had their way, the colony would have been dominated by an aristocracy. They were forced to let all church members take part in the selection of a governor and a General Court. Neither aristocratic nor democratic, the colony was theocratic. Away from England, the Puritans of the Bay refused allegiance to the English church, built Congregational ones. Not closely united to each other, these were tightly linked with the state. It is perhaps needless to say that heretics, including Anglicans, were persecuted in the colony. Its leaders never intended to establish religious freedom for all, so to encourage men to lose their souls.

Massachusetts Bay and Plymouth served as mothers and stepmothers to the other New England colonies. From them families went in search of economic opportunity to Connecticut, Rhode Island, New Hampshire, and Maine, in the 1630s and later. With them migrated others who were banished or who fled because they could not or would not support the established order in Massachusetts Bay and Plymouth. Newcomers from England often preferred to go to the newer settlements. Rhode Island was a haven for men and women who were heretical or rebellious, or both, who were unhappy in Massachusetts Bay and Plymouth. Some of them, including the able and generous-spirited Roger Williams and the talented Mrs. Ann Hutchinson,

were driven away because of their heterodoxies. The Reverend
Thomas Hooker, a principal figure in the migration to Connecticut, was dissatisfied with the Massachusetts Bay regime.
However, Connecticut drew many settlers because of the rich
lands in the valley of the river after which the colony was
named. Some of its first English residents, in and about the town
of New Haven, were puritanical Puritans. Connecticut, embracing a varied collection of settlements, was chartered as a corporate colony in 1662 and became a younger Massachusetts Bay.
So did New Hampshire and Maine. The Mason family acquired
a proprietary claim to New Hampshire from the Council for
New England; the Gorges family similarly secured Maine.
These proprietors feebly encouraged occupation of their domains, but many of the early inhabitants were people who
moved northward from Massachusetts Bay and Plymouth. The
Bay Colony contested both the Mason and the Gorges claims.
Maine, with Plymouth, definitely became a part of Massachu-
setts in 1691. The Masons were unable to hold New Hampshire,
but the efforts of Massachusetts Bay to annex it ultimately failed.
It was turned into a royal colony in 1679.

Rhode Island was in New England but not quite of it for
several generations. The outcasts and fugitives who were its
first settlers gave it a special complexion that faded but slowly.
Under the leadership of Roger Williams, who flirted briefly
with the Baptists, who could not firmly decide which
variety of Protestantism was God-chosen, church and state
were divorced. (Williams would not persecute even the
Quakers, who were, in their early days, detested and punished
by all right-thinking Christians. Nevertheless, such was the
temper of his time that even he, gentle but obsessed by
doctrinal niceties, at one time refused communion to his
wife). Nor was political authority concentrated in the hands
of men who claimed superiority because they commanded
the keys to heaven or to money. For some years the Rhode
Islanders managed to live with little government and fewer
taxes. Their neighbors looked upon them as both heretics and
anarchists. When they did establish a political regime for their
colony, it was corporate, and its powers were limited. Ultimately, when her neighbors ceased to insist upon the Congrega-

tional way, Rhode Island became truly a part of New England.

Forming solid bastions of empire about Chesapeake Bay and in New England in the first half of the seventeenth century, the English failed to fill the coastal territories between. They were forestalled by the Dutch, whose New Netherland threatened permanently to keep separate the English possessions on the North American mainland. In the second half of the seventeenth century the English transformed New Netherland into New York and New Jersey, and they founded Pennsylvania and Delaware, thus securing a firm grip upon the Atlantic coast line from Maine to Virginia. They also flowed into the Carolinas.

England never admitted the right of the Dutch republicans to undertake imperial adventure in North America. However, the Dutch refused to be warned off. Two years after the English planted themselves at Jamestown, the Dutch explored the Hudson River. Soon claiming all the lands between the Connecticut and Delaware rivers, they put down in the valley of the Hudson and on Manhattan. They pushed eastward to the Connecticut; and they spread southward across the Delaware, taking over in 1655 small settlements made along its banks by the Swedes. New Netherland, owned by the Dutch West India Company after 1621, was misgoverned. But the company granted religious toleration, and it permitted Protestants of various descriptions from several countries, and Jews as well, to make their home in the colony. Its capital, New Amsterdam, profiting from a magnificent situation for trade, became a prosperous town. Basic for New Netherland was a commercial and military alliance with the Iroquois confederacy. Supplied with guns by the Dutch, its warriors held back the French advancing southward from the St. Lawrence River. At last, in 1664, the English attacked and captured New Netherland, almost without a struggle. Nine years later the Dutch recaptured New Amsterdam, but they did not try to keep it. They had built a great empire, but they were too few to retain all of it. They needed English help to stave off French advances across their flat homeland. They returned New Netherland to the English in 1674. The bulk of it became the larger part of the colony of New York, owned by James, Duke of York. New York became a royal colony in 1685 when he ascended the English throne as

James II. From New Netherland was also carved New Jersey, which James conveyed to friends. That colony was definitely royalized early in the eighteenth century. The English inherited from the Dutch rich provinces, the valuable Iroquois alliance, and some thousands of sturdy citizens, including ancestors of many distinguished American families, such as the Roosevelts, Schuylers, and Livingstons. New York and New Jersey, especially the former, long retained a Dutch cast. Blessed by nature, both colonies grew steadily.

Less than a generation after the fall of New Netherland, the English were firmly established in Pennsylvania and Delaware. Many persecuted Quakers sought asylum in New Jersey, and others pursued profit there. William Penn, the richest Quaker in England and one of their prominent leaders, was asked to arbitrate a furious quarrel between Friends over property rights in New Jersey. He was increasingly attracted to investment in a "Holy Experiment" to the west of that region. He was a close friend of Charles II and his brother James. Charles II gave him Pennsylvania, to pay off a debt owed to Penn by the Crown; and James made a present to him of Delaware. Himself a victim of Anglican oppression, Penn wished to provide a safe sanctuary for his fellow Friends. He also hoped to make money. His domains contained a few hundred settlers when he acquired them. Beginning in 1681, several thousands of Quakers and other exotic Protestants, including Mennonites and Moravians, swiftly moved from England and the European continent to fair and fertile lands west of the broad Delaware. There, given religious freedom, they thrived. Sharing political authority with Penn, they bickered with him. He made no immediate financial profit, but he created a rich estate for his descendants. He also made two colonies, for Delaware was gradually separated from Pennsylvania.

During the years in which the English closed the gap between their possessions beside the Chesapeake and in New England they also made the Carolinas their own. At the middle of the seventeenth century Spain still claimed all the lands between the southern boundary of Virginia and their outpost at St. Augustine. However, no Spaniard lived north of the Savannah River. The English ignored the pretensions of Spain. By 1653 farmers seeping southward from Virginia had put down in North Carolina. A decade later Charles II gave to eight of his courtiers and friends a "Carolina" that extended from Virginia to the outposts of the Spanish in Florida. These proprietors yearned for income without investment. Nevertheless, they sent out one ship which carried settlers from England and the English West Indies to their domain. These founded Charleston in 1670. The proprietors also encouraged others to settle in and near that place. The center of a growing trade with the southern Indians, it became the nucleus of South Carolina. The owners also welcomed new settlers in the northern part of their grant. There gradually grew the colony of North Carolina. The Anglican Church was established in both of the Carolinas. The two became distinct political entities early in the eighteenth century. By that time rice-growing assured the prosperity of South Carolina. North Carolina long remained an inconspicuous home for plain farmers who were neither rich nor eminent.

Let us consider the prospect of the flourishing English colonies along the Atlantic seaboard from Maine to South Carolina in the year 1713, at the end of the War of the Spanish Succession, a little more than a century after the founding of Jamestown. Holland had withdrawn from the contest for empire in North America, Spain had ceased to be an aggressive competitor, and France had become England's chief rival. The flag of the Bourbon king of France, Louis XIV, flew over Canada, and he claimed to own all of the Mississippi Valley, named Louisiana in his honor. But there were then no more than a few scores of Frenchmen settled in all of Louisiana, and Canada was thinly peopled. Something like 400,000 persons lived in the English colonies to the east and south, and their number was rapidly increasing. That year, in the Treaty of Utrecht, France formally abandoned Nova Scotia, Newfoundland, and the Hudson Bay country to England. Moreover, after the crushing defeat of the French fleet at La Hogue in 1692, Louis had conceded naval superiority, so important in the struggle for empire beyond the Atlantic, to the English. It was already doubtful that France, or France and Spain in combination, could prevent English dominance in North America. It was by no means obvious at the time to policy-makers on either side of the Channel that such was the fact. A half-century later the French empire on that continent collapsed, and Napoleon himself could not revive it.

CHAPTER 3

Jewels of Empire

❀

THE ENGLISH COLONIES THAT became American states prospered, expanded, and matured during the fifty years following the Treaty of Utrecht. Their inhabitants quadrupled in number. They became more numerous on the coastal plain, on Tidewater; they moved into Georgia, the last of the Thirteen Colonies to be settled; pushing inland, they occupied much of the Piedmont; as early as 1745 they began to pass over the Appalachian Mountains into the valley of the Mississippi. They obtained rich harvests from soil and sea; their commerce increased steadily; they developed infant industries. They did not suffer very seriously from the exertion of British authority. When, at the close of the Seven Years' War in 1763, the Bourbon rulers of France and Spain were compelled to accept the consequences of overwhelming defeat in the New World, the entire eastern third of North America came under the English flag. The way opened for advance of the colonists to the Mississippi River, even beyond it, and a noble vista lay before them.

The natural wealth of the regions between the Atlantic and the Appalachians does not, and did not then, match that to be found west of the mountains. Precious metals were relatively scarce, and the vast and immensely rich black lands of the Mississippi Valley had no counterpart on the Atlantic seaboard. Nevertheless, with its sandy shores and stony hills, with its swamps and wilderness, the seaboard also offered opportunities to tillers of the soil that did not exist either in the British Isles or on the European continent. Opulent and virgin lands in the valley of the Connecticut River and in southeastern Pennsylvania lured men to America. Quantities of land not quite so fertile were nowhere lacking, and these also beckoned insistently to tenants and peasants of the Old World. A generous Nature supplied wide reaches suitable for horticulture and grazing. Almost untouched forests—a traveler saw no treeless landscape—plenteously offered pine, oak, and other kinds of wood, to make ships, houses, churches, and every sort of furniture from cradle to coffin. Birds—ducks, turkeys, and quail—abounded. Fish were plentiful in the rivers. Coastal waters were crowded with cod, halibut, salmon, and mackerel. They contained so many fish that even edible ones were long used to fertilize the thinner soils of Long Island and New England. There were millions of deer; from them and from beaver men could secure skins and furs desired across the Atlantic. Fine harbors were frequent all along the coast from Maine to Virginia and were not lacking in South Carolina. They made easy the inlet and outlet of men and goods; and many rivers, including the broad Connecticut, the majestic Hudson, and the lordly Delaware, served as channels of travel and trade. Nature also offered climates in which men could thrive. Rainfall was usually sufficient, even ample, everywhere east of the Appalachians. To the north, winters were harsher than they were in western Europe and the British Isles, but they were bearable; summers were warmer, only occasionally uncomfortable. To the south, it was otherwise. There the winters were mild, somewhat softer than those of southern England; but summers were warm and humid, nearly tropical. In New England the immigrant from Europe shivered when the temperature fell to minus 30 degrees Fahrenheit; in the Carolinas, often, whites and Negroes alike sweated and sought refuge from a burning sun. The newcomer from Europe deplored the extremes of American weather; nevertheless, he enjoyed and profited from its changes and its customary moderation.

The Indians had made so little use of the natural treasures east of the Appalachians that they were nearly untouched. The whites, in seeking to exploit them, encountered difficulties, hardships, misery, disease, and death. But they persevered, and they more and more effectively made use of the largesse extended to them on land and sea. By the end of the seventeenth century many of them were comfortably established, by the standards of

that time, along the western edge of the Atlantic; two generations later, tens of thousands of them were living well on the
uplands ascending westward to the Appalachians. A century and
a half after the founding of Jamestown, it was evident that her
mainland colonies in North America were easily the most valuable possessions of Great Britain overseas.

Athough the English colonists inexorably drove back or
subjugated the Indians, they and their American descendants
advanced westward by fits and starts. Unlike the Spanish, they
did not swiftly conquer many tribes and exert their sway over
vast regions. Their wars with the Indians, chronic and regional
rather than total and continental, were nonetheless sufficiently
harassing and brutal. The Indians long hindered the efforts of
the English and the Americans to take advantage of the natural
resources of North America. Defending their hunting grounds,
their homes, and their independence, they restricted the westward march of the whites. They continued to struggle even
after all hope of successful resistance had been lost; hence, warfare between the whites and the Indians began soon after the
founding of Jamestown and continued intermittently until the
last of the resisting warriors put down their guns and knives far
to the west nearly three centuries later. The colonists traded
with the redmen, made treaties of peace and alliance with them,
and even sought to Christianize and civilize them. William Penn
and the Pennsylvania Quakers managed for a time to maintain
peace with those Indians who resided west of the Delaware
River. Almost invariably, however, when the men of sallow skin
coveted and purchased, or took, Indian lands, they sooner or
later encountered armed resistance. Thus, warfare with the Indians was frequent on the frontiers of the colonies. Combat with
them was not courteous; it was not fought in accordance with
the rules laid down by the whites. The Indians considered neither ambuscade nor treachery to be immoral; they slew men,
women, and children; and they viciously tortured male captives
before putting them to death by fire. To the whites who
suffered at their hands they were shrieking devils. The whites in
their turn resorted to perfidy, wreaked barbarous vengeance.
The Indians set fire to log cabins and forts of the colonists, and
they in turn burned towns of the Indians. Gradually, in the

seventeenth century, the Indians were either exterminated or driven back from the seacoast between Maine and South Carolina. In the following century they were forced back across the Appalachians.

Suffering grievously at the hands of the Indians, the colonists were tried less dramatically but woefully by sickness and death from disease. The salty air of the wide Atlantic did not prevent the passage across the ocean of bacteria and viruses; nor did it cure hereditary infirmities; nor did it add to the knowledge and wisdom of physicians. In England and on the European continent during the seventeenth century and much of the eighteenth, population grew slowly. Not so on the western side of the Atlantic. Nevertheless, the colonists were by no means immortal, except in the minds of some of their descendants. Death often carried away infants and children, before they could heap up a debt to Nature or to God. Old graveyards along the Atlantic seaboard tell again and again their brief and pitiful tale. Their tombstones cluster about those of their parents, and those of their stepfathers and stepmothers too, for husbands and wives also died, often young, and were replaced. Malaria, yellow fever, and smallpox took heavy tolls. The great pox—syphilis—seems to have been uncommon in the colonies, but smallpox was endemic in the eighteenth century. The colonists burgeoned from natural increase, but only because they produced babies in astonishing numbers.

One will not seriously err if he races to the conclusion that the lives of the colonists were not only short but less than Arcadian. For they, with few exceptions, encountered daily and nightly discomforts, afflictions, and toils that tested the bodies and spirits of those who did not soon succumb to the assaults of disease or of the savages. They did not secure shelter without physical exertion, or food without effort, or clothing without labor. Comforts only gradually accumulated, and luxuries even more slowly. The colonies, much as they had to offer, were not permeated by earthly bliss. Many of the difficulties that confronted settlers were aggravated by their inexperience. English ways and means did not always lead to sound American solutions.

Cover, against cold, heat, snow, rain, and insects, posed various problems, some of them almost beyond resolution. The roughest of huts supplied the first shelter for many of those who went early to North America. At Jamestown men attending divine service sat on logs under a canopy. Chopping and sawing oak and pine, New Englanders raised up wooden houses much like those with which they were familiar in England. Thus, by habit, they covered the sides of their houses with boards. The log cabin, which was warmer in winter and cooler in summer than the clapboard house, made its first American appearance in the Swedish settlements along the Delaware River. Thin walls and scanty heat from a hearth fire did not entirely check the chill of winter in Maine, or in Rhode Island. To be sure, the New England house was aesthetically superior to the log cabin, which could hardly be made so as to delight the eye and which was not to be an important permanent part of the American landscape. By the eighteenth century houses, and churches, north of Long Island Sound were commonly as weather-tight as might then be, and they frequently possessed beauty and charm. In Virginia and the Carolinas wooden houses with two hearth places, one at each end, were the rule. Later they were replaced to a degree by structures of brick. Settlers in the Southern colonies suffered less from cold than those who lived in Massachusetts or Connecticut, but they were pestered, if not tormented, by lice and bedbugs, and especially by flies and mosquitoes. Until the colonists obtained windows and screens—screens were long a comfort enjoyed only by the prosperous—the stings and stabs of the insects, thriving in the milder American climates, both irked and infected the flesh, within the home and without.

In a new country nearly all domestic and field tasks were more difficult than in Europe. Men, women, and children toiled. To clear land of trees and brush, so that it might produce crops, was work that tried strong males. Women were endlessly busy, spinning, weaving, sewing, making candles and soap, cooking, and nursing the children. Only the Lord's Day provided relief from physical labor. Leisure was long a rarity in the colonies.

Despite all their trials and adversities, the colonists, taken as a whole, prospered. Gradually, they achieved comfort and acquired some luxuries. Many, perhaps most, people in England

and on the European continent then ate meat only on Sunday; in America it was part of the daily diet. There men grew taller and stronger. Moreover, they bred so quickly and so steadily that their numbers, heavy casualties notwithstanding, multiplied. They were not sorely vexed by the social diseases; prostitutes were almost unknown in the colonies until the eighteenth century was well advanced. For several generations a bachelor or spinster could hardly live alone at ease. Nor could widows or widowers maintain a happy household. The colonists married early and remarried early and late. Thus Benjamin Franklin was one of a brood of seventeen, and that other father of the American nation, Patrick Henry, sired fourteen children. The colonists desired, or were at least willing to have, offspring. Children could be useful on the farm or in the shop, were assets rather than burdens. Besides, when they reached maturity, there would be farm lands for them, and also gainful crafts and trades. Parents did not need to be much concerned lest their sons and daughters starve, or languish in poverty, or turn to crime. There were no beggars, such as one saw in the streets of London and Paris, in the colonies. Nor were the roads infested by highwaymen, at a time when highway robbers were numerous in England. Above all, the abundance of tillable earth, of which possession was not very difficult to obtain, encouraged large families.

So wide were the American portals of opportunity that they easily accommodated later immigrants from Europe along with the descendants of the first ones. The colonists grew vastly in numbers because of continuing additions from London, La Rochelle, Belfast, and Hamburg, as well as from the prodigal production of young. In one colony or another every variety of Christian except for the Roman Catholic could gain relief from religious oppression; and members of the Church of Rome were not usually barred from the American Eden. Nor were Jews denied admission. Hence, oppression in the Old World on the score of faith, or lack of it, drove the persecuted across the ocean throughout the seventeenth century and into the eighteenth. Fleeing Puritans and Anglicans were followed by Quakers, French Calvinists, Lutherans, Mennonites, Moravians, German Calvinists, and Sephardic Jews. Tens of thousands poured across the Atlantic so that they might worship as they would. The tyrannies of rulers and nobles, and their wars, also persuaded maltreated men to seek haven in America. At a time when John, Hans, and Jean were forced to fight one another, to destroy one another's homes and fields, without knowing why, America beckoned insistently. Above all, however, those who left Europe behind sought economic advantage.

Assuredly the motives of those who made off for America were mixed, tangled beyond neat analysis and smooth description. Some went there for adventure, and some merely drifted away from their old homes. In the main, nevertheless, it is apparent that open lands, and opportunity for artisans as well as peasants and laborers, were alluring to the poor and dissatisfied on both sides of the English Channel. Did any emigrating Puritan fail to give thought to the things of this world? Few of those who went to Virginia and Maryland, few who went to the colonies, were truly aristocratic—that is, actually of gentle birth. The privileged do not usually flee from their privileges. Tenants and farm laborers who could hardly hope to become landowners in England, Scotland, or the Germanies learned that they might have their own spacious acres in the English colonies; and they went to get them. Some of the colonies actually gave them land. Craftsmen equally unknown to fame and of not much greater repute in the Old World crossed the Atlantic so that they might have their own shops and businesses. It was the poor and the middling sort that streamed to the New World.

Indeed, many of those who went to America were at least technically servants. Most of the men and women classified as servants were legally bound to work for others for a period of four or five years after their arrival. Such persons more or less willingly, in one way and another, entered into service in exchange for passage across the ocean. They were so eager to escape from the Old World that they risked their lives and accepted temporary bondage in order to enter the New. They were commonly crammed into little space in ancient and frail vessels, and they were sometimes treated as if they were unfeeling freight. In America their masters and mistresses were not uniformly benevolent. Such servants toiled at every task, in field and forest as well as store and home. Often the servant was a temporary member, if an inferior one, of his master's family.

Released at the end of the stipulated period of service, he or she was given complete freedom, clothing, and perhaps best wishes and a bit of cash by a grateful farmer or saddler. Then the former servant, like other immigrants who had been able to transport themselves to the colonies, could acquire land or open a shop, marry, and beget children. Usually men and women who entered into such servitude profited ultimately. If they did not, their descendants did, beginning life on nearly equal terms with the progeny of more prosperous immigrants.

It may surprise that the governments of Great Britain and her colonies did not try severely to limit emigration from the European continent, but so it was. Parliament imposed an oath of allegiance upon those who would be naturalized in England, one that an honest Roman Catholic could not take. Nor were adherents of the Roman Church welcomed in America. There they were on occasion refused permission to land, and were subjected to political and religious discrimination. However, if born in English America, they could not be denied citizenship there. Only a few Roman Catholics, chiefly Irish and English, crossed the ocean before the American Revolution. Foreign Protestants were allowed, encouraged, even urged and helped, both by the Mother Country and the colonies, to emigrate from France, Holland, western Germany, and Switzerland. It was correctly assumed that they would be as loyal to England as colonists of English ancestry. Most of them were easily absorbed, both politically and culturally.

Extending a friendly hand to sturdy and useful foreign Protestants who would go to the colonies, England in the eighteenth century frowned upon the emigration of worthy people of her own, but exported thousands of criminals, vagrants, and unwanted to the colonies. Englishmen in that century were usually satisfied at home. Merchants, artisans, farmers, and others from the southern side of the Tweed continued to emigrate but in relatively small numbers. Much larger contingents of Scotch-Irish (or Ulster Scots) crossed the ocean after 1700, together with uprooted Highlanders and not a few Lowlanders. Conspicuous among those who went from the British Isles to America after 1717 were convicts permitted to accept transportation as servants in lieu of execution or other punishment. Sentenced to seven years of service in the colonies for a minor crime, or

fourteen for a major crime, the convicts were often unfortunate
rather than vicious. Nevertheless, England thus reduced both
her stock of undesirables and the expense incurred in dealing
with them. It was contended in England that this social refuse
filled a colonial need for laborers. As many as 20,000 men and
women were transported to North America before the Revolution, large numbers of them to Virginia and Maryland. Neither
the "seven-year" servants nor those bound for fourteen years
were wanted in the colonies, several of which tried to bar them
by law. To no avail, since transportation was intended to improve England rather than her American possessions. Such laws
were uniformly "disallowed," that is, declared null and void, by
the English Privy Council. In North America, as afterward in
Australia, the depraved and the unfortunate people exported
from England presumably helped to populate. When the inhabitants of the Thirteen Colonies began their struggle for independence, that perceptive but bad-tempered John Bull, Dr.
Samuel Johnson, described them as a "race of convicts." As he
often did, Johnson exaggerated somewhat. England was not relieved of all her male scoundrels and wicked women; and it has
not been demonstrated that the practice of transportation
debased the American people, or the Australian.

Convicts were not the only persons who went willy-nilly to
America. Far more numerous than they were the Negroes who
were taken away from the western shores of the "Dark Continent," or on occasion purchased in the West Indies. They came
from various tribes and societies in Africa. Commonly they
were captives of their fellow blacks, who sold them as slaves to
white traders at steamy African ports. They were crammed into
ships and carried to market across the Atlantic, if they survived
the voyage. Seldom did a slave ship arrive with her human cargo
intact; closely packed in noisome quarters, suffering from the
tropical sun, intimately exposed to contagious diseases, sometimes deprived of sufficient food and water, the Negroes died in
large numbers and were cast into the sea. Even so, the brutal
oceanic trade in slaves was lucrative, and fortunes of merchants
in Liverpool, Newport, Rhode Island, and Charleston, South
Carolina, were based, at least in part, upon it. The price of a
slave was low in Africa, much higher in America, where Negroes were much wanted for field labor after 1700. Ultimately,

in the middle of the eighteenth century, the voice of humanity began fervently to condemn the iniquities of the oceanic traffic in black bodies and souls. By that time the demand for slaves in the Thirteen Colonies had diminished; moreover, in the Southern colonies, where Negroes were numerous, thoughtful whites had become concerned because of the difficulties raised and to be raised by the presence of a massive minority of blacks among the whites. Accordingly, several colonial assemblies tried to stop or interrupt the importation of the Africans, with little success. Slave traders, both English and American, slave owners, royal governors, and English Cabinet members desired that the wicked commerce continue, and it was impossible legally to stop it so long as the English flag flew over the colonies.

Of such magnitude was the Atlantic slave trade that the Negroes, the "invisible men," became by far the largest non-English element in the colonies. They did not cease to reproduce in America; white men and Negro women united to supply mulattoes and others of mixed blood. As American independence approached, one out of every five colonists had a black, brown, or yellow skin. However much white blood he had in his veins, he remained a Negro.

The colonies grew in goods as well as numbers. A decade before they became independent, they were exporting about one hundred million pounds of tobacco annually to the British Isles, and they were buying yearly about £2,000,000 worth of goods from the Mother Country. A third of the British merchant marine was owned and sailed by Americans. By that time there were American merchants who rode in their coaches and who measured their wealth in thousands of English pounds, American country gentlemen who rode in their coaches and possessed thousands of good acres. However, surer proof of American prosperity and basic evidence concerning its nature is to be found in the reminiscence of an old farmer published in 1787:

> At this time my farm gave me and my whole family a good living on the produce of it, and left me one year with another one hundred and fifty silver dollars, for I never spent more than ten dollars a year which was for salt, nails, and the like. Nothing to eat, drink or wear was bought, as my farm provided all.

Impressive as the maritime commerce of the Americans was, imposing as the estates of country gentlemen were, especially in the Southern colonies, American riches were principally in the hands of plain, land-owning farmers.

What did England do to hinder or foster the economic advance of her North American colonies? That question has often been asked, and it has been variously answered. Certainly, when the English, in the second half of the seventeenth century, gradually formed a policy regarding the colonies, they gazed at them through mercantilist eyes. Indeed, England's interest in the colonists remained principally economic, and mercantilist, until after the middle of the eighteenth century. Political questions concerning the relationship between Britain and the colonists were often ignored or set aside for a future day. Not so with respect to matters of money, trade, and manufacture. After 1651 Parliament, by a series of laws, including the famous Navigation Acts and the Molasses Act of 1733, severely restricted the maritime commerce of the colonists. They were not permitted to sell breadstuffs in England, and they were required to take to England tobacco, furs, and rice to be used or consumed in northern Europe. Similarly, the colonists had to buy European goods from British merchants. The Molasses Act was intended to prevent them from trading with the foreign islands of the West Indies. Other laws limited colonial manufacture of woolens, hats, iron, and steel. In general, England sought to create a self-sufficient economic community within her empire, each part of it serving the other. In the main, the colonies were valued as producers of raw materials and as consumers of English finished goods. English manufacturers and merchants were favored against colonial competitors. On the other hand, England paid bounties to Americans who grew indigo, also to those who supplied tar, pitch, and turpentine, the so-called "naval stores." On the whole, the restricting English laws were less injurious to the Americans than they seem to be. They were not all rigidly enforced; and they often required the colonies to do what they would have done in any case. The tobacco planters of Virginia and Maryland suffered more from the laws than did other Americans. Admitting that the laws offered greater benefits to the English than to the colonists, London politicians declared that both profited at the expense of foreigners, that the account between England and America was balanced by the protection which the British army and navy extended to the colonists. It is doubtful that the account was so balanced, since the Americans had to spend money on and fight in wars declared in London to defend the interests of the English as well as their own.

Whatever were the consequences to the colonists of English mercantilist notions, it is apparent that the Americans were allowed greater religious and political freedom than French, Spanish, or Dutch colonials. Now and again dignitaries of the Anglican Church, eager for establishment of it in America, asked help from London politicians, but they seldom got it. They were not permitted even to send a bishop across the ocean to promote the Episcopalian cause. Although England, after the Glorious Revolution of 1688, insisted that Anglicans be given religious liberty in Massachusetts, Connecticut, and New Hampshire, the Puritan Congregational Church was not deprived of its official status in the three colonies. To secure efficiency, greater exercise of English authority, and better defense against the French, Indians, and other enemies, the makers of English colonial policy slowly moved toward the conclusion that every colony, ideally, should have a royal governor and council; also, that reduction in the number of colonies, or centralization of some sort, was highly desirable. However, although many schemes to unify or federate the colonies were brought forward, only one was attempted. A Dominion of New England, created by King James II in 1686, soon expanded to cover New York and New Jersey, and governed by royal officials, was allowed to die when James was driven from his throne two years later. Nor did London insist that every colony be royalized. Connecticut and Rhode Island remained corporate; Pennsylvania, Delaware, and Maryland proprietary. Only eight of the Thirteen Colonies that broke away from Britain in 1776 drove off royal governors and royal councilors.

In every colony appeared an elected legislative body which asserted itself ever more powerfully. Given various titles, it aspired and claimed to be an equivalent of the English House of Commons. It secured dominance over taxation and domestic affairs, and it encroached upon the authority of governors and councils, whether royal or proprietary. Governors and councils might, and often did, check the aggressive elected representatives of the colonists; occasionally the English Privy Council also used the weapon of disallowance to curb them. Nevertheless, amidst chronic and vexing struggles, the defenders of royal and proprietary prerogative lost ground. In English political theory the House of Burgesses of Virginia and its counterparts in other colonies might be looked upon as legislative bodies that met by British permission. In America it was increasingly assumed that they met as a matter of right. In practice, as the colonial time drew to an end, they had very largely made good their claim to be American Houses of Commons.

Clash between American representatives on the one side and British and proprietary officials on the other did not arise from a long and powerful campaign on the part of the colonists to create new institutions. On the contrary, the Americans followed English patterns. Their new parliaments resembled that at Westminster, and their governors the King. Their courts functioned much as courts did in England, if less elegantly, and their laws were basically English. They valued vastly the personal rights of Englishmen—trial by jury, freedom from arbitrary arrest, the right to reasonable bail, and the others—and they strove mightily to protect them. The colonists also brought over from England their systems of town and county government, their parishes, their sheriffs, their coroners, their justices of the peace, their constables. In time, American institutions diverged from the English ones upon which they were molded. However, they remained similar in spirit and in essence two centuries after the Americans became an independent people.

Permitting her authority over the internal affairs of the Americans to dwindle, Britain would not let the French and Spanish prevent colonial expansion. The contest for empire in North America was only temporarily interrupted by the Treaty of Utrecht. Eight years later England moved toward the founding of Georgia, building a fort on the Altamaha River. In 1732 a charter for Georgia was issued. Much has been said about the benevolence of its sponsors, including General James Oglethorpe. However, the colony was also intended to foster trade with the Indians, and especially to serve as a bulwark against the

French in Louisiana and the Spanish in Florida. No more than six debtors are known to have gone to Georgia. However, Oglethorpe established Savannah in 1733, and the colony soon acquired a mixed population of English immigrants, Germans, Scottish Highlanders, and South Carolinians. Oglethorpe guarded it for some years with British regulars. Exposed to attack from Spanish Florida, ill-governed by trustees for almost two decades, it grew slowly. A royal colony after 1751, Georgia was for many years a newer and weaker South Carolina. The British treasury contributed to its governmental expenses until Georgia became an American state.

The founding of Georgia was no more than an important incident in the continuing struggle for North America. England and Spain again assailed each other after 1739 in the War of Jenkins' Ear, which later merged with the War of the Austrian Succession. In the later years of that conflict the English fought against both the Spanish and the French in North America, without decisive result. In 1754 began that climactic clash of arms between England and the French Bourbons which became a part of the great dynastic and colonial struggle known as the Seven Years' War. In North America the French, helped by Indian allies, won impressive early victories in the unsettled regions between the English colonies and Canada. However, the British navy dominated the sea lanes of the Atlantic, making it difficult for France to convey reinforcements across the ocean, or even to communicate with Canada and Louisiana. Besides, the French were pouring soldiers and money into the war in the European theater, where they had to deal with Anglo-German forces and those of Frederick the Great of Prussia. England sent more and more of her red-coated regular troops to North America. More and more thousands of colonials took the field with them. In 1759 Quebec fell to the English, in the following year Montreal and all of Canada. Spain, entering the war toward its close, also suffered humiliating defeats. When peace was made at Paris between George III of England and the Bourbon monarchs in 1763, Spain abandoned Florida to England, and France ceded Canada and all that part of the French empire that lay east of the Mississippi, except for the town of New Orleans. Thus all of the eastern third of North America became English

soil. Before the treaty was signed, France gave Louisiana, including New Orleans and the French possessions west of the
Mississippi, to Spain. France discarded her dreams of North
American empire. It was obvious that Spain could not for-
midably oppose English expansion beyond the Mississippi,
that the way was opening for English advance to the Pacific
Ocean. As it turned out, Canada remained within the British
Empire and Commonwealth, and the English language
and culture triumphed over those of France nearly everywhere north of Mexico. These were no small things. Twenty
years later, however, George III was forced to acknowledge
the independence of his most valuable domains in the New
World, of the United States of America. The American flag
would be raised over California, Oregon, and Washington.

CHAPTER 4

The Colonial Americans

𝄞

WHEN THE FRENCH WITHDREW from North America, it was not obvious to every casual observer that the Americans were an important people. Nevertheless, it is clear enough in retrospect that their condition, except for that of the Negro slaves, was nearly as comfortable, commodious, and secure as might be in a brutal and most uncertain world. So long as the British navy continued to dominate the Atlantic—and it seemed likely to maintain its sway for decades—they did not need to fear invasion by Bourbon armies. Nor must they be fundamentally concerned about an Indian threat, even though the red-skinned warriors, with or without European allies, could create havoc and agony on the western frontiers. They were not only as safe as a people might be from alien enemies in the North Atlantic world but were endowed by the Treaty of Paris with a vast prospect of expansion, even to the shores of California. The astute Benjamin Franklin, and with him John Adams, considering the maturity, the numbers, and the wealth of the Americans, and observing their rapid and continuing increase in both population and riches, had already discerned that they would become truly powerful in the British Empire, or conceivably as citizens of an independent nation. Less penetrating eyes saw the Americans as mere colonists, thinly scattered along the edge of a vast continent; divided from one another by clashing economic interests; set apart by antagonistic social structures; linguistically and culturally diverse; provincially jealous and hostile because of quarrels over boundaries, lands, and commerce; and kept apart by distance and bad roads. It was doubted they were even

a people. Were they not Yankees, Pennsylvanians, and Carolinians, rather than Americans? Unquestionably there was remarkable variety among them, and one may readily distinguish
among three regions, the Southern colonies, New England, and
the Middle colonies. Divergence and conflict between East and
West—between Tidewater and interior—also existed. But the
Americans, though heterogeneous, had much in common. Indic-
ative of their true unity is the fact that they had come to be
called "Americans." That name was in part applied to them for
convenience. More important, it recognized that they were a
people not basically different from one another, and that they
were not merely Englishmen who happened to reside in North
America.

To say that the Southern colonies, Maryland, Virginia, the
Carolinas, and Georgia, differed economically and socially from
the others is not to offer a novel or dramatic insight. The long
growing season and plentiful rainfall in those regions made possible, even relatively easy, the production of tobacco in Virginia
and Maryland, and of rice and indigo in the Low Country of the
Carolinas and Georgia centering upon Charleston. Tobacco and
rice could profitably be sold abroad; and England after 1748
paid a bounty on and supplied a market for indigo, used in the
making of dyes. All three could be raised in quantity by unskilled labor, under direction. Hence the bringing in of large
numbers of Negro slaves, the very cheapest of workers, at least
in the short run. Hence also, in great part, the rise of plantations.
After 1700, sanguinely hoping for big crops obtained at low cost
and sold at high prices, many Marylanders and Virginians grew
more and more of the "yellow weed," acquired more land upon
which to grow it and more slaves to care for it. In the Low
Country rice and indigo planters similarly dreamed of easy
wealth and expanded their land and slaveholdings. The plantation owners prospered, although their debts often mounted
almost as swiftly as their assets. Thus agriculture in the South
acquired a special cast, and there was frequently, alas, one plantation where several homestead farmers and their families could
have lived in freedom and comfort. Trade did not thrive in that
region as it did elsewhere in the colonies. Charleston, colonial
capital of South Carolina and busy port of the Low Country,

grew into a small city. It was the only one in the entire Southern region.

The social order in the South, principally based upon its special economy, was also distinctive. It was peculiar in that its bottom was composed of a mass of Negroes, who were, with few exceptions, slaves. Nine out of every ten American Negroes lived, or at least existed, in the Southern colonies. About one third of the people in the entire South were Negro. Some of the blacks were household servants and mechanics; most of them were valued because they cared for crops and produced progeny. Above the Negroes were all the whites, among whom the English element was principal, although Scotch-Irish, Germans, and Scots were also numerous. Above all the other whites was a gentry, an untitled American aristocracy, composed almost exclusively of plantation owners. It was a relatively new aristocracy, membership in it being founded on the possession of wealth rather than patrician ancestors. The worthy person, even the unworthy one, was not barred from it because his father had engaged in commerce; a man who belonged to it might himself be occupied in trade as well as agriculture. At the end of the colonial era, gentry included George Washington, whose father was not quite of it; Edmund Pendleton, who was descended from a bond servant; and Benjamin Powell, in youth a wheelwright, a carpenter, who had earned himself the title of "Gent" by merit. Below that gentry, and often confused with it, were many not-so-rich planters and substantial homestead farmers. These, along with shopkeepers and a few professional folk, composed a middle class. This middle class has escaped the attention it deserves because it lacks the glamor of aristocracy, the brutal charm of slavery. Beneath the middle class were the bond servants, numerous only in Virginia and Maryland, whose status was, of course, temporary. Above the slaves were the "poor white trash," not yet known by that name but real enough. The "trash" should be distinguished from the many whites who were poor only in possessions. Ignorant, lazy, quarrelsome, lawless, and fecund, those degraded people were more numerous than the Southern gentry. It should be added that white men of all classes contributed to the blood stock of the Negroes, who were moving biologically toward their masters and mistresses.

Fascinating as life in the country may be, rural lanes are not the smoothest or broadest highways to learning and the arts. Roads in the Southern colonies were bad, and the region lagged in terms of educational and intellectual advance. Education largely remained a private affair, and elementary schools supported by churches and individual benevolence were available only to a minority of children. The offspring of the slaves were seldom taught more than the performance of physical tasks. The young, male and female, of plain farmers often learned only to write their names. The sons of the aristocracy were commonly instructed by tutors—their sisters learned but to read and write, to play a musical instrument, to dance, and to pursue the domestic arts. Not infrequently a young gentleman continued his studies at the College of William and Mary, founded in 1693, for several generations the only institution of higher learning in the South, or at a college to the north, or at an English private school or university. One finds some of them studying Latin at Westminster School, law at the Inns of Court in London, medicine in Edinburgh and Leyden. However, formal education at the higher levels was not easily available to the middle class, and it was not sought by the majority of young gentlemen. It could not be secured in Charleston, for there was no college there during the colonial time. Nor was Charleston remarkable as a city that nourished literary and artistic talent, although her richer residents wrote essays and verse.

Something more should be said about the males of the Southern aristocracy, for it contributed great men to America and to the world. From it came Thomas Jefferson and James Madison, who were college men, scholars, and cultivated gentlemen as well as philosophers and statesmen. However, the usual man of the gentry was less given to intellectual pursuits. He was comparable to an English squire. He belonged to the Anglican Church, which was established in all the Southern colonies, but he was not devout. He managed his lands and his slaves, hunted, danced, watched cockfights, gambled, and frequently visited his neighbors. Most important, he engaged in politics. The gentry dominated local government in parish and county, and usually both houses of the Southern colonial legislatures—not so thoroughly in North Carolina as elsewhere, for that "valley of humility between two mountains of conceit" contained fewer aristocrats and more homestead farmers than did her neighbors. The aristocrats were splendidly schooled in public affairs, read and wrote about them, acquired breadth of view in statecraft, and gained the polish of men of the world. Of such was the Virginian, George Washington. He and his like offered both sturdy and informed leadership.

In his time New England produced no heroic figure equal to Washington, but many worthy men sprang from its thin soil and stony hillsides. The Yankees, as the inhabitants of the region north of Long Island Sound and east of the Hudson River were commonly designated after the middle of the eighteenth century, varied from the Southerners in both appearance and reality. If New England was not lavishly endowed with natural resources, its people were energetic, thrifty, and ingenious, like those of the Dutch provinces and the Swiss cantons. Moreover, the Yankees commanded more good land than the Dutch, far more generous forests than the Swiss. Most of them were tillers of the soil, farmers who owned their fields, wood lots, and orchards. Many, however, were carpenters, masons, mechanics of all sorts, and traders. The same man might engage in two or more pursuits, farming and fishing, lumbering and shipbuilding, trading and tavern-keeping. Cramped by the lack of fertile soil, the Yankees made ships and went to sea. They gathered abundant crops of fish off their own coasts and on the Grand Banks of Newfoundland; and they turned to maritime commerce with singular success. It is often said that the increasingly evident affluence of Massachusetts rested upon the carcasses of codfish; underneath it also were the trunks of pines and oaks, potent rum, and the bodies of slaves carried from Africa. Merchants grew wealthy in Massachusetts, and in New England, from oceanic traffic as well as fishing.

There were few slaves in New England; few citizens equivalent to the "poor white trash"; few bond servants; and an aristocracy less conspicuous, less powerful, and less glamorous than that of the Southern colonies. Upon the stable and diversified economy of the Yankee country was based a large middle class. Its members usually had the right to vote, and their will was potent in public affairs. Aristocrats did not dominate in Massa-

chusetts or Connecticut as they did in Virginia and South Carolina. A distinction made in the seventeenth century between the
"gentleman" and the "goodman" had softened. Moreover, the
Congregationalist clergy had lost prestige and influence. The
men of the cloth had been, to a degree, displaced by men of
money. Nevertheless, New England had its first families of
wealthy merchants, landowners, officeholders, lawyers, and
clergy. With strong support from the middle class, they were
the leaders in that region. So firm was their grasp upon the body
politic in Connecticut that they formed a "standing order"
which endured for generations. Even so, Hutchinsons, Salton-
stalls, Trumbulls, and Griswolds did not have the social and
political stature of the Southern Lees, Carters, and Pinckneys.
New England society was semi-democratic.

Before the end of the colonial time the prosperous New Englanders offered outward evidence of their wealth in their
clothes, coaches, carriages, and homes. The well-to-do wore
garb like that of English gentlemen and ladies, like that of
Southern aristocrats. They had their wines as well as their rum,
and their big houses. More impressive than their mansions were
the New England churches in austere elegance; more pleasing to
the generous-minded observer than those mansions were the
neat, attractive homes of tens of thousands of villagers and
farmers. The New England village had acquired a charm and
beauty which long endured. New England also had cities—
Newport, which would afterward cease to grow rapidly; and
Boston, which was the second largest American city and would
retain importance in commerce, in banking, in education, and in
the sight of its citizens. English travelers visiting the Yankee
country in the eighteenth century, and later, remarked that it
bore a greater resemblance to Old England than other parts of
America. Its people continued to be almost entirely of English
descent until the nineteenth century was well under way.

The Yankees were also the best educated of the colonists.
Elementary instruction was quite readily available to them,
often at public expense. As the American Revolution approached, the New Englander was usually literate. Moreover,
there were many men among the Yankees who were college
graduates. Harvard was the only college in New England until

Yale was founded in 1701. Nevertheless, the two colleges sent forth hundreds of informed and thoughtful men in the eighteenth century. After 1764 the College of Rhode Island (Brown University) and after 1769 Dartmouth contributed to the supply of well-educated men in the colonies. It was further increased by private study and reading, for those who earnestly sought to learn often had access to books.

Instruction of the young, even in New England, was interrupted by the tasks of transplanting from Old England, and learning and the arts did not flourish steadily from the beginning of settlement. There was, to be sure, a transit of European civilization, at least the English variety of it. However, all of that civilization did not promptly pass over the ocean, and things physical during many decades occupied minds and energies at the expense of things intellectual and artistic in New England. So it was everywhere in America as people flooded into wild new territories. Included among those who went to New England in the second quarter of the seventeenth century were many scholars, both clerical and lay. Moreover, Harvard produced gifted and learned men even in its first years. Nevertheless, there was a cultural sag in New England; it could not and did not keep pace with the Mother Country.

Nevertheless, New England spawned scholars, writers, and even a distinguished artist in the colonial time. In the South, William Byrd II of Westover, author of charming sketches of life in Virginia and North Carolina, stands out because so few men in that region distinguished themselves in letters before the onset of the American Revolution. He would have had more literary company among the Yankees. But let us not make too much of New Englanders who studied, wrote, or dabbled in the arts. We should not praise highly men—or women—who would in no way have been remarkable on the eastern side of the Atlantic. Eschewing ancestor worship, no American will classify the New England poet Edward Taylor, who was born in Old England, with John Milton, or match Cotton Mather of Massachusetts against John Locke. Mather was only a bright star in a sequestered corner of America. If he presciently declared that disease was caused by tiny invisible animals, he also believed that witches were both real and visible. His intellect was chaotic as well as brilliant. Of the Reverend Jonathan Edwards, who has been sufficiently admired by later American generations, it may be said that he was a gifted theologian and an acute philosopher, that he put the case for freedom of the human will in the face of an omniscient God as well as the logician may do it. In the London of his day Edwards would not have been a man of small repute. Another New Englander, John Singleton Copley, of a later generation than Edwards, actually did win fame in England. Copley went abroad to study painting, was acclaimed in London for his artistry, remained in England, and fathered a lord chancellor. His best work, however, was done before he left his native country. Portraits that he painted of various Americans are remarkable for their realism and craftsmanship. However, he is not usually ranked with his English contemporaries Sir Joshua Reynolds and Thomas Gainsborough.

Material, educational, and intellectual advances, so important in themselves, also profoundly affected the Congregational establishment in New England. Almost united with the state, except in Rhode Island, the Puritan church wielded vast power in seventeenth-century New England. The will of the orthodox Puritan clergy and laymen was dominant alike in public and personal affairs. Punishing heresy, even Anglican deviations, they most earnestly strove to preserve the true church and the Puritan way. Congregations vied with legislatures in the curbing of the unfaithful, the heedless, the willful, and the wicked. Idolatry and blasphemy were at one time capital crimes in Massachusetts, and persons who denied belief in the resurrection of the body or in the validity of infant baptism, even persons who withdrew from communion, could be banished. On the other hand, Puritan congregations formally inquired into the behavior of their members and excommunicated men and women of heretical belief and unpleasing conduct; in 1640 Captain John Underhill was driven from communion in Boston because he had committed and had tried to commit adultery—and would not offer a suitable confession. Far less heinous offenses were similarly punished. Without the confession and repentance of the parents, a child conceived before their marriage might be denied baptism. It was widely believed among the Puritans that a child born on Sunday was conceived on a Sunday and so was especially burdened with sin. The true New England Puritan feared that even he, the seemingly anointed, might at last be disappointed, and he kept both his own and his brother's conscience. It ought to be added that, to his credit, he was not a prohibitionist. Congregational clergymen drank rum, and Harvard students were daily served beer with bread and beef. The "steady habits" for which the men of Connecticut have long been famous included toping. It is claimed, in fact, that some New England towns required by law the maintenance of an ordinary, or tavern, conveniently near the village place of worship. It is notorious that the Puritans of eastern Massachusetts hanged nineteen persons found guilty of witchcraft after 1688. They were not the first to suffer for that crime in Massachusetts. One ought not exaggerate the significance of the hysteria about witches that convulsed Salem—and Boston—toward the close of the seventeenth century. Belief in witchcraft was not confined to the Puritans—nor were barbarous punishments. In England in 1765 a woman convicted of poisoning her husband was burned at the stake. The execution of innocent victims accused of witchcraft is evidence of a sort that Puritanism was in decline.

So it was, but in slow descent. The New Englanders, as their lives on earth became longer and more pleasant, worried less about their existence beyond the grave. Doubtless they became more tolerant in their beliefs as they voyaged distantly and conversed with men subscribing to creeds other than their own. Deism, which obtained many converts in Europe subsequent to the discoveries of Isaac Newton, spread to America. Even Puritan clergymen increasingly preached about the God of love, saying less about the God of justice, before whom even well-educated Puritans had bowed in utter fear. Some of the ministers slipped toward Unitarianism. Weakened by assaults from worldly prosperity and secular learning, orthodox Puritanism lost communicants, especially those with social pretensions, to newly founded Anglican churches. It suffered further from schism. It was hit hard in the 1740s by a wave of pietistic and emotional revivalism, the "Great Awakening." The ravings, the rantings, and the frenzies of the "Great Awakening," which Jonathan Edwards, who ought to have known better, helped to

stimulate, grievously offended the Congregationalists who clung
to traditional Puritan emphasis upon religious law and logic. As
the American Revolution approached, the Congregational establishment was not what it had been. In 1755 at Marblehead, Massachusetts, Mrs. John Glover confessed in open church that she
had engaged in sexual intercourse with her husband before their
marriage. But there is no record that Glover, later a valiant and
most useful officer who served under General Washington,
humbled himself in church before he defied his King.

Let it not be thought that the New Englanders internally led
dark, dismal, and desperate lives. Their religious notions and
moral codes were their own and hence were not utterly un-
suited to them. One may not say that they were an unhappy
people. Were the Spartans, with their rigid rules? Or the
Samurai, because of their Bushido? If not gay or frivolous, the
Yankee could nevertheless be contented, even joyful. Consider
the radiant and touching lines addressed by the Puritan poet
Mrs. Anne Broadstreet "To my Dear and Loving Husband."

> My love is such that Rivers cannot quench,
> Nor ought but love from thee give recompence.
> Thy love is such I can no way repay;
> The heavens reward thee manifold I pray.
> Then while we live, in love let's so persever,
> That when we live no more, we may live ever.

Between the colonial extremes were the Middle colonies, New
York, New Jersey, Pennsylvania, and Delaware, moderate in
climate, immoderately furnished with good soil, great rivers,
and splendid harbors. They were the "bread colonies," sending
grain and flour to distant places. But their lands bounteously
gave forth iron as well as wheat and corn, and manufacturers of
the black metal in the Middle colonies offered dangerous competition to those of Sheffield and other English cities before 1750.
Water-borne craft in large numbers plowed the Hudson and the
Delaware. Philadelphia and New York were centers of both
river and oceanic traffic. As the era of the Revolution drew
near, Philadelphia, with more than 20,000 citizens, was the
largest American city, and New York threatened to pass Boston
in population. Had they been located in England, the two cities

would have been important there. Their well-to-do merchants, such as John Watts of Manhattan and Israel Pemberton of Philadelphia, together with country magnates, gladly supplied a gentry in the region between Connecticut and Maryland. That aristocracy was a trifle closer to the Southern aristocracy than was the patrician class of New England. Some of its members, such as the Philipses, Livingstons, and Van Rensselaers of New York, owned wide estates and dictated to numerous tenants and white servants. In Delaware the masters and mistresses of Negro slaves lived much like their counterparts in Virginia. The Middle colonies had their sharp social gradations but also a middle class almost as large proportionately as that of New England. Plain farmers who owned their good land were numerous, and artisans and traders thrived in cities, towns, and villages.

Remarkable in that early Middle America was the variety of its people, for it was the home of large non-English minorities, notably German, Scotch-Irish, and Dutch. The ancestors of the Pennsylvanians were as much German as they were English; and the Scotch-Irish settled thickly in the interior of William Penn's colony. Preachers exhorted their congregations in Dutch in several communities of New York and New Jersey until the end of the eighteenth century; and the use of German, at least of a sort, persisted in German enclaves of Pennsylvania into the twentieth century. Equally various were the churches, none of them established, except that the Anglican Church was officially recognized in three New York counties. The followers of Calvin, English, Scotch-Irish, German, and Dutch, were numerous; Lutherans, Moravians, Anglicans, Quakers, and Jews worshiped the Creator in their several ways. These were all the more diverse because the "Great Awakening" and its emotional Christianity disturbed and divided several of the sects. That Christianity of enthusiasm, of hell-fire and brimstone, indeed, spread throughout the colonies, and waves of it were to assail the American people again and again.

The "Great Awakening" does not offer testimony to educational and intellectual advance. Men and women who lost their self-control in eagerness to save their souls might speak in "strange tongues" but not in Latin. Their religious frolicking might lead them to read the Holy Scriptures but hardly the plays of Shakespeare. However, there were other awakenings in the Middle colonies. Schools maintained at public expense were less common than in New England, but many privately managed ones, often maintained by clergymen and churches, purveyed elementary instruction. That devotion to learning so characteristic of the Scots was displayed by Scottish and Scotch-Irish Presbyterians in America; the Dutch and many of the Germans also set high value upon knowledge. The task of civilizing the young was not neglected in the Middle colonies. In that region no fewer than four universities were born before the Revolution: Princeton, founded in 1746; the University of Pennsylvania, established as an academy at Philadelphia in 1751; Columbia, appearing three years later as King's College; and Rutgers, which began as Queen's College in 1766.

Those central colonies had their full colonial share of talented and learned men in the eighteenth century. In New York the Scottish-born official, Cadwallader Colden, wrote a worthy history of the Iroquois and more than dabbled in medicine and physics. He erroneously believed that he had made discoveries correcting mistakes of Newton. William Livingston of New York and New Jersey was a poet, essayist, polemicist, and politician. In Pennsylvania the Bartrams, John and William, father and son, distinguished themselves as botanists; the charming *Travels* of the younger Bartram would supply imagery for Samuel Coleridge's "Kubla Khan." By far the most distinguished man in all the colonies before the Revolution was, of course, Benjamin Franklin, Boston-born but a Philadelphian during most of his long and busy life. One may not properly describe in a brief space his many-faceted genius, his diverse achievements. Born the son of an artisan, he became a printer, philosopher, essayist, postal official, superb propagandist, inventor, politician, and diplomat. He contributed importantly to knowledge about electricity, and he wrote his classic autobiography. His education was largely informal, his donations to mankind cardinal and profuse. Not without faults—there was a strain of grating smugness in him—he was the very model of the self-made and well-made man in the American "land of opportunity."

It is apparent enough that variety and contrariety were char-

acteristics of the American scene after the middle of the eighteenth century. Nor have all the colonial divergencies and
clashes been mentioned, for they existed between East and West
as well as North and South. Indeed, division between East and
West, in one form or another, like that between North and
South, was to endure into the twentieth century. It appeared as
soon as the colonists moved inland, from the coastal plain to the
Piedmont above it, into the so-called Old West. The people of
the Old West, especially those from Pennsylvania southward,
were poorer, less educated, less European, and more American
than those of the Atlantic Tidewater. The Tidewater leaned
toward the aristocratic, the Old West toward the democratic.
The interior folk were often indebted to their more prosperous
fellows of the coastal plain. The Tidewater did not always exert
itself to help defend the Old West against the Indians; it was
reluctant to give the newly settled areas representation in the
colonial assemblies in proportion to numbers; and it sometimes
discriminated against the people of the interior with respect to
taxation. In the Southern colonies the homestead farmer of the
interior, owning few or no slaves, was set against the wealthy
planter to the east. Hence came political collisions, and even
unsuccessful rebellions by the people of the interior. They
took up arms under Nathaniel Bacon in Virginia in 1676. In
Pennsylvania they marched against Philadelphia in 1764; soon
afterward, as Regulators, they created uproar in the Carolinas.
Bacon's Rebellion was not put down without bloodshed, and an
uprising of the Regulators in North Carolina continued until
they were crushed by Governor William Tryon and provincial
militia in the pitched battle of the Alamance in 1771.

One may be tempted to magnify the cleavages among the
colonial Americans. For they had much in common from the
beginning, and they became more alike. One may think too
much about their varied ancestral roots in Europe and Africa,
English, Welsh, Scottish Lowland and Scottish Highland,
Scotch-Irish, Irish, Dutch, Flemish, German, Swedish, Finnish,
French, Swiss, Jewish, and Negro. It should be observed that
virtually all of the European forebears of the colonists lived on
the lands and islands north of the Pyrenees and west of the Elbe
River. They were west Europeans, and both they and their

descendants in America were overwhelmingly Protestant, if of many sects. Moreover, the English element in America was easily principal in the colonial bloodstock, and the English language, modified somewhat in the American environment, prevailed without serious contest over other European, and African, ones. English ways of thought, English institutions retained an easy ascendancy. Karl Schmidt became Charles Smith, and Hans Fuchs became John Fox, and the Smiths and Foxes gradually learned to think like their English-speaking neighbors. Besides, although German, Dutch, and French elements persisted, there was much intermarriage between the English and European parts of the colonial population before the beginning of the Revolution—it would accelerate.

Tending to fuse, even with the Negroes, the colonists also became less and less like the English at home.

> Leaving the old, both worlds at once they view
> That stand upon the threshold of the new.

Not too different from one another when they emigrated to the New World, the settlers were brought closer together by common experiences and interests in America, these being other than those influencing their brethren in the Old World. From 1607 onward they encountered similar troubles in subduing Nature. They had the same enemies, the Indians, the Spanish, and the French. They had a common experience of contest with English authority. Hence they grew together, and at the same time apart from their kin on the European continent and in the British Isles. That they had become like one another and unlike their blood relatives beyond the Atlantic was recognized by the observant and assumed by the less perceptive among them well before the Americans and the English exchanged shots at Lexington. It is significant that the terms "America" and "American," to indicate Britain's colonies on the mainland of North American and one of their inhabitants, had come into everyday use by the 1760s. While it is clear that these names were increasingly employed because of convenience—there were no brief equivalent terms—they were also used because they were needed to identify a distinct area and people. Thus the question posed by J. Hector St. John de Crèvecoeur and so often quoted, "What then is this American, this new man?" To be sure, the wide and growing gap between the American and the Englishman was not yet seen by all in America or England. An American in the 1760s might still refer to the Mother Country as "home"; and an Englishman might assume that a citizen of New London, Connecticut, if not the equal of one of Old London, if only a "poor relation," was nevertheless English. But that gap between the Englishman and the American became ever greater after the collapse of the French empire in North America. After 1783, when England recognized the independence of the United States, there could be no serious question that its citizens, an incomplete compound of old breeds, had become a distinct and new one.

CHAPTER 5

The Onset of the Revolution

THE AGE OF THE American Revolution is now about two centuries in the past. Few who have mused upon the vicissitudes and triumphs of mankind will deny that the rupture of the first British Empire and the founding of the American republic in the third and fourth quarters of the eighteenth century have had vast consequences. They may not be nicely and shortly described with easy assurance; indeed, the causes, the course, and the immediate and remote outcomes of the Revolution continue to supply materials for scholarly, subtle, and seemingly endless debate. Such contests, although the issues must at length become segments of an ancient chronicle, even parts of a prehistory, may be expected to endure. Not so merely because the more and less learned cannot refrain from engaging in intellectual rivalry; nor even because the Americans broke free from the British Empire, important, even God-given, as their independence afterward seemed to them. Not yet may it be said that the divorce between Britain and America has been finally decreed. Nor did the Revolution destroy the British Empire, which reached a new majesty in the nineteenth and twentieth centuries before it fell into a second decline. But the Americans of the Revolutionary time did tear from their backs the yokes of oppressive European royalty and nobility, created a more decent order for themselves, and opened the way for a still happier society for those who came after them in the republic they created. The American achievement of freedom, gained at the expense of one of the most powerful of modern empires, also struck a heavy blow against colonialism, of whatever sort. During scores of years to come, the Declaration of Independence of the American subjects of George III would inspire other peoples in all parts of the world to seek their own national liberty. Moreover, the republic formed by the patriots not only proved that potent monarchy, hereditary privilege, and other hallowed inequities and injustices were not indispensable to the avoidance of anarchy, but also offered for many generations a respectable model of humane and successful self-government. These offspring of the Revolution were surely of the first magnitude in the history of mankind.

The wheel of national fortunes has spun and will spin. At one time and another in the modern era, Spain, France, England, and Germany have enjoyed hegemony in Europe. At the close of the Seven Years' War, England was easily the primary nation. The Treaty of Paris of 1763 marked the nadir for France and Spain; in central Europe the rising state of Prussia, exhausted by warfare but directed by Frederick the Great, counterbalanced the weakened empire of the Austrian Habsburgs; and Romanov Russia was still on the fringe of eastern Europe. England had already embarked upon the Industrial Revolution, well in advance of her neighbors; her foreign commerce was as ample as that of France; British ascendancy on the seas could not then be questioned; and the British Empire was at a zenith. Peculiarly valuable and impressive were Britain's overseas possessions, including the eastern third of North America; Jamaica, Barbados, and many other rich islands in the Caribbean; footholds in Central America; Gibraltar and the Balearic island of Minorca, bases that, with the navy, assured control of the western Mediterranean; colonies on the west coast of Africa; and rich parts of India. In India, as in North America, the French had been routed; and that vast subcontinent was open to British exploitation. Immediately after the Treaty of Paris, English milords, if their behavior puzzled continental Europeans, were also looked upon with profound respect, were envied and copied.

But Britain was not so potent as she seemed. The population of her home islands was much less than half that of France. True, her island position gave her great military advantage, making defense relatively easy so long as she controlled the adjacent

waters. It may be believed that conquest of the British Isles by a
European assailant was then unlikely, and that it would become
even less likely for some generations as the English made effective use of their stores of coal and iron and as their numbers
multiplied. Nevertheless, it is evident that sea power was essential to the maintenance and expansion of the Empire, if not
indispensable for the preservation of the British state. It had
been, and could be, used to check enemies on the European
continent, to protect British commerce and to attack that of
foes, to safeguard British colonies, and to conquer those of ad-
versaries. In 1763 the British navy was unquestionably the
strongest in the world, powerful enough to meet a challenge
from the combined fleets of France and Spain. Would it retain
its superiority? Its dominance had been attained as much by the
weakness of its rivals as by its own strength. Deeply humiliated
in the Seven Years' War and well aware that feebleness at sea
was responsible for many of the disasters they had encountered,
the ministers of Louis XV of France began to build a new navy
even before the close of that conflict—and to restore the French
army. The inferiority of the French and Spanish on salt water
was not in the nature of things or of men. There was nothing in
the British climate which assured to Britain greater admirals or
sturdier sailors; nor was Britain the only nation with access to
pine and oak; nor was seamanship confined to men born west of
the North Sea. It could not be assumed that the French would
never be lords of the Channel. Prudence declared that Britain
must keep her powder dry and her warships wet, numerous, and
efficient.

It has been observed that British prestige was founded to a
degree on the divisions of Europe. Here again, it was not safe to
believe that rulers and states beyond Calais would continue
without interruption to struggle against one another, so as to
help maintain some sort of balance of power on the Continent,
and thus to lessen the military dangers to which even England
was exposed. To be sure, it was not likely that all of Europe
would combine against England. Even so, experience asserted
that the last great European war had not yet been fought, that
another would come within no long time. For several generations Britain had had at least one powerful ally on the Continent

in each of the major convulsions of Europe. Obviously, a potent ally, or several allies, would be most useful, possibly indispensable, when the day of military danger again came. Yet Britain had no reliable friend among the rulers of the great powers in 1763. In time of need she could rely only upon feeble Hanover and weak Portugal. The French and Spanish Bourbons had to be looked upon as inveterate enemies—and Spain, like France, was mending her military machine. An alliance with Frederick the Great of Prussia had served Britain very well in the Seven Years' War. The British had allowed it to collapse before the end of that conflict, leaving Frederick, as he saw his situation, in the lurch. He survived the assaults of his many Continental enemies; he would not rely upon a partnership with Britain in the future. The Austrian and Russian empires had no reason to support Britain, unless she suffered so greatly that the balance of power in Europe was badly upset to their own disadvantage. It is apparent that Britain's position was diplomatically weak in 1763, also that it would not easily be strenthened.

That England was not all-powerful was recognized by perceptive Englishmen. Some of these, after the capture of Quebec in 1759, while church bells were ringing frequently in London to celebrate a string of British victories, urged that Canada be given back to France when peace was made. Contemplating the numbers and the riches of the English colonists in North America, they proclaimed that the Americans had gained ever greater freedom within the empire and were moving toward independence. So long as they were menaced by French Canada, they would value the protection they received from the British army and navy. But, relieved of the French danger, the colonists would continue to reduce British authority. It was wise to return Canada to France rather than keep it and add to the risk of losing the Thirteen Colonies. Canada had little economic value—not so much as a West Indian island or islands that Britain could demand from France instead; it would be prudent to demand sugar fields rather than snowbanks. The Thirteen Colonies were of the very first importance to England, if only because they offered a splendid market for English goods. These arguments appeared in newspapers and pamphlets. They did not persuade

the British Cabinet to abandon Canada. Must England conquer
it a third time? Even so, concern in London lest the colonists
seek greater freedom at the expense of Britain increased.

Some men in the imperial capital distrusted the loyalty of the
Americans to Britain, and more believed that they had not done
their duty in the Seven Years' War. The colonies had spent
large sums, and they had raised many thousands of troops toward winning that struggle. But their assemblies had not, in the
opinion of fault-finding Englishmen, contributed enough,
quickly enough, to the war effort. With greater justice, the
behavior of American merchants during the war was bitterly
condemned. Not a few of them, while the British navy sought
to prevent reinforcements and supplies from reaching the
French possessions, had traded with and had supplied the enemy
with foodstuffs. And had not colonial merchants frequently violated the Navigation Acts in peace as well as war?

It is true that the conduct of the Americans in the Seven
Years' War was not beyond reproach, that British authority
over them had diminished, and that it would continue to de-
crease, unless measures were taken to defend it. As early as 1759
in the flush of victory, the British Cabinet began efforts to restrict the growing power of the American assemblies, to assert
more positively the royal prerogative. Its measures aroused
American discontent, the more so because they were accompanied by a rising wave of Anglican activity in New England
and the Middle colonies, together with an attempt by the Anglican clergy to get permission to send a bishop to America. Such
permission was not given, then or later, although fear of Anglican aggression disturbed American Congregationalists, Presbyterians, and even laymen of the Episcopal faith. But the Americans were not yet gravely vexed because Britain tried to retard
the colonial clock. When, after the end of the war with the
Bourbons, Britain sought to turn back that clock, when Parliament undertook to tax the colonists for revenue to support a
British standing army in North America, they angrily resisted.
Looking back, the student of the affairs of men and of states
may declare with confidence that the relationship between England and her colonies inevitably altered. But it cannot be said
with equal assurance that complete separation was destined. To

claim that the cleavage had to come through force of arms, in the War of Independence, requires superhuman knowledge of the will of God or of unchangeable fate. After Anglo-American contest had become severe, Benjamin Franklin could still conceive that America might become the center of power in a continuing British Empire, that the capital of that empire might in time move across the Atlantic. It was not impossible that separation should come in the course of generations, with England consenting to gradual destruction of her authority. Other outcomes may plausibly be conjectured, provided that the growing numbers and wealth of the Americans are properly taken into account. In the longer run, there could be no change they were unwilling to accept.

The English politicians who unwittingly goaded the Americans into revolt were not philosophers who could see far into time to come. Not one of them had ever visited North America —they knew more about Paris and Florence than they did about Philadelphia and Boston. Even so, had they been cautious, had they been indifferent toward things American, they would not have become involved in a fundamental clash. Instead, they acted with undue assurance and misplaced vigor, daring the colonists to challenge Britain. Less than three years after the Treaty of Paris the Americans forthrightly defied their parent state in the Stamp Act crisis. England then undertook to placate them—but English sovereignty had been questioned. Those who made English policy could not accept defeat. They made two more attempts to bring the Americans to heel, and they at length provoked armed rebellion.

Within the brief space of twenty-eight months after the Treaty of Paris, English ministries led by the Earl of Bute and George Grenville carried through a long series of measures that affected the colonists in many ways and aroused almost universal resentment among them. The young King George III, who had ascended the throne in 1760, was not the framer of these measures. Bute, who was prime minister in the early months of 1763, was responsible for two momentous decisions, both of them acceptable to Grenville. One of these was that the British army, enlarged during the Seven Years' War, should not be reduced to its former size. An important part of the army, under General Jeffery Amherst, commander in chief with headquarters at New York, was doing garrison duty in numerous forts in the North American interior. Parliament agreed with the Bute ministry that the army ought to have for the future seventeen regiments—on paper about 8,500 men—on the North American continent and adjacent islands. The ministry consented to the dispersal of the troops in the forts by Amherst. His forces were to be twice the number that had been thought sufficient for defense against Indian and European enemies before 1754. The decision to maintain so many troops in itself created colonial unrest. Moreover, the decision was taken upon the assumption that the troops could not be supported by English taxpayers and that the money needed for their maintenance must come from colonial pockets. A decision was made in principle that Parliament must levy taxes upon the Americans to get the funds. It was left to the Grenville ministry to choose the sort and size of the taxes.

Had they been astute, Bute and his colleagues would have reduced British garrison troops in North America to a few regiments to be stationed in the St. Lawrence Valley to keep the French Canadians in order and one or two at Pensacola or Mobile to keep watch against the Spanish. Had they done so, had they compelled the Americans to provide soldiers for their own defense, they would have escaped many troubles, and would have given the colonists a vent for their energies. Almost at the very time that Parliament undertook to maintain a standing army in North America, many Indian nations of the Ohio Valley and the region of the Great Lakes, fearing that they would be despoiled of their lands, attacked British garrisons in several forts located between the frontiers of the Thirteen Colonies and the upper Mississippi. They waged the struggle known as Pontiac's War alike against British soldiers and colonials. The regulars could not prevent punishing raids by the Indians upon the frontiers. Moreover, several posts defended by the redcoats were taken, and they suffered humiliating, ghastly defeats. At length, weary of conflict and assailed by regulars and American militia under the command of General Thomas Gage, who succeeded Amherst, the Indians were forced to make peace. The war was embarrassing and expensive to Britain.

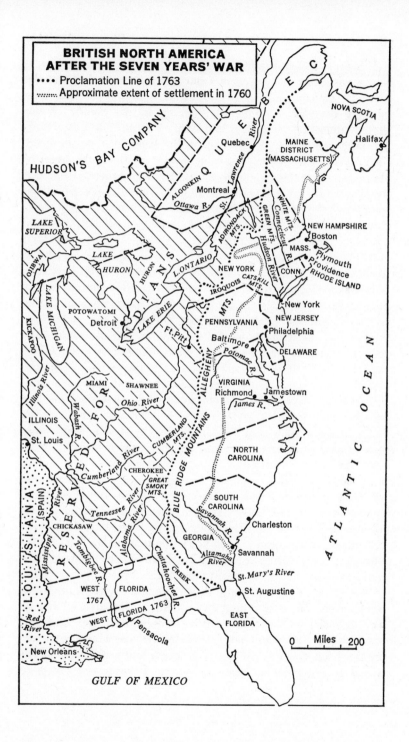

**BRITISH NORTH AMERICA
AFTER THE SEVEN YEARS' WAR**

•••• Proclamation Line of 1763
········· Approximate extent of settlement in 1760

However, Pontiac's War persuaded the Grenville ministry, not to withdraw the redcoats from exposed forts, but to take energetic steps to avert future clashes with the redmen. The ministry determined to maintain in office two royally chosen Indian superintendents who had been appointed to foster English influence among the savages at the beginning of the Seven Years' War. On October 7, 1763, toward soothing the fears of the Indians that they would lose their lands and their freedom, it issued a royal proclamation intended to curb the westward expansion of the colonists. The Indians were recognized as communal owners of their villages and hunting grounds; they were not to sell any part of them except at a public meeting presided over by a royal official; and settlement by whites beyond the Appalachian divide was forbidden. The Grenville ministry also —again to placate the redmen—encouraged the Indian superintendents to do what they could toward removing abuses suffered by the savages at the hands of white traders. All of these decisions, magnifying British authority at the expense of colonial, aroused discontent among the Americans. Especially offensive were those clauses of the Proclamation of 1763 that placed limits upon colonial expansion. Frontier folk who wanted new lands and homes beyond the mountains were angered; they defied royal authority and crossed the Appalachians into the valley of the Mississippi. Also vexed by the Proclamation were some richer Americans, usually organized in companies, who hoped to buy lands over the mountains cheaply and to sell them profitably in the future. Among these were many merchants and planters, influential men, including Washingtons, Lees, and Carters of Virginia. These speculators did not abandon their schemes because of the Proclamation; they tried to circumvent it, to secure revision of it, and not without success. The Proclamation was not firmly enforced, but it added to the anger created among the Americans by other British measures.

The decision to maintain larger garrison forces in North America had other untoward consequences. The men who made it would have been wise to consult the colonists beforehand, but they did not. They did not intend to use the troops to coerce the Americans; very few of the soldiers were stationed in the settled parts of the Thirteen Colonies. Nevertheless, the presence of regiments of redcoats at no great distance from them nourished among the Americans feelings against Britain arising from other parts of the Bute-Grenville program. The presence of even small detachments in colonial towns and cities led to fracases between soldiers and civilians. From that decision also proceeded the Quartering Act of 1765, which required the colonists to provide barracks of one sort or another, with firewood, candles, and some foodstuffs and drink, for soldiers located among them. Many colonists condemned this law because it forced them, willy-nilly, to spend their money. They coupled it with other British laws designed to extract much larger sums from them. The Quartering Act, renewed each year, became a greater grievance when the troops were employed to repress the Americans. And they were later so used, for the standing army presented a standing invitation to British politicians to resort to force. They succumbed to that temptation within five years.

Important as they were, the actions of Crown and Parliament concerning defense, the Indians, and the West after the Treaty of Paris would not in themselves have raised revolt. Nor would the Americans have been driven to it by a campaign begun in 1763 by the Grenville ministry to enforce the Navigation Acts and to restrict their overseas commerce. However, it also gave them pain. Grenville demanded of customs officers on the American coasts that they do their duties and collect those imposed by Parliament; ordered the commanding officer of a British naval squadron stationed at Halifax to help the customs men; and arranged for the establishment of a special admiralty court at Halifax to try persons accused of violating the British laws that regulated maritime trade. What was more serious, Grenville pushed through Parliament in the spring of 1764 a revenue law that raised taxes on wines and other goods imported by the colonists. Most injurious was a levy—in the so-called Sugar Act —of threepence per gallon upon molasses brought in from the foreign islands of the West Indies. This tax replaced one of sixpence per gallon that had been on the books since 1733 but that had not actually been collected. The new duty obviously was to be exacted. Intended to force American merchants to buy molasses from British West Indian planters, the duty caused injury in several ways. Molasses, used by common folk for sweetening, was also the principal ingredient of rum. The sticky stuff was more than trifling in the American economy. Moreover, the new duty was so high that it threatened to interrupt seriously all trade with the French, Spanish, Dutch, and Danish islands. Traffic with them was profitable to the colonists, who could hardly expect to sell to foreigners if they did not buy from them. In addition, trade with them had supplied the Americans with Spanish and French coins, useful to a people whose balance of trade with Britain was steadily unfavorable. The new duty on molasses was not made more palatable by a Currency Act of 1764, which forbade the colonial assemblies to issue legal tender paper money, so offering another threat to colonial means of exchange.

But the Sugar Act was not intended merely to channel trade. Its preamble flatly declared that it was intended to get money to support, in part, the British army under General Gage. So was raised a great issue. Perceptive and aggressive Americans denounced the levy on molasses as iniquitous because it injured their economy, as unconstitutional because it undertook to tax them for revenue without their consent.

An American might not see clearly, nakedly, the intent of Parliament in the Sugar Act to tax him toward the support of the British army. He could have no doubt whatever about the purpose of the Stamp Act. In the spring of 1764, Grenville announced that he would introduce it in the following year. Income from the Sugar Act would probably fall well below £40,-000. The Americans must contribute much more. A stamp tax might produce £100,000. Grenville said he would consider an alternative; but he was actually determined to impose the tax. He did not intently listen to suggestions from Americans that he try to raise money in more acceptable ways. Declarations from the colonies that such a tax was unconstitutional merely hardened his will. In the spring of 1765 he brought forward his bill; it required of the inhabitants of the British colonies in the New World that they buy stamps at various prices, that the stamps be placed upon newspapers, playing cards, diplomas, ship papers, and legal documents. A minority in Parliament doubted the wisdom of the tax; one member of the House of Lords declared that Parliament lacked the constitutional right to exact payment of it, since the colonists did not send members to Westminster. The Stamp Act was swiftly enacted, for there was little doubt in Parliament about its authority over America, not much more that the Americans must be forced to contribute handsomely to the defense of the Empire. England was suffering from a postwar depression; her public debt and taxes were high; and American public debts and taxes were low. It was forgotten that the laws of trade and navigation added to British wealth at the expense of the Americans. At one and the same moment Britain was made to assert her power and her poverty. As much money as might reasonably have been secured from the Americans could have been saved by abolishing unearned pensions and sinecure offices given to favored aristocrats in England. But Grenville did not dare to attack deep-rooted public corruption at home.

To the Americans the Stamp Act was the last, and by far the worst, of a long series of blows aimed at them. They saw in the Bute-Grenville measures a pattern of tyranny. They, too, suffered from a postwar depression. Vehemently and almost unanimously they defied Britain. They declared that a tax levied for revenue without their consent or that of their elected representatives violated their rights as Englishmen; it was unconstitutional as well as unjust. Some of them said that it trampled upon the natural rights of mankind. A few stamps were sold and used in Georgia, none in the colonies stretching from Massachusetts to South Carolina. Britain was not challenged from the West Indies, or from her newly established colonies of East and West Florida, or from Nova Scotia, or from French Canada. But Patrick Henry, a "wilderness Demosthenes," persuaded the House of Burgesses to resist. With Virginia taking the lead, the inhabitants of the Old Thirteen destroyed or sequestered stamps sent across the ocean, and they forced men who had accepted office as stamp distributors to resign their appointments. They threatened violence against those who would try to collect the stamp tax; and here and there American mobs destroyed the property of men, chiefly officials, who asserted British authority. Americans also postponed paying debts to British merchants and declined to buy British goods. Their assemblies and the Stamp Act Congress, an extralegal gathering held in New York in the fall of 1765, demanded repeal of the stamp duties and also of the one upon molasses. Concentrating upon the detested stamp tax, the Americans did not unequivocally declare that the import duty on molasses, inasmuch as it was partly intended to secure revenue, was also unconstitutional.

Few in Britain, including Americans there, had expected colonial defiance, and the news that the colonists had dared to resist was shocking. Suddenly there was an imperial crisis. What to do? Wisdom from the future declares that, if the Americans were to remain permanently in the Empire, they must be satisfied, then, and afterward. The voice of the past proclaimed the right and necessity of suppressing revolt. Few colonials subject to European states had dared to disobey their decrees, none successfully. George Grenville, and many with him, declared that British sovereignty had been questioned, that it must be forcibly asserted; there must be no weakness. However, when the crisis came, Grenville was no longer prime minister. The most admired man in British public life, William Pitt, pronounced the American argument against taxation without representation to be valid. He called for repeal of the duties. So did a new prime minister, the Marquis of Rockingham. That wealthy nobleman believed that Parliamentary authority was no less in North America than it was in England, but he desired to avert a struggle with the colonists. He urged that the Stamp Act, not his mistake but Grenville's, be rescinded. It was repealed in the spring of 1766. Almost simultaneously Parliament passed a Declaratory Act, which asserted English power over the colonies "in all cases whatsoever."

So the crisis passed, for the Americans were delighted by the withdrawal of the stamp duties. They fervently voiced their gratitude to Pitt, avowed their profound loyalty to George III. All was well again. But it was not. The cancellation of the duties did not mean that England would thereafter steadily seek to avoid contest with America. It happened that the Marquis of Rockingham and his friends, who were disposed to conciliate the colonists, controlled the British ministry when the Americans first defied the Mother Country. The Rockinghamites formed only one of several factions in Parliament. The repeal of the Stamp Act was carried through without enthusiasm; and it was, to a degree, extorted. Many in Parliament regretted that Britain had bent under the American assault. These would exert powerful influence in ministries that followed Rockingham's, those of the Duke of Grafton and Lord North. On the other hand, the Americans, having achieved unity and victory, were less devoted to Britain than they had been and had not been persuaded that they must more modestly define their rights within the British Empire. A yawning gulf had appeared between Britain and America; it had not been finally closed; and it would widen again.

The Grafton ministry would not let well enough alone. Composed of disparate elements, it was dominated during the year 1767–68 by Charles Townshend and others disposed to proclaim and employ British authority over the colonies. Hence the imprudent passage of the Townshend duties on papers, lead, painter's colors, and tea landed in American ports. Again it was asserted that the colonists must contribute toward imperial defense. Townshend recklessly claimed that the Americans had not objected and could not object to the constitutionality of levies for revenue collected in their ports, that they had made a case only against "internal" taxation. The Grafton ministry also established an American Board of Customs Commissioners at Boston, the better to collect the Townshend duties and others imposed earlier. Further, it established a new boundary line between the colonists and the Indians that permitted new settlements immediately west of the Appalachians. That boundary did not satisfy land-hungry pioneers and speculators. Moreover, the Grafton ministry arranged to concentrate General Gage's army on the Atlantic seaboard, where it might be more effectively used, if necessary, against the Americans.

Thus arrogantly and carelessly provoked, the Americans again resisted. They had not violently attacked the Sugar Act as unconstitutional, nor had they gone into uproar in 1766 when the duty on molasses was reduced to one penny per gallon but applied to British as well as foreign molasses. It could hardly be claimed that the tax, as then revised, was intended to control trade. But the Townshend Act, rashly and explicitly put forward as a money-raising measure, unquestionably revived the issue that had been presented by the stamp tax. It seemed, espe-

cially since Britain was requiring colonial contributions under
the Quartering Act, that English politicians were firmly determined to get an American revenue. Denouncing the Townshend
levies as taxation without representation, the colonists insistently
called for their repeal. To enforce that demand, they resorted to
a widespread boycott of British merchants. They again indulged
in mob action and in minor assaults upon British officials, particularly customs men. Britain again bent before the storm, and the
Townshend duties were withdrawn, except for that on tea, in
the spring of 1770. The duty on tea was retained to assert the
right of Parliament to tax. The second Anglo-American crisis
then passed, although the colonists agreed among themselves not
to buy the taxed tea. Before the crisis ended, however, the British Cabinet, in 1768, ordered troops into Boston to defend the
customs commissioners there. Eighteen months later they were
withdrawn, but only after a squad of redcoats had killed five
civilians and wounded six others in the so-called "Boston Massacre." Inevitably England was charged with military tyranny.

The bloodshed in Boston quickened passions. In that city
Samuel Adams, Puritan, tireless politician, and astute propagandist, a man who could not be satisfied by the British, who was
moving toward American independence as an ideal, persistently
sought to turn those passions into rage, but without success,
during the three years that followed the Massacre. It was not
yet possible for him to find a maddening issue. There was in
both England and America a prevailing disposition to let sleep-
ing dogs lie. Except for the planters of the Chesapeake region,
both the English and the colonists felt the pleasure of a pervasive prosperity. Many Americans, negligent of constitutional
principle, purchased and used Townshend-taxed tea. More of
them enjoyed beverages made from smuggled Dutch tea. Lord
North, who had played a principal part in the withdrawal of the
bulk of the Townshend duties, and who was prime minister
after 1770, was indolent and ordinarily cautious. Nevertheless,
in 1773 he imprudently put the Americans to the test for the
third time. Under his leadership Parliament undertook to help
the British East India Company sell to the Americans millions of
pounds of tea that it had in its warehouses. Parliament made it

possible for the company to sell its tea at prices well below those of Dutch competitors. It was hoped that the colonists would buy the cheaper stuff—and pay Townshend duties in large sums. And if they did so, how could the Americans protest against other taxation for revenue?

The colonists saw the trap. Samuel Adams was given the exasperating issue he had earlier sought in vain. Even colonial merchants who had been much opposed to renewed commotion were angered, because the East India Company decided to sell its tea only through a few favored persons. To prevent its sale, aggressive Americans, notoriously in the Boston Tea Party, destroyed some of the tea sent across the ocean by the company. Other shipments were sequestered; still others were carried back to England. Defied a third time, the British government resolved to reduce Boston and Massachusetts to obedience, to make examples of them. Parliament closed Boston harbor to commerce and undertook to revise the charter of Massachusetts so as to increase royal authority within its bounds. General Gage was appointed governor, ordered to execute these Coercive Acts, and instructed to employ troops to maintain order in the troublesome colony. The port of Boston was to remain closed until there was reparation, or at least repentance, for its Tea Party.

Coupling the Coercive Acts with the Quebec Act, passed about the same time, the Americans denounced them as "Intolerable." They saw in the law for Quebec what was not intended, a scheme to set up an arbitrary government in Canada and to persuade the French-Canadians to accept it by offering favor to Roman Catholicism and other benefits at American expense. Massachusetts refused to bend to British authority, and British officials and their sympathizers, threatened by their neighbors, fled from the countryside into Boston. Bringing in troops as rapidly as possible, Gage was able to maintain British authority there and in neighboring villages. In September 1774 he prudently began to fortify the city. Gathering about 5,000 men and reporting an ugly impasse to London, he remained quiet until April 1775.

Meanwhile, the Massachusetts Patriots organized a revolutionary regime, began to prepare for armed conflict, and called for help from their fellow Americans. They received it. Twelve

of the colonies, stretching from Maine to the Savannah River,
without much concern for legal niceties, sent delegates to the
First Continental Congress which met in Philadelphia in the
autumn of 1774. Among its many distinguished members were
George Washington, Patrick Henry, John Adams, and John
Rutledge. It declared that it would not permit the subjugation
of Massachusetts. Appealing to the rights of Englishmen and
those of mankind, the Congress demanded the repeal of the
Coercive Acts and of several others enacted by Parliament after
1763. It called for a return to the Anglo-American situation as it
was at the close of the Seven Years' War. Toward compelling
Britain to listen, it established machinery to prevent the importation and consumption of British goods, and, if necessary, to
cut off exports to Britain. The delegates called for a second
congress, to meet in May 1775; it would consider the British
reply to the American challenge and would act accordingly.
During the following winter Patriot regimes like that of Massachusetts began to appear in several colonies. Men who declared
themselves against the boycott of British goods, or who indicated sympathy for the Mother Country, were silenced, except
in Boston; some of them were brutally tar-and-feathered. Militiamen drilled.

In the early weeks of 1775, British orators such as Lord
Chatham, Edmund Burke, and John Wilkes, reading the news
from America as ominous, urged that the colonists be concili-
ated. Politicians not in power warned against stronger repressive
measures; they said the colonists would fight, that France and
Spain would very likely join them. But George III and the North
ministry had to decide. They reached the conclusion that England could not appease. With the support of a large majority in
Parliament and probably a majority of the English people, they
resolved to reinforce the army in America, to put it in motion,
and to use the navy. Under their leadership, Parliament made a
gesture toward accommodation in Lord North's Conciliatory
Resolution of February 1775. It offered to exempt from Parliamentary taxation for revenue any and all colonies that voted
money toward paying their fair share of the costs of imperial
defense. This proposal was addressed to the several colonies
rather than to the American Congress. It was certain to be

viewed beyond the Atlantic as a device to divide rather than to satisfy the colonists. It was also too late.

With a copy of the Conciliatory Resolution sent to General Gage went orders to him to use his army immediately. These reached him in Boston on April 14. Accordingly he sent out a detachment of about 700 men to destroy military stores collected by the Patriots at the village of Concord, west of Boston. En route, the British troops fired into a band of militia gathered at Lexington, killing five of them and wounding more. They engaged other Americans at Concord. On their return journey, they, and a larger body of redcoats sent to their assistance, were assailed by swarms of Yankees. The British troops, after suffering heavy losses, reached the outskirts of Boston and safety. However, the militia of New England promptly invested the city. The War of Independence had begun. Soon there was talk about an armistice, and later there was much more talk about a peace by the terms of which the Americans would remain within the British Empire. The war went on until Britain reluctantly acknowledged American independence.

CHAPTER 6

The Revolutionary Climax

FOR MORE THAN FOURTEEN months the Patriots, at least by their public declarations, fought for their rights within the British Empire; then, early in July 1776, they proclaimed American independence. During most of that period the British army in America was much too weak to take the offensive; it was driven from Boston and almost from Quebec. Before England could mount major attacks upon them, the Patriots not only announced their separation from the Empire but began to lay the foundations of both the American states and the American union. Whether these would endure remained doubtful for many campaigns. In 1776 and 1777 the Patriots were sternly tested by British offensives. Thereafter, the war widened, with France, Spain, and Holland taking up arms against England; and the struggle became basically one of endurance for the Patriots. But it did not remain such; British offensives in the Southern states led to a final triumph for the Patriots at Yorktown in 1781. Two years later Britain formally and grudgingly admitted that America had become free.

The outcome was dramatic, stunning to those who had entertained exalted notions of British power. It has puzzled scholars who have made too much of British might and of American weakness. Hence have arisen curious, sometimes delightful, explanations of England's final defeat. The American historian George Bancroft concluded that God, in much the same fashion that He rescued the Israelites from the Egyptians, had decisively intervened at critical moments to save the American cause. Why He permitted the Patriots to suffer so much before He acted,

Bancroft did not quite make clear. Other historians have been able to explain the American triumph only by ascribing almost fabulous incompetence, even treachery, to high British officers who were in fact neither astonishingly deficient nor unfaithful. Actually, a sober assessment of the vigors and infirmities of the British and American combatants must persuade that they were not remarkably unequal. It may well be that the Patriots would have secured their independence without French and Spanish intervention and help. The Americans were virile as well as numerous; if necessary, they could feed, clothe, and arm themselves; and Nature gave them powerful and utterly reliable allies, the wide and stormy Atlantic and the broad, rough, forested, hilly, and remote spaces of North America. United, they could not have been permanently subdued. If divided among themselves, the Americans would obviously lose part of the advantage of their strong defensive position. They were divided in the War of Independence, but not to such a degree that the Patriot cause was fatally weakened. Moreover, the British were by no means unanimously or zealously determined to suppress the rebellion across the ocean. There were many in England who would not lift a hand to assist George III and his Cabinet, not a few who wished the Patriots well.

At no time during the decade before the outbreak of hostilities did all the colonists insist that, at whatever cost, Britain must yield to them. Even in the days of the Stamp Act crisis, when feelings against British "tyranny" ran high, there were colonists who stood for obedience. The number of such persons swelled with the passing years. The grudging concessions made by England, even though interspersed with assertions of power, had an effect. Moreover, mob violence alarmed pacific and cautious Americans, including many of means. Might not the workmen, the sailors, the artisans, the ignorant, if unrestrained, at length assail economic and social as well as political order? As the fighting approached, more and more colonists drew back. After the beginning of the war, when the Patriots moved toward independence as their great goal, they suffered further defections. When they solemnly cut the tie with Britain, the Patriots—or the Americans, as we may call them—were far more numerous than their neighbors who clung to Britain, who were known as

Loyalists or Tories. It is probable that more than one-half of the white colonists were devoted Patriots; that less than one-quarter of them were Loyalists; that the remainder were neutral, or nearly so. The Negroes had little reason to choose the one side or the other. Few of them fought; they rendered far greater service to the Americans than they did to the British.

What sort of people were the Tories? It has been said that they were the more prosperous, the socially superior colonists, that the Patriots were the humbler and poorer colonists. Evidence to support such a distinction has not been brought forward; it existed in the minds of the Loyalists, and it can be found in the minds of those who have pitied the Tories because of their hard lot. But that there was such a difference in reality remains to be demonstrated. Most of the Patriot leaders came from the gentry. The officers of the Continental army were commonly young gentlemen of the "best families," few of whom served with the British. Actually, both the Tories and the Patriots came from all occupations, all social levels, all parts of America. Nor may one distinguish between the parties on the score of ancestry, although Virginia and New England, largely populated by people of English blood, were Patriot strongholds. In no large part of America were the Loyalists dominant; they were proportionately more numerous in New York, Pennsylvania, and the Far South than elsewhere. Royal and proprietary officeholders were likely to be Tories, also Anglican clergymen, also latecomers from Britain. People of Scottish descent, doubtless because they were often recently arrived from their native country, were conspicuous among the Tories. One may not assume that every man who was Scottish-born was a Loyalist, however. The Reverend Doctor John Witherspoon, a latecomer and president of Princeton, signed the Declaration of Independence. It should be added that the Loyalists were not all utterly committed to Britain. Such men there were among them, the always faithful who chose ruin, exile, and death rather than bow to the will of the Patriots. The majority of the Tories were not so absolutely devoted. Most of them ultimately, if reluctantly, became citizens of the American republic.

If the Patriots lost adherents as they drove on toward separation from Britain, they displayed undiminished energy and ardor. They expelled royal governors and other civil officers who opposed them. They did such men no bodily harm, but they locked up William Franklin, Tory son of Benjamin Franklin and governor of New Jersey for several months. When royal Indian Superintendent John Stuart fled from Charleston to safety among British troops at St. Augustine, they held his wife for two years as hostage for his good behavior. Patriot conventions and congresses derived from the lower houses of assembly seized legislative authority everywhere from Maine to Georgia by July 1775; and committees of safety assumed executive powers. Moreover, the Second Continental Congress, gathering at Philadelphia in May 1775, undertook to supply leadership to the American cause. The delegates were largely the same men who had met at the Pennsylvania capital in the preceding year. Added to them was Benjamin Franklin, who had fled from England to escape arrest, and later Thomas Jefferson, who had already made a name for himself as a polemicist. Delegates from Georgia also at length appeared. Thereafter all of the Thirteen Colonies were represented. The new Congress considered Lord North's Conciliatory Resolution and mistakenly concluded, as did other Patriot bodies, that it was merely a device to split the Patriots apart. Congress sent off a final Olive Branch Petition to the King. Demanding that Britain make much larger concessions, it was voted without enthusiasm—to please members who desired to try a last gesture toward accommodation—and with little hope that it would be gravely weighed in London. The Congress saw the march of Gage's troops from Boston to Concord as Britain's answer to earlier demands for redress of grievances. It met force with force. It appointed George Washington as commander in chief of a Continental army and sent him to take command of the Patriots who had invested Boston. It undertook in 1775 to make, not only a Continental army, but also a navy and marine corps. It promptly began to print paper money, established a postal service, appointed commissioners to deal with the Indians, and in general took upon itself the powers formerly exercised in America by Crown and Parliament. Later it would declare American independence, borrow money abroad, enter into foreign alliances, and make the first constitution of the United States. It was itself, in fact, the first American national government.

The Patriots were as aggressive in the field as they were in council, and they took as much advantage as they could of British military weakness in the first stages of the war. Gage received reinforcements at Boston in 1775, but these did little more than replace his losses. He might have broken through the motley forces gathered beyond his trenches. To what avail? An advance into the New England countryside would have been suicidal. He had not enough men or supplies or transport to undertake it. In the Battle of Bunker Hill on June 17, 1775, he gained control of one lofty eminence that commanded the city, at dreadful expense. His small army sustained 1,054 casualties. So he made Boston temporarily safe for his troops and for a British naval squadron in its harbor. General William Howe, who succeeded Gage at Boston in the fall of 1775, was forced to abandon the city in the following March. Washington did not quite dare to assail the British trenches. At length, however, he acquired cannon captured at Fort Ticonderoga. He mounted these on Dorchester Heights, overlooking Boston from the south. Rather than risk an attack, Howe then prudently evacuated Boston, sailing away to Halifax.

Unprepared for the Patriot onslaughts, the British were ousted from the Thirteen Colonies and almost from Canada. Heterogeneous forces collected by the Earl of Dunmore, the last royal governor of Virginia, failed to maintain a foothold in the Old Dominion. Scottish Highlanders recently settled in North Carolina took up arms for the King but were crushed at Moore's Creek Bridge in February 1776. In the following June a British naval squadron carrying a small army was repulsed by American batteries on Sullivan's Island in Charleston harbor. Meanwhile, Forts Ticonderoga and Crown Point, weakly garrisoned by redcoat invalids, easily fell to Patriot arms. Thus the way opened for an invasion of Canada, which was thinly protected by British regulars. One Patriot army under General Richard Montgomery captured Montreal and moved down the St. Lawrence River against Quebec. Outside the city it was joined by a second American force under Benedict Arnold that had made its way northward through the woods of Maine. However, in Quebec, General Guy Carleton, governor of Canada, vigorously defended the city. A desperate assault upon it on December 31, 1775, failed, and Montgomery was slain. The

Patriots vainly maintained a siege of the city until the following May. They hoped that the French-Canadians would take up arms against Britain, that Canada would become a fourteenth colony—and state. But most of the French-Canadians, loving the Americans no more than they did the British, remained indifferent and idle spectators. When a British fleet and army came up the St. Lawrence in the spring of 1776, the Americans fled, retreating all the way to Fort Ticonderoga. The hope of making Canada a part of the American union endured some time longer among the Patriots, and they planned to resume their offensive. They were never able to move northward again to the St. Lawrence. It had been decided that Canada would remain British. Nevertheless, the Patriots profited from their invasion of Canada, for it persuaded strategists in London not only to send an army to Quebec but to appoint two commanders in chief in America, one to serve in Canada, the other in the Thirteen. Later, that division in command, when Britain put large forces in the field, proved to be most valuable to the Patriots.

The news of Lexington and Concord, of Bunker Hill, of the overthrow of British authority in the Thirteen Colonies, created dismay in England. Again a vociferous minority demanded that efforts be made to placate the Patriots, that the attempt to subdue them be abandoned. But George III and the North ministry, with the hearty consent of Parliament, decided to use greater force. They were advised by some military men to rely principally upon the navy. It could inexpensively maintain a blockade of the American coasts which might ultimately compel the Patriots to submit, or at least to negotiate. These experts doubted that Britain could raise enough troops to overrun the Thirteen Colonies. French and Spanish intervention was to be feared, in the event that Britain became heavily involved in America. However, King and Cabinet, grossly undervaluing the strength of the Patriots and exaggerating that of the Loyalists, chose to believe that British troops, with the help of the navy, could quickly crush American resistance. Before the end of 1775 the American ports were declared to be under blockade, and the King solemnly withdrew his protection from the colonists. The services of thousands of German mercenary troops—the so-called Hessians—were hired, and so many troops were sent

across the ocean in 1776 that the British forces in North America numbered about 45,000 by the fall of that year.

What did George III and the North ministry intend to do to
the Patriots, after they had been compelled to yield? The Patriots, not surprisingly, feared that they would be bloodily punished if they were defeated; and American historians have often
asserted, or suggested, that the heads of the Patriot leaders were
at stake. However, appointing Richard Howe, Admiral Lord
Howe, to the command of British naval forces in American
waters, placing his younger brother, General William Howe,
over the British army in the Thirteen Colonies, and separately
entrusting the British detachments stationed in the St. Lawrence
Valley to General Guy Carleton, the British government also
authorized the Howes, as peace commissioners, to offer terms
toward an enduring settlement, *after* the Patriots had put down
their arms. The brothers were empowered to pardon all rebels.
Rhode Island and Connecticut were to be made royal colonies.
The Americans were to contribute between 5 per cent and 10
per cent of the costs of imperial defense, each of the colonies
paying in the same proportion that the Continental Congress had
established for the retirement of its paper money.

The peace terms carried by the Howes were not made public;
the brothers were not permitted to announce them, except for
their power to pardon, until the Patriot cause had collapsed. The
Howes might, and did, declare that Britain was disposed to be
generous toward achieving a final accommodation. But although
the Patriots entertained respect for the Howe brothers, they
hardly dared to trust themselves to British mercy. Moreover,
even had the Howes disobeyed their instructions, had they informed the Patriots of British intentions, they would have been
too late. General Howe, with British troops, arrived in New
York Harbor on July 2, 1776. That same day the Congress
proclaimed American independence. Shortly afterward the
admiral joined his brother. Over a period of months they vainly
sought to persuade the Americans to lay down their arms; they
also unsuccessfully tried to compel them to yield.

The Patriots, embittered by their losses in battle, became less
and less disposed to bargain with Britain as the struggle continued. The emotional gap between them and the Mother Coun-

try widened. When Lord Dunmore, promising them freedom, enlisted Negro slaves, they were exasperated. When it became apparent that Britain would make use of Indian allies, so bringing onto the American frontiers all the horrors of Indian warfare, they found it difficult to think of England as an affectionate parent. Learning that Hessian soldiers would be sent against them, they saw themselves as exposed to the attacks of brutal foreign troops. Indeed, then, did Britain intend, not only to crush them, but to subject them to all sorts of horrors? Sentimental ties to Britain continued to snap. Nevertheless, many of the Patriots were loath to separate. If they successfully asserted their independence, they must try to form a republic. Could they, so varied in their interests, so scattered over such great distances, govern themselves decently under republican forms? No other people had done so in similar circumstances since the days of the Romans. If they called upon the Bourbons for help, as they must, might not the French and Spanish behave toward them as the Anglo-Saxons behaved when the Britons invited Hengist and Horsa to come to England to help them fight against the wild Picts? They would not be happy under French or Spanish masters. Social revolution was also to be feared. Was it not better to deal with Britain, to accept British tyranny, which would be relatively mild? The Patriots increasingly resolved to put aside all doubts and fears, to risk everything.

Before the end of 1775, Washington and several high officers in the Continental army were ready to take the last step. In January 1776, Thomas Paine, who had come from England only fourteen months earlier, trenchantly and tellingly, in his famous pamphlet *Common Sense*, urged that the time had come to part. Patriot of Patriots, Paine savagely attacked monarchy as an institution vicious in origin and wicked in practice. In the beginning kings were aggressive brutes, and they had not improved. America, he said, must be freed of ancient tyranny and royal despotism, must fight for independence and the rights of mankind everywhere. *Common Sense* was widely circulated and read; after its appearance, more and more Americans announced that they wanted a complete separation. In April 1776, North Carolina's revolutionary legislature authorized its delegates to the Continental Congress to vote for independence. On May 15 the

legislature of Virginia instructed its deputies to introduce a motion to cut the last tie. Accordingly, on June 7, Richard Henry
Lee of the Virginia delegation at Philadelphia so moved. Many
members of the Congress were not yet ready to vote for independence. However, the Congress appointed a committee to
prepare a statement to justify separation, should it be resolved
that nothing less would do. By June, indeed, the great majority
of the delegates were determined to part from Britain. Not a few,
however, favored delay—in order to form a stable government
and to get assurances of French aid before acting irrevocably.
Even that firebrand Patrick Henry spoke out in Virginia
against a precipitate decision. John Dickinson of Pennsylvania led those in Congress who hesitated. Probably no more
than two or three delegates were definitely opposed to separation. On July 1 nine colonies, through their deputies, voted for
it. On the following day, the delegations of twelve colonies—
with that of New York abstaining only because it had not been
given power to act—solemnly resolved "That these United
Colonies are and of right ought to be free and independent
states; that they are absolved from all allegiance to the British
crown, and that all political connexion between them and the
state of Great Britain, is and ought to be totally dissolved."

The deed was done. Two days later, after amending it, the
Congress—again without the consent of New York, which was
given soon afterward—gave its approval to that memorable
document, the so-called Declaration of Independence, drawn up
to justify separation. Thomas Jefferson, John Adams, Benjamin
Franklin, Roger Sherman, and Robert R. Livingston had been
given the task of preparing it. Jefferson was its principal author.
The Declaration of Independence was, and remains, an extraordinary pronunciamento. Abandoning all argument based on the
rights of Englishmen, the Patriots now proclaimed that their
cause rested upon the natural rights of mankind. Men were created equal, and they accepted the rule of a governor or governors in return for protection of life and liberty. The bargain
made was a sacred compact. If it was gravely and persistently
violated, if he or they who wielded power abused it at the
expense of the governed, then they had the right, the duty, to
rebel and to make a new compact. The Patriots might have

applied this doctrine explicitly to both King and Parliament. They did not. They now assumed that Parliament had never possessed authority over them, referring to its acts as "pretended legislation." Asserting that their duty had been only to the King, they denounced George III as a tyrant. He, with the assistance of others, including Parliament, had inflicted upon them many grievous injuries. Offering a long list of these, the Congress solemnly affirmed that they amply warranted severance of all bonds between America and Britain. The great Declaration repeated the resolution of July 2 "That these United Colonies are and of Right ought to be Free and Independent States." Toward that end the delegates pledged "our lives, our fortunes, and our sacred honour."

The Declaration of Independence has been subjected to much criticism. John Adams, jealous of the fame that it brought to Jefferson, said that it contained nothing new. It did not, to be sure; but Jefferson, borrowing and even paraphrasing the ideas of Algernon Sidney, John Locke, and other English political philosophers, clothed them in melodious and vibrant language that summoned the Patriots and mankind to make a new and better order. The theory of natural rights propounded in the document has been found to be historically defective; it has not been shown that a political regime resting upon the consent of citizens is outrageous. Scholars have emphasized that George III, a commonplace rather than a wicked man, was not personally responsible for many of the misdeeds for which he, his Cabinets, and Parliament were indicted. It is also true that the entire list of charges brought against them will not bear scrutiny. The accusations were colored by passion, and British intentions were misconstrued so as to put Crown and Parliament in the worst light. Shortening and softening the indictment, one nevertheless concludes that the American cause was essentially just. Such, in fact, was the belief of many Englishmen at the time, and afterward of almost all thoughtful Englishmen. In a sense, in 1776, the Americans were more English than the English, for they had inherited their allegiance to the cause of freedom from the noblest traditions of the Mother Country.

However great may be the ultimate influence of the Declaration of Independence, it did not blunt British bayonets, Hessian

swords, or Indian tomahawks. In the summer and autumn of
1776 the Patriots suffered defeat after defeat. George Washington, commanding the main American army, undertook to
defend New York City, but was easily driven from it by General Howe. With dwindling ranks, Washington was compelled
to retreat across the Delaware River in December. The American cause then seemed to be in desperate straits. However, General Carleton, advancing southward from Canada, chose, because
of the approach of winter, not to assail an American garrison
force that barred his way at Fort Ticonderoga. He withdrew
toward his bases, planning to resume his march in the following
spring. The coming of winter also persuaded Howe to put an
end to campaigning. Then, the morning after Christmas, Washington made a brilliant surprise attack upon a Hessian garrison
at Trenton. At trifling cost, the American general captured more
than one thousand Hessians. Moreover, he eluded pursuit by
British troops led forward by General Lord Cornwallis in an
effort to punish him for his rashness, and he won another victory over part of them, at Princeton, early in January 1777,
before seeking shelter from the cold in the hills of northern
New Jersey. Washington's splendid little triumphs over the
Hessians and the British, reviving Patriot morale, marked a turning point in the war.

The Americans needed the confidence they gained from
Washington's exploits at Trenton and Princeton, for they were
attacked by many Indian tribes and by two British armies in the
campaign of 1777. The powerful Indian nations, except for the
Cherokee, had hitherto remained neutral. The Cherokee, taking
up arms in the preceding summer, had been driven back through
their mountain fortresses by Southern militia. In 1777, however,
most of the Iroquois, together with several Ohio Valley tribes,
took the field as allies of King George. Thousands of other
warriors later carried their muskets and tomahawks to war.
With and without British leadership the Indians sooner or later
struck against every part of the American frontier, continuing
their assaults even after the British had ceased to fight. Staggered, the American backwoodsmen stubbornly resisted amidst
the horrors of warfare as waged by the redmen. Militia and
Continentals went to help them and put the torch to the villages

of the Iroquois, the Shawnee, and the Cherokee. The Americans struck blows from which the Iroquois and the Cherokee never fully recovered. At the close of hostilities, after bloody and savage fighting, the Americans were firmly planted in Kentucky and Tennessee, far beyond the heights of the Appalachians.

The Patriots also survived the onslaughts of the two British armies. In July 1777, General John Burgoyne led a mixed force of British and German regulars, Tories, and Indians southward from Canada toward Albany, while a second and larger army under Sir William Howe moved from New York against Philadelphia by sea. Howe advanced against that city from the south, from Chesapeake Bay. Fortunately for the Patriots, the British failed to concentrate their efforts. Moreover, having received "secret" aid, including large quantities of muskets and other military equipment, from France and Spain, the Americans were better prepared to resist than they had been in 1776. They had acquired experience and some discipline. Washington strove to defend the American "capital." Sir William Howe drove him back at Brandywine in September, captured Philadelphia, and repelled a surprise attack by the American commander at Germantown early in October. But at the end of the campaign Washington's army, encamped west of Philadelphia, was still able to fight. Meanwhile Burgoyne encountered disaster. He easily captured Ticonderoga in early July. However, in August the Patriots drove back a mixed force of British troops and Indians under Colonel Barry St. Leger that was moving down the Mohawk Valley toward Albany from the west in an attempt to help Burgoyne. The British general himself, plunging down the valley of the Hudson, was checked, was beaten back in two battles by American Continentals and militia under General Horatio Gates, and was forced to lay down his arms at Saratoga in October. Even more than Trenton, Saratoga was a heavy blow to Britain.

After the campaign had ended, Washington went into winter camp at Valley Forge, where his troops suffered bitterly from the cold and lack of food. But his army had not been routed, and it would revive with the coming of spring. Britain derived little benefit from Howe's victories. The news that Washington's army survived, that Burgoyne's was gone, made certain the

entrance of France into the war. The news shocked London.
Refused permission to resign as prime minister, Lord North did
his feeble best to meet the emergency. A commission led by the
Earl of Carlisle was sent from England to America with authority to offer the Patriots peace and autonomy within the Empire.
General Sir Henry Clinton, who succeeded William Howe, was
instructed to evacuate Philadelphia and temporarily to take the
defensive. It was feared in London, with the best of reasons, that
a French fleet and army would swiftly appear on the American
coast.

The news that brought dismay to London was gladly received
in Paris. The French foreign minister, the Comte de Vergennes,
had long desired that France should intervene. He had been
restrained by more prudent men in the ministry of Louis XVI.
Vergennes had been allowed only to give clandestine help to the
Americans. The royal treasury was embarrassed. And was it
wise to aid republicans? If successful, would they not offer a
bad example to the French people? But now, urging that France
had been given a heaven-sent opportunity to reduce the power
of her ancient enemy, that France might wrench from England
her lucrative and nourishing trade with the Americans, Vergennes had his way. In small part the French decision to enter
the war must be ascribed to Benjamin Franklin, who had been
sent by Congress to Paris with two other commissioners to
solicit assistance. Franklin had ingeniously done everything possible to create a favorable opinion of the Patriots' cause in the
French capital. On February 6, 1778, he and his colleagues
signed at Versailles two pregnant treaties. In these France recognized the United States of America and undertook to fight
against the British until American independence was assured.
Early in May the Continental Congress unanimously and gladly
endorsed the treaties. The Carlisle commissioners arrived too
late to prevent the formation of the alliance. Besides, they could
not offer enough to satisfy the Patriots, who would accept nothing less than independence.

Hostilities began between England and France in June 1778.
Spain hesitated until the following spring. The advisers of King
Charles III at Madrid did not favor an American republic, one
that might move even more aggressively against Spain's New

World empire than had the British. Spain finally took up arms when France promised to make the capture of Gibraltar a great goal of the conflict. Spain did not become an ally of the United States. Before the end of 1780, England declared war against Holland, that small nation being too helpful as a neutral to England's enemies. Indeed, almost all of Europe was either at war with Britain or unfriendly in the later years of the struggle. The League of Armed Neutrality, including the Baltic powers, appeared as a champion of the rights of nonbelligerents on the seas. After 1778, Britain was increasingly isolated, and was forced to fight on many new fronts, in the Floridas, the West Indies, at Gibraltar, in the Mediterranean, on the west coast of Africa, in the Indian Ocean. England even had to prepare against a French invasion from the Channel.

Under increasing strain, Britain could not give Sir Henry Clinton all the reinforcements he desired, nor was it possible to bar the French navy from North American waters. Retreating from Philadelphia, Clinton concentrated his forces in New York City. He was briefly threatened by a combined attack on the part of Washington's army and a French fleet under the Comte d'Estaing which operated off the American shores in the summer of 1778. He undertook no great offensive from that place. With Washington hovering outside his defenses, Clinton carried on a raiding war against ports of the Northern states and in Virginia. In 1780, General Benedict Arnold treacherously deserted the Patriots. His defection proved to be unimportant. The Patriots, suffering from war weariness and inflation, persevered. That same year a French squadron and a small French army established themselves at Newport, Rhode Island. These could be held in check. However, Clinton's situation at New York City was by no means easy, and he continued to fear that he would be assailed simultaneously from the land and the sea.

Clinton knew that the same danger existed wherever British troops gathered in numbers on the American coast. Nevertheless, after December 1778, when Savannah fell to British arms without serious resistance, he became increasingly committed to action in the southernmost American states. They contained many Loyalists, and it was believed in London and New York that much could be accomplished in Georgia and the Carolinas with relatively small forces. Success lured the British on to expensive and hazardous adventures. In May 1780, Clinton himself captured Charleston, together with an American army of 5,000 men. By the following summer both South Carolina and Georgia seemed to be firmly in British hands. But Lord Cornwallis, assuming command in the Southern theatre when Clinton was forced to return to New York, was menaced by local partisans and also by militia and Continentals who moved against him from the north. Bold and aggressive, he chose, not to defend his positions, but to drive the Americans from North Carolina. He won battles; his subordinates on detached service lost battles. In the spring of 1781, after suffering heavy losses, he left the care of the British conquests in South Carolina and Georgia to others and marched to Virginia with 1,600 men. As he moved northward, the American forces that he had failed to destroy pressed southward. Led by General Nathanael Greene, they captured all the British strong places in the Carolinas and Georgia, except for Charleston and Savannah, before the end of 1781.

Meanwhile, Cornwallis himself encountered disaster. He collected about 7,000 troops in Virginia. Suddenly he was surrounded in the fall of that year at Yorktown on Chesapeake Bay. A powerful French fleet under Admiral de Grasse came to the Chesapeake, drove away a smaller British fleet, and secured control of the bay. Washington, swiftly leaving the vicinity of New York City, gathered about 17,000 American and French soldiers in Virginia and prevented the escape of Cornwallis by land. Then Washington began assaults upon the British entrenchments at Yorktown. Clinton, a British army, and a British fleet set out from New York to rescue Cornwallis. They were too late. He was forced to surrender on October 19, 1781. As the redcoats laid down their weapons, a British band played "The World Turned Upside Down." The world was indeed changed.

The stunning Franco-American triumph at Yorktown forced out the North ministry in England; Parliament would support no more offensives in North America; and it became necessary for England to recognize American independence. An American delegation consisting of Benjamin Franklin, John Adams, John Jay, and Henry Laurens signed a preliminary treaty of peace

with the British in 1782. In the following year, after the final
failure of Franco-Spanish attacks upon Gibraltar, it became part
of a general peace made at the same city. By its terms England
formally recognized the existence of the American republic and
conceded generous boundaries to it. The Floridas passed from
British to Spanish hands—Spanish troops had taken Mobile and
Pensacola—but England retained Canada. With those exceptions, all of North America east of the Mississippi River became
American territory.

The Americans were to encounter many troubles, although
these were fewer than those of most European peoples during
several generations. The security of the republic was virtually
assured, provided that its citizens did not engage in fratricidal
struggles. It derived safety from the divided nations of Europe
and from the undivided Atlantic. Fortunately for the republic,
most of the Loyalists remained within it, gave it their allegiance,
and were completely absorbed into the body politic. There
were no Tory revolts after 1783. A Loyalist minority, including
some thousands of men who had fought for Britain, went into
exile. The bulk of these, numbering perhaps 38,000, settled in
Canada. There they and their descendants displayed a special
and fervent loyalty to Britain. The republic engaged in many
quarrels and in a war with England and Canada. At length
Canada also became independent from England. In the twentieth
century, confronted by common and dangerous foes, the peoples of the three countries moved toward a military, if not a
political, reunion.

CHAPTER 7

A New Order

❋

THE PATRIOT AND BRITISH armies that engaged in battle in the War of Independence were relatively small, and so were the numbers of the slain and wounded. Nevertheless, and even though there were areas where the farmer and villager were little disturbed by the sounds of combat, the war brought with it much suffering. Homes were burned; Negroes, horses, cattle, poultry, and grain were seized and carried off by the British and by the Loyalists. If an owner was paid for property taken by the Patriots, he might be forced to accept depreciated paper money. Most civilians were injured by inflation. Goods ordinarily imported from England and the West Indies became scarce during the conflict, and their prices rose high. Moreover, the Congress and the states put out excessive quantities of paper currency that lost value. In fact, about $200 million worth of paper money printed for the Congress became utterly worthless long before the end of the War. Attempts by several of the states to regulate prices failed. Economic dislocation hurt grievously. The years of the war were hard ones for nearly all the Americans, and their troubles did not entirely cease with the coming of peace. The prosperity they had enjoyed in 1775 did not substantially return until 1787. Even so, those twelve years brought with them extraordinary civil achievements. These were of such great consequence that historians have been tempted to believe that the Americans almost simultaneously executed two revolutions, an "external" one, referring to the separation from England, and an "internal" one, designating the creation of a new political, social, and economic order within America. The term

"Internal Revolution" is grandiose, but America was basically reformed. It would be absurd to suggest that, had England and America remained together, the course of American history would have been the same.

It was not obvious to all at the time that the Americans were laying solid foundations for a better future for themselves and their progeny, and even for the rest of mankind. Europeans who desired no change in their own world, and who preferred to believe that efforts to reform the American one must lead to anarchy and disaster, fancied that the Americans were indeed plunging into poverty and confusion. Not a few Americans were profoundly disturbed by the course of civil events and saw about them disorder and approaching ruin. Historians of later times, meditating upon the glories of the Constitution of 1787, magnified them by exaggerating the troubles that preceded the adoption of that document. Such troubles there were, but the Constitution, important as it was, was not a vehicle by which the Americans climbed from an abyss. It is unquestionably true that they were in good health in the summer of 1787—before the Constitution was made. It was a crowning achievement; it did not solve every American problem.

Remodeling their political institutions during and after the war, the Americans encountered many difficulties and did not immediately find the solution to every one of them. It was clear enough that it would not do to establish thirteen independent states. It was essential that the Americans form some sort of union, indispensable both to the winning and to the preservation of American freedom. Moreover, although local allegiances continued among them, although men gave loyalty to the states in which they resided, devotion to the nation also became a potent force during the war. But it was no more possible, because of jealousies and fears of tyranny, to concentrate power in one government than it was to divide it among thirteen. Accordingly, the Congress, seeking to distribute power between a central regime and the states, devised the Articles of Confederation, the first national constitution of the United States. Ratified by the states, after much delay, in 1781, it was deficient in several ways. It was basically defective because it gave insufficient authority to the national government, too much to the states.

The powers that were given to the former were largely vested in a Congress, they being much the same as those that the Congress had exercised as a revolutionary body after 1775. Under the Articles the Congress was given substantial authority over foreign and Indian affairs, and it acquired authority over vast lands beyond the Appalachian Mountains. It was authorized to emit currency, to borrow money, to establish a postal system, to build a navy, and to maintain (with the help of the states) an army. But it was largely dependent upon requisitions from the states for funds; the states were often delinquent; and Congress was therefore almost constantly threatened by bankruptcy. The national regime included neither a vigorous executive nor potent courts. It could not coerce the citizen; and its authority could be and was defied by several of the states. The Congress was quite unable to solve all the problems of the nation. Within five years after the Articles were put into effect, it was obvious to most thoughtful Americans that they must be revised or replaced, if the nation was to endure.

Which is by no means to say that the Americans achieved little or nothing politically before *the* Constitution of 1787 was put into effect. Had they accomplished nothing more during the twelve years after the battle of Lexington and Concord than to establish republican institutions, they would have made no trifling change. And republicanism did triumph. Neither in the states nor at the seat of Congress did a king appear—or a dictator. An occasional American, influenced by European practice and tradition, or convinced that monarchy was requisite to the preservation of an orderly society, wanted a royal master and family. But an overwhelming majority of Americans detested George III and all kings and emperors. Moreover, there was no European prince who would fit an American throne; and the only American who could have occupied one was Washington, who had no desire to be a monarch. It was twice suggested to him in 1782, by one of his officers, that he ought to be king or dictator; he rejected the proposals with disdain. Happily for his countrymen, Washington never entertained such an unworthy ambition. Respected, trusted, and admired as he was, Washington could not have become a sovereign or a tyrant without causing a civil war; and it is most doubtful that he would have been victorious in such a contest. In 1787, Alexander Hamilton, a believer in limited monarchy in the English style, saw that it could not be imposed upon the Americans; he accepted republican government as inevitable. So, after the Peace of Paris, did most of the Loyalists who remained in the United States. The overwhelming majority of Americans, it should be repeated, were devoted to the republican principle. It became a fundamental part of the American credo.

Again, that America became republican was no small thing. Much later, kings and queens in Europe would disappear, would become useful and attractive figureheads, would be replaced in some instances by dictators far more tyrannical and vicious than crowned heads. But in the eighteenth century kings and emperors wielded vast power on the European continent, and English rulers were not merely adornments. Then George followed George, Karl succeeded Karl, and Louis took the place of Louis, almost in the nature of things, even by divine right. George III and his immediate successors in England were by no means the worst of royalty in their time. Yet the Americans were fortunate to be rid of them. The destruction of monarchy in America was valuable also because it weakened the principle of aristocracy; European monarchy and aristocracy supported each other. Gaining the benefits of republicanism for themselves, the Americans struck a blow at dominating royalty everywhere. They proved that a republic could stand and flourish even in a vast territory, and the example they offered was not ignored. It inspired the Italian Giuseppe Mazzini, the South American Antonio de Nariño, and many another revolutionary. It had something to do with the slow conversion of Britain into a socialist monarchy.

Another important political innovation was the written constitution, framed by a convention especially elected for that purpose and ratified by the voters. Many Americans were familiar with descriptions of government in the form of colonial charters; the educated men among them believed that government should be based upon compact; and it seemed imperative, to prevent tyranny, if for no other reason, to put down in writing the powers and duties of lawmakers, executives, and judges. The Americans framed such a basic instrument, not only for the nation, but for every one of their thirteen states before the end of the war. Some of the state constitutions were made even before the Declaration of Independence, some were only temporary, some long endured. Several of them were made by Revolutionary assemblies in the same fashion as ordinary laws. However, thoughtful Patriots began to insist that constitution-making ought not to be entrusted to legislators, men elected to do other and various tasks. They declared that such fundamental documents should be prepared by bodies especially elected for the purpose. They had their way, and the constitutional convention became, in the 1780s, an American institution. The constitutional referendum appeared almost simultaneously. Early in the war men who would not put entire trust in any group of human beings declared that any document that laid the very foundations of government must be sanctioned by the voters. Within ten years the constitutional referendum was generally recognized as indispensable. In accordance with this principle, the national Constitution of 1787 was submitted to conventions in the several states.

Striving to prevent tyranny, the Americans especially sought to protect the life, liberty, and property of the individual by solemn declarations of their sanctity. Every state promulgated a Bill of Rights, in which those rights were listed and were asserted to be inviolable, beyond infringement by governor, legislature, or judge. Such a charter of personal safeguards, in some states, was inserted in the constitution; in others, it was separately declared to be fundamental law. Believing that the Creator had established the rights of mankind, and familiar with the defenses established for them in English law, the Americans commonly considered those personal freedoms to be almost sacred, more important even than governmental machinery. Varying somewhat from state to state, the Bills of Rights were designed, among other things, to assure trial by jury; the efficacy of the writ of *habeas corpus;* and freedom to speak, to petition, to assemble peacefully, and to bear arms. Unhappily, these forthright, even hallowed affirmations, afterward repeated again and again in American basic laws, did not positively assure the liberties of the individual. They did announce ideals that tended to become realities in America.

The new state constitutions did not establish political democracy in the United States. Not one of them gave the vote to all white males. In every state the male voter had to be at least a taxpayer; in some he was required to be an owner of property. (In Vermont, not recognized as a state until 1791, adult males could vote after 1777.) Moreover, some of the American commonwealths demanded that legislators and executives be men of much property. Most of the states, in accordance with colonial practice, established a bicameral legislature; the members of the upper house, or senate, were often men of wealth, elected for long terms and devoted to the protection of property. Such senators were sometimes indirectly elected; and electoral districts for both houses were not infrequently drawn so as to favor the few and the rich, to indulge the resident of the Tidewater at the expense of the Piedmont farmer or backwoodsman. The first constitutions of Maryland and New York were well designed to prevent domination by the unlettered and the poor. It was actually easier to secure the suffrage in colonial New York than it was in New York freed from English tyranny. Moreover, the governors and judges who replaced English and proprietary governors and judges were very generally persons of means.

Why did that American generation fail to establish political democracy in the new states? The fact is that many Americans of the time had no faith in it, were bitterly opposed to it. These, often called Conservatives by historians, conceived that the great purpose of the War of Independence was to throw off the English yoke, that there should be as few other changes as possible. They desired that the power formerly wielded by the English should pass into the hands of those Americans who had formerly shared authority with the English. Led by aristocrats and would-be aristocrats, the Conservatives wanted neither economic nor social leveling. Vigorously opposed to the Conservatives was another group, commonly called Radicals or Democrats, that stood for majority rule, destruction of privilege, and social equality. Between the Conservatives and the Radicals were Liberals or Moderates, men like Jefferson and James Madison, who sought to make changes but who thought it unwise to make every one of them immediately. These groups clashed seriously. For a time the Radicals had their way in

Georgia, the Conservatives in Maryland. In most of the states the outcome was compromise.

But if the Radicals were not victorious everywhere and immediately, it is nevertheless true that long strides were taken toward the establishment of political democracy in America. Most white men could vote. Power was placed in legislatures rather than in governors and judges. Elections became frequent and regular. Representation in the legislatures was less inequitable than it had been in the past, the Piedmont securing seats at the expense of the Tidewater. There was a major shift of power toward the left, and it would continue. Aristocratic republicanism would go down.

There was much less economic than political leveling in the Revolutionary era. During and after the War of Independence some Patriots, like the merchants Robert Morris and William Bingham, became rich, and others slipped down the economic ladder. However, few poor Patriots became wealthy, and few opulent ones descended to poverty. Certainly no class was deprived of its property, and no class acquired it. It is true that there was a shift of wealth from Loyalists to Patriots. The lands of some Tory landlords, which had been seized and sold by the states, fell into the hands of Patriot tenants. But other Tory lands were bought by Patriot army officers, merchants, and lawyers. Moreover, the bulk of the Tories escaped confiscation. Even so, had it become public policy, as the result of the Revolution, to make it easy for every man who did not own land to acquire it, we should be forced to declare that there was an "Internal Revolution." America possessed tens of millions of fertile acres that might have been given at no or little cost to poor men. However, if speculators were less favored after 1776 than they were in the colonial time, if it became somewhat more difficult for men of wealth and influence cheaply to secure vast grants of land and handsome estates, neither the American states nor the central government undertook to give a farm to every landless man. Those who had served in the Patriot forces often received acres of soil for their services. Generally, however, public lands were sold, in order to secure badly needed revenue; and the terms of sale were not remarkably generous. Not until 1862, by the Homestead Act of that year, did the federal government actually give land to settlers. On the whole, it was probably easier for the poor man to get a farm because America separated from England. But here, again, is not massive economic overturn.

Although the Revolutionary upheaval did not lead to vast economic change, it did inspire efforts to prevent hereditary fortunes and so to strike at aristocracy. In Europe the aristocracy was buttressed by primogeniture and entail. In America, before the War of Independence, the principle of primogeniture was legally recognized everywhere, and property could be entailed in every colony except South Carolina. The first-born son of a person who died intestate received a larger share of his or her estate than younger brothers and sisters; in some colonies he inherited the entire estate. Entail was more important than primogeniture, for it enabled the owner of property to assure possession of it to his offspring. He could arrange for the passage of an estate from eldest son to eldest son into the indefinite future, despite the wishes of his descendants. In Virginia even slaves could be placed under entail. It is apparent enough that entail encouraged the perpetuation of wealth, social position, and political power in one line of descent, that it was a prop of aristocracy. Jefferson and other reformers demanded that entail and primogeniture, which were unjust to younger children and encouraged hereditary concentration of wealth, power, and privilege, be abolished. They were, in every state, within thirty years after the Declaration of Independence. It has been pointed out by scholars that relatively few estates were entailed before 1776, and it has been suggested that these legal changes were not of the greatest moment. But they were important in that they struck blows against both current and future inequities. To be sure, it remained possible for families to gain and to keep economic and social superiority. Inheritance taxes did not disturb the rich in America until the twentieth century.

It is an ancient practice of mankind to distinguish between supposedly superior and presumably inferior human beings by means of hereditary titles of nobility. On the continent of Europe in the eighteenth century dukes and counts were far above the common herd, almost of a different human species. They were almost as far removed as kings and emperors from peasants and traders. In England the gulf between common folk and those who bore hereditary titles was not so immense but was great nevertheless. There, too, dukes, earls, viscounts, barons, and baronets—and their kin—were privileged. They consorted with the King and other members of the royal family. Offices, pensions, and honors came easily to them. So firmly established was their right to favor, so clear was it that the aristocrats belonged to a higher order of humanity, that farmers, cobblers, traders, and clerks conceded that they themselves were of meaner stuff. The renowned elegance, beauty, and charm of the eighteenth century in England were not for them but were reserved for their betters. Turning against monarchy, the Americans would have no nobility. Several states, in their constitutions, forbade hereditary distinctions. They would doubtless have been forbidden by every state constitution had it seemed necessary. It was not, for the Articles of Confederation and the Constitution of 1787 denied to the states and to the United States the right to grant a title of nobility. The Constitution also forbade American officeholders to accept one, without the consent of Congress, from a foreign ruler or nation. Very few Americans had hereditary titles before 1776; happily, no more were permitted. The evils inherent in such distinctions were only too evident. Some of Washington's officers, including the Baron von Steuben, who was not truly a baron, and General Henry Knox, who was not modest, formed the Order of the Cincinnati after the War of Independence, restricting membership to officers of the Continental army. On the other hand, they proposed to include the eldest sons of officers, their eldest sons, and so on. Hereditary membership in the order was bitterly denounced, especially in New England. As the first head of the society, Washington, upon the advice of Jefferson and James Madison, declared himself against it, and a national meeting of the order decided that membership should die with the officers. Nevertheless, some of the state chapters of the Cincinnati admitted eldest sons. The order languished.

Inevitably, many Americans afterward yearned for honors, for themselves and their descendants. American heiresses would marry foreign noblemen. The principle of aristocracy was not

dead in the United States. American young ladies eagerly sought
to be received at court by English monarchs. "Old" families,
especially those located on the Atlantic seaboard and in the
Southern states, continued to claim to be socially superior and
were often admitted to be such. Members of such clans, and of
others with even more slender claims to special and enduring
status, often projected family trees across the Atlantic until they
reached William the Conqueror, Charlemagne, a Dutch nobleman, or a German prince. An American untitled aristocracy—or
well-bred plutocracy—persisted into the twentieth century. The
republic had its *Social Registers*, trans-Atlantic equivalents of
Burke, Debrett, and the *Almanach de Gotha*.

Casting aside shackles imposed by kings and nobilities, the
Americans could hardly fail to move against the tyranny of the
church. They did so. At the beginning of the War of Independence they enjoyed a larger measure of religious freedom than
any other people in the Western world. However, it will be
recalled that the Episcopal Church was established in the five
Southern colonies and three New York counties; and that the
Congregational Church was favored in three New England commonwealths. Legal privilege was everywhere extended to Christians of orthodox belief. Although the fraction of Americans
who were church members was smaller than at any later time,
religious discrimination was not trifling. It was grievous that
Roman Catholics could not vote in Maryland, that non-
Episcopalians were compelled to support the Anglican Church
in Virginia. Many of the Revolutionary leaders, although they
usually retained church membership, held unorthodox beliefs.
Jefferson and John Adams were Unitarians; in maturity Tom
Paine, Franklin, and Washington were deists. Nowhere in his
writings does Washington refer to Christ, although it was long
afterward reported that the dignified and reserved Virginia gentlemen prayed in the snow at Valley Forge. In the Declaration
of Independence the Patriots appealed, not to the Jewish Yah-
weh or the Christian Lord, but to "Nature's God," a "Creator,"
and a "Divine Providence." Since sectarians often feared and
detested one another, it was possible to advance far toward complete religious freedom. Episcopal and Congregational clergymen fought to maintain the legal privileges of their churches.

The Congregational Church retained some of those privileges in Massachusetts and Connecticut until well into the nineteenth century. Elsewhere, however, it was possible quickly to cut most of the ties between church and state. Only in Virginia were the Episcopalians sufficiently numerous and influential to make a stout defense of their favored position. There Jefferson and James Madison, insisting upon complete religious liberty, led an onslaught against the Anglican establishment. Other Virginia leaders, including Washington, Patrick Henry, and John Marshall, did not wish to go so far. They favored a "general assessment" scheme, by which all Virginians would contribute through taxation to the support of the churches of their choice, or to charity. After a decade of struggle the Virginia Assembly finally enacted Jefferson's Statute of Religious Liberty, which made belief or the lack of it a personal matter in the Old Dominion. Here and there minor discriminations persisted, such as a requirement that an officeholder declare his belief in God or the Trinity. In general, the states threw up walls between church and state. Moreover, by the First Amendment to the Constitution of 1787, Congress was denied power to create "an establishment of religion," to limit religious liberty. Achievement of that freedom was not the smallest outcome of Revolutionary ferment. It was not absolute. Christianity received moral support from federal and state governments far into the twentieth century, and even indirect financial aid, notably by way of subsidies for the education of children in private church schools. The Protestant sects regained members and power in the nineteenth century. Roman Catholics also became numerous in America. Many Protestants and nearly all adherents of Rome, convinced that their religious revelations were entirely and singularly valid, declared that America was a "Christian country," that it must remain such. Jews, Baptists, many other Protestants, deists, agnostics, and atheists continued the campaign for a complete divorce between church and government.

Proclaiming that the rights of man were the gift of Nature, that "all men are created equal," the thoughtful and sensitive Patriots conceded as a corollary that Negro slavery ought to be ended. The great men of the Revolutionary time, almost without exception—Washington, Jefferson, Hamilton, Patrick

Henry, Henry Laurens, James Madison, and many another—said that the bondage of the blacks could not be morally justified. Believing, erroneously, that the Negro was inferior by heredity, Jefferson nevertheless declared that he ought to be free. Men from Maine to Georgia denounced slavery. It was assailed as unjust to the blacks and injurious alike to master and man. Sentiment against Negro servitude rose high enough so that it was possible substantially to put an end to it above the Mason-Dixon line within thirty years after the Declaration of Independence. After 1780, Pennsylvania and the states to the north, one by one, declared slavery illegal; and in the great Northwest Ordinance of 1787 Congress forbade the institution in the wide region between the Great Lakes and the Mississippi and Ohio rivers. Alas, it was easy to strike at Negro servitude in areas where slaves were few, where they were almost unknown, where their liberation was not costly; in the South it was otherwise. There abolition of Negro bondage might bring immediate and heavy economic losses to slave owners. Moreover, to free the slaves would create new social difficulties in that region. What would be the relationship between the numerous freed blacks and the whites? In Virginia and Maryland sentiment against slavery was strong enough to permit the passage of laws that allowed masters to release slaves—to manumit them. Thus, some thousands of Negroes gained their liberty. But it was not possible, even in those states, to proceed massively against the institution. After a time even Maryland and Virginia made manumission difficult. In the Carolinas and Georgia it would have been idle to urge the abolition of slavery by law. Jefferson and other Southern reformers came to believe that it was necessary to put off action against Negro servitude to a future time.

Feeling among the Patriots against the oceanic slave trade ran higher than it did against slavery itself. Arguments against the swift destruction of slavery could be brought forth; the oceanic traffic in Negro bodies and souls could not be defended. Of course, it *was* defended, by those who profited from it. But many a slaveholder wanted no more slaves introduced from abroad. State after state forbade their importation. In South Carolina and Georgia, where slave labor was much wanted after the war, action was delayed, but Georgia made it illegal to import slaves in 1793. South Carolina, banning the traffic between 1787 and 1804, thereafter permitted introduction of Negroes from Africa but not from the West Indies. After 1808 the oceanic trade was forbidden by federal law, and it dwindled. It was well that the flow of slaves across the Atlantic was reduced to an illegal trickle. But Negro servitude remained; the institution was not seriously weakened. What to do about it, and what to do about the larger problem of relations between whites and Negroes, would perplex future generations.

If the future was to be bright, far-seeing Revolutionary leaders asserted, America must spend generously for the instruction of her young. As early as 1765, John Adams declared that the English colonization of North America was "the opening of a grand design for the illumination of the ignorant, and the emancipation of the slavish part of mankind all over the earth." Adams later proclaimed the necessity of devoting large sums of tax money to education. He and other thoughtful men realized full well that the winning of independence made education more important than ever, for a republic could hardly succeed without an enlightened citizenry. Jefferson urged that Virginia provide elementary instruction for all her young, that Virginia make secondary schooling available for talented sons of the poor, and that a few of these be sent at public expense to the College of William and Mary, which should be remolded into a university. The distinguished Patriot and physician of Philadelphia, Dr. Benjamin Rush, and George Washington desired a national university. The war and the economic troubles that followed hindered educational advance. There were many Americans, then as later, who would not gladly pay for the instruction of the children of others. Several states made generous provision, on paper, for elementary schools, also for academies, colleges, and universities. Many of these institutions, because money was not forthcoming, were stillborn or died in infancy. Sales of public lands did provide some funds for elementary schools; private schools and colleges were also assisted; and one state university, that of North Carolina, finally and very modestly opened its doors in 1795. Only very gradually did the states actually assume fiscal responsibility for elementary instruction, and higher education was long reserved for those who were born to prosperous parents and those who were willing to make great sacrifices to pursue it. It is doubtful that the American people were much better educated a half century after the Declaration of Independence than they were when they separated from England. Education was and remained an immense American problem. It also offered vast opportunities.

More could be said about reforms and attempted reforms in the states, of efforts to codify laws, to improve prisons, and to assist debtors to a new life. But it is necessary to turn our attention westward, to the broad lands beyond the Appalachians. Congress laid solid foundations for the development of the eastern half of the Mississippi valley. Managing to survive Indian attacks during the War of Independence, and even expanding, the settlements of Kentucky and Tennessee continued to grow after the Peace of Paris. But all was not well in that West. Indian attacks did not cease. They were encouraged by the English in Canada; and the English, violating the treaty of 1783, maintained garrisons on American soil, south of the Great Lakes. The Spanish encouraged the Indians of the Old Southwest, and they restricted the passage of American shipping through the lower Mississippi River Valley. Congress was unable to act vigorously against the Indians, the British, or the Spanish. Nor could Virginia or North Carolina offer much help to the pioneers of Kentucky and Tennessee, their citizens beyond the mountains. Discouraged, a few of those pioneers even made overtures to the Spanish and the English. A stronger central government would come to the assistance of the backwoodsmen after 1789. But even in 1785, Congress could and did lay down a plan for the orderly distribution of lands on the far side of the Appalachians. Two years later, in the extraordinary Northwest Ordinance, it framed a political regime for the Old Northwest. That region was not to be a mere colony. It was to be a territory, and it was to have a representative assembly as soon as the number of settlers within it reached 5,000. Their private rights, including freedom of worship, were guaranteed. It will be recalled that slavery was forbidden. No fewer than three and no more than five states were to be carved from the territory. As soon as any part of it had 60,000 inhabitants, it would be admitted to the Union as a state and would be placed "on an equal footing with

the original States in all respects whatever." Five commonwealths were eventually formed from the territory. Thus it was
decided that the region and its people were not to be held in
subjection but were to receive equal treatment with older American regions and their people. The foundation of American
"colonial" policy was laid, since similar liberal arrangements
were afterward made for other western areas. Ultimately even
Alaska and Hawaii were added to the Union as perfect political
equals of the other states. Here was a generous statesmanship.

Again, America was transformed during and after the War of
Independence. If the term "Internal Revolution" is extravagant
to describe that transformation, it is nevertheless true that American institutions were profoundly altered. In no other brief
period of American history were they so radically improved.

CHAPTER 8

A Stronger Union

※※※

THE REVOLUTIONARY GENERATION WAS neither composed of nor led by demigods. In the summer of 1787, eleven years after the Declaration of Independence, fifty-five of its principal men made *the* Constitution. It was ratified within less than one year, and the political machinery described in it began to turn in the spring of 1789. The achievement of the men who framed it and who secured its adoption, the "Founding Fathers," has been magnificently lauded, and not without reason. In praise of them it has been urged that they saved the American people from dire distress and virtual anarchy, that they altruistically devised an almost perfect governmental instrument. To the contrary it has been contended that they were largely men of the Conservative stripe, who primarily sought economic benefit for themselves, who carefully inserted in that Constitution clauses toward that end, together with political devices that would enable them to dominate the stronger central government for which it provided. It has even been suggested that their triumph was the American equivalent of the later Thermidorian reaction in the French Revolution, that swing toward the right in 1794 which followed the Great Terror. America had neither a great terror nor a little one. Not one of her numerous politicians was hanged or shot as a public enemy in the 1780s. One ought not to look upon the Founding Fathers as saviors; on the other hand, one may not believe that they were swayed almost exclusively by narrow and selfish motives. The situation of the American people in that summer of 1787, if not at all desperate, was truly awkward; the Founding Fathers did, with their assent, create a splendid federal Union; if they were principally Conservatives in America, they were Radicals from English and European viewpoints; if they temporarily slowed the tide of political and social change, they preserved and provided future protection for the great gains of the Revolution.

It was apparent to many thoughtful Americans, even before the Articles of Confederation were endorsed by the states in 1781, that they did not prescribe a sound federal system. Fearing concentration of power, alarmed lest an American tyranny replace an English one, the makers of the Articles had recognized the need for some sort of American union, had declared, indeed, that they were founding a "perpetual" one. How could they protect their freedom against a dominating central government and at the same time give it strength enough to defend the nation, to meet all needs that were general rather than local? Here was a truly awkward problem. The men who prepared the Articles not only dreaded tyranny but harbored loyalties to their states; men from the small states were concerned lest they be dominated by the large ones; and Southerners, quarreling with Northerners over economic and even social issues, wanted no Northern masters. Hence came the too weak central government based upon the Articles. That mistake was aggravated by failure to provide proper machinery for it.

The defects of the Articles of Confederation became ever more apparent. In 1784 it was difficult to collect enough members of Congress to ratify the treaty of peace. States tardily honored requisitions upon them for funds, or did not even respond to pleas from Congress for cash. Without sufficient money, that body was unable to exert all the authority, limited as it was, that had been vested in it by the Articles. The new United States of America, too poor to maintain armed forces to assert its rights and claims against England, Spain, and the Indians, could not stop bickering among the states, could not prevent them from violating provisions of the Peace of Paris. The nation was intermittently menaced by bankruptcy. England cramped the overseas commerce of the Americans by applying the Navigation Acts to them as aliens—to the surprise of some Americans who wished both to be independent from England and to have the rights of British citizens. England did not even bother to send a minister to the American capital. Where was the American capital? Congress could not decide where it should be, and the delegates met here and there, at Philadelphia, Trenton, Annapolis, and New York. So evident were the shortcomings of the Articles of Confederation that efforts to amend them began in 1781, the very year in which they were adopted. These efforts continued for five years. It was urged that Congress be given at least a measure of control over internal and foreign commerce, and especially that it be authorized to impose duties upon imports. It was apparent that the proceeds from such duties would assure the solvency of the central government and give it vigor. But all such efforts failed, for the Articles could not be changed without the unanimous consent of the thirteen state legislatures. That could not be secured. It became only too clear that extraordinary action was necessary if the American system was to be soon and suitably altered.

Fortunately, in the year 1786, sentiment in favor of constitutional change began to rise rapidly. Then, as later, the Americans were disposed to believe that government was largely responsible for their troubles. They had not yet recovered from the postwar economic depression. Some of the states were levying heavy taxes to reduce their war debts. Toward the end of 1786, farmers of western Massachusetts who could not pay their taxes, and who feared that they would lose their homes and farms, took up arms to defend their property. Led by Daniel Shays, a Revolutionary officer, the farmers resisted the Massachusetts militia and did not abandon the struggle until four of them had been killed in open fighting and it had become apparent that their rebellion could not succeed. In other states emission, and the fear of emission, of legal tender paper money, to ease the burden of debt, aroused creditors and persons who dreaded inflation. Many Americans began to think of constitutional change as the remedy for every difficulty.

Those who had long urged the creation of a stronger central government, including George Washington, now had their opportunity. Especially eager to seize it were men of the Conservative cast. On the whole they had not been very successful in their contest in the states with the Radicals and Liberals. Might they not gain control of a strong central government? And might it not be possible to give it authority to issue a sound currency and to protect property against attack by the states? Many of the Conservatives desired to infuse vigor into that central government because they were its creditors; they were not being paid, and they could hope that a solvent regime would honorably meet all the obligations of the United States.

Rather curiously, those who desired to do something about the Articles of Confederation found a vehicle in the Annapolis Convention of 1786. Called to consider means to remove economic barriers between the states, the convention was attended by delegates from only five of them. It could not accomplish its purpose. However, Alexander Hamilton and James Madison, who were present, persuaded the gathering to go beyond its original purpose, to ask the states to send men to another convention which should propose changes toward making "the constitution of the federal government adequate to the exigencies of the Union." This scheme was endorsed without enthusiasm by Congress—after five states had chosen delegates. The device of a constitutional convention offered promise. Shays' Rebellion spurred the timid and the reluctant. Eventually every state, except the smallest one, Rhode Island, sent delegates. In consequence the Federal Convention met at Philadelphia in the Pennsylvania Statehouse from May to September 1787. Of the fifty-five men who took part in its work, thirty-nine put their names to the Constitution that it produced.

Whatever may be said about the motives of the men who made the Constitution, it is the settled and sound opinion of historians that they formed a truly distinguished body of men. There was genius among them, and much talent. More than half of them were lawyers; some were planters and merchants; a few were physicians and professors. A majority of them had attended college, and many were veteran politicians. Several of the dominating figures of the Revolutionary generation did not attend the Convention. Thomas Jefferson and John Adams were absent, Jefferson serving his country at Paris and Adams representing it at London. Their counsel would have been valuable in the Convention. Also missing were two American folk heroes, Patrick Henry and Samuel Adams, who saw no compelling reason for constitutional change. In the time of the Stamp Act troubles

Henry had quickly and boldly come forward as a champion of American liberty. However, neither he nor Samuel Adams was famed for his constructive abilities. But Washington was present. He presided over the Convention. No orator, no subtle contriver, he had little to say. No other American was trusted as he was; he gave dignity to the Convention; and his support of the Constitution that it made was to be vital. Franklin was there, old and tired, his ingenuity at last almost exhausted. Amiable and venerable, he by his very presence soothed antagonism, reminding delegates of past trials victoriously endured, offering steady hope of triumph over others to come. Also there was James Madison, a Virginia planter, a small, smiling, diffident, kindly scholar, a constructive genius. He would do more than any other man to solve the vexing questions the Convention had to face; he would earn the magnificent sobriquet, "Father of the Constitution." In the Virginia delegation with Washington and Madison was George Mason, who often spoke usefully in defense of personal liberty and who insisted that the oceanic slave trade must be ended. Lawyer James Wilson of Pennsylvania contributed helpfully. John Rutledge, Charles Cotesworth Pinckney, and Charles Pinckney, South Carolina aristocrats, displayed statesmanship; defending the special interests of South Carolina, they nevertheless refused to place them above the general good. Oliver Ellsworth and Roger Sherman of Connecticut, without fanfare, found a middle way in hot disputes and led furious debaters into it. John Dickinson, respected, sensible, honorable, was a member from Delaware. Among the men from Pennsylvania was Gouverneur Morris, a one-legged, amorous, and snobbish aristocrat who was chiefly responsible for the surprisingly good English into which the Constitution was put. One of the three delegates from New York was Alexander Hamilton. He possessed abilities of the very first order but played a very small part in the Convention. Declaring that he favored limited monarchy in principle, he abandoned his chance to sway the Convention. He attended few of its sessions.

It was quickly decided that it would not do to try to patch up the Articles of Confederation, that they must be replaced by a new instrument. Arriving early at Philadelphia, the Virginia delegates prepared and submitted to the Convention a so-called

"Virginia Plan." It would have concentrated great power in the central government, giving it authority to coerce both the states and the people. It was sharply condemned by many speakers, and it was, after much debate, set aside. However, the convention made use of fundamentally important parts of it. By June 19 the delegates had decided both to make a new constitution and to vest sufficient authority in the central government so that it would be both federal and national.

The Convention did not reach these decisions without qualms and heartburnings, and its members had to face many more—and perplexing—problems, sometimes in tropical temperatures. Summer in Philadelphia is often warm and humid. During late June and early July the Convention was riven by a quarrel between the small and the large states. The Virginia Plan called for a bicameral Congress. Seats in its lower house were to be apportioned in accordance with population; the House of Representatives, as it came to be known, was to elect the members of a second chamber, later named the Senate, from lists of names submitted by the states; and the national legislature was to choose the national executive. Delegates from the small states furiously assailed these arrangements. They were intended, it was charged, to assure domination of the central government by the large states, Virginia, Pennsylvania, and Massachusetts. The men elected to the lower house from those states would combine, and those commonwealths would control both the legislative and the executive branches of government. Gunning Bedford of Delaware heatedly asserted that it might be better to take the hand of George III rather than to accept mastery by the large states, and William Paterson of New Jersey came forward with a "New Jersey Plan." It would certainly have prevented the ascendancy of Virginia, Pennsylvania, and Massachusetts. It provided for a unicameral legislature in which each state would have one vote. Moreover, that assembly would have rather modest powers. That the Founding Fathers were not all demigods appears clearly in the debates over the merits of the opposing provisions of the Virginia and New Jersey plans. Madison pointed out that the lawmakers would assert the wishes of their constituents; that the interests of citizens of the large states did not necessarily clash with those of the citizens of the small ones;

that interests were regional, economic, and social; hence, that legislators from Massachusetts would tend to vote with those of New Hampshire rather than with those of Virginia, men from Delaware to side with those of Pennsylvania rather than with those from Rhode Island. The argument offered by Madison was irrefutable, but it did not persuade the champions of the small states. Swayed by particularistic jealousies, they obstinately clung to their fears.

If the Convention was to accomplish anything, it was necessary to placate Bedford, Paterson, and their allies. They were finally satisfied, by the Connecticut Compromise, so named because the delegates from Connecticut, a state that was neither large nor small, played an important part in the making of it. Accordingly, it was at last decided that the Congress should contain two chambers, the House of Representatives and the Senate. No law could be passed without the consent of both. Each state legislature was empowered to elect two senators, and it was stipulated that the states were always to be equally represented in the Senate. However, population was largely to determine the number of persons sent by each state to the House of Representatives. Delegates from the smaller commonwealths were much pleased by the bargain. Assured that the Congress would not be ruled by the large states, they were thereafter quite willing to give handsome powers to the central government.

One may assess too highly the abilities of the Founding Fathers, and also their desire to act for the common good, and so conclude that the quarrel between the large and small states, being in some part artificial, was not truly difficult to settle. The stupidities and perversities of mankind suggest only too emphatically that the controversy was real and bitter. Certainly few will say that there were no burning issues between South and North in the Convention.

Clash between North and South began with the republic and would wax and wane for generations. It was apparent even in 1775 that there were jarring regional elements among the Patriots, that these would not be easily reconciled in a new nation. In 1775 and 1776, American soldiers whose homes lay west and south of the Hudson River, suspecting that the Yankees intended not only to drive off the English but to dominate the rest of the Americans, declared that they would, if necessary, fight against their comrades in arms. Tory writers hopefully warned the Patriots who resided south of the Susquehanna River that flight from the gentle rule of England would lead them under the yoke of the Northern Patriots. During the war it became steadily clearer that Maryland, Virginia, the Carolinas, and Georgia formed a distinct region. It came to be called the "Southern states;" later it was known as the "South." Thus it was that the boundary between Maryland and Pennsylvania, the Mason-Dixon line, acquired fame as the northern limit of the South, and as the southern limit of the North. The South, with its warmer climate, special agriculture, plantations, slaves, aristocracy, exports of tobacco, rice, and indigo, and imports of manufactures, was posed against the North, with its colder climate, general agriculture, burgeoning commerce, infant industries, and growing merchant marine.

Southerners and Northerners bickered and fought in and outside Congress during the War of Independence and after. Should Negro slaves be enlisted in the Continental army with a promise of freedom as a reward for service? Northerners and Southerners did not give the same answer to this question. Nor could they easily agree that slaves should or should not be taken into account as property in apportioning the sums to be paid by the states toward meeting national expenses under the Articles of Confederation. South Carolina at one time even suggested that, to prevent Northern domination, every action taken by the Congress under that feeble instrument be approved by no fewer than eleven of the thirteen state delegations in it. Before and after the Peace of Paris, Southerners who sought to promote the growth of their settlements in Kentucky and Tennessee eagerly strove to open the Mississippi River to American traffic; Northerners opposed drastic measures toward that end. Northerners and Southerners engaged in chronic and irritating controversy over the location of the national capital. Immediately before the Federal Convention feeling ran so high among Northern and Southern leaders that there was talk of separation on both sides of the Mason-Dixon line.

In the Convention delegates from the South, with the striking exception of George Washington, stoutly defended Southern interests. Washington, convinced as early as 1780 that vigor must be infused into the central government, if for no other reason than because as commander in chief of the army he had suffered from its weakness, was not alarmed lest the North rule the nation and the South. But even Madison, at that time a fervent nationalist, desired the insertion of clauses in the Constitution that would protect the South against the North. John Rutledge and Charles Cotesworth Pinckney agreed with Madison. Other Southern delegates, including George Mason, were determined at almost any cost to prevent Northern tyranny.

There was no struggle over slavery in the convention. Northerners did not attack it, and Southerners were not goaded to a defense of it. But were slaves to be counted when seats in the House of Representatives were apportioned? And—Congress being given the right to levy direct taxes—were slaves to be counted like whites when such levies were imposed? Southerners wished to number Negroes with whites for the purpose of representation but said they ought not to be counted as equal to white persons for the purpose of taxation. Northerners declared that slaves should be considered the equals of whites for taxation but not for representation. A hot quarrel arose. It was at length settled by a compromise. In accordance with a formula proposed by Madison, it was agreed that five slaves were to be counted as three whites for both purposes.

North and South also wrangled about the measure of authority to be given to Congress to levy external taxes and to regulate maritime commerce. All agreed that there must be import duties; proceeds from them would put the nation on its financial feet. However, the South exported far more than the North, and Southerners would not have taxes placed upon the produce sent out from their region. Moreover, many Southerners, fearing that both their imports and their exports would be entirely carried in Yankee ships and that the Yankees would profit at their expense, sought to prevent those evils. They were jealous of the rapid growth of the Northern merchant marine. They wished to deny to Congress power to injure foreign, especially English, shipping to the benefit of the American merchant marine. Further, men from the Deep South—from South Carolina and Georgia—were alarmed lest Congress be authorized to take immediate action against the oceanic slave trade. On the other hand, Northerners desired to give Congress authority to impose all sorts of taxes and duties in American ports, in order to defend American shipping against foreign competition and to put an end to the oceanic traffic in slaves. Feeling ran high between the two sections. At length, with the delegations of Connecticut and South Carolina leading the way, they made a bargain. It was agreed that Congress might impose import, but not export, duties; regulate foreign commerce; and act against the oceanic traffic in slaves, but not until the Constitution had been in force for twenty years. This arrangement pleased John Rutledge and Charles Cotesworth Pinckney. George Mason, because he believed that it did not sufficiently protect Southern interests, bitterly condemned it. In fact, largely because he feared that the Constitution would enable the North to dominate the South, he refused to sign it.

The Convention had its squabbles as well as its great debates. However, the public was not informed about them, for the convention excluded spectators and toiled in secrecy. At last, finishing their labors, its members knew that they had not found a wondrous answer to every question they had faced. When, in September, the time came to sign the Constitution, only forty-two men were present. Three of these refused to put their names upon it, and those who did sign it believed that the document was far from ideal. Nevertheless, despite many shortcomings, the Constitution was superbly drawn. It provided splendidly for the governmental needs of the Americans at that time. With changes, it would endure for many generations and would become almost sacred to the Americans. They have offered it that loyalty which other peoples have given to kings and queens. It has not often been altered by formal amendment. However, the less it has been so changed, the more it has become different through custom, laws made by Congress, and interpretation by the Supreme Court of the United States.

The Constitution provided for that strong "general" government so much desired by many Americans. It, like those of the states, was to rest upon the people, and it could enforce its will, within specified limits, upon the people. Its powers were listed in the Constitution and were confined to those listed. Besides, the central government was restricted by specific prohibitions. Nevertheless, it was tendered such large authority that it was unquestionably "national." It retained the powers given it by the Articles of Confederation. It was authorized also to levy import and internal taxes; to regulate interstate and foreign commerce; to establish a sound currency; and to maintain an army and navy. It was to have three branches: the two-house legislature described above; an executive headed by a President, chosen by indirect election and endowed with large authority; and an independent judiciary consisting of a Supreme Court and such other tribunals as might later be created. "Checks and balances" were inserted in the Constitution to prevent encroachment by one of the three branches upon the others. Curiously, the Constitution did not contain a Bill of Rights. In part, that omission is to be explained by the fact that the new central government was to have only its listed, or enumerated powers. Presumably it would not go beyond them, and a Bill of Rights was therefore unnecessary. It is also likely that some members of the Convention did not wish to cramp Congress, President, and federal judges.

In making the Constitution instead of revising the Articles of Confederation, the Convention, in a sense, went beyond its announced purpose. To be sure, it might have proposed amendments to the Articles that would have made that instrument a very clumsy version of the Constitution. The delegates certainly did go far beyond their instructions in another way, for they declared that the Constitution should go into force when it was ratified in nine states by conventions especially elected to consider it. This procedure clearly violated the provisions of the Articles, which demanded that amendments be unanimously approved by the state legislatures. It was pointed out by some members of the Congress of the Confederation that the Constitution, if adopted, would be unconstitutional. However, it would have been very difficult to get the endorsement of every state, and it could be contended that decision by special conventions was sounder in theory, even more democratic, than decision by legislatures. The old Congress, half-dead already, refused to interfere in behalf of the Articles, and the Constitution was referred to the states.

There followed a long, and sometimes bitter, struggle over the merits of the Constitution. Everywhere it was denounced by men of the Radical cast, and they received support from the camp of the Liberals. Its enemies, called Antifederalists, accused its framers and defenders of trying to create a "consolidated" union, a central government that would be all-powerful and tyrannical. They said that the rich and the well born—the Conservatives—intended to use it to put themselves in the saddle. They made much of the fact that the Constitution did not contain a Bill of Rights. Was not omission of a list of protections of the person in itself proof of tyrannical intentions? Many mechanics and many plain farmers, especially farmers who resided in the interior, both disliked the instrument and distrusted its sponsors. In the South the Constitution was vehemently attacked, not only as as a vehicle for arbitrary rule, but also as a device to injure Southern interests and to open the way for domination of the South by the North.

It has often been said, and it may be true, that a majority of the American people disliked the Constitution. If so, it was nevertheless endorsed in truly republican fashion. Had a plebiscite been held in each of the states, the Constitution would indeed have been set aside. It is not so certain that it would have been condemned in a nation-wide poll. Fortunately, the Americans made their decision through the state conventions. The men who were elected to those bodies were far more familiar with constitutional and political intricacies than were the voters who chose them. The champions of the Constitution, except perhaps in the South, obviously had the weight of argument on their side; they convinced many doubters; and they were victorious. The famous series of essays called *The Federalist*, written by Hamilton, Madison, and John Jay and devoted to defending the Constitution, probably had little effect. They appeared in many newspapers, but they were too abstruse and too dull to win over many waverers. Doubtless they convinced the already persuaded. Not superb propaganda, they continue to offer valuable evidence concerning the intentions of the framers of the Constitution. But the *Federalist* essays were only one of many means employed by the defenders of the Constitution to advance their cause. Admitting that it was not perfect, they pointed out that it called for a strong central government but not an all-powerful one; that that government would rest upon the voters; and that it would be, at least ultimately, responsible to them. Adoption of the Constitution would lead to national solvency, encourage commerce, enable the United States to deal with the Indian problem, permit it to assert its rights against foreign countries, and give dignity and respectability to the American nation. These arguments were impressive. They had pocketbook appeal, and they touched the spirit of patriotism, of nationalism, that had risen high in the War of Independence. Also in favor of the Constitution was the fact that Washington was for it. And would he not be the first President under it?

In the Northern states the strongest argument against the Constitution was that it lacked a Bill of Rights. The Delaware, Pennsylvania, New Jersey, and Connecticut conventions ratified it without remarkable struggle. The consent of Massachusetts and New Hampshire was secured by promises on the part of the Federalists that they would not oppose, that they would support, amendments adding a Bill of Rights after the Constitution was put in force. By June 21, 1788, six Northern states had voted in the affirmative. At that time New York was still wavering. Sentiment in tiny Rhode Island was so much against the Constitution that the legislature of that state had not even bothered to call a convention.

Meanwhile, three Southern states, Georgia, Maryland, and South Carolina, had endorsed the instrument. Thus, by that June 21, it had been approved by nine states. However, there could be no union without Virginia and North Carolina, and there was much, even rancorous, feeling against the Constitution in those commonwealths. The fear of tyranny was potent in the South, for many Southerners continued to be alarmed lest the Constitution enable a Northern majority to dictate to a Southern minority. They desired both a Bill of Rights and additional safeguards against Northern tyranny. In South Carolina the powerful planter aristocracy had set aside those fears and had compelled ratification. However, it was apparent that North Carolina would not consent unless Virginia did. The contest in Virginia was therefore decisive. There the fate of the Constitution hung in the balance until June 25. Its enemies, led by Patrick

Henry, fought almost desperately. He was supported by George
Mason, Richard Henry Lee, and other notables. Henry so forcefully insisted upon massive protection for the South that Washington expressed the suspicion that Henry, a great orator rather
than a statesman, desired to form a separate Southern confederacy. However, in the Virginia convention, Madison, Henry Lee,
John Marshall, George Innes, and other friends of the Constitution defeated Henry and his allies in debate. Henry quite correctly predicted that the national government, if not restrained,
would eventually move against slavery. But he made the mistake
of finding faults where none existed. Madison, replying calmly,
was most convincing. Besides, it then seemed that the South,
having already extended into Kentucky and Tennessee, would
grow more rapidly than the North, hence that the South would
easily be able to defend its interests at the national capital. Although he was not a member of the Virginia convention, the
wishes of Washington, relayed from his home beside the Potomac River, were well known. His influence made itself felt. He
would very likely be the first President under the Constitution;
and—nationalist that he was—he was hardly an enemy of the
South. At last, by promising to push for a Bill of Rights after the
new regime should be formed, the friends of the Constitution
won a narrow victory.

The final triumph of the champions of the new system was
then assured. Feeling against the Constitution was strong in New
York. In its convention Alexander Hamilton, struggling ardently
in behalf of a document he did not admire, one that he favored
only because it was superior to the Articles of Confederation,
managed to avert a decisive vote until news came that Virginia
had endorsed it. It was then possible for him to lead New York
to the "band wagon," by a slender majority of three votes.
Again it was necessary to promise support for a Bill of Rights in
order to get approval. North Carolina and Rhode Island were
then virtually forced to join the new Union, for it was obvious
that they could not survive or flourish as independent republics.
North Carolina waited until 1789, when the passage of the much
desired Bill of Rights was virtually assured. Rhode Island, without any real choice, reluctantly endorsed the Constitution in
1790.

Too much should not be asked of mortals. Forging a new and greater Union, the Founding Fathers did not solve every American problem. The antagonism between South and North would continue, would darken the American scene, and would at last erupt in a bloody civil war. The men who made the Constitution could hardly have done better than they did. Let it not be forgotten that the Americans as a whole were a healthy and vigorous people, that their condition was not dismal in 1787 or 1788. One may believe that they would surely have found passable solutions to their political problems. They displayed a splendid capacity for government in those years. In the debates over the merits of the Constitution there was little violence, and no American was killed. The Antifederalists accepted their defeat with much good grace. Most of their fears were not well founded. Many enemies of the Constitution at length became ardent admirers of it.

In the first elections held under the Constitution the Conservatives were successful. The advantage they secured was only temporary, and the political and social gains of the Revolution were not destroyed. In a larger sense—from a world view—the Constitution was itself the great and culminating innovation of the Revolution. Moreover, infusing vigor into the American nation, it removed barriers against economic advance, and it reduced the military dangers to which the republic was exposed. And so it ensured that the American Reformation of the Revolutionary era would continue.

CHAPTER 9

The Federalists in the Saddle

To the surprise of almost no one, George Washington became the first American President. Under the Constitution, electors chosen by the state legislatures cast two ballots toward electing the President and a Vice-President. They unanimously named Washington, and he soberly accepted the highest office that the Republic could bestow. John Adams secured the Vice-Presidency. In the late spring of 1789 the Virginian solemnly took his oath of office at New York. At fifty-seven he was not yet old. No European ruler of that time was his equal, and his very presence at the head of the republic gave it a simple majesty. He had much more than dignity to contribute, for he was intelligent, industrious, honest, and utterly devoted to his country. No Caesar, no Napoleon, he had not frequently displayed military genius in the War of Independence; but he was amply endowed with both physical and moral courage. There was a romantic and pathetic episode in his youth. He fell in love with Mrs. Sally Fairfax, the charming wife of one of his friends. She told him that his cause was hopeless. Forty years afterward, he recalled that he had spent the most joyous time of his life with her. Entering into a marriage of affection and convenience with a wealthy widow, Mrs. Martha Custis, no beauty, he became a contented country gentleman. He liked his wine and an earthy story, but he stood for no nonsense about land or money. As President, he and "Lady Washington" maintained a "republican court." But he was the "old planter" to a Revolutionary comrade. He was rather dull company; he deeply resented adverse criticism; and he was susceptible to flattery, especially from

Alexander Hamilton. He possessed solid virtues rather than smooth graces. When he chose to act, he towered above his contemporaries, above even the splendid figures of Jefferson and Hamilton. His trials in the Presidency often exasperated him. They were not so grave as those he had faced in the War of Independence. Even so, his achievements as the first magistrate under the Constitution were of the first order.

Under the leadership of Washington the American Republic acquired stability and muscle. Prosperity had already returned when he took his oath of office; it pleasantly persisted. The central government quickly became solvent and almost potent. Its debt was refunded; its army was put upon a respectable footing; hostile Indians learned that the "Great White Father" could strike as well as talk; and Spain and England were forced to give heed to the wishes of a lusty, if infant, member of the family of nations. The French Revolution, and the great European wars which began in 1792, posed many awkward questions for America. Washington clung to a policy of neutrality and secured advantages for his country from the distresses of Europe. Although he would not have it so, two quarreling parties sprang up at home while he was in the Presidency. Against his will, he became the leader, at least the patron, of one, the Federalists. He was succeeded by a Federalist, John Adams, who served as the chief executive until March 1801. Adams won only one great victory—he cut short an undeclared war with France. Losing control of the Presidency and Congress in 1801, the Federalists were never able to regain it. Frustrated and embittered, they might have consoled themselves with the thought that they had built well.

The older Washington, like the younger George III, disliked factions and parties. So did the Federal Convention, which made no provision for them. As George III desired to be a patriot King, George Washington yearned to be a patriot President. Therefore, he chose as his principal advisers the ablest men, regardless of political affiliation, that he could get. By far the most important of these for several years were Jefferson and Hamilton. Washington brought Jefferson home from Paris, appointing him Secretary of State, so as to get the benefit of his experience in foreign affairs. For his Secretary of the Treasury

Washington chose Hamilton, once his trusted aide de camp in
the Continental army. Leaning heavily on these two men, and
also seeking the advice of other heads of executive departments,
Washington soon began to consult them collectively, so forming
the Cabinet. It was a useful device, and it endured. However,
Washington learned, to his vexation and to his sorrow, that he
could not have Jefferson, Hamilton, and harmony in his Cabinet.
Political parties began to emerge within two years, the Federalists and the Democratic-Republicans. Hamilton was a champion
of the Federalists, Jefferson of their enemies. The two men
quarreled sharply in the Cabinet even before their followings
acquired solidity. Washington tended, especially upon domestic
questions, to listen to Hamilton rather than to his fellow Virginian. Despite his wishes, he gradually became more and more
associated with the Federalists.

Even before the end of 1789 the new regime carried through
three basic constructive measures. That summer the financial
troubles of the United States were virtually, if only temporarily,
resolved. Every thoughtful public man knew the remedy for
them, levies upon imports—such taxes were to be the principal
source of federal income for more than a century. In the summer of 1789, Congress imposed duties that brought nourishing
cash into the treasury, so making it possible to meet the current
expenses of the national government, also offering evidence that
it could and would pay its debts. In September, Congress endorsed the Federal Bill of Rights and asked the states to consider
it. It offered many of the protections to persons—and states—
against national tyranny that the Antifederalists had so insistently demanded. As it was sent to the states, the Bill of Rights
contained twelve amendments to the Constitution. Ten of these
were ratified by 1791. They assured trial by jury, freedom from
self-incrimination, reasonable bail, and other safeguards to individuals accused of crimes against the United States. That same
September, Congress devised a system of federal courts in a
Judiciary Act. They were organized in three layers, the highest
tribunal being the Supreme Court. It was some time before these
courts and the judges who sat in them acquired business and
prestige. At first distinguished lawyers did not eagerly seek to be
Chief Justice of the United States, to preside over its loftiest

tribunal. Eventually that court, becoming *the* interpreter of the Constitution, would make so much and such important law that it came to be known as a "third legislature."

The American Republic was healthy and sturdy at the end of 1789. One could then believe that provision for the national debt and for a currency were all that were necessary to put American domestic affairs in splendid order. Alexander Hamilton thought otherwise. During the years 1790 and 1791 he came forward as an ingenious and thoroughgoing "planner," thus winning applause from Socialists and even Communists in the twentieth century, although his sympathies went to creditors, financiers, merchants, and industrialists. He desired to employ national power to remodel the American economy in a hurry, to secure a balance between industry, commerce, and agriculture.

Also, by encouraging and assisting capitalists, bankers, shipowners, manufacturers, and major traders, Hamilton hoped to secure from them stout support of the new regime. Indeed, he desired that he and they should be masters of a national government far more potent than that described in the Constitution. For Hamilton had no faith in the common run and ruck of mankind; he believed that a qualified few, of whom he was one, should rule. He was not an aristocrat by birth, although various dignified Scottish Hamiltons claimed him as their own after he became Secretary of the Treasury. He came into the world on the West Indian island of Nevis in 1755 as the illegitimate son of an unsuccessful Scottish merchant. Migrating to New York in his youth, he had embraced the Patriot cause, had served it loyally and well, and as an officer had won the enduring confidence of Washington. A hero of the War of Independence, he had married Elizabeth Schuyler, a daughter of the Schuyler family of New York, and so had become associated with the American aristocracy. Becoming a lawyer, politician, and writer, he had played a very small part in the federal Convention. In it he had openly declared his belief in limited constitutional monarchy as ideal. It will be recalled that he championed the Constitution, not because he thought it splendid, but because, poor as it might be, he saw that it was an improvement over the Articles of Confederation. He was adventurous and ambitious in both his earlier and later years. A small man physically, he was to be tempted, in the last years of his life, by notions of dictatorship. Like most politicians, he was not as scrupulous as he might have been. In a defective and workday world he was not shocked by misconduct, financial or otherwise, on the part of his friends. He himself could not be corrupted by money; he died almost a poor man. Industrious, courageous, possessed of a penetrating intellect, Hamilton was an extraordinary combination of genius and snob. Speculators, persons seeking governmental favor, aristocrats, and would-be aristocrats gathered about him. He was a formidable antagonist. A most useful servant of the new nation, he fell short of his goals, fortunately for the republic.

To a degree, Hamilton was checked within his own gradually emerging Federalist party. It acquired a large following among New England farmers, and many Southern planters adhered to it. But these were often merely conservative-minded men who did not wish to extend special or great favors to commerce and industry. Hamilton himself had little appeal for voters. New England Federalists tended to put their trust in one of themselves, John Adams; and Southern planters who joined the Federalists admired, after Washington, John Rutledge and the brothers Thomas and Charles Cotesworth Pinckney. John Adams was to wreck one of Hamilton's biggest schemes, and he learned to hate its author.

But Madison and Jefferson were the two men who most persistently and most effectively fought against Hamilton and his works. Elected to the first House of Representatives, the "Father of the Constitution" learned that the Secretary of the Treasury intended to use to the uttermost the powers vested in the central government by that document and to employ them to the special benefit of Northerners, some of them not distinguished for probity. The diffident, thoughtful Virginia planter became alarmed. He had not helped to make, had not fought for, the Constitution in order to assist aristocrats, speculators, and favorites; he did what he could to prevent the giving of pelf and privilege to Northerners—and some Southerners; and he strove to check excessive expansion of national authority. Jefferson soon became his stout ally; the two Virginia planters formed a close friendship that was both personal and political; and the more vigorous, the more assertive Jefferson became the dominant figure in a remarkable partnership. Gradually Jefferson, with Madison as his chief lieutenant, developed the Democratic-Republican party in the South. Moreover, they entered into an alliance with Northern politicians, notably George Clinton of New York and Aaron Burr of the same state. The Democratic-Republican party, strongest in the South, acquired adherents throughout the Union.

The statues which admiring Americans have erected to honor and to preserve the memory of the creators of their republic deceive their beholders. Their makers have straightened Hamilton's nose and have endowed him with a personal beauty he did not possess. The sculptors are even more generous to Jefferson; in stone he appears as a tall, strikingly handsome, majestic, and magnanimous man. He was actually lanky, not very graceful, and relaxed rather than erect in posture. He was red-faced and freckled, and in his later years his long nose reached toward his chin. Jefferson was not remarkable for grandeur, even for tidiness, in dress. Quite human, he was imperfect in substance as well as in outward appearance. Born in 1743, he was about twelve years older than Hamilton, eleven years younger than Washington. Fortune was far more generous to him than to Hamilton, than to men generally. His mother came from the Randolphs, one of the fabled FFV, or First Families of Virginia; his father was a surveyor and a successful land speculator. Reared just behind the frontier of Virginia, he was a sturdy country gentleman. He went to the College of William and Mary, and continued to study into his old age. Architect, inventor, writer, amateur scientist, philosopher, diplomat, and politician, he was the only American of his time who approached Franklin in versatility. Unlike Franklin, he had almost no sense of humor. A truly civilized man, he pondered English law and philosophy and learned to love liberty; he became a devout republican. He was an idealist and a reformer; he desired that America should escape from the ancient injustices, corruptions, and political and religious tyrannies of Europe. Like other children of the Enlightenment whom he met in France after the War of Independence, he conceived that commerce and industry debased the persons engaged in them. He wished America to have no more commerce, no more industry than was necessary; that America

be a nation largely of landowning, vigorous, virtuous, and informed farmers. Let it not be thought that he was hopelessly
romantic, naïve, unworldly. He was also a realistic and gifted
politician; if he believed that the American breed could be improved, he was certain that some of his enemies were beyond
repair; in the heat of political battle he was not unworldly, not
always utterly scrupulous.

Adept as he was in politics, Jefferson soon learned that Hamilton was a resolute and resourceful enemy. Jefferson, Madison,
and their allies vainly tried to check the aggressive Secretary of
the Treasury for many months. In 1790, Hamilton persuaded
Congress to accept an expensive scheme he had framed to deal
with public debts and to establish beyond cavil the credit of the
United States. At his urging Congress undertook to pay in full
all the debts incurred by the central government before 1789.

Those obligations included many millions of dollars in the
form of official "certificates of indebtedness," given to individuals for goods and services during and after the War of Independence. The certificates had fallen far below par, and a large
part of them had been acquired by speculators. Should the speculators be rewarded for their shrewdness? Madison, to no avail,
declared that the original receivers of the certificates, they who
had helped the nation in time of need, ought not to be forgotten.
Hamilton asserted that it was impossible to distinguish between
such men and speculators, that only those who held the certificates could be paid. He had his way; the speculators profited;
and several members of Congress and others hastily arranged to
buy as many of the papers as they could before it became widely
known that they would be honored at par. Hamilton also insisted that the federal government assume debts of $21.5 million
accumulated by the states in their efforts to win the War of
Independence. It was hardly essential to the credit of the nation
that this be done. Moreover, some states, chiefly Southern ones,
had paid off all or most of their war debts, while others, principally in New England, had done little or nothing about them.
It was obvious that this measure would not recognize Southern
virtue, and that it would reward Northern delinquency. Again
Hamilton, eager to change creditors of the states into creditors
of the United States, and so to attach them to the central gov-

ernment, had his way. However, to get it, he had to make a
bargain with Jefferson and Madison. In return for their consent
to the assumption of the state debts, he had to agree to the
moving of the national capital from New York City to Philadelphia for ten years, thence to the banks of the Potomac River.
Neither part of the bargain was utterly beneficial. Established in
the city of Washington, a part of a federal District of Columbia,
the servant-masters of the nation would swelter in the damp heat
of summer in that badly placed capital.

For all his abilities, Hamilton was unable to concoct a scheme
that was completely defensible. In order to assure a supply of
sound paper currency, to create an agency that could hold federal funds and that could lend money to the national government in time of need, he urged the chartering of a Bank of the
United States for a period of twenty years. Why did not the
brilliant Secretary make use of his own Department of the
Treasury to achieve those ends? His bank was modeled after
that of England—to avert censure, he said it was copied from the
Bank of Amsterdam. He desired an institution that would be
partly public, partly private; one fifth of its stock was to be held
by the United States. The private persons who bought its stock
could hope to gain from their association with the national government. Hamilton's contrivance had another defect, since it
was doubtful that the national government had been given
power to charter such a bank. Denouncing Hamilton's scheme,
Jefferson, in a carefully reasoned paper, told President Washington that the bank would be unconstitutional. He pointed out
that the Constitution contained no reference to such an instrument, that its establishment would increase the authority of the
central government as defined in the Constitution. However,
Hamilton, defending his proposal in a written opinion submitted
to Washington, subtly responded to Jefferson's attack. Doubtless
Jefferson, urging "strict construction" of the Constitution, had
logic on his side. But Hamilton cleverly urged the doctrine of
"implied" powers. He said that Congress was authorized to collect taxes, to regulate currency and trade. Toward those ends his
Bank of the United States would be most useful, even necessary.
Declared he: "If the *end* be clearly comprehended within any of
the specified powers, and if the measure have an obvious relation

to that *end*, and is not forbidden by any particular provision of the Constitution, it may safely be deemed to come within the compass of the national authority." Hamilton offered a line of argument that actually permitted vast extension of that authority; in time, in important part through the application of the doctrine of "implied" powers, it would grow far beyond any reasonable definition of it offered in 1787. At length that authority was increased even by inference from the "implied" powers.

The specious argument offered by Hamilton was to be most useful, for it permitted, without cumbersome resort to constitutional amendment, expansion of national action to provide for the needs and to deal with the ills of a changing and complex American society. Moreover, he got his bank. Washington doubted the validity of the argument but chose to accept the views of his Secretary of the Treasury rather than those of his Secretary of State upon a matter of money. Congress also approved the charter. The First Bank of the United States did perform its basic functions, and it gave strength to the American economy. So many investors rushed forward to purchase stock in the bank that its price soared. Those who bought it at a very high price lost heavily when the market value of the stock soon sank.

At last, Hamilton went so far with his economic measures that Congress balked. Toward the end of 1791 he urged protective tariffs to encourage American industry, bounties to stimulate agriculture, and the building of roads and canals. Eventually Congress would adopt all of those measures, but it did not seriously consider them when they were first offered by Hamilton. They seemed extraordinary even to some of his admirers, and it was doubted that Congress possessed authority to adopt them.

Hamilton was too gracious to speculators, including greedy men who secured advance information about his schemes and made—or tried to make—profitable use of it. He was not too scrupulous in his efforts to mobilize men of birth and money into a political force. On the other hand, he did not hesitate to goad plain farmers into hopeless rebellion. He persuaded Congress to impose an excise tax upon whisky, in part to give the federal government an excuse to display its newly acquired power. He knew that the tax would be detested, that its collection was likely to be resisted by farmers who lived in the interior of Pennsylvania and other states to the south. If they dared to challenge federal authority, he expected Washington to use armed force to reduce them to obedience. So it worked out. The farmers of the interior, for lack of currency, used whisky as a means of exchange. The tax was a burden upon them. Many of them, in western Pennsylvania, took up arms to prevent its collection in 1794. When they gathered in bodies and refused to disperse, Washington called thousands of militiamen into service, placed them under the command of General Henry Lee, and ordered him to crush the "Whisky Insurrection." Hamilton accompanied Lee as he marched against the malcontents. They did not dare to fight Lee but fled to their homes. Two of their leaders were convicted of treason, but Washington prudently pardoned them.

The vigor of the new central government was much more suitably displayed in its dealings with the Indians. Furnished arms and liquor by traders who lived in Spanish Florida, some Cherokee and Creek warriors harried the frontier settlements of the Old Southwest throughout the 1780s. During the same years, Indian braves of the Old Northwest made savage raids across the Ohio River. They obtained their guns, tomahawks, and firewater from Canadian merchants. Washington achieved a troubled peace in the Old Southwest in 1790. In that year the President invited Alexander McGillivray, a halfbreed "King of the Creeks," to New York, where he signed a treaty of friendship. Washington had to use the rod against the hostile tribes of the Ohio Valley. In 1791 they defeated a mixed force of regular troops and militia under General Arthur St. Clair. Washington then entrusted the task of subduing them to General Anthony Wayne, an impetuous hero of the War of Independence. Wayne assiduously and slowly drilled a small army and then drove forward through hostile Indian country in 1794. Attacked by the Indians on the banks of the Maumee River, in northwestern Ohio, he routed them in the Battle of Fallen Timbers. A large part of the Old Northwest was thus opened to settlement.

In 1792, urged by both Jefferson and Hamilton to accept a second term in the Presidency, Washington was again honored by the unanimous vote of the electors. But his two advisers gave him no peace, for they had become bitter personal enemies. In the following year they quarreled over foreign policy; Washington listened sympathetically to Hamilton; and Jefferson temporarily retired to private life in his beloved Monticello home in Virginia.

The shattering French Revolution that began in 1789 and the wars that broke out between revolutionary France and most of the monarchs of Europe aroused American passions and affected American interests. In the early stages of that upheaval the Americans very generally applauded the French reformers. Were they not striving to remodel France in the American image? However, the formation of the First French Republic in 1792, the execution of Louis XVI, of Queen Marie Antoinette, of bishops, and of officers of the French army and navy who had fought in the War of Independence alarmed many Americans of the Federalist persuasion. They feared that atheistic, savage, destructive French republicanism would spread across the ocean. When England and France fell to blows early in 1793, they gave their favor to England and her allies. Among them was Hamilton, who had sought close friendship with England from the time he entered the Treasury. On the other hand, deploring the excesses of the French republicans, Jefferson and his friends believed that they fought for humanity. Both Hamilton and Jefferson advised Washington that America ought to keep out of the war, and the President issued a proclamation of neutrality. However, the two Secretaries engaged in ever sharper disputes over foreign as well as domestic policy. The pro-French Jeffersonians and the pro-English Hamiltonians engaged in violent warfare in the newspapers. The honors and dishonors in that struggle were about equal. Perhaps a third of the Americans looked coolly at both England and France. It became evident to Jefferson that Washington leaned toward Hamilton's views, even on foreign affairs, and he left the Cabinet at the end of 1793. Hamilton resigned from it, for personal reasons, early in 1795. However, his influence in it continued; in fact, before the end of the following summer, the Cabinet became completely Federalist.

Washington resented the arrogance of the French republicans, who claimed credit for the help that the French monarchy had given America in the War of Independence and who tended to look upon the new nation as a "client" of France. On the other hand, he harbored no affection for England. He strove to avoid a choice between the antagonists and to do what he could for America. He would not let the French use America as a base for attacks upon the shipping and allies of Britain. Nor would he offer the slightest help to the English. Indeed, he was exasperated by their behavior. They restrained American maritime commerce when American merchants were eagerly seeking to do business with all the European antagonists. Needing able seamen in the royal navy, they forcibly impressed English sailors from American merchant vessels, and sometimes Americans they claimed to be English. They continued to hold forts on the American side of the boundary between the United States and Canada, in violation of the Peace of 1783. Washington sent Chief Justice John Jay to London to demand that England change her ways. Privately assured by Hamilton that they need not fear an American declaration of war, the ministers of George III knew that it was not necessary to concede all that Jay asked. He was able to secure a treaty in which England promised to withdraw the troops from the forts on American soil. But other Anglo-American issues persisted, issues that did not soothe the hatred aroused in the War of Independence. Jay's Treaty was bitterly condemned, in and out of Congress, because England conceded so little. Washington successfully insisted that it be ratified by the Senate. He had doubtless gained from England nearly all that he could without taking up arms. The English promise to evacuate the forts was no small thing, and the pledge was kept. Washington was more successful in bargaining with Spain. In Pinckney's Treaty, also concluded in 1795, Spain conceded that her province of West Florida did not extend north of the thirty-first parallel, and opened the lower Mississippi, at least temporarily, to American shipping.

Had he desired it, Washington would have been elected a third time to the Presidency. He preferred to retire to his Mount Vernon home, where he died in 1799, "first in war, first in peace, and first in the hearts of his countrymen." Before departing from office he published his "Farewell Address," advising his fellow citizens to avoid "permanent" foreign alliances, not to indulge in partisan rage, not to let themselves be drawn into contest between North and South. Some of the Democratic-Republicans declared their delight that Washington the Federalist was leaving the public scene. His departure from it brought no distress to John Adams, who lusted to succeed him and who could not believe that Washington gladly retired from office. Adams had not yet learned that there was less joy than care in power. Washington knew that fame did not bring unalloyed bliss. The year before he died he wrote to Mrs. Sally Fairfax, then widowed and living in England, that the events of forty years had not erased from his mind "the recollection of those happy moments, the happiest in my life, which I have enjoyed in your company."

The Democratic-Republicans who were not pleased with Washington did not admire John Adams, who achieved the Presidency he so keenly desired. In 1796 they put forward Jefferson against Adams, but they were not quite strong enough to dislodge the Federalists. Adams was a vain, small, plump man who seemed to follow Washington like a fat barge after a battleship. He was a better man than he appeared to be. Behind an unimpressive exterior, he was intelligent, studious, and courageous. Moreover, unlike many Federalists, who joined a love for England to hatred for republican France, he gave his heart only to his own country. In truth, he was a very moderate Federalist; his principles were not remote from those of Jefferson. However, Adams maintained Washington's Cabinet and listened too much to its members. Two of them were Hamilton's men rather than his own. They and other extreme Federalists persuaded him to move most vigorously against France. The Directory which controlled that country after 1795 also goaded Adams. It not only authorized the seizure of American merchant vessels but grossly insulted American envoys. Aggressive Federalists clamored for a declaration of war, for additions to a small navy begun by Washington, and for a large army. Adams consented to the establishment of a Department of the Navy and the building of several frigates. He also agreed, in principle though with reluctance, to raise an army, officially to be led by Washington. But it was unlikely that Washington would take the field, and the Virginian insisted that Hamilton be his second in command.

Adams would have chosen General Henry Knox for that post. He gave in to Washington. But why, Adams asked himself, was the former President so determined to give power to Hamilton, who had never been more than a colonel? In 1798 undeclared naval warfare began with France, enduring for two years. The new American warships performed very well. His Hamiltonian advisers continued to urge Adams on toward a declaration of war. He balked. Why were they so eager? For what would that army under Hamilton's command be used? Not against the French, who had no troops in North America and who would hardly send any across the ocean. Presumably against the Spanish in the Floridas or Louisiana, because Spain was an ally of France at that time. Was it certain that the French would not negotiate? What would America gain by fighting France? Adams saw that he had been hoodwinked. He dismissed the extreme Federalists from his Cabinet, discreetly and unofficially inquired of the Directory whether it would bargain. The French answer was in the affirmative. Becoming master of France during the negotiations that followed, Napoleon gave his consent to the Convention of 1800 which formally set aside the alliance made between the two nations in 1778; put an end to the undeclared war on the sea; and temporarily reduced Franco-American friction.

Adams was not rewarded in this world for his good sense and patience in foreign affairs. Hamilton angrily schemed to secure the election of another Federalist to the Presidency in 1800. Nor did the Democratic-Republicans gratefully acknowledge that Adams had served his country well. Repressive measures taken against them by the Federalists, especially the Sedition Act of 1798, embittered them. The purpose of the Sedition Act was to suppress Democratic-Republican editors and publishers. It provided for the punishment of any person who published "any false, scandalous, and malicious writing" concerning the President, Congress, or the national government generally. It clearly infringed upon the freedom of the press guaranteed by the Constitution. Federalist judges enthusiastically and injudiciously enforced the law, fining or sending to prison several editors and printers who had forthrightly declared that the Federalists in office were less than admirable. Jefferson and his followers struck back as best they might, even calling upon the states, in the Virginia and Kentucky Resolutions of 1798, to stand forth as defenders of personal liberty against federal tyranny. More to the purpose, they violently assailed the divided Federalists in the election campaign of 1800, winning control of both the Presidency and Congress.

The triumph of the Democratic-Republicans was almost snatched away from them. Their electors had cast 73 votes for Jefferson and 73 for Aaron Burr of New York, most of them intending to put Burr in the Vice-Presidency. However, the two men were legally tied for the Presidency, since the Constitution did not then require separate balloting for the two offices—it was required by the clarifying Twelfth Amendment, added to the Constitution four years later. Burr could have prevented dispute by insisting that he would accept only the Vice-Presidency; but, brilliant and ambitious, he kept silent. A House of Representatives that had not yet passed under the control of the Democratic-Republicans had to decide between Jefferson and Burr. The Federalists in that body played with fire. Some of them hoped to prevent a choice, and so to have an excuse to keep Adams in office. Others sought to bargain with Burr, to form an alliance with him. He would not listen to them. At length, more prudent men among the Federalists, including Hamilton, who distrusted Burr even more than he did Jefferson, threw their support to Jefferson, and he was formally elected to the Presidency by the House of Representatives.

CHAPTER 10

The Jeffersonian Republic

❀❀❀

WALKING FROM HIS BOARDING house down the unfinished streets of the new and raw city of Washington to the Capitol, Thomas Jefferson took the oath of office as President on March 4, 1801. Later he would see his plain but dignified entrance into power as a great American turning point. He would refer to his own victory and that of his followers as the "Revolution of 1800." Yet it was not certain on that March day that the Jeffersonians had won an enduring ascendancy. The clever Aaron Burr, who took his oath with the Virginian, was not a reliable lieutenant. Should Jefferson die before the end of his term of office, Burr would succeed him. Moreover, the danger remained that Burr would ally himself with the Federalists. If Burr was less than a friend, the man who administered the oath to Jefferson, Chief Justice John Marshall, was the President's open and perennial foe. A distant cousin of Jefferson, Marshall had broken with him many years earlier and had become a devoted Federalist. There was no sympathy for Jefferson in the small sharp eyes of the Revolutionary veteran who had only recently been appointed by John Adams to preside over the Supreme Court. Marshall and a phalanx of judges who shared his political opinions would do what they might to thwart Jefferson. The astute and ambitious Hamilton was still alive, and the Federalist party was by no means dead.

Nevertheless, time and the tide of events were with Jefferson and his disciples. In his inaugural address he proclaimed his allegiance to a liberal republicanism, to the principle of majority rule, to civil rights, economy, and peace. He would not carry his

country into "entangling" foreign alliances. He did not condemn every one of his political antagonists. Rather, saying "we
are all republicans, we are all federalists," he invited them to join
him. Many of them, at length, did that very thing. Jefferson's
most bitter enemies, except for Marshall, vanished from the
public scene, within six years; and Marshall was never more than
a sharp and irritating thorn in Jefferson's side. The Federalist
party failed to win a national election after 1798, and the Jeffersonians changed the course of the republic. To say that there
was a "Revolution of 1800" is doubtless to exaggerate. It is
nevertheless true that the downfall of the Federalists, whose
leaders were commonly aristocratic, snobbish, and hostile to political democracy, was no mere incident. The triumph of the
Jeffersonians, many of them as sincere, devoted, and generous-
minded republicans as their leader, was an enduring one. Besides
it opened the way for the establishment of a thoroughgoing
political democracy. Jefferson was also instrumental in opening
the way for a massive advance of that democracy toward the
Pacific Ocean, for it was he, fortunate man, who seized a heaven-
sent opportunity to buy the vast territory of Louisiana from
France.

Not that Jefferson as President was uniformly victorious over
his enemies. He and his adherents were checked when they attacked the Federalist judges who dominated the national courts.
During his last weeks, even his last days, in office, Adams and
the Federalists had been busy creating new courts and new
judges, the new judges being, of course, chosen from among
their own ranks. One of them was John Marshall, who had
served Adams as Secretary of State. The Jeffersonians soon disposed of several of those judges by destroying the recently established circuit courts in which they sat. But when Jefferson and
Secretary of State James Madison sought to keep from the bench
an obscure Federalist named William Marbury, who had been
given a minor post as Justice of the Peace in the District of Columbia, they suffered an embarrassing defeat. They refused to
give Marbury his commission, even though he had been legally
appointed during the final hours of the Adams Presidency. He
unwisely sought from the Supreme Court a writ of *mandamus*
ordering Madison to deliver the commission. Marshall and his

colleagues knew that Madison would not comply with the writ, that he and Jefferson would only laugh at the impudence of the Court. Marshall managed both to avoid humiliation and to enlarge the Court's power. Under his clever guidance, in *Marbury v. Madison* (1803), the Court unanimously ruled that a part of the Judiciary Act of 1789 permitted it to issue the writ that Marbury requested. However, it also declared that section of the law to be null and void, on the ground that it clashed with the Constitution. By refusing the writ to Marbury, the Court denied Jefferson and Madison an opportunity to flout its authority. At the same time, declaring part of a law passed by Congress to be unconstitutional and therefore not law, the Court set a most important precedent. To be sure, it did not again rule against the validity of a federal statute until 1857. But the precedent had been established; under Marshall, the Court set aside several state laws as unconstitutional; and, after the middle of the nineteenth century, it rendered null and void many state and national laws. To a degree, following in the path marked out by Marshall, the Supreme Court ultimately became a "super-legislature."

The ingenious Marshall had won a triumph. He knew that his enemies would seek revenge. He believed they would try to limit the authority of his Court by law. Instead, Jefferson undertook to remove Federalists from the bench through impeachment. Several of them had behaved very badly, had persecuted Democratic-Republicans on trial before them in most unjudicial fashion. Again, Jefferson finally encountered defeat. One Federalist district judge, an insane man and a drunkard, was successfully impeached. However, the Constitution specified that judges were to serve during good behavior, that they were to be impeached only for the commission of a crime or the acceptance of a bribe. When the Jeffersonians in the House of Representatives impeached Samuel Chase, an Associate Justice of the Supreme Court and a judge who had waged savage political warfare in the courtroom, they overreached themselves. It could not be shown that Chase had committed a crime or accepted a bribe. Some Democratic-Republicans in the Senate joined the Federalist minority there in voting Chase not guilty, and he was acquitted. Jefferson and his loyal allies decided that they could not swiftly cleanse the federal bench. As vacancies arose, as Federalist justices died, the Jeffersonians replaced them with their own men. But the Federalist magistrates did not hurry into eternity to plead their own cases before the ultimate tribunal. Marshall continued to preside over the Supreme Court until 1835. Moreover, he insidiously converted several Jeffersonians who became his colleagues to Federalist principles. He dominated that Court almost to his death.

Too much should not be made of the failure of the Jeffersonians to win early control of the national judiciary. They held sway over the Presidency and Congress. Not one of their important measures was set aside by Marshall-minded judges. Jefferson was re-elected in 1804 by an overwhelming majority, and his friend Madison succeeded him in 1809. The Federalists, divided, out of touch with a changing America, were never able to reverse the political tide that ran against them. Even John Quincy Adams, the talented son of John Adams, joined the Jeffersonians. After the passage of some years, in fact, Jefferson was almost as much troubled by divisions in his own triumphant party as he was by the assaults of the Federalists. Those divisions were even more vexing to Madison.

With Jefferson republican simplicity entered the Executive Mansion, which had been called the Palace in Washington's time. Jefferson lived comfortably in it like an easygoing Virginia gentleman rather than as a pale copy of a king. On one occasion he personally opened the door of the White House for a British envoy—and he was wearing house slippers instead of shoes. Though unable to manage his personal finances—like Hamilton, he died poor—Jefferson, with the help of his able Secretary of the Treasury, Albert Gallatin, conserved the public money. He and Gallatin wiped out internal taxes, economized, and reduced the national debt from $83 millions to $57 millions, despite heavy unexpected demands upon the Treasury. Unfortunately, as it turned out, Jefferson saved too much money. He and his followers founded the military academy at West Point in 1802, but they starved the army, and they barely maintained the splendid little navy built by the Federalists. Napoleon Bonaparte became the master of France before Jefferson entered the Presidency. The long wars waged by Napoleon, especially the contest between France and England that began in 1803 and continued for twelve years, injured America. Prudence demanded that America be prepared to fight, perhaps against France, more likely against England. Strong as the American military position was defensively, the nation was not invulnerable, and its people needed protection, especially on the oceans. Versatile as he was, Jefferson had neither taste nor talent for warfare, and he neglected America's land and sea defenses in years of danger.

Nevertheless, while Jefferson was in the Presidency, the young American republic proudly and successfully waged war against the pirates of North Africa, against those led by the Pasha of Tripoli. European monarchies had long paid tribute to the robber rulers of the Barbary States on the southern shore of the Mediterranean. America had followed their example, preferring to bribe those pirates rather than to suffer seizures of American merchant vessels by them. But when the corsair master of Tripoli, being refused an increase in tribute, declared war on the United States, Jefferson accepted his challenge. American warships and marines blockaded Tripoli and forcibly persuaded its ruler to sign a treaty of peace in 1805. He consented to accept an occasional small present in lieu of the bribes he had customarily received. A decade later, after another campaign by the navy in the Mediterranean, all the robbers of the North African coast reluctantly agreed neither to exact tribute nor to molest American shipping.

No military genius, Jefferson nevertheless had the pleasure of signing a treaty that doubled the territory of the republic. If the Napoleonic Wars posed awkward questions for America, if they finally forced America to take up arms, they also offered her opportunities, by far the greatest of which was a chance to buy the far-spread colony of Louisiana. It came in a curious fashion; a French menace turned out to be a blessing. In 1800, Napoleon, grandiosely meditating the revival of the French empire in the New World, forced Spain, in the secret Treaty of San Ildefonso, to cede Louisiana to France in exchange for a concession in Europe. In the following year news of the bargain, which was a profoundly disturbing one for the United States, reached Jefferson. He was especially alarmed because Louisiana included New Orleans and the French had thus gained control of both banks of the lower Mississippi. It had been difficult enough to deal with the Spanish when they were masters of the lower reaches of the great river. To reach foreign markets, and even the American east coast, the produce of Trans-Appalachia had to be sent down the river on small craft and transferred to ocean-going vessels at or near New Orleans. Spain had reluctantly permitted such transfers. Would Napoleonic France? Moreover, Spain being weak, that nation might have been compelled to sell New Orleans and its vicinity to the United States; if necessary, force could have been used against the dons to gain sure access to the Gulf of Mexico from the river. But, planted at New Orleans, the French would not be easily dislodged; they would be, in fact, a formidable barrier against both American commerce and American westward expansion. Alarmed, Jefferson sent his trusted friend, James Monroe, to Paris to join the American envoy there, Robert Livingston. He ordered the two to try to secure a perpetual guarantee that would enable American commerce to flow along the river. He hoped, almost against hope, that Napoleon would sell New Orleans and West Florida, and he empowered Monroe to offer as much as $10 million for them. Livingston and Monroe were to bring as much pressure as they could upon France, to hint that French possession of New Orleans would compel America to seek an alliance with England. Did Napoleon wish America to marry herself to the British fleet? Suddenly, before Monroe arrived in Paris, the French threat turned into an astonishing opportunity. The Anglo-French war, which had temporarily ceased, was about to resume. It was to be expected that New Orleans, in French hands, would be attacked by the English. It would be better, thought Napoleon, to sell it to the Americans rather than let it fall to his hated antagonists. Besides, the French were in deep distress on the island of Haiti, their steppingstone between France and New Orleans. A revolt of Negro slaves on that island and yellow fever were destroying a French army sent to reduce it to obedience. Napoleon, in April 1803, asked Livingston how much the United States would give for all of Louisiana. Monroe entered the French capital in the nick of time. Ignoring their instructions, the two Americans boldly said that America would pay about $15 million for Louisiana. Napoleon accepted the offer, a bargain was quickly struck, and a treaty outlining the terms of the purchase was sent to Washington.

Had some Federalists had their way, the treaty with Napoleon would have been rejected. With every westward advance of the republic, their party, having little appeal for the farmers of the interior, lost ground. Standing forth against the purchase, many Federalists denounced it as unconstitutional, expensive, and unwise. Controlling neither the Presidency nor Congress, they turned against the doctrine of implied powers—every American party would tend to take a narrower view of national authority when its enemies held the reins in Washington. The Constitution did not specifically authorize the acquisition of territory. It could be inferred that the national government possessed such power, since it was given authority to wage war and to make treaties. Federalists who had been willing to stretch the Constitution to justify the First Bank of the United States would not construe it liberally to get Louisiana. They were borne down by a Democratic-Republican plalanx. Jefferson and his followers were determined to seize the chance that had come their way. What to do about the constitutional difficulty? Some of Jefferson's advisers who had earlier assailed the doctrine of implied powers now did a turnabout and recognized its merit and its validity. Jefferson himself could not so easily or so swiftly reverse his interpretation of the Constitution. He believed that the purchase of Louisiana violated that document, that it ought to be amended so as to permit endorsement of the treaty. But the passage of such an amendment, requiring the consent of Congress and of three-quarters of the states, would take time. Napoleon might change his mind and withdraw from the bargain; the English might take New Orleans before it could be transferred to the United States. Jefferson insisted that the treaty be confirmed. Conceding that it was bad to violate the Constitution, he trusted that the American government would not do it again, except in the case of dire need. He placed the destiny of the nation above constitutional technicality. The treaty was ratified. Twenty-five years later the Supreme Court decided that the Constitution had not been violated, that the United States did indeed have the power, by implication, to acquire territory.

Jefferson was sure that America had made a splendid bargain.

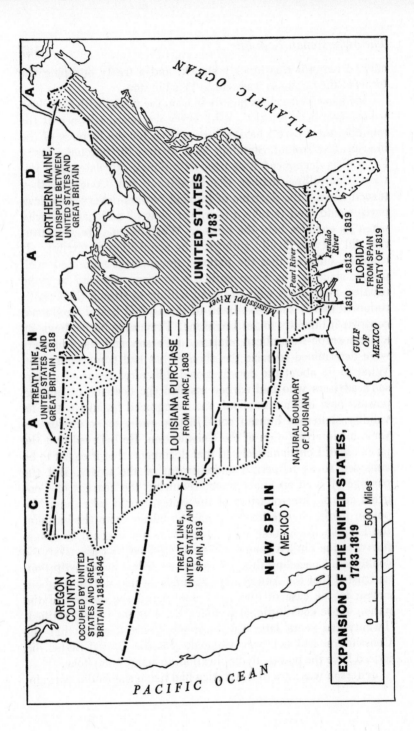

EXPANSION OF THE UNITED STATES, 1783-1819

0   500 Miles

PACIFIC OCEAN

ATLANTIC OCEAN

C A N A D A

UNITED STATES 1783

NORTHERN MAINE, IN DISPUTE BETWEEN UNITED STATES AND GREAT BRITAIN

TREATY LINE, UNITED STATES AND GREAT BRITAIN, 1818

OREGON COUNTRY OCCUPIED BY UNITED STATES AND GREAT BRITAIN, 1818-1846

LOUISIANA PURCHASE FROM FRANCE, 1803

Mississippi River

TREATY LINE, UNITED STATES AND SPAIN, 1819

NATURAL BOUNDARY OF LOUISIANA

NEW SPAIN (MEXICO)

Pearl River

Perdido River

1810   1813   1819

FLORIDA FROM SPAIN TREATY OF 1819

GULF OF MEXICO

There was some doubt that France had secured from Spain the right to sell Louisiana. Moreover, its boundaries were uncertain. But Jefferson rightly concluded that Spain lacked energy to try to regain Louisiana. Also, it was to America's advantage that its limits were vague. The nation had obtained effective title to New Orleans and the whole western half of the Mississippi Valley, an empire. The United States doubled in size. Besides, America secured claims to West Florida and Texas, claims that could be asserted against a weak neighbor. They soon were.

Afterward Jefferson declared that he wished to be remembered as the author of the Declaration of Independence and of the Virginia Statute of Religious Liberty, and as the founder of the University of Virginia. He might well have included the securing of Louisiana as one of his extraordinary deeds. And yet—did he set too high a value upon things of the mind?—he rejoiced over the magnitude of Louisiana. He fancied that, with the wide stretches of America east of the Mississippi still unsettled, it would supply farm land for his countrymen for ages to come. Thus a semi-utopian dream that he nourished for the nation seemed likely to be fulfilled. He saw trade, manufacturing, and cities as corruptive forces. He desired no more of them than was indispensable. Envisioning an ideal republic of honest, sturdy, economically independent husbandmen, he even desired that the Americans keep away from the sea. The most sagacious of men have often misjudged their own time, have been unable to pierce the fog of the future. Americans later fell into the habit of seeking answers to harassing questions in the statements of the founders of the republic. These may supply inspiration and example; but they do not offer a solution to every puzzling public issue. Both Jefferson's hopes and estimates for the future were ill founded. Within three generations there were no fertile vacant lands in America; there were within her boundaries throbbing industry, immense trade, and huge cities.

Himself an ardent and inquisitive naturalist, Jefferson keenly desired more information about Louisiana. He arranged, in 1804, to send Meriwether Lewis and William Clark to explore the northern part of it, to get information about its resources, possible routes for roads, and the Indians who dwelled beyond the Mississippi. In a remarkable journey that lasted for more than three years Lewis and Clark traveled up the Missouri River, crossed the Rocky Mountains, passed down the Columbia River Valley to the Pacific Ocean, and returned safely. They not only executed their mission but gave substance to a later American claim to the Oregon Country. More data about Louisiana was brought back by Lieutenant Zebulon Pike, who searched for the source of the Mississippi River, then made his way into what are now Colorado and New Mexico. Wandering into Spanish-held territory, Pike was put in prison but was later released and permitted to report about the vast regions he had seen. American settlers soon made their way to New Orleans and to St. Louis. They pushed on westward from the Mississippi. The state of Louisiana made its appearance as early as 1812, the state of Missouri eight years later.

The purchase of Louisiana, an unexpected triumph for Jefferson, also had something to do with the death of one of his bitter enemies and the downfall of another. Timothy Pickering, passionate Massachusetts Federalist, fearing that the acquisition of Louisiana would put the South and the West permanently in power at Washington, schemed to separate New England from a republic in which its interests were not and would not be cherished. He hoped that New York might be induced to join his proposed new nation, and he desired to enlist the help of Alexander Hamilton and Vice-President Aaron Burr toward achieving that end. Hamilton, who practiced law in that state, was also politically unhappy, but he refused to take part in Pickering's conspiracy. Instead, because he disliked and distrusted Burr, he freely attacked Burr's character in private conversation. At length Burr demanded that Hamilton give him satisfaction, either in words or on the dueling field. As a former military officer and a man of honor, Hamilton reluctantly chose to fight. At Weehawken, New Jersey, in July 1804, he was shot and mortally wounded by Burr. Not yet fifty years of age, Hamilton, who was so out of harmony with the changing spirit of his country, could hardly have made any further great contribution to it. If he was too scrupulous about his honor as a gentleman, he nevertheless left the world in dignity.

It was otherwise with Burr. The archaic notion that men had to defend their honor in personal combat attained vogue in

America during the War of Independence. It was brought across the ocean by European officers who served with the Patriots. It persisted in the South for two generations after the Burr-Hamilton duel, and even longer, in cruder form, in the West. However, Burr was looked upon as a murderer in the Northern states, and he was indicted in New York and New Jersey. The Vice-President of the United States, continuing to preside over the Senate, became a fugitive from justice. He was a ruined man. He was replaced as Vice-President by a loyal Jeffersonian in 1805. Soon afterward he embarked upon an extraordinary adventure. He had courage and charm, and he persuaded about eighty men to follow him in an expedition down the Mississippi River in 1806. Largely because Burr habitually kept his plans to himself, his intention remains uncertain. Did he mean merely to settle with his followers in Louisiana, to conquer for himself Texas, then held by Spain, or to make himself ruler of territory taken from his own country? He and his men were threatened with arrest on the lower Mississippi. Fleeing toward Spanish Florida, he was captured and tried for treason in Richmond, Virginia, in 1807. Jefferson did all that he could to assure the conviction of Burr. But Chief Justice Marshall, who presided over the trial in a federal circuit court, was not eager to condemn him. Marshall rigidly—and fortunately—insisted that the Constitution, which declares that "No Person shall be convicted of Treason unless on the Testimony of two Witnesses to the same overt Act," be strictly obeyed. Such evidence could not be brought forward, and Burr admitted nothing. He was acquitted in the courtroom. Tried again and again by historians, that reticent man has had several judgments passed upon him. He fled to Europe to escape further legal proceedings. There he emptily pursued other romantic enterprises. When public excitement died, he returned to New York and died there in obscurity.

If the rivalries and torments of Europe presented opportunities to America, if they enabled America to buy Louisiana, they also created embarrassment and vexation during the decade after the purchase of Louisiana. In 1812 America a second time entered into a war against England, despite the very real fondness of Jefferson and Madison for peace.

The great European struggle that had begun in 1792 resumed

in 1804. The Emperor Napoleon and his armies won victory after victory, and France dominated western and central Europe for some years. However, England, destroying the fleets of Napoleon and his allies, gained a firm and unquestionable control of the water approaches to Europe. Since Napoleon could not be checked on land until he invaded Russia in 1812, England, straining to bring him down, desperately tried to choke him by means of a naval blockade. In turn Napoleon did what he could to deprive the English of foodstuffs, raw materials, and markets. England and France struck heavy economic blows at each other, and in doing so, they also injured neutrals. America was the neutral that suffered most. As they had in the 1790s, the Federalists tended to sympathize with England, and the Democratic-Republicans continued to offer a measure of favor to France. In the main, the Americans did not wish to fight on either side. But, if they sought to maintain neutrality, many American merchants nevertheless desired to sell and buy goods in English and European ports. They were the more eager to transport grain and other American produce across the ocean because they could get very high prices for their cargoes. Moreover, American farmers profited from the traffic. Accordingly, the immediate economic interests of many Americans entangled America in the European war. Both the British and the French seized American ships and cargoes. Demands for redress and revenge came from harbors and inland hamlets alike.

Napoleon and his advisers were not only high-handed but unscrupulous in their treatment of American ships and cargoes. The British were only arrogant and rigorous. However, needing sailors, the British continued to insist upon their right to board neutral vessels and to impress into their service British subjects found on those vessels. Their sea captains could not always distinguish between an Englishman and an American, and sometimes they seized men who were unquestionably American. On occasion they were indifferent to the nationality of the sailors they took. In 1807 the commander of the British frigate *Leopard* flagrantly violated international law. He haughtily demanded from Commodore James Barron of the American frigate *Chesapeake*, as Barron moved out to sea from Norfolk, Virginia, that he surrender four men, presumably British deserters, from his crew. Barron's ship was not ready for action, but he refused. The *Leopard* then opened fire, killing three and wounding eighteen American sailors, and took the four men by force. Such a remarkable display of contempt for the American flag led to clamor for war in the United States. Jefferson resisted it, even though an apology and amends for the attack upon the warship came tardily, even though the English continued to take men from American merchant ships.

Jefferson sought to assert American interests and to defend American rights on the seas by using economic weapons. The only thing he did to strengthen the armed forces was to build, uselessly, gunboats to defend the Atlantic shoreline. He believed that he could compel France or England, or both, to behave by denying access to American markets, by holding American foodstuffs on the western side of the Atlantic. He tried to play the antagonists against each other. For a time American trade with Europe was virtually cut off by law. The economic weapons wielded by Jefferson, and by his successor, James Madison, hurt America as much as they did England, and more than they injured France. At last, however, England, suffering from economic distress and concerned lest America declare war, undertook, in 1812, to reduce her interference with American shipping.

That decision came too late to avert conflict. Mild, peaceable, and no longer young, James Madison did not yearn for hostilities. However, younger and more aggressive men of his party who entered Congress in 1811 bitterly resented the indignities inflicted upon the American flag by British sea captains, the "enslavement" of American sailors, and the injuries done to American maritime commerce. How long must English insults and outrages be endured? They clamored for revenge. These "War Hawks," as they were called, chiefly Westerners and Southerners, also held against England the fact that English traders sold supplies to Indians of the Old Northwest and Old Southwest with whom the United States was at war. Besides, they were moved by a lust for land. What better way to punish England than to seize Ontario in Canada? And, since Spain had become the ally of England, why not take the Floridas from her? The Federalists were hotly opposed to war. They contended that there was as much reason to fight France as there was to strike at England. New England merchants, who profited handsomely if two of three ships they sent across the Atlantic escaped seizure, insisted that armed clash be avoided. The War Hawks, with the reluctant consent of Madison, pushed on. Congress declared war on England on June 18, 1812, two days after it was announced in London that England would make important concessions.

Once begun, the war had to be fought. Fortunately for the United States, England could not concentrate her forces against her American enemy until 1814, until the power of Napoleon had been broken. America was almost utterly unprepared for war. The quality of the navy was superb, but it contained only sixteen vessels, not one of them as large as the most powerful of the British ships. The regular army was small and decrepit. Money could not be easily obtained, especially since the Jeffersonians had allowed the First Bank of the United States to die when its charter expired in 1811. Sentiment against the war in New England and New York was so strong that it was not easy to get either men or money from the northeastern part of the nation. America possessed great defensive strength but, as in the War of Independence, found it difficult to mount successful offensives against Canada.

The war began brilliantly for the Americans on the ocean, but British sea power gradually asserted itself. In 1812, in a series of duels with British ships, American frigates and smaller craft were almost uniformly victorious, thus demonstrating that the English had no special or exclusive gift for sea warfare. Then the British navy established a tight blockade of the Atlantic seaboard. However, American cruisers and privateers continued to slip out into the ocean. These severely damaged the British merchant marine during 1814, capturing and sinking vessels in the waters adjacent to the United Kingdom.

The war began badly for the Americans on land, and ended with a smashing victory. American attempts to invade Canada in 1812 failed dismally. Supported by an Indian confederacy organized by the brave chief Tecumseh, Canadian militia and British regulars captured Detroit. Besides, American threats against Quebec and lower Ontario were checked in 1813. However, things went better in that year for the Americans in the region of the Great Lakes. Commodore Oliver Hazard Perry defeated a British naval squadron on Lake Erie and won control of it; and General William Henry Harrison invaded upper Ontario, defeated the British and their allies in the Battle of the Thames, and destroyed the confederacy of Tecumseh, who was killed in the struggle. Meanwhile, General Andrew Jackson, the great American hero of the war, began his swift rise to military glory in the Old Southwest. American forces entered West Florida even before the declaration of war against England and took Mobile in 1813. Jackson was sent against the powerful Creek nation, which had obtained arms from British merchants. After several bloody engagements, he crushed the Creek in the Battle of Horseshoe Bend, in March 1814. Some weeks later the British, now able to send to America thousands of veteran soldiers no longer needed in Europe, opened a series of offensives. Two of these, mounted from Canada, were stopped, one on the Niagara frontier, the other on Lake Champlain. A third drive by the British was more successful. They made their way into Chesapeake Bay, captured Washington, were checked at Baltimore, and then withdrew—after sorely injuring American pride. It was restored by Jackson, who defended New Orleans against a fourth offensive by a British expeditionary force under General Edward Pakenham. In January 1815, Jackson repelled an attack by Pakenham's army, inflicting upon it such heavy losses that the British were forced to abandon their hope of taking New Orleans.

It turned out that the Americans had won this, their most decisive victory, after the peace treaty had been signed. Toward the end of 1813, England officially offered to begin negotiations. The invitation was accepted by Madison, and five American commissioners bargained with English representatives at Ghent, Belgium, in 1814. No agreement was possible until it became apparent that neither side could establish military superiority. At last the Americans, since the issues that had arisen from the impressment of sailors and from invasion of the rights of neutral shipping would vanish with the end of the Napoleonic Wars, ceased to demand that England abandon the practices on the ocean that had been so exasperating. They could not claim English territory on the basis of conquest. On the other hand, the English, asking for territorial compensation on the basis of victories on land, later had to admit that they had made no real military progress. Accordingly, in December 1814, the parties signed a treaty which said little except that peace was to be restored. The only American conquest of the War of 1812 was West Florida, taken from the Spanish and kept.

If the Treaty of Ghent settled none of the issues between America and England, it is nevertheless true that the War of 1812 persuaded the leaders of both countries that it was preferable to compromise rather than fight. In consequence, the two nations entered into a series of conventions during the years 1815–18 that pointed toward a more harmonious future. They agreed to keep their armed forces on the Canadian-American boundary to a minimum; they placed that boundary at the forty-ninth parallel between the Lake of the Woods and the Rocky Mountains; and they put the Oregon Country temporarily under joint rule. For the Americans, the War of 1812 was not, as they once regarded it, a Second War of Independence. The existence of the republic had not been seriously threatened. The war's outcome convinced all sensible British politicians that America would not go away. On the other hand, most Americans were thenceforth willing to follow a policy of live-and-let-live with respect to Canada. Not that every Anglo-American question was settled for all future time.

CHAPTER 11

Over the Appalachians

✦✦✦

BEFORE THE END OF the War of Independence the Americans were building log cabins, planting corn, and raising pigs far to the west of the Appalachian mountain wall. At that time, however, most of them lived at no great distance from salt water. When Washington became President, the center of population in the United States was on the shore of Chesapeake Bay. Four decades later it was in western Virginia, almost precisely at the Appalachian divide. During those forty years the American population tripled, and the number of states swelled from thirteen to twenty-five. The course of American empire moved westward. A large minority of Americans resided beyond the mountains in 1830. Moreover, the Americans as a whole then looked westward rather than eastward, inward rather than outward, at themselves rather than at Europeans. They remained a farming people, although commerce, and even industry, flourished. The passage of the Americans from the aristocratic republicanism of the Federalists via the benevolent republicanism of Jefferson to a generous political democracy virtually ended with the election of Andrew Jackson to the Presidency in 1828. Social leveling proceeded with political, though not for Negroes or women. Vulgarity also made progress; education lagged; and American arts and letters remained colonial and imitative. There was no great influx of immigrants from Europe; and the Americans, having been first cousins, once removed, to the English, became first cousins, twice removed. Their story was one of plain grandeur. But there was no Homer, no Gibbon among the Americans of that era to tell it. Indeed, its simple majesty has not yet been limned by an epic poet or a superb historian.

After the achievement of independence the American did not commonly or promptly become a contemplative genius. Rather, he busied himself with family, farm, shop, and sometimes factory. He continued generously to reproduce himself, for the multiplying numbers of the Americans during the first forty years of the republic came from generation rather than immigration. About 350,000 persons, a large fraction of them from the British Isles, found new homes in the United States during that period. But the number of Americans increased by one-third in every decade. Babies continued to be looked upon as casual bounty; not until the twentieth century would they be considered burdens in America. They were born in New England farmhouses, Southern mansions, Kentucky log cabins, in westward-moving wagons.

Remarkable was the export of bodies, large and small, from New England after the War of Independence. Yankeeland, at least its countryside, seemed to be crowded, seemed to offer little economic opportunity. New Englanders poured by the thousands into western New York and western Pennsylvania, into the Western Reserve of Ohio, into the fertile woodlands of southern Michigan, across the black grassy prairies of northern Indiana and northern Illinois. They walked, rode horseback, jounced in wagons, and floated on rivers and lakes toward a setting and rising sun. They carried with them the names of their New England villages, building new Plymouths, Concords, and Bostons. They did not leave behind Yankee diligence, shrewdness, or thrift. They prospered in the valley of New York's Genesee River, on the south shore of Lake Erie, in the valley of Michigan's Huron River, and also in Cincinnati and St. Louis, for they occasionally went southward as well as westward. In less picturesque but richer country than New England afforded, they built schools and churches like those they had left behind them. Their new and more spacious farms, yielding vast quantities of grain, comfortably supported a sturdy people. Mingled with them were industrious self-reliant "Pennsylvania Dutch," New York Dutch, and Jerseymen.

Southerners also sought and found new Canaans beyond the

ridges of the Appalachians. From the uplands of Maryland, Virginia, and the Carolinas they surged into the watershed of the Ohio River. They filled the rich limestone lands of central Kentucky and moved on into Missouri. Many of them, partly because they detested slavery, put down in the lower parts of Ohio, Indiana, and Illinois, to which they gave a Southern complexion that long endured. Above all, however, the Southerners streamed into the Old Southwest, into Tennessee, Alabama, and Mississippi, and across the "Father of Waters" into Arkansas and Louisiana. The fat soil of the Black Belt of the northern stretches of Alabama and Mississippi was as seductive to them as was the dark rich earth of the Old Northwest to the Yankees. Not that they wished to grow grain or cattle, as did the New Englanders. They wanted fields to fill with cotton plants, and they found them. Bodies were multiplying in England and western Europe as well as in America, for the Industrial Revolution brought with it a domestic revolution. Convention and the weather required that all those bodies be covered. Eli Whitney had invented the cotton gin in 1793, a machine that made it possible for the first time quickly to separate the seeds from the only kind of cotton that could be grown in the Southern interior. Machines to turn that cotton into cloth reached out for it, in Old and New England, and Southerners gladly undertook to feed them. Cotton culture spread rapidly from the Carolinas and Georgia to the Mississippi and beyond, and a Cotton Kingdom, with its center beyond the Appalachians, began to emerge. With it grew a tobacco principality—for cultivation of the "weed" became important in Kentucky and Tennessee—as well as a duchy of sugar in Louisiana. Slavery and the plantation expanded with cotton, tobacco, and sugar fields.

Let it not be thought that all Americans were entranced by siren voices from the west. The Atlantic coast was not denuded of people. True, numbers increased less rapidly on the Southern seaboard than they had in the past. In that region tens of thousands of once fertile acres had been ruined by tobacco growers who neglected to fertilize the soil, impoverished by the lusty appetite of the tobacco plant. The British bounty upon indigo vanished with the British flag; and indigo culture, ceasing to be profitable, also came to an end, early in the nineteenth century.

Cotton fields east of the Appalachians did not match those of the Black Belt. Agriculture did not flourish on the Southern seaboard. From Maryland to Maine it was otherwise. Homestead and diversified farming continued to be profitable north of Chesapeake Bay, in part because of the rise of great cities. Indeed, the farmers of New Jersey and Connecticut prospered. Part of their progeny remained on family land. Perhaps more of their sons went to nearby towns and cities to seek their fortune than moved westward. Many who drifted away from the farm found their way to New York City, to Baltimore, to Albany.

America remained rural—and often rustic—but villages grew into towns, towns into cities, and cities into larger cities. The sturdy noble agrarian society of which Jefferson dreamed became ever less likely; before his death in 1826, the dim outline of an urban America became discernible. In 1800 Philadelphia contained 70,000 inhabitants, in 1830 more that 150,000. Even more striking was the growth of New York City, which housed about 60,000 persons at the beginning of the nineteenth century; within the following generation the city at the mouth of the Hudson became the largest in America. Its leadership in numbers would long be unchallenged. During that generation Baltimore, Pittsburgh, Cincinnati, St. Louis, and New Orleans also grew amazingly. Even Boston, which did not keep pace with its colonial rivals, had more than 50,000 inhabitants in 1830. However, there were those who believed that Boston, falling behind in quantity of citizens, retained quality.

The cities were nourished by commerce rather than industry. Those that grew so remarkably were internal and external ports, centers for trafficking. New York City was a gateway for goods as well as persons. Its splendid harbor and magnificent location assured its supremacy in size. After 1825 the Erie Canal, opening a water route between New York City and the Old Northwest, brought to the city both dollars and people. Ships from Boston went to the shores of China, providing occupation for sailors and bringing handsome profits to their owners. Produce from the farms of Maryland and Pennsylvania was put aboard ship and sent to sea from Baltimore. River traffic enriched Cincinnati, St. Louis, and New Orleans. Cincinnati was, for a time, a great meat-packing center, acquiring the ugly title of "Porkopolis."

Bales of cotton began to crowd the wharves of New Orleans. Pittsburgh flourished as the center of a web of commerce long before it became noted for the making of iron and steel.

All of which is not meant to suggest that people and products moved about easily and quickly before the nineteenth century was thirty years old. They continued to be propelled principally by the muscles of men, horses, and oxen on land, and by the winds on water. The journeys of men and of goods were slow, and remained tedious, laborious, and dangerous. Nevertheless, travel and transport had become easier. The turnpike, a good road financed by tolls, made its appearance in Pennsylvania in 1790. Soon afterward that kind of highway was built in New York, New Jersey, and New England. Most remarkable of all the turnpikes was the Cumberland Road, also called the Old National Road, a paved thoroughfare that began to extend westward from Cumberland, Maryland, in 1811 and ultimately reached Vandalia, Illinois. It was much used as an avenue to the Mississippi. Before that road was finished, canals became more popular than turnpikes. Small ones were cut before the end of the eighteenth century. Most extraordinary of these was the Erie Canal, which linked the Hudson River with Lake Erie after 1825. A heavy traffic moved along it for several decades. Thousands of New Englanders and New Yorkers used it to reach the Great Lakes and new homes in the regions south and west of the lakes. But advance in water transport was by no means confined to canal-building. When Robert Fulton's *Clermont*, in 1807, chugged its way from New York City to Albany and back, it became evident that the steamboat was more than an interesting big toy. Only ten years later the paddlewheels of the steamboat *Washington* moved it from Louisville to New Orleans and back to Louisville. The steamboat soon became a familiar sight on the Ohio and Mississippi rivers and on the Great Lakes. In 1819 the steamship *Savannah* crossed the Atlantic. However, the bulk of ocean traffic long continued to be carried in sailing vessels, and the building of the first railroad to carry passengers was not begun until 1828.

If American towns and cities were centers of commerce rather than manufacturing, it is also true that the Industrial Revolution was under way. Before the War of Independence raw

materials were processed and made into finished goods in the
home and in the artisan's shop. After that struggle had ended,
the Americans eagerly imported inventions and industrial techniques from Europe in general and from England in particular.
The English government vainly tried to stop the flow of manufacturing secrets across the Atlantic. The English mechanic-
engineer Samuel Slater built the first American cotton factory in
Rhode Island in 1790–91. A quarter of a century later there were
more than one hundred such factories in that state. At the end of
the War of 1812, in fact, the making of cotton goods had become truly important in the economy of New England. All
along the seaboard sprang up forges, mills, and factories where
iron, flour, and leather goods were made. The Yankees used
water power to turn their machines; west and south of the Hudson steam was increasingly employed to propel them. After the
close of the War of 1812, British manufacturers flooded American markets with cheap goods and ruined many American factory owners. The setback was only temporary. American entrepreneurs were so successful that the shrewd observer Alexis
de Tocqueville predicted soon after 1830 that they might become the aristocrats of America. American inventors contributed to the rise of industry. They became even more prolific
after 1815 than their English counterparts. Among them was Eli
Whitney, whose cotton gin was not his most ingenious contribution. In 1798 that brilliant Yankee applied the principle of
interchangeable parts in the making of muskets. Moreover, he
devised machine tools to make those parts. A year later, Simeon
North of Connecticut began to make pistols in the same fashion.
Whitney's clever techniques would later supply the foundation
for gigantic industrial advance.

A quarter-century after the Louisiana Purchase it was already
apparent that Jefferson's splendid society of yeomen living
sturdily and independently on the land would not include all
Americans. The city and the factory, with their evils—and
their benefits—were enticing men, women, and children from
the farm. Offering economic opportunity, the city, with the
exception of Boston, was neither neat nor clean nor healthy.
Sewers were hardly more common than they were in the country; water and milk were often contaminated; and typhoid and

William Pitt, first Earl of Chatham. Painting by William Hoare. The artist caught the imperious spirit of Pitt, the Englishman most admired by the Americans of the Revolutionary generation.

Washington and his Family. Painting by Edward Savage. Engrav-Engraving by J. Sartain.

Andrew Jackson. Painting by Ralph Earl.

A Pennsylvania Farm Scene. The painting of "The Residence of David Twining, 1787" is by Edward Hicks, who in 1846 painted his boyhood home as it was before 1800. The painter himself, at the age of five, stands at the knee of his foster mother, Beulah Twining; also in the picture are his foster father, David Twining, and his foster sisters. The farmhouse is still standing.

Kitchen Ball at White Sulphur Springs. Painting by Christian Mayr. The Negro servants enjoy their own party at a fashionable Virginia resort.

Edgar Allan Poe.
Daguerreotype.

The Bloomer girl. The famous costume is shown on the cover of a popular song book.

Camp Meeting. Lithograph by Kennedy Lucas. Many camp meetings were much less decorous than the one depicted here.

Kindred Spirits. Painting by Asher B. Durand. Of the Hudson River school, Durand painted William Cullen Bryant and Thomas Cole in a scene in the Catskill Mountains.

The Banjo Player. Painting by William S. Mount. Mount was a self-taught artist who declined to study in Europe. Called a "rural Rembrandt," he fondly painted scenes of his native Long Island.

other fevers were endemic and epidemic. Bathtubs were almost unknown. Noisome odors assailed the nostrils of the fastidious. In summer the fly and the mosquito grew big at the expense of the citizens. In winter the poor shivered in ill-made houses that did not give enough protection against the cold and the north winds. Protection against fire and criminals was rudimentary. The factory had a specially ugly side. The "hands" earned little more than their subsistence, for factory owners squeezed out as much profit as possible to build fortunes and more machines. Men toiled from dawn to dark, except on Sunday, and with them women and children. Most of the employees in the cotton mills were female or young, or both. Children who should have been in school, children who were not old enough to go to school, spent 70 hours per week and more attending machines. There were well-intentioned entrepreneurs, in Waltham and Lowell, Massachusetts, who provided decent housing, churches, libraries, and other cultural opportunities for the girls who worked in their textile mills. To one English observer Lowell looked like "a commercial utopia" and "a philanthropical manufacturing college." But Waltham and Lowell were un-usual. Moreover, they were at best only generously managed "company towns." Before long even the mill owners of Waltham and Lowell lost interest in the education and happiness of their workers, and the two towns became like others in New England. Fortunately for the employees, the supply of labor in America was limited. They were not so dependent upon their jobs for a livelihood as factory workers afterward were. They were not so viciously exploited as were laborers in England at the beginning of the Industrial Revolution in that country. They did not inhabit an urban paradise.

It is notorious that the onset of the Industrial Revolution was everywhere accompanied by the abuse of workers, and one is tempted to exaggerate both the sufferings and the numbers of American factory hands before 1830. Relatively few people were tied to machines. Most Americans still lived on the land. Those who remained on farms east of the Appalachians, who resisted the siren calls of factory whistles, fared well. Their markets expanded. However, they worked long and hard, for toil was as necessary in the fields as it was at the machine, or at the counter. Moreover, for many, the transit from the land to commerce and industry led to a better life. The abler and the more fortunate prospered in mercantile and industrial pursuits. Wealthy merchants became numerous in Boston, New York City, and Baltimore. Many thousands of merchants merely did well. The owners of factories did not invariably become insolvent. Eli Whitney eventually gained substantially from the sales of his cotton gin, and he profitably made muskets for many years for the American army. Bankers, builders, lawyers, and newspaper publishers flourished.

If the allure of the Eastern towns and cities was often false, it ought not to be assumed that migration to the beckoning West led to swift sure prosperity. Jefferson might dream of tens of thousands of worthy farmers, men who inhabited comfortable homes and owned broad acres, men whose family trees were great oaks or magnolias shading their houses from the afternoon sun. And there were such men, in large numbers, in the valley of the Mississippi and on the Great Lakes watershed by 1830. But not every man who traversed the Appalachians was virtuous, industrious, and fortunate, and the poor man who secured a commodious homestead without suffering hardships, without much toil, was lucky indeed. Nor did his sufferings, his labors, necessarily ennoble the pioneer, although romanticists ask us to believe that they did. There was opportunity beyond the mountains, and it was often successfully seized. Most of those who went westward doubtless did well, if not for themselves, for their children. Never before were so much rich virgin land, such vast resources, within the reach of common—and uncommon— men. Even so, it should not be forgotten that many a pioneer ended his days in rural or village poverty.

Certain it is that the pioneers were not all magnificent men and women. The trappers and fur-traders, who led the van, might be brave and venturesome; they were also harum-scarum, irresponsible, and often downright vicious. Mingled with the farming folk who followed them were ne'er-do-wells, gamblers, shiftless wanderers, fleeing debtors, and men who lowered their eyes when they saw sheriffs and judges. Nor were all the tillers of the soil who wended their way westward splendid specimens of manhood and womanhood. Among those who moved into the

Old Southwest was much "poor white trash," that shiftless, brutish, and depraved variety of humanity whose mean, sordid, tragic lives in the old Southern states would be repeated, generation after generation, in the newer Southern commonwealths. The "trash" also settled in the parts of the Old Northwest, immediately north of the Ohio River, called "Egypt." They were so conspicuous in "Egypt" that the many sound and vigorous Southerners who put down in that region have often been thoughtlessly labeled as inferior folk—as if all those who migrated from the old Southern states were "trash." Scoundrels, cheats, and careless people who migrated from New England and New York were comparatively less numerous, were not so obviously undesirable as the "trash."

It has often been said that the pioneers, by overcoming the trials and dangers of life in newly settled regions, became hardy, self-reliant, and democratic both socially and politically, almost as if they became a better breed than those from whom they sprang. Surely environment affected those people, but it did not alter them utterly. Fundamental qualities of family, good and bad, persisted, as did ways of thought, and prejudices, and institutions. Moreover, the effects of environment, important as they were, were not uniformly beneficent.

It will not be denied that one of the immediate consequences of migration westward was intellectual and cultural loss. The pioneer carried with him a bag of beans rather than a knapsack of books; to be sure, he often squeezed a Bible into a safe niche amidst his belongings. He might take with him a violin. His wagon did not usually contain a piano. At the end of its westward journey, the first tasks of a pioneer family were physical rather than intellectual. Unmarried hunters, Indian traders, and wanderers who preceded farmers often lived like the redmen; some of them sank into a degraded savagery. Encompassed by Nature, such men might acquire a noble simplicity; more often, they merely became more primitive. Rural, uncouth, roistering bullies were only too common among the farmer folk, as were rowdies and ruffians in the river ports. Such men engaged in fights in which they employed feet, teeth, skulls, and knives as weapons. They did not think it improper to bite off the ear of an opponent or to gouge out his eyes. They were by no means in the majority; but even the majority of pioneers lost respect for law in the new and less orderly communities.

The decent and industrious people who formed the mass of the immigrants were forced, for some years, to devote themselves to the needs of the body rather than to those of the mind. Except for Revolutionary veterans, they were seldom given land. The states did not present farms to all comers, nor did the federal government before the passage of the Homestead Act in 1862. In fact, until 1820, federal law did not permit the sale of national lands in small quantities and at low prices; and the states often sold land to speculators. A farm was not to be had for the asking. Clearing one of trees in southern Michigan was an almost back-breaking task. The building of a log cabin, even with the help of neighbors, demanded muscle and skill. The plowing and the planting of virgin soil was not work for weaklings. Women and children labored with the men. Only gradually did the clapboard house replace the log cabin. The mansion of Virginia was not swiftly reproduced in large numbers, nor were the commodious homes of New York country magnates. The federal government set aside one thirty-sixth, later one eighteenth, of its lands for the support of education. But even elementary instruction was at first costly, and the children of the pioneers seldom learned more than how to read, write, and cipher. Colleges and universities were conceived, declared in existence, and commonly remained on paper. Educationally and culturally the Americans west of the Appalachians long lagged behind those who remained on the Atlantic littoral. The Yankees who settled in the Old Northwest occupied a region as favored as might be by Nature in resources and climate, and they were accustomed to labor, thrift, and intellectual pursuits. They built Congregational churches and schools with remarkable speed. Even so, they could not immediately reproduce New England. In the lower Mississippi Valley intellectual and cultural lag was only too obvious.

Westward expansion unquestionably fostered social and political democracy. Like the men and women who forsook the Old World for America, those who turned their backs to the Atlantic and migrated far into the interior of the continent were

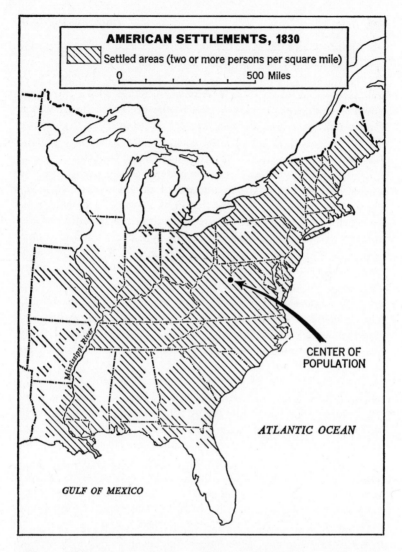

AMERICAN SETTLEMENTS, 1830

Settled areas (two or more persons per square mile)

0 _____ 500 Miles

CENTER OF
POPULATION

ATLANTIC OCEAN

GULF OF MEXICO

Mississippi River

seldom either aristocratic or wealthy. In the newer society far removed from Europe, in a society where few were rich and few were condemned to poverty, it could be believed that men —except for Negroes—were equal. White manhood suffrage quickly became the rule in the states added to the original thirteen, with Vermont, Kentucky, and Tennessee taking the lead even before 1800. Somewhat less rapidly the right to vote was extended to white males in the seaboard states also, for they too, though to a lesser degree, felt the force of leveling influences, among them the example of Trans-Appalachia. In the presidential election of 1828 few American white men, except in Rhode Island, were denied access to the polls. Its result was a triumph for political democracy, for it placed in the White House Andrew Jackson of Tennessee, not a gentleman by birth, not a scholar, not a man removed in spirit from the crowd.

So intimately associated was the name of Jackson with the rise of that democracy in which almost all except women and Negroes were permitted to vote that it is commonly called Jacksonian democracy. With it came more than the widening of the suffrage. Political and judicial machinery was changed to enable the voters to express their will more decisively. It became standard practice to elect rather than to appoint state judges. More and more commonly, presidential electors were deprived of freedom of choice, becoming mere instruments to report the wishes of the voters. More and more often, men were nominated for office by party conventions. In the 1830s the national party convention, meeting for the purpose of naming candidates for the Presidency and the Vice-Presidency, appeared. It was to remain a basic part of American political machinery. Men in public life became more and more responsive to the desires of the masses. Often in the colonial time the voters merely chose between two gentlemen who differed not at all from each other in principle. Then the gentleman in office might consult only his own conscience. With the coming of the generous, if not complete, Jacksonian democracy, he who would gain office, he who would keep it, had to consider seriously the wishes of the voters, even to pander to them. The belief sprang up that any man, regardless of education, skill, or experience, could perform the duties of almost any office. It became easier to win elections by making promises to the electorate that could not be kept. The politician who served as a messenger for his constituents was often the victor at the polls. Jacksonian democracy had its darker side. Educated men, refined men, conscientious men declined to enter into the hurly-burly of political contest, to try to please the vulgar, to trim their sails to fit the changing winds of public sentiment.

The decline of the Roman Empire, said Edward Gibbon, marked the triumph of barbarism and religion. The rise of democracy in America was accompanied by the growth of vulgarity and revivalistic Protestantism. As colonials the Americans detested Englishmen who placed themselves on the throne with George III and condescendingly referred to their "subjects" across the sea; as citizens of a free and magnificent republic some Americans saw themselves not only as superior to the slaves of kings but also as the consorts of the Goddess Liberty. Boasting of their republican simplicity, they proclaimed the backwardness of other peoples. The march toward democracy was not accompanied by an improvement in manners, although the Americans continued to display a remarkable kindliness toward one another and toward strangers. American males were invariably gracious, at least in their way, to women. They were buoyant in spirit and action. Nevertheless, their behavior in dining rooms, stagecoaches, taverns, and other public places often offended the fastidious, whether American or foreign. The tobacco-spitting American man was not one of Jefferson's noble farmers. The niceties of civilization were often abandoned on the frontiers of settlement, and they were not uniformly respected in American cities. English travelers often found fault with American manners, except for those of prosperous Bostonians and Southern planter aristocrats. They also suffered from American cooking, describing it in the same terms of anguish and amusement that American travelers would employ with regard to English food at the middle of the twentieth century.

If an increase in church membership and in the number of persons professing faith be the true measures of religious advance, Christianity flourished in America after the Revolution. The Protestant sects acquired tens of thousands of converts and reconverts. That the nation gained in religious health may be doubted. Unitarianism continued to acquire believers in New England, especially in Boston, but the generous intellectual approach to religion of the great leaders of the Revolutionary generation did not attract uneducated citizens. These accepted the dictates of the past and desired personal assurance. The various orthodoxies of the Congregational, Presbyterian, and Baptist churches acquired adherents. The Methodists became a principal sect. More important, however, was the remarkable growth of emotional Christianity, within and without the familiar churches. Waves of a revivalism that was lugubrious, impetuous, and indecorous swept across the nation, especially after the beginning of the nineteenth century. These rose high in rural regions, especially those beyond the Appalachians. Exhorters such as Charles Grandison Finney and Peter Cartwright proclaimed a feeling Gospel to tens of thousands. The camp meeting became an American institution. Sheltering themselves in tents and huts, men and women often spent several days at such gatherings. They were bombarded from crude pulpits by batteries of black-clad preachers who belched eternal hell-fire for the unregenerate and announced the blisses of heaven for the penitent. These rural apostles, these wilderness Whitefields and Wesleys, aroused their listeners to frenzy, drove them to gibbering in "strange tongues," and so thoroughly released some of them from customary restraints that they committed at night the sexual sin the preachers denounced during the day. Invocations of the wrath of God had the same ultimate effect for some worshipers as the flutes that beguiled the Babylonian devotees of the Goddess Ishtar to their religious and amorous revels. That camp-meeting harangues and frolics served either religion or civilization may be doubted. To be sure, men and women who came to faith via such emotional orgies often went on to embrace a more sensible Christianity.

One may easily make too much of the primitive and the unlovely in American society during the first decades of the republic. John Dryden declared:

> For colleges on bounteous kings depend,
> And never rebel was to arts a friend.

And it is true that independence was not quickly followed by a golden age of American civilization. Ralph Waldo Emerson, who did not despise his native New England, afterward declared that, in the entire region between 1790 and 1820, "not a book, not a speech, a conversation, or a thought" deserved notice. Nevertheless, New England was not then a cultural desert. In fact, during the half-century after the achievement of independence, poets, novelists, artists, and architects became numerous on the Atlantic seaboard. During that period dozens of young Americans, among them the talented John Vanderlyn and Washington Allston, went abroad to study painting; even more wrote verses; and writers of prose became almost abundant. Unfortunately, perhaps inevitably, most of them lacked originality. They sought to cast things American in European, chiefly English, molds. Usually, they came forth with anemic imitations of European models. Culturally, America remained colonial more than fifty years after the Declaration of Independence. America could not place beside her numerous brilliant inventors as many splendid authors and artists. Even so, the sea captain Philip Freneau, who celebrated the virtues of America in grandiloquent verse, also wrote the delicate haunting poem, "The Indian Burying Ground," containing lines of which any English poet of his time might have been proud. He touchingly addressed "The Wild Honey Suckle":

> From morning suns and evening dews
> At first thy little being came:
> If nothing once, you nothing lose,
> For when you die you are the same;
> The space between, is but an hour,
> The frail duration of a flower.

Freneau's best work was done before the end of the eighteenth century. William Cullen Bryant also found his truest inspiration in Nature. In 1815 he composed "To a Water Fowl," a poem that was praised on both sides of the Atlantic. But neither Freneau nor Bryant, who soon settled for respectable journalism, achieved the renown of Washington Irving, the New Yorker, whose talents as a writer of essays and tales won him fame both in England and America before 1820. The charm of his "Rip Van Winkle" and "The Legend of Sleepy Hollow" endures. So does the repute of James Fenimore Cooper, also a New Yorker, whose many novels of life on the frontier and at sea retain vigor and appeal. Cooper's books gained many readers in Europe. They continued to fascinate Europeans for generations and to give them a distorted and antiquated view of America long after his fellow countrymen, unwisely allowing themselves to be irked by his verbosity and slow pace, had turned away from *The Deer-*

slayer and *The Prairie*. Cooper created one remarkable character, Natty Bumppo, the first hero of an American "Western"
story.

If letters and arts did not swiftly and abundantly flower in the
new republic, its schools were even less distinguished for scholarship, whether they were newer beyond the Appalachians or
older on the Atlantic coast. Thoughtful men, during and after
the Revolution, might and did proclaim the compelling need for
elementary and secondary schools, and also for colleges and universities, and they urged that public as well as private money be
spent to build and maintain them. But many Americans were not
so enlightened; among them were men, including prosperous
ones, who disliked taxes, especially when the revenue therefrom
was used for the instruction of the children of others; and not a
few Americans preferred to entrust education to the clergy.
The principle of elementary instruction at public expense did
gain adherents; two free public high schools, at Boston and at
Portland, Maine, opened their doors at the end of the second
decade of the nineteenth century; and the University of Virginia, in its early years the most important of the state universities, was founded almost simultaneously. However, secondary
education continued to be offered chiefly at private academies,
these becoming numerous. Sectarian and other private colleges
abounded on paper. However, all schools at every level, of
whatever type, were impressive in form and number rather than
in substance. Too often the sectarian ones stressed the preservation of faith rather than the advance of learning. In 1816, compared to that of the German University of Göttingen, the Harvard College library was somewhat better than pitiful. Teachers
and professors received low pay and often deserved no more
than they were given. No more than two out of every hundred
Americans went to a college of any kind immediately after the
War of 1812; and no female was admitted to such an institution.
Time would bring great improvements. Meanwhile, a massive
spread of newspapers and books contributed largely to public
enlightenment. The foundations were being laid for an American Renaissance.

At the end of the third decade of the nineteenth century the
American condition was not ideal, but it was healthy. European

ladies and gentlemen, ignoring the shortcomings of their own society, could, after three months in America, write two volumes about the new nation and many paragraphs concerning the crudity and delinquencies of its citizens. The famous survey of the *Domestic Manners of the Americans* by the waspish Frances Trollope, who deplored the lack of refinement among the Americans, pleased English readers, exasperated American ones. The citizens of the republic preferred views of their country such as that offered by the English engraver Thomas Bewick, who had not visited the United States:

> When its immense territory is filled with an enlightened population, and its government, like a rock, founded on the liberties and rights of man, it is beyond human comprehension to forsee the strides the nation will make towards perfection. It is likely they will cast a compassionate eye on the rest of mankind, grovelling under arbitrary power, banish it from the face of the earth, and kill despots with a frown.

Many Americans then and later believed that they knew the remedies for all human woes, that they had a mission to perfect the world.

CHAPTER 12

Gentlemen and Democrats in Washington

❀❀❀

So BITTERLY DID THE New England Federalists detest the War of 1812 that some of them proposed to leave the Union. More of them demanded changes in the Constitution, to reduce the power of Virginia and to prevent the nation from waging wars without Federalist consent. This demand for constitutional revision, conveyed through the Hartford Convention of 1814, reached Washington along with the news that the struggle with England had ended, and with reports that Andrew Jackson had shattered the British at New Orleans. New England regionalism was thus made ridiculous. It did not die, but the Yankees thenceforward gave their allegiance to the nation. After the War of 1812 the interests and wishes of the New Englanders were not long or much neglected in Washington; and they drew away from doctrines of states' rights and secession. Indeed, immediately after that conflict, a wave of nationalism swept across America. Political animosities also temporarily softened. The Democratic-Republican James Monroe of Virginia was elected to the Presidency in 1816 without keen contest; two years later the Federalist party died; and in 1820 Monroe was re-elected without a war of words. The period during which he resided in the White House was, and often still is, called "The Era of Good Feelings." The announcement of the Monroe Doctrine appealed to national pride and was acclaimed in all parts of the republic. But hostility toward the central government, while diminishing in New England, grew in the South. Slavery and tariff protection became bitter political issues. The South began to turn away from the North and the nation; and new men in new parties, including the redoubtable Andrew Jackson, were not able to close the widening gap. The coming of political democracy did not assure statesmanship of the very highest order in Washington.

Just after the War of 1812 the Democratic-Republicans were not what they had been when they came into power in Washington. Most of them were far less hostile than they had earlier been to the concentration of authority in the national capital, in part, no doubt, because it was in their own trustworthy hands. War Hawks John C. Calhoun and Henry Clay, who did not become timid doves with the coming of peace, urged the creation of a new Bank of the United States, protective tariffs, and the building of roads and canals at national expense. All of these had been Federalist measures in the past. As "New Nationalists" they carried many of the Democratic-Republicans with them. Moreover, Federalists who deserted their party in its death throes often retained Hamiltonian notions; and they also rallied behind Calhoun and Clay.

To the dismay of Jeffersonians who clung to the original tenets of their party, the New Nationalism was for a few years the dominant philosophy in Congress. It was not entirely pleasing to President Madison or President Monroe. Nevertheless, with the consent of Madison, the Second Bank of the United States was chartered in April 1816, with a capital of $35 million. It resembled closely its predecessor, one-fifth of its stock being held by the nation. It was at first badly run; but it prospered, after 1823, under the leadership of Nicholas Biddle. With headquarters in Philadelphia, it established twenty-five branches, and it supplied a sound paper currency. It performed another public service, for it condemned dubious and sometimes worthless paper money issued by state-chartered banks. American bankers then, and until well into the twentieth century, were only too often sanguine, speculative, careless men, and they were not seriously restricted by law. Biddle insisted that the money they issued be supported by something more than a promise to pay. He therefore became an ogre, and the Second Bank of the

United States a monopolistic "Monster" that devoured and destroyed its weaker but more deserving rivals. With better logic, they, and various politicians, denounced Biddle's bank because its private stockholders profited from their association with the national government. Inevitably, it was also, like its predecessor, assailed as unconstitutional.

In that April in which the "Monster" was created, Congress took another and even longer step. Hitherto American import duties had been collected primarily for revenue, had offered little protection against foreign goods. A flood of British manufactures into American markets immediately after the War of 1812 threatened to wash away American "infant" industries; and demands for bulwarks against imports from England poured into Washington. Calhoun, who hoped that his state, South Carolina, would become a manufacturing center, helped to erect tariff walls. The Yankee Daniel Webster, fearing that such barriers would injure the shipping of New England, opposed them, as did many men of New England. Constitutional scruples—there were those who doubted that Congress could impose duties except for revenue—were set aside. A tariff act that partly dammed the flow of British goods was signed by Madison. Thereafter, protection in one degree or another for one item and another was part of the American economic structure, the rates fluctuating in accordance with public opinion and regional politicking.

Calhoun, Clay, and other New Nationalists also desired to disburse federal funds to build roads and canals but could not persuade Congress to act. New Englanders were hostile to such spending. They were the most prosperous Americans and would be compelled to pay higher taxes than the Southerners and Westerners. Moreover, they would get fewer highways and waterways than the Southerners and Westerners. They were averse to "internal improvements" at their expense that would specially benefit their fellow countrymen. Besides, both Madison and Monroe doubted that the Constitution permitted such expenditures; they asked for an amendment, impossible to secure, that would place beyond question the power of Congress to vote funds for such purposes. The campaign for internal improvements therefore lost headway. It would be revived, especially by Clay.

The New Nationalists likewise clamored, but in vain, for a stronger army and navy, for a federal university, and for other means of encouraging the arts and sciences. Memory of the War of 1812 faded; the danger of attack by Britain or any other European power lessened; and the unifying force of a common powerful enemy lost its potency. Americans could manage without a further increase in federal activity; and the doctrine of states' rights, weakening in the Northern states, soon grew apace in the South when it seemed that federal authority would be used to benefit those who lived in the North and to hurt the South.

The New Nationalism endured longer in the Supreme Court, where it was not new and where John Marshall continued for many years to assert the American whole against its parts. In 1816, in *Cohens v. Virginia*, the Court emphatically declared that a citizen seeking to gain his constitutional rights could appeal to it from the highest court of a state. Three years later, in the famous case of *McCulloch v. Maryland*, the Court, adopting the Hamiltonian doctrine of implied powers, proclaimed not only that the Second Bank of the United States was constitutional but also that a state could tax neither the bank nor one of its branches, for "the power to tax involves the power to destroy." The bank was a federal instrument; the states were forbidden to use taxes to injure it—and so to limit federal authority. In 1824, in *Gibbons v. Ogden*, the Marshall Court liberally interpreted the power of the central government to regulate interstate and foreign commerce. However, even before Marshall's death in 1835, his colleagues were turning away from him; after he departed from the high tribunal it was long dominated by men sympathetic to states' rights.

That the New Nationalism did not bring enduring domestic harmony, that discord within the Union continued to threaten its very existence, was apparent as early as 1818, when Missouri asked for admission as a state with slavery. Collision between East and West could be softened. But could a desperate clash between North and South be prevented? The petition from Missouri was bitterly assailed by many Northerners. Slavery was then confined by the Mason-Dixon Line—the southern boundary of Pennsylvania—and the Ohio River. It must not be allowed to advance westward or even northwestward into the

Louisiana Territory bought from France. Those Northerners
were also unhappy because the acceptance of Missouri as a slave
state would destroy a balance in the Senate between slave and
free states. Southerners were as determined that the request of
Missouri be granted as Northerners were that it be denied.
Debate was hot, even furious, alarming the watching Jefferson,
who saw only too clearly the menace to the Union for which he
and his generation had sacrificed so much. At length, in 1820, it
was possible to make a bargain between North and South that
settled immediate questions. In the Missouri Compromise of that
year, Missouri was admitted as a slave state, counterbalanced by
Maine, which was separated by Massachusetts and recognized as
a free state. It was also stipulated that slavery be barred from all
that part of the Louisiana Territory north of the line 36° 30'.
Issues arising from the servitude of the blacks then temporarily
faded. Wise men, such as John Quincy Adams, knew that
slavery remained a source of fundamental and dangerous discord
within the Union.

The talents of James Monroe were no more than respectable;
but the disappearance of the Federalist party, despite sectional
antagonisms, gave him a second term in the White House without contest. In the election of 1820 he received the votes of all
the Presidential electors except one; that was idealistically cast
by William Plummer of New Hampshire for Secretary of State
John Quincy Adams because his abilities were superior to those
of the President under whom he served. However, it may be
said for Monroe that he saw and made use of the talents of
Adams. Together they secured the final cession by Spain of all
her territories and claims in the Floridas; together they astutely
put forward the Monroe Doctrine.

Andrew Jackson also had something to do with the departure
of the Spanish from the northern shores of the Gulf of Mexico.
Angered because British merchants in the Floridas were permitted by Spain to supply arms and liquor to Indians who raided
the southern American frontiers, General Jackson, responsible
for the defense of those frontiers, marched into Spanish lands
and seized Pensacola in 1818. He captured and executed two of
the British traders. Spain protested, and Jackson withdrew from
the town. Several members of Monroe's Cabinet urged that the

highhanded behavior of the general required punishment. Adams quietly but firmly supported Jackson, informing Spain that such troubles could be prevented only by Spanish withdrawal from the Floridas. Monroe, aware that the stand taken by Adams was a popular one, stood with his general and his Secretary of State. Weak, torn by dissension at home, and staggered by uprisings in her American empire, Spain decided that it was wiser to get something for the Floridas than to try vainly to hold them. By a treaty of 1819, ratified two years later, America agreed to accept the Sabine River as her boundary on the southwest, thus abandoning her claim that Texas was included in the Louisiana Purchase; Spain, on the other hand, gave the United States title to all her remaining possessions in the Floridas, including the peninsula, then thought to be peculiarly suited to mosquitoes rather than to people.

The agonies of Spain brought worry as well as opportunity to Monroe and Adams. After 1808, one after another, the Spanish colonies in Central and South America rose in revolt. There followed a series of wars that endured for eighteen years, with English and American volunteers helping the rebels. In 1822, Russia, France, Austria, and Prussia, as members of the Quadruple Alliance, not only established firmly the authority of King Ferdinand VII in Spain, but began to consider intervention in his behalf in the New World. The rulers of the countries in the Alliance detested revolution, and they did not admire the republics springing up in Spanish America. That they would have taken military action is uncertain. In any event, George Canning, the British minister responsible for foreign policy, became alarmed. The rebels had opened their ports, hitherto closed by the Spanish, to all foreign vessels. Canning desired that they remain open to British shipping. Moreover, he feared that French troops would go to, and perhaps remain in, Spanish America. He asked America to join England in warning off the Alliance. The Americans also desired to trade with their neighbors to the south; besides, they sympathized with fellow republicans. Nevertheless, Monroe hesitated to accept the British invitation. Adams was more worried about Russian expansion from Alaska than he was about the appearance of a French army in the New World—Russia had recently announced a claim (soon afterward withdrawn) to the eastern shore of the Pacific as far south as the fifty-first parallel. He did not wish America to appear to be "a cock-boat in the wake of the British men-of-war." He advised Monroe to proclaim that America would not permit European intervention or aggression in the New World. Accordingly, in a message to Congress in December 1823, Monroe laid down four principles in the Monroe Doctrine. There must be no more colonization upon the American continents by European powers; America would look upon any attempt to extend European monarchy to the Western Hemisphere as a hostile act; America would not interfere with existing European colonies in the New World; America would not meddle in the internal affairs of European nations.

So America declared herself to be the guardian of the Western Hemisphere. And the doctrine was not immediately challenged, for Canning had already warned France that intervention in Latin America by the European monarchies must not be attempted. The Quadruple Alliance put neither troops nor ships in motion. Monroe and Adams successfully asserted the special authority of the United States in the New World, without cost. Moreover, their doctrine was astutely applied to England as well as to the nations of the European continent. Refused help, Spain was driven from the Americas, except for Cuba and Puerto Rico, by 1826. From the ruins of the Spanish empire sprang many republics. With them appeared, without much commotion, the empire, later the republic, of Portuguese-speaking Brazil. The rulers of the new nations, like the monarchs of Europe, would find arrogance in the Monroe Doctrine. It nevertheless became and long remained a cornerstone of American foreign policy.

Monroe was the last American President to have played an important part in the Revolution. He was also the last to wear knee-breeches. Moreover, when he left office, it was not assumed that his successor must be a gentleman born. Gentlemanly John Quincy Adams succeeded Monroe, but only after sharp contest. He was only the best qualified of four men who struggled for the prize in 1824. The contest was one of persons rather than of principles, an internal one among the Democratic-Republicans. Like his father, Adams was respected rather than adored. His chief antagonist was Andrew Jackson, the hero of the War of 1812, whose exploits as a civilian were not impressive. Jackson was not born a patrician, and he could hardly have been a serious candidate at an earlier time. The rise of political democracy, coupled with Jackson's glamor, gave the victor of New Orleans more popular votes and even more electoral votes than Adams. However, the general did not get a majority in the electoral college, and the House of Representatives had to choose the President from the three leading aspirants. Henry Clay, whose views were much like those of Adams, and whose own campaign for the office had failed, successfully exerted his influence in behalf of the New Englander. It would have been better, perhaps, for Adams had he been defeated.

John Quincy Adams was almost as uncomfortable in the Presidency as his father had been. Many followers of Jackson believed that Clay had thwarted the popular will and sought revenge for an imagined wrong. When Adams, disregarding political clamor, chose Clay as his Secretary of State, he exposed himself and Clay to the charge of a "corrupt bargain." Jackson himself—he was inclined to look upon those who disagreed with him as mortal enemies—came to believe that the accusation was true. His friends heaped abuse upon Adams, and together they began a long campaign to secure the defeat of Adams in 1828. Allies of the President responded with calumnies against Jackson and Mrs. Jackson. Adams himself would not stoop to such political warfare. Out of perverse high-mindedness, he did not even discharge federal employees who struck against him. He demanded no more of them than that they do their official duties. Adams wished to use federal power liberally toward the building of roads and canals, also toward the encouragement of science and the arts. But the only truly important measure of his Presidency was the tariff law of 1828, which was designed by the Jacksonians to embarrass Adams and to ensure his defeat in the approaching election. The cynical maneuvers of the Jacksonians in Congress led to the establishment of high rates not desired by many Jacksonians. Their "Tariff of Abominations" provoked a national crisis, but first it helped Jackson to reach the White House.

In 1828 the monolithic Democratic-Republican party van-

ished. From it sprang the National Republicans, the combined
followings of Adams and Clay. With recruits, they would become known as the Whig party by 1836. Meanwhile, the
Jacksonians formed the Democratic party, which was to have a
lengthy history. Jackson led it to its first great victory. He, like
his lieutenants, avoided issues. His allies thumped away at the
"corrupt bargain," contending, with some success, that the voter
must choose between the personalities of Jackson and Adams.
The general was portrayed as a man of the "common people."
Much more was made of his military prowess. Many plain folk,
farmers and workmen, admired him. By no great margin the
nation expressed its preference for the martial hero as opposed
to the civilian statesman. On Inaugural Day in 1829, Adams
retired bitterly to private life. He would return to Washington
as a member of the House of Representatives. Jackson went into
office with a wild celebration at the White House. It was in-
decorously invaded by the "common people," who rejoiced over
their triumph and spilled wine on the furniture.

What manner of man was Andrew Jackson? He has often
been portrayed—carelessly—as a child and a champion of the
masses, as a knight of democracy. His many admirers among
historians concede that he had some faults but declare them to
be minor defects in a great man. It is admitted that he dealt
roughly with domestic foes as well as foreign ones. A more
detailed assessment of the lanky, stern-visaged, gray-haired man
who became President in his early sixties forces a refinement of
the general notions about him. To understand him, it is necessary to recall that he was born in the backwoods of the Carolinas, of that Scotch-Irish stock from which sprang Calhoun and
Presidents Andrew Johnson and Woodrow Wilson. Jackson,
like many of that breed, was sturdy, brave, willful, and fond of
feuds. Even in his later years he rather primitively considered all
men to be either friends or enemies. Moving to Tennessee in his
youth, he spent little time in schools; nor did he, as Franklin did,
acquire a liberal education by his own independent efforts. He
learned enough to be accepted at the bar in Tennessee and to
practice law there. He moved steadily upward in politics, reaching the United States Senate; he climbed the ranks in the Tennessee militia; and he acquired land and money. He was a suc-

cessful civilian before he rose to military glory. He also gained gentlemanly polish, but he remained socially democratic, though not catholic in his friendships. In youth he engaged in brawls, in maturity he did not shrink from duels. In one affair of honor he shot to death a man who gossiped maliciously about Mrs. Jackson. The general, dignified, imperious, irascible, was pleased by the flattery of "friends." He had an iron will. Those who admired him gave him the sobriquet of "Old Hickory"; others referred to the President as "King Andrew." Like most of the military heroes who followed him into the Executive Mansion, he was not well versed in civil questions. He had positively committed himself upon no issue of the day, and his followers had informed the public that he was on both sides in every dispute. He seemed disposed to limit federal authority, but he was also a patriot.

Unquestionably the election of Jackson marked the triumph of political democracy in the United States, even though women and Negro slaves cast no ballots. The White House was no longer reserved for the elite, or for the choice of the gentry. Few historians will say that the change was unwholesome. With Jackson also came a larger measure of social democracy, except with regard to Negroes. Several of his most trusted lieutenants were self-made men, such as Martin Van Buren of New York. It is also true, however, that his intimate advisers were often skilled in vote-getting rather than versed in statecraft. He and they, devoted to the proposition that one white man was as good as another, discharged many veteran and proficient public servants who had supported Adams and replaced them with persons less competent who had discerned and extolled the merits of General Jackson. In fact, subscribing to the principle that "to the victors belong the spoils," the President and his allies firmly established the "spoils system" in Washington. Henceforth, for several generations, the federal bureaucracy was gutted whenever the Presidency passed from one party to another. The same unwholesome "system" was similarly established at the state capitals.

Anyone who fancied that President Jackson, as he approached old age, was more flexible, less resolute than General Jackson, erred sadly. He dodged issues in the campaign of 1828, for he

knew how to win and how to avoid losing votes. When he had
to commit himself, he was as vigorous, as determined as ever—
and as sure that he was in the right and that his opponents were
rascals. John C. Calhoun and South Carolina, Nicholas Biddle
and the Second Bank of the United States, felt the force of his
wrath.

Jackson's friends created a crisis when, for his benefit, they
helped to put the "Tariff of Abominations" on the statute books.
The barriers which it erected against foreign goods aroused
furious resentment in South Carolina. Factories were not springing up in that state, and its agriculture was lagging. The South
Carolinians decided that tariff rates which raised the prices of
the things they bought injured them to the benefit of Northerners who had successfully engaged in manufacturing. By 1828
Calhoun, ever solicitous for the welfare of his state, had abandoned nationalism for states' rights. In that year the South Carolina legislature endorsed and published an extraordinary "Exposition and Protest" secretly written by Calhoun. It condemned
the "Tariff of Abominations" as both wicked and unconstitutional. But it went much further. Others before Calhoun, including Jefferson, had declared that a state might nullify a federal
law. Appealing elaborately to history and to logic, Calhoun asserted that the Union was merely an agreement ratified by sovereign conventions of the states. He proclaimed that the state
convention retained sovereign authority, that it could accordingly nullify any federal law it considered to be unconstitutional.
If so nullified, a national law could be made legal only through a
constitutional amendment, which required the consent of three-
quarters of the states. Later, Calhoun, pursuing his argument,
said that a state convention, if nullification produced no remedy,
could legally dissolve the bond between a state and the Union.
Thus, he would have it that a state might separate from the
Union, both by right of revolution and by a lawful ordinance of
secession.

Such a creed could hardly be reconciled with national existence. The history and the logic that supported it were not
unassailable. When it was defended in the Senate by Senator
Robert Y. Hayne of South Carolina, it was attacked by Senator
Daniel Webster, earlier a champion of states' rights but now a

champion of the Union. The fervid, rolling sentences of Webster's oratory did not discourage South Carolina. The tariff rates were revised in 1832 but only slightly. The nullificationists then struck. A South Carolina convention solemnly declared that the tariffs of 1828 and 1832 were unconstitutional and void, and that they must not be collected in the ports of the state. From South Carolina came threats of resistance and secession, if there was an attempt to coerce the state. Having expressed sympathy for states' rights, Jackson had also declared that the Union must be preserved. He had learned that Calhoun, ostensibly his friend, had not supported him when his behavior in Florida had been questioned in the Cabinet in 1818. Jackson's response was predictable. He issued a proclamation declaring to the people of South Carolina that nullification was nonsense, that they would do well to avoid treason, that he would do whatever was necessary to execute federal law. Privately the President talked about hanging Calhoun. He was prepared, if necessary, to lead troops into the state. A minority within it asserted loyalty to the nation. No other Southern state endorsed nullification. Those who gave allegiance to the doctrine became more conciliatory. Then Congress, in 1833, announcing in a Force Bill that it would supply the President with men and weapons, also undertook to reduce tariff rates during a nine-year period. Jackson and South Carolina accepted this "Compromise of 1833." The state withdrew its ordinance of nullification, then nullified the Force Bill in a final gesture of defiance. South Carolina had felt the weight of federal authority, but her protest had not been in vain. In 1833 a Southern President and the bulk of the Southern people would not countenance disunion. But opinion in the South would alter. A generation later, most of the Southern states, in accordance with the doctrines of Calhoun, tried legally to secede.

The intricacies of banking were as foreign to Andrew Jackson when he was chosen President as were tariff schedules. In his campaign for the Presidency he had not committed himself for or against the Second Bank of the United States. However, many of his cohorts, especially from the South and the West, detested the bank and all its branches, and Jackson attacked it in his inaugural address. That institution, because of its awkward coupling of public service and private profit, was basically vulnerable to attack. Moreover, its guiding spirit, Nicholas Biddle of Philadelphia, a man who possessed literary as well as financial ability, was less scrupulous than he might have been. The bank lent money to members of Congress, and it retained the legal services of Senator Daniel Webster—it gave favors to politicians whose votes and influence might be important for its continued existence. In any case, it could not escape assault by men associated with state-chartered banks that were hurt by the competition and the sound currency practices of the national one. Biddle feared that it would be difficult to secure renewal of its charter, which would lapse in 1836. Encouraged by Henry Clay, he decided early in 1832 to challenge the President immediately rather than to wait until it was necessary for him to act. Clay secured the passage by both Houses of Congress of a bill to recharter the bank. Jackson angrily vetoed it, and Clay could not muster enough votes to pass it over the veto. Clay was not too unhappy. A Presidential election was approaching. Might he not, with rechartering of the bank as a principal issue, defeat Jackson in it? A national convention of National Republicans nominated him. A national convention of Democrats—the major parties thereafter steadily used that device—named Jackson. He came forward as the champion of the plain people, the enemy of monopolistic bankers and privileged aristocrats. Had the contest taken place in the halls of Congress, Clay might have won. Farmers and workmen did not love Biddle's bank; they did not turn against their old warrior hero. He won an easy victory at the polls.

Once engaged in a struggle, Jackson was accustomed to fight to a finish. Nor would Clay, supported by a majority in Congress, let the bank issue die. It pained Jackson even that the bank should live until 1836. He decided to withdraw the federal deposits from it, so as to weaken public confidence in it. Two successive Secretaries of the Treasury would not execute his will; he removed them; and he found a third, Roger B. Taney, who gladly did his bidding. Taney put federal funds in several state banks. The Second Bank of the United States languished; Jackson slew the "Monster." His enemies denounced him as an ignoramus, a tyrant, a violator of the Constitution; and the

Senate formally censured him. John Quincy Adams said he was a "barbarian." But he routed his antagonists. Before he left the Presidency, the Senate "expunged" the censure from its records.

Indomitable, inflexible when challenged, Jackson was neither an informed financier nor a political philosopher. He was not a cruder Hamilton, not a homespun Jefferson. He provided no substitute for the Second Bank of the United States that performed its useful services. He actually encouraged state-chartered banks to continue vicious currency practices. Then, learning that their depreciating bills were profitably used to buy federal lands, he ordered the land offices to demand gold or silver instead of the dubious or worthless paper. He thus proclaimed the weakness of many state-chartered banks. A large number of them tottered and fell, precipitating an economic crisis and a depression that Jackson bequeathed to his successor, Martin Van Buren. Nor did Jackson find any generous answer to the troubles created by the lust of white men for the lands of the Indians of the Old Southwest and Old Northwest. His solution was their removal of the Indians beyond the Mississippi. Following a "Trail of Tears," Cherokee, Creek, and Choctaw warriors and women were forced to vacate their familiar fields and to put down again in an Indian Territory far to the west.

Before he retired to his much-loved plantation in Tennessee, "King Andrew" ordered his Democratic party to put Van Buren in the Presidency. It was done. The Democrats nominated the smooth fat little politician from New York. The Whigs, not sufficiently united to rally behind one candidate, put forward several men, each of them popular in his state or region. That curious procedure gained them nothing; the voters, like the Democratic politicians, did as Jackson desired. But Van Buren could not fill the general's shoes. He established branches of the Treasury to hold federal moneys. Otherwise, he accomplished little. The economic depression continued, even though the national debt was then trifling. The Democrats, nominating Van Buren a second time in 1840, were unable to magnify his modest talents. The Whigs, seriously divided among themselves, agreed that it was important above all to defeat Van Buren. They set aside Clay, still their principal leader, and offered the nation a "balanced ticket" shrewdly prepared to get votes. They copied the Democrats, naming for the Presidency William Henry Harrison, like Jackson a hero of the War of 1812; for the Vice-Presidency they selected John Tyler, a Virginia gentleman and a champion of states' rights. When a Democratic editor nastily described Harrison as a man who should be content with a log cabin and a supply of hard cider—Harrison was actually a descendant of a proud Virginia family who lived quite commodiously—the Whigs gladly and not very truthfully declared that he was indeed a man of the people. On the other hand, they portrayed Van Buren, whose lineage was humble enough, as an aristocrat who was fond of wine and good living. The unworthy strategy of the Whigs succeeded. Issues were submerged; Van Buren was blamed for the continuing depression; and Harrison was elected. The Whigs controlled both the Presidency and Congress.

Suddenly the Whig party was called to account for its sins. Clay expected that Harrison, who was nearly seventy years of age but an utter novice in politics, would do his bidding. But Harrison died less than a month after taking the oath of office, and Tyler took his place. Tyler had never promised to be Clay's man. In his philosophy and prejudices he was closer to Calhoun than to the Kentuckian. To please Clay, he finally consented to an upward division of tariff rates. However, determined to be his own man, he could not conscientiously satisfy his fellow Whig. Twice Clay drove through Congress a bill chartering a third Bank of the United States; twice Tyler successfully vetoed it. At length Tyler broke completely with Clay and the bulk of the Northern Whigs. Finally he even brought Calhoun into his Cabinet and joined the Democrats. The tub-thumping triumph of the Whigs in 1840 led them to frustration.

Tyler's time was not without achievements in foreign affairs. On the whole, however, it cannot be said that he or his immediate predecessors who rose to authority with the advent of political democracy, possessed the merits of the earlier heads of the republic.

CHAPTER 13

The Peculiar South

꧁꧂

ENEMIES OF THE REPUBLIC, when it was created, hopefully predicted that it would divide and disappear. Not the least of the weaknesses they perceived in it was the separation between South and the North at the Mason-Dixon Line. It was evident enough that the Southern states differed from the Northern ones in climate, economy, racial composition, and social order. It will be recalled that Patrick Henry and other Southerners of the Revolutionary generation condemned the Constitution because it would enable a Northern majority at the federal capital to strike at a Southern minority. It could then be believed that the South would form the larger part of the Union; that clashes between the two regions would be less than vital; and that slavery—vanishing in the South as well as in the North—would cease to be a source of discord. But the growth of the South did not keep pace with that of the North, and economic and social divergence between the two sections increased. Negro slavery, dying on one side of the Mason-Dixon Line, persisted and spread on the other. The Old South appeared, a peculiar South, with a very special economy, society, and outlook. It made its appearance soon after the War of 1812, and it acquired solidity in the second quarter of the nineteenth century. It requires description for many reasons. One of these is that the Southerners, being in a minority position, and unwilling to alter their institutions to please a majority pressing from the North, at last slipped into civil war with their fellow countrymen.

If the Southern states failed to keep step with the Northern states in extent, wealth, or in numbers of people, it is nevertheless true that the Old South was of imperial proportions. It was larger than western Europe, more extensive than the Confederacy which sprang from it and engaged the Union in deadly combat in 1861. The South of the Revolutionary era, although it included Kentucky and Tennessee, centered on the Atlantic seaboard between the Mason-Dixon Line and the southern boundary of Georgia. The Old South, by 1845, stretched to the Gulf of Mexico and to the plains of Texas. It covered fourteen states, including Maryland, Kentucky, and Missouri, for its limits were basically the same as those of Negro slavery. Wherever there were large numbers of blacks in servitude, there was the Old South. Where slavery did not exist, neither did that storied South. There should be no doubt that the presence of large numbers of Negroes, they being, with few exceptions, slaves, set apart the Old South from the North. There would be deep cleavage at the Mason-Dixon Line far into the twentieth century, until the Negroes should spread more or less evenly across the nation. In 1860 nearly four million blacks constituted one-third of the inhabitants of the Old South; Negroes—free Negroes—in the Northern states could be counted only in tens of thousands. The gap between the Old South and the North was all the greater because the many blacks on one side of the line were nearly all enslaved, while the few on the other side were free.

Other reasons for division between the Old South and the North can be, and have been, brought forward. And these have been magnified, for scholars, like other sophisticated human beings, often prefer subtle error to plain truth. Many questions have been befogged by professorial revelations, verbosities, and pomposities. Differences in climate have been stressed. They were less than fundamental; the one region was not tropical, or the other polar. It has been urged that they were sundered by clashing economies. True, the one section was devoted to agriculture, and that of a special sort, while the other was turning toward commerce and industry. From that divergence came political squabbling, in which the issue of tariff rates was central. But economic differences between the two regions—and the resulting political struggles—did not menace the Union. After the Compromise of 1833 there was no desperate struggle over tariffs. It has been said that the Old South was basically different because aristocracy, introduced by the coming of Cavaliers to Virginia during the period of the English Commonwealth, survived within the South, after the triumph of social equality—and vulgarity and plutocracy—in the North. But this sort of social separation was far from absolute. Few Cavaliers settled in Virginia in the seventeenth century. The Southern aristocracy was neither ancient nor all-powerful in its own country. It has been declared that ancestry divided the sections, the whites of the Old South being English by descent, those of the North being more European than English. Here again, the two regions were not utterly opposite. One must believe that the Old South, dissimilar from the North in many ways, was set apart, above all, by the presence within its confines of several millions of Negro slaves. Without slavery, as Abraham Lincoln sensibly declared, there would have been no Civil War.

Indeed, the massive bondage of the blacks also, to a degree, divorced the Old South from all other regions of the civilized, the more advanced parts of the Western world. Slavery had long since vanished in Europe, and even serfdom was dying upon that continent. Unfortunately, while Europe was moving toward the extinction of the grossest of her many social injustices, Negro slavery in the United States persisted and even flourished. It was never firmly rooted in the Northern colonies and states, where slave labor was unprofitable. Most Negroes in bondage were illiterate and ignorant and could perform only simple tasks under direction. They could do the manual toil necessary for the raising of tobacco, rice, sugar cane, and cotton. But Nature, declaring that cotton, rice, and sugar cane, and even tobacco, should not grow in New York or Michigan or Iowa, forbade the northward extension of black servitude. It was possible to confirm the decision of Nature by federal and state laws. It was otherwise to the south, where temperatures and rainfall were only too suitable for the growing of cotton. The invention of the cotton gin, and the growing need in the first half of the nineteenth century for clothing to cover multiplying human bodies, ensured profits, sometimes immense ones, for Southern landowners. Requiring work that could be performed by unskilled labor, cotton raising provided employment for tens of thousands of slaves, men, women, and children. Had such not been the case, how could the white masters have made valuable use of their slaves, who were constantly increasing in number? Cotton raising gave new vigor to the institution of slavery, and it spread wherever it seemed that the "white weed" would spring from the ground. Cotton growing also served to perpetuate the plantation and much of the special Southern society of the eighteenth century.

The Old South, vanishing in the flames of the Civil War, endured less than a half-century. There was romancing enough about it while it lasted. Afterward, in memory, in myth, in political fantasy, it became other than what it was. Southern eyes that looked back upon it often saw an idyllic agrarian society dominated by brave, courtly, and generous-minded patricians who lived in stately mansions, presided over broad plantations, and were surrounded by swarms of loyal and affectionate slaves. Admirers of that never-never land conceded, sometimes reluctantly, that not all the Southern whites were benevolent gentlemen or charming ladies, that among them were the poverty-stricken, ignorant, and brutish "poor white trash." However, those misbegotten people could be, and they were, placed in romantic contrast against the superior whites and against the blacks. Such an image of the Old South is both unfinished and false. Nor is it possible to endorse another distorted view that afterward gained thoughtless credence. Held chiefly by more or less sophisticated Northerners who did not love the Southern whites, it was different only in that the aristocrats were seen as polished brutes who both exploited the Negroes and kept the "poor white trash" in cruel subjection. Stereotypes should be avoided.

The Old South was not monolithic, and it defies swift and sweeping description. It is not preposterous to say that the Old South was a collection of Souths. The great plantations were not continuous, and the Negro slaves were not ubiquitous within its wide borders. In the narrow valleys of the Southern Appalachians, stretching from Virginia to Alabama, broad fields of cotton, gangs of sweating slaves, and patricians were rare. In that far-spreading hill country a man was usually a homestead farmer, white but not wealthy. The big plantations and the bulk of the slaves were to be found in the lowlands of the South. And their masters and mistresses were not necessarily aristrocrats, either in birth or in bearing. The economic and social systems of Virginia and Mississippi were not identical, nor were those of North Carolina and South Carolina. It is a fact that the Old South was riven by political discord. It will be recalled that the Southerners did not hasten in mass to the defense of South Carolina in the squabble over nullification. They fought one another, sometimes bitterly, as Whigs and Democrats. They moved rapidly toward political unity when slavery was threatened from Washington.

Whatever else may be said about the Old South, it will not be denied that it was fundamentally rural. There was no large city between the banks of the Potomac and those of the Rio Grande, except for New Orleans. Neither manufacturing nor internal commerce flourished in the Old South as they did in the North. Railroads appeared early in the region, but they did not spread as rapidly as they did beyond the Mason-Dixon Line; and Southern cities that were centers of railroad traffic, such as Richmond and Atlanta, remained relatively small. Atlanta, despite its strategic location for trade, had fewer than 10,000 residents at the time of the Civil War. Several of the principal cities of the region, such as Baltimore, Louisville, and St. Louis, were situated upon its fringes; they were ocean and river ports. The Old South contained dozens of towns and hundreds of villages. Essentially, nevertheless, it looked like the South of the Revolutionary era. Those who traversed it gazed upon extensive fields and thick forests. They saw far more of sandy or muddy country roads than they did of broad highways or city streets.

The plantation, with its fields of tobacco, cotton, rice, or sugar cane, did indeed dominate the landscape of the Southern lowlands. As the Civil War approached, there were thousands of Southern estates containing more than 1,000 acres. Their owners were the "great planters," the true Southern aristocrats. Their landholdings were baronial, and they counted their slaves in hundreds. Some of them were proprietors of plantations larger than 5,000 acres. A second and far more numerous class of planters, perhaps 10,000 of them, owned fewer than 1,000 acres and

50 to 100 Negroes. A third class of "small planters," as many as 90,000, owned plantations that could be described as large farms with fewer than 50 slaves. To say that the plantation was principal in Southern scenes is not to assert that the admired mansions of the gentry were constantly in the eye of the traveler. The lordly homes of the Southern aristocracy existed, especially in the Deep South, in Alabama, Mississippi, and Louisiana. However, the abodes of most planters were not very impressive, were inferior to those of prosperous Northern farmers; and everywhere in the Old South were rude cottages, cabins, and shacks that sheltered whites who were poor in worldly goods and blacks who possessed almost none. Southern vistas were often dismal and depressing, whether one observed the countryside or looked at towns and cities.

For the Old South did not keep economic pace with the new and thriving North. The wealth of the great planters, who formed its fabled aristocracy, was less than it appeared to be. After 1830 the rising price of land and especially of slaves constantly added to the capital value of their holdings. However, the income from their crops did not increase in proportion. A great planter could be land-poor and slave-poor. Nor was the middle class both extensive and possessed of vast riches. It has been mentioned that romantic views of the Old South would have it that it had no middle class, that its whites belonged either to the aristocracy or to a rural proletariat of "poor white trash." Nevertheless, lacking the charm of aristocracy or the drama of poverty—like all middle classes—it was real enough. It embraced not only tens of thousands of the less affluent planters, but also several million persons who owned few or no Negroes—homestead farmers, mechanics, tradesmen, clergymen, teachers, lawyers, and others. Those of the middle class who possessed more money and more slaves have often been promoted to the aristocracy by their descendants, and by others who have refused to concede that an aristocracy must be of the few. On the other hand, worthy folk of the less prosperous part of the middle class have been carelessly confused with the "poor white trash." Those wretched people are by no means mythical; there were many tens of thousands of them. They could look down only upon the slaves.

In nostalgic and mistaken memory the aristocracy of the Old South was not only extensive in numbers and English Cavalier by descent but Episcopalian in faith and composed of educated and cultured gentlemen and charming ladies. Actually, its relatively few members were not usually patrician by birth. There were well-to-do planters who lived east of the Southern Appalachians and who belonged to families that had possessed lands and slaves for several generations. Occasionally an aristocrat of similar background was to be found west of the great ridge, but many of the "great planters" were "new men" who had rapidly acquired acres and Negroes west of the Appalachians. They resembled Andrew Jackson rather than Thomas Jefferson. Gallantry does not require that their wives be given distinguished forebears. Nor were the "great planters," except on the Atlantic seaboard, remarkably addicted to Episcopalianism; the lower Mississippi Valley was crowded with Baptists, Methodists, and Presbyterians but contained very few Episcopalians. In some ways the aristocrats of the Old South certainly did resemble the aristocrats of the South of the eighteenth century. They were not usually remarkable for their learning. It has often been remarked that the novels of Sir Walter Scott and the poetry of Lord Byron were much read in the Old South. However, its aristocrats spent much more time with account books than upon fiction. They went from the cotton field to the hunting field rather than to the realms of literature; and they devoted more of their leisure to cards than to the study of statecraft. William Gilmore Simms, the prolific novelist of South Carolina, did not find patrons among the rich planters as Benvenuto Cellini did among the rulers of Renaissance Italy and France. The aristocrats were usually busy "practical" men. Legend would have it that they were extraordinarily fond of gambling and dueling, but they were not usually either reckless or irresponsible or vicious. Their manners were gracious; they were generous in spirit, even chivalrous; they were brave and accustomed to the use of arms. Holding arbitrary sway over their slaves, they were often proud and imperious.

Side by side with that aristocracy, but worlds away from it, lived, or existed, the "poor white trash," also known as "crackers," "hillbillies," and "clay-eaters." Alas, there were more of

those shiftless, degraded, and ignorant folk than there were
patricians. Their like could be found outside the South but not
in such large numbers. Whence they came is somewhat of a
mystery. It has been romantically suggested that they were the
descendants of the vagrants and criminals expelled from England
and transported to America in the colonial time. It may safely be
assumed that the men and women deported from England reproduced in America, but it is no more certain that they were
the ancestors of the "poor white trash" than it is that the aristocracy was descended from proud and worthy English families. If
the trash were to a degree inferior by inheritance, one may not
question that they were also molded by environment—and even
by chance. Losing out in economic competition with their fellow whites, occupying inferior lands, the trash suffered from a
vicious cycle of poverty, ignorance, disease, and apathy. The
traveler might see the shabby, unpainted, rickety homes of those
wretched people in narrow mountain valleys, upon islands in the
swamps of the Southern lowlands, upon Piedmont lands that had
once been good but that had been ruined by pernicious tillage.
The men were often surly, pale-faced, lanky, lounging idlers, ill-
favored males who preferred hunting and fishing to farming.
Their women were slatternly, as indolent and slovenly within
the house as were the men outside it. The trash possessed sufficient energy to reproduce too many of their kind. They were
devoted to whisky and to primitive and emotional Protestant
sects. The presence in large numbers of those ill-fed, illiterate,
and lethargic people is evidence enough that all was not well in
the Old South.

Those who are unfamiliar with the South have on occasion
succumbed to a temptation to swell the ranks of the "poor white
trash" by including within it many, even all, of the plain farmers
of the Old South who did not own slaves. However, to do so is
to create misunderstanding. The Old South contained a large
body of yeoman farmers who were industrious, owned good
land, lived in shabby comfort, were sturdy, and were not
depraved. They were numerous on the Piedmont between Virginia and Alabama, but they were to be found in all parts of the
South. God-fearing in the Baptist or Methodist way, they and
their wives and children were not usually committed to despair.

The yeoman was not well educated. Often he could write no more than his name. But there was a gulf between the yeomen and the trash, and the former could, and often did, rise in the world. It is therefore appropriate to place them in the large Southern middle class. Forming the lowest stratum of that class, the yeomen were not sharply separated from the merchants, the not-so-rich planters, and others who composed its higher levels. That virile middle class, more rural than urban, less remarkable for its intellectual pursuits than for its physical and moral vigor, gave basic strength to the society of the Old South.

There is room for dispute about the status of many whites in the Old South, but that of the Negroes is obvious. They, whether free or slave, were below all whites. Only one white person in four owned slaves, but every white person, even if he was of the trash, could comfort himself with the thought that he was above every Negro. There were tens of thousands of free Negroes in Virginia and Maryland, and not a few in other parts of the Old South. They were not set apart by the dominant whites from the bulk of the Negroes, who were slaves. In the eyes of all the whites, all those who had some African blood in their veins, no matter in what proportion, were Negro and inferior.

The slave of the Old South was not the slave of the eighteenth century. The Negro of the colonial time was often African by birth; if born on the western side of the Atlantic, he was, with exceptions, widely separated, both biologically and culturally, from the white man. With the passing generations, the races came closer. The stoppage—almost total—of the oceanic slave trade cut off African influences. Unions between white men and Negro women, producing mulattoes, quadroons, octaroons, and others of mixed blood, altered more than the skin color of the Negroes. A Negro lass could not refuse her body to her master, or to the son of her master; she was not protected from the embraces of other white men. Infusions of white patrician blood, and of much that was plebeian, changed the Negroes. Isaac Jefferson, a slave of Thomas Jefferson, observed that several of his fellow servants in his master's household strongly resembled Mrs. Jefferson's father. In the twentieth century, perhaps correctly, some Negroes claimed to be descended from

Mrs. Martha Washington through the President's stepson. Certainly, the blacks, with Africa becoming ever more remote, became more like their white rulers in language, in modes of thought, in religion. Conversely, the speech of the whites seems to have been affected by that of the Negroes. Thus is explained the Southern drawl. Whatever else they might be, the Negroes of the Old South were American.

That the blacks, whether of black, brown, yellow, or white skin, were not what they had been, is evident from their occupations. Those who were free were not, of course, confined to household service and field labor. They were also clerks and artisans, and even, in a few remarkable instances, owners of slaves. But many of those in bondage were likewise carpenters, masons, clerks, drivers of stagecoaches and steam engines—skilled and semi-skilled workers. Such men were often "hired out" by their masters. Some of them were literate. Occasionally such a man, saving small sums given him for good performance, was able to buy his freedom, and at last even that of his wife and children.

However, most of the slaves were still engaged in menial and field tasks—and worked far more often in cotton and tobacco rows than in the mansions of their owners. A dozen or more Negroes might be maids and footmen in the "Big House," and slaves cooked for its occupants in a kitchen behind it. The young of the aristocracy were usually cared for by a "Mammy," who was almost a second mother to them. But most of the slaves, men, women, and older children, worked in the fields from dawn to dusk. A master who possessed only a few Negroes might toil side by side with them. On a large plantation the slaves labored in gangs under the direction of white overseers. Household slaves, if they spent their days caring for the needs and executing the whims of their owners, were rewarded; they were treated as human or at least half human. The field hand might be looked upon as little more than a piece of moving property.

The lot of the slave varied, not only in duties imposed, but from place to place and from master to master. In general, the slaves of the Upper South—Virginia, North Carolina, Tennessee, and Arkansas—were better treated than those of the

Lower South—the states stretching from South Carolina to Texas. A Negro reared in Virginia dreaded transfer to Alabama; a Tennessee slave did not wish to be sent "down the river" to Louisiana. Unfortunately for them, many Negroes were sold southward by owners who could not afford to keep them. The market for slaves in the Lower South was only too good. The threat of sale to a Mississippi planter could daunt a refractory Virginia slave. To be sure, indulgent proprietors were to be found everywhere—and others who were stern masters. In the main, the slaves, in part because they were valuable, were not harshly treated. There were masters who treated their slaves as if they were their own children—which they sometimes were. There were also planters, and overseers, who cursed, cuffed, flogged, and even killed slaves.

Whatever may be said in defense of slavery, however cogent may be the extenuating arguments offered in its behalf, the institution was inherently vicious. When it was ardently assailed, after 1830, it was almost as warmly praised by Southern apologists. Their case was fundamentally feeble. A planter could not do much for his slaves and still make a profit, partly because the blacks softly condemned their condition by their good-natured indolence and inefficiency. The Negro father and his family were housed in the plainest cabins, in which the furnishings hardly deserved the name. They were given little and cheap clothing, and monotonous and inexpensive food. Except for a fortunate few, they were not allowed to learn to read and write. They were not usually permitted to marry legally. Their owners carelessly encouraged casual unions among them, and slave families were unstable. American folklore would have it that powerful young Negro males were used for stud. Convincing evidence of such a practice is lacking. Nevertheless, it is only too clear that the marriage tie between slaves was often disregarded by whites, who separated husbands and wives for their own advantage. The slave did not possess the dignity of a surname. He might be called "Sam" or "Mr. Darby's Sam." Oppressive "slave codes" enacted by the Southern legislatures restricted the movements of the blacks, forbade manumission, and imposed heavy penalties upon slaves who rebelled. Such codes did not allow a slave to testify in court against his master. No legal punishment was imposed upon the master or overseer who brutally flogged a lazy or tired field hand. The behavior of a master who killed his slave might be denounced by his fellow whites; but he would not be imprisoned for his crime. The Southern states protected the property rights of the owners; they offered almost no safeguards to the persons who were property.

One of the ugliest facets of slavery in the Old South was the trade in Negro bodies—and souls. Negroes were bought and sold, privately and publicly. Considerate masters tried to keep their slaves. If forced to dispose of Negroes, they attempted to sell husband, wife, and children to men and women who would not abuse them. However, the blacks only too often passed from one owner to another as mere commodities. They were frequently sold at public auction. In Savannah and St. Louis, in Richmond and New Orleans, even in Washington, human beings were placed upon the block as if they were cattle or bales of tobacco. Prospective purchasers inspected their teeth, tested their muscles, and estimated their reproductive value. To see a human being sold to the highest bidder, perhaps an obvious brute, was pitiful; when the husband and wife were bought by separate purchasers, the scene might be heart-rending. Another distressing sight was that of a coffle of slaves chained together and walking from the Upper South to market in the Lower South. Not so wantonly cruel as the oceanic traffic in slaves that had been condemned and outlawed by the civilized nations, that internal commerce nevertheless had its horrors.

It has been urged by historians that the slaves were nearly as happy as the whites among whom they lived, by other historians that the Negroes were continuously and even desperately discontented. Instances enough may be adduced of love and loyalty from slaves to their masters and mistresses, indeed of reciprocal devotion. On the other hand, much may be made of the attempts, usually unsuccessful, of many thousands of Negroes to escape. Emphasis may be put upon slave revolts. The truth, as usual, lies between the extremes. It would be ridiculous to contend that most blacks were content, much less happy, in bondage; occasional local insurrections prove beyond doubt that there were Negroes who preferred savage punishment and death to subjection. In the summer of 1822, Denmark Vesey, a free

Negro, plotted an uprising in Charleston, South Carolina. It was discovered, and 37 Negroes were put to death. In the biggest of the slave risings of the nineteenth century, that led by Nat Turner in Southampton County, Virginia, in 1831, Turner and 59 followers killed 61 whites, chiefly women and children. Alarmed and vengeful whites hunted down and slew a hundred or more slaves. If most of the blacks neither tried to escape nor engaged in hopeless rebellion, if some of them were satisfied with their lot, it is certain that most of the slaves desired freedom. The good humor that the Negroes commonly displayed in bondage is to be ascribed to acceptance of the inevitable rather than to a pervading happiness. It has been remarked that they subtly indicated their discontent daily by doing no more work than they were compelled to do. The Negro, like the German slave in ancient Rome, was not pleased with his status.

With the advantage of hindsight, it may be asserted that slavery and the Old South of which it was so large a part were anachronisms, that they would die. Scholars have suggested that the slave owners, had they not been forced to release the blacks, would later have willingly freed them, if for no other reason than that time would have demonstrated that free labor was more profitable and less trouble than slave. It was not evident in 1830, or 1850, that the bondage of the blacks would be destroyed by insurgent Negroes, by dissatisfied Southern whites, or by the two in combination. As it happened, both slavery and the Old South went down under attack from the North. It began while General Jackson lived in the White House. Himself a slave owner, he did not think it necessary, because he was devoted to democracy, to direct that assault.

CHAPTER 14

The American Renaissance

❀❀❀

IF, TOWARD THE MIDDLE of the nineteenth century, the Southern scene was soberly shadowed, all was not radiant and sweet to the north. There, too, human beings, white-skinned ones, were exploited. There, factories, multiplying, sucked in men, and women, and children and spewed them out worn and broken. The many cities of the North were not uniformly lovely. Thoughtful men and women saw many and grievous ills in that region. However, economic advance, creating social ulcers, was not entirely or permanently baneful. There, machines pledged a better future, if the benefits from them were decently shared. The "Old Immigrants" from Ireland and the northwestern part of Europe poured into Northern harbors to participate in that future. They added to an ever-growing population. Bright on the Northern scene was a literary Renaissance, a surge in the world of letters.

Many American scholars, looking back from the twentieth century to praise the gifted poets and distinguished novelists of the fourth and fifth decades of the nineteenth century in America, have failed to see the mechanical geniuses of those twenty years. Nevertheless, in the 1830s and 1840s when Ralph Waldo Emerson, Edgar Allan Poe, and many another literary light began to shine, the fertility of American inventors more than matched that of American writers. They were also more productive than the inventors of England and western Europe. The patents they obtained in Washington soared in number, averaging 646 per annum in the 1840s. Eli Whitney and Robert Fulton were followed by Cyrus H. McCormick, Samuel Colt, John

Ericsson, Charles Goodyear, Samuel F. B. Morse, Elias Howe, and Walter Hunt, by a galaxy of constructive geniuses. In 1830, Peter Cooper built the first American locomotive. Soon afterward McCormick and Obed Hussey independently invented the mechanical reaper. In 1835, Colt obtained a patent for his revolver, the weapon that was to make the American cowboy something more than a herder of cattle. Ericsson devised an efficient screw propeller for steamships, a recoil mechanism for gun carriages, various scientific instruments, and later the iron-clad warship *Monitor*. It was Goodyear who learned how to vulcanize rubber, who made the rubber tree a vital natural resource. When his fellow countrymen would not buy his paintings, artist Samuel Morse turned from oils and watercolors to the wonders of electricity. A Congress that ignored Morse the painter gave money to help Morse the inventor. In 1844 the magnetic telegraph developed by him carried from Baltimore to Washington the message, "What hath God wrought?" Soon afterward Elias Howe wrought a sewing machine which could be used both in the home and in the factory. He became rich. Like Howe, Walter Hunt was interested in fastening together pieces of cloth. He made that useful thing, a reliable safety pin. Almost simultaneously, other men learned how to preserve food in cans. The Emersons, Poes, and Nathaniel Hawthornes of the mechanical world gave impulse to the Industrial Revolution. Perhaps even more than the literary men of their time, they shaped both the immediate and the remote future.

The devices of the inventors, usually created to meet specific needs, made possible a remarkable advance in manufacturing. Entrepreneurs, some of whom were inventors, put them to use. Before 1830 more goods were finished in American homes than in factories; after that year domestic fabrication rapidly lost importance. Enterprising men, such as Nathan Appleton and Patrick Tracy Jackson, built factories in New England and used water power to fashion large quantities of cotton. During the twenty years after 1830 the number of spindles used in the making of cotton goods in America almost doubled; they numbered more than three million in 1850. New England also began to make machine tools and smaller metal products, such as clocks, cutlery, pans, and guns, in quantity. Manufacturing in

New York, New Jersey, and Pennsylvania kept pace with that
of New England. The entrepreneurs of those states had easy
access to iron ore, coal, and large markets. Employing steam as
well as water power, they made locomotives, stoves, woolen
goods, flour, and machinery of all sorts. Nor did industry fail to
develop in the Ohio Valley. There, the distilling of whisky and
tobacco manufacturing flourished with the processing of flour
and meat. Lagging far behind industrially, the South nevertheless had its factories, including the Tredegar iron works at
Richmond. As the Civil War approached, the value of the things
that came from American industry actually exceeded the value
of those which came from her farmlands.

The swift growth of American industry was accompanied by
an astonishing and far-reaching change in transport. The railroad train began to replace the wagon, the stagecoach, and the
steamer. The first true railroad was built in England in 1825, but
the Americans soon afterward began to form railroad companies, build engines and cars, and lay tracks. The Baltimore
and Ohio Railroad, the first to carry passengers in America, was
chartered in 1827. English and American capitalists invested
large sums in the new companies, and several American states
gave subsidies to encourage them to proceed. They did, so
swiftly that America had 3,328 miles of railroad in 1840, when
all of Europe had only 1,818 miles. The depression that began
in 1837 temporarily interrupted the progress of the "iron
horses," and several states repudiated bonds that they had floated
in order to assist the railroad entrepreneurs. However, the railroad builders were almost feverishly active in the 1840s. By the
end of that decade tracks and trains were common sights east of
the Mississippi River. Not that the railroads then offered smooth
safe transportation over very long distances. Their engines,
burning wood or coal, were not very powerful; the tracks upon
which they ran were only wooden strips thinly covered by iron;
and passenger cars, at first modeled after the stagecoach, retained much of the discomfort of that carriage. The bridges
over which trains passed were often made of wood; brakes were
uncertain; and accidents were frequent. In part because the railroads did not use the same track gauge, they were not articu-
lated. Nevertheless, by the mid-century, they were altering the

patterns of commerce, industry, and American life. Internal traffic, before the coming of the railroads, had followed water-courses. The trains tended to run from east to west and from west to east, rather than from north to south and south to north. The railroads helped to establish ever stronger economic links between the Old Northwest and the seaboard states north of Chesapeake Bay. Railroad traffic contributed to the continuing growth of New York City and to the rise of Chicago.

Let it not be thought that the Northern states at the mid-century were thick with factories and cities. If New York City then contained more than half a million people, if the number of Philadelphians approached that figure, it is also true that only 125 out of every 1,000 Americans lived in cities containing more than 8,000 inhabitants. There were at that time only eighty-five such cities in the entire nation. The great majority of Americans still lived in villages, in hamlets, on the land. Those who dwelled in the Northern states were less rural than the Southerners; but they were not, in the main, an urban people. The homestead farmer was still the most typical man in the North.

If the Northerners moved toward the factory and the city, they also, like the Southerners, continued to move westward. By the mid-century, indeed, almost half of all the Americans lived beyond the Appalachian Mountains; and the center of American population was moving steadily toward the setting sun. The upper parts of the Mississippi Valley attracted far more settlers than the lower ones. By river and lake steamers, in Conestoga wagons, on horseback, by railroad, they poured over the amazingly rich prairie lands of Illinois and Iowa and through the fertile woodlands of Michigan and Wisconsin. Between 1837 and 1848, Michigan, Iowa, and Wisconsin were admitted to the Union as thriving commonwealths.

Shifting westward, the Americans continued to increase in number. They also became less Protestant and less English. During the two decades after 1830 their numbers almost doubled; they were more than 23,000,000 in 1850. That phenomenal figure does not indicate that the Americans were reproducing themselves as never before. In New England the birth rate actually began to fall. The Old Immigration from Europe added heavily to the American stock. In the period 1831–50 about 2,300,000

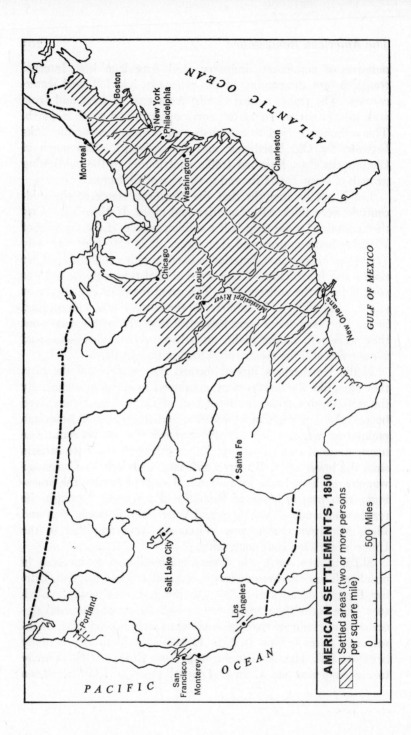

AMERICAN SETTLEMENTS, 1850

Settled areas (two or more persons per square mile)

0   500 Miles

aliens entered the Atlantic ports. At least 2,000,000 of those travelers came to stay. Among them were a few Scandinavians; more Dutch, who put down in Michigan and Iowa; and many Irish and Germans. In the 1840s both the Irish and the Germans fled to America from economic distress and political tyranny in their homelands. They did not prosper swiftly in their new country. The Irish, mostly Roman Catholic, settled chiefly in the cities of the Atlantic seaboard, especially in New York and Boston. Usually unskilled, they had to perform physical labor. The Germans, many of them also Roman Catholic, commonly sought new homes beyond the Appalachians. They often became American farmers, but they also congregated in Cincinnati, St. Louis, and Milwaukee; in those cities "Little Germanys" appeared. Few of the Old Immigrants went to the Old South, where economic opportunity was more limited, where they had to compete with slave labor. The Southerners were little altered by the Old Immigration. It added variety and vigor as well as numbers to the population of the Northern states.

The Schmidts and the O'Briens did not find that all was exceeding well in the Northern states. It may be true, as one Irishman asserted, that a laborer could support himself and save enough money every two weeks to buy three acres of fertile land. If so, in a little more than two years he could purchase 160 acres, a farm large enough to maintain a family in comfort. But such arithmetic is misleading. To achieve so much, the laborer would need to be steadily employed, single, and thrifty. Moreover, he could not successfully till the soil without some knowledge of farming, without a little capital, without tools. The Old Immigrant bettered his lot by fleeing from the Old World. The O'Briens gladly added meat to the potatoes upon which they had lived in Ireland. However, handicapped by his lack of money, perhaps by his ignorance of English, even by his religion, the Old Immigrant usually made slow economic progress. To be sure, if he at last acquired a farm or a shop, as he often did, he certainly did not toil in vain, and his descendants gained immensely.

If the Old Immigrants learned that arrival in the land of Canaan did not put an end to their toils and troubles, those

Americans born in the Northern states did not uniformly prosper either. Among them were entrepreneurs who became rich,
who shouldered their way into the Northern aristocracy. Or
should one say that they, with bankers and merchants, combined
with the descendants of the colonial aristocracy to form a gen-
teel plutocracy? In any event, the upper class of men and
women of wealth grew in numbers, if not in polite learning,
manners, and graces. The middle class in the North, remaining
broad and numerous, continued to contain the bulk of the population there. However, its less affluent members, such as masons,
carpenters, and mechanics, found it difficult to maintain their
families and their status during the depression of 1837, indeed
throughout the period 1837–50. Their wages did not keep pace
with rising prices. They might derive consolation from the
harsh fact that unskilled laborers were slipping downward into a
lower class not too different from a European proletariat. As the
mid-century approached, the North had larger proportions of
rich and poor than in the past.

The Americans have been reluctant to apply the word "proletariat" to themselves or to their fellows. It may nevertheless be
said that a proletariat, American style, appeared before the middle of the nineteenth century. It differed from European prole-
tariats in several ways. It was relatively small; its members often
escaped from it; and the children of those who remained in it
had a good chance to climb the economic and social ladder.
Even so, unskilled laborers—and they were not all recent immigrants—fared badly in the later 1830s and in the 1840s and
formed a special class of the poor. An observer reported that one
out of every seven persons who lived in New York City at the
middle of the nineteenth century was a pauper. There, as in
London, wealth and want, opulence and indigence existed side
by side.

Whatever might be his temporal destiny, the laborer, like
almost all Americans, was consoled by expectations of "pie in
the sky," of joy and glory after death. For the Christian
churches continued to flourish in the North as well as in the Old
South. They also spawned new sects. Here and there, in New
York City and Boston, were educated Unitarians and thoughtful
agnostics; and not every untutored man was a devout Christian.

In the main, however, the Northern Protestants were as fervent as those of the Old South, and Roman Catholic immigrants clung to their faith, which was a comforting certainty to men and women who had left their native country behind them. Remaining enthusiastic, the Protestants engaged in theological contests and created new varieties of Christianity. Among these were such exotics as the General Six Principle Baptists and the Seed-in-the-Spirit Predestinarian Baptists. Also of Baptist origins was William Miller, from whom the Seventh Day Adventists derived inspiration. Miller, a New England farmer, observed that the Second Coming of Christ was set by the New Testament at no distant time. In 1831, like some other evangelists, he began to preach that it was scheduled for the near future. He was persuasive in many pulpits, and his message circulated through magazines. His announcement that the end of the world was at hand aroused fear and faith in tens of thousands. At last he proclaimed the awful day, March 21, 1843. The Millerites, dressed in their best clothes or in white robes, gathered on roofs and on hills at dawn to greet the Saviour and to enter the eternal. It turned out that Miller had not correctly read the Biblical calendar. Disconcerted, he decided that he had made a small error, but he was never able to correct it. From his following sprang the Seventh Day Adventists. Clinging to the notion that the world could not last long, they prematurely deprived themselves of several of its pleasures, including meat, alcohol, tobacco, and dancing.

The largest of the new sects, the Church of Latter-day Saints, was not so hostile to earthly enjoyments during its first decades. It was founded in 1830 by Joseph Smith, a New York Moses, who announced that an angel had told him to go to a cave near the village of Palmyra, wherein he had found golden plates inscribed in an unknown language. He translated the writings into English and published them as *The Book of Mormon*, which he declared to be an addition to the Old and New Testaments. Later other revelations came to Smith. He swiftly won converts whom he promised to lead to a new Zion. Missionaries whom he sent to England gained several thousand adherents for him. Smith offered a private socialism as a cure for the evils of this world as well as assurance of joy to come. He and his followers

were persecuted by their neighbors. They moved westward, to
Missouri, and thence to Nauvoo in Illinois. Industrious and
thrifty, they thrived at Nauvoo, and their numbers multiplied.
To make sure that they would continue to increase, Smith announced in 1843 that polygamy was divinely sanctioned. He and
his disciples undertook to follow the example of Solomon, and
the spinster became a rarity among the Saints. Smith did not
long enjoy the pleasures or endure the sorrows of plural matrimony, however. In the following year he and his brother
Hyrum were charged with various offenses against the law and
were put in jail by officers who knew not Zion. There they were
seized and murdered by a mob of ignorant lawless men. The
church founded by the martyred Smith survived him and grew.
Not long after his death his followers, under a brilliant new
leader, Brigham Young, trekked to the deserts of Utah, which
they made bloom. His church afterward spread throughout the
world.

That the early histories of most respectable churches and religions contain antics and logical discrepancies is not unknown.
Nevertheless, the spectacle of many thousands of Americans
confusing the arrival of spring with the Second Coming of
Christ suggests that the Americans as a whole were not too well
informed in the year 1843. Such was the fact. However, they
had opened a massive and continuing attack upon illiteracy and
ignorance; they had entered upon the "Common School Revolution." In the 1830s and 1840s states, counties, and cities, chiefly
in the North, established public elementary schools in almost
astonishing numbers. Overcoming the resistance of the thrifty,
of the childless, of those who favored Christian and private instruction, the champions of elementary education at public expense won victory after victory. Indeed, the principle became
firmly fixed that tax money must be liberally spent to begin the
process of civilizing the young. At the mid-century there were
no fewer than 80,000 elementary school houses in the nation,
with 90,000 teachers striving to pound reading, writing, and
arithmetic into the resisting heads of 3,500,000 children. The
teachers were more impressive in quantity than they were in
quality. They were neither well paid nor well trained. They and
their students would improve, even though the problem of edu-

cating ever larger numbers of children placed a heavier and heavier burden upon American adults. They bore it with an increasing cheerfulness for which they have not always received their due.

The Americans were not then ready to spend public funds liberally for secondary or advanced education. Several state universities opened narrow doors, but they did not thrive. Dozens of church-connected colleges were established, but men who disliked "godless" state universities did not lavish money upon institutions that combined religious and secular instruction. The denominational colleges were at least as successful in preserving the faith of Methodists, Presbyterians, and Baptists as they were in turning out scholars. If the course of study in private institutions was confined, classical, and theological, it was merely restricted and classical in the public ones. Only a small fraction of American males found the way to the campus.

The process of learning has never been imprisoned within academic walls. The Americans had the benefit of multiplying newspapers, some of which sold for only a penny. They bought many magazines. A few of these circulated widely. After 1830 the lyceum, a society for the advancement of learning, became a powerful engine for the spread of learning. By 1835 there were three thousand lyceums scattered over the nation. The members of such groups studied books and listened to lectures by traveling scholars and writers, including Ralph Waldo Emerson and Charles Dickens. They, with other Americans, even bought books, and the publishing of them became an important and even profitable enterprise in Eastern cities. In one way or another, information spread more rapidly through the mass of Americans than ever before.

If Presidents Andrew Jackson and Martin Van Buren read little more than governmental prose, President John Tyler graciously received Charles Dickens in the White House when Dickens was on his first and dyspeptic tour of America, and was described by the great novelist as a gentleman. For, as the midcentury approached, many Americans eagerly sought "culture." So avid they were for it that the novels of Sir Walter Scott and Dickens found a handsome market in America. To be sure, more Americans, less sophisticated, read the Scriptures, newspapers,

and books of etiquette. Nor were those who eagerly sought
"culture" remarkable for their sensitive judgment of books and
of authors. They knew and cared little about music or architecture. Many of them preferred mediocre writings by Englishmen
to meritorious works by their own countrymen. Since there was
then no international copyright, American publishers profited
from "pirating" the books of English authors—English publishers would later cheat American writers in the same fashion. To a
large degree, English prestige in the realm of literature was justified. American writers had molded themselves after English
ones, and many of them would continue to be anemic imitators
of their English superiors.

Nowhere were the English so sedulously copied as in Boston.
There the "Brahmins," an educated, polished, and almost sterile
elite, ruled both socially and intellectually. They were of old
New England stock, from families that possessed "old" money.
Born in proper parts of Boston or Cambridge, the Brahmin, if
male, was a college graduate. Ideally, he was a Harvard man and
a member of a learned profession. If female, the Brahmin was a
well-bred bookish lady. To these chosen persons of both sexes,
all Americans who lived at an inconvenient distance from Boston
were residents of barbarous outlying regions. They would have
it that their city was the "hub of the solar system." They desired
to be considered as equals by similar English gentlemen and
ladies. Indeed, they were, along with Southern aristocrats, often
praised by the English as the best of the Americans. However,
there were English snobs who saw Boston as the capital of a
small and distant planet palely lit by the glowing English sun.
How could Boston, or America as a whole, without kings,
nobles, castles, ancient colleges, antique church, or traditions,
achieve much intellectually or artistically? Many Brahmins entered the republic of letters; lusting for praise from imperial
England, they failed to achieve great power or remarkable originality. Of such, ironically, was Dr. Oliver Wendell Holmes,
who described and named the Brahmins.

Nevertheless, Boston was the center of an American—chiefly
Northern—Renaissance. In the fourth and fifth decades of the
nineteenth century the Yankees were both prolific and creative
in the world of letters. Drawing inspiration from Europe and

from Transcendentalism, New England burst into literary flower. Returning from his studies in Germany, George Ticknor sought, with some success, to breathe intellectual life into Harvard. Henry Wadsworth Longfellow, after studying at Bowdoin College and in several European countries, became a professor and a poet. He learned foreign languages easily; he was long a shining light at Harvard; and he eventually became the most popular poet in both America and England. Unfortunately, he was also bookish, imitative, and devoid of passion. Most of his verse was commonplace; his long narrative poem "Evangeline" and one or two others contain charming passages. But there was vigor and enduring vitality in Transcendentalists Ralph Waldo Emerson and Henry Thoreau, who declined to spend their energies pouring thin American wine into old European bottles; and in Nathaniel Hawthorne, Longfellow's classmate at Bowdoin, who deeply felt the internal strife of the New England Puritan.

Transcendentalism, of which Emerson became the high priest, was a potent fermentive force. Not the same thing to all of its devotees, who were many in New England, it replaced Unitarianism among rebellious Yankee intellectuals. They denounced all religious rituals and creeds. They believed that God was present in all places and at all times, and that He constantly revealed Himself to those who attuned themselves to the Divine. Such beliefs, heretical even to Unitarians, required personal thought and action; they were immensely stimulating, especially to writers. Emerson did not create Transcendentalism, but he was its most brilliant apostle. He was a Harvard man, but he earned part of his expenses at the college as a waiter. He looked far more like a statesman than most American Presidents. Leaving a Unitarian pulpit because his conscience would not permit him to partake of communion, he began to lecture and to write. He composed poetry that was cold and unappealing, except for his "Concord Hymn," in which he celebrated the resistance of the American militia to the British troops at Concord in 1775. He wrote pithy prose that was less than fluent. He was not even a good speaker. A scholar, he has been excessively praised by scholars who have forgiven him their own faults. Nevertheless, Emerson exerted a profound influence; his calls for courage, for self-reliance, for the independent pursuit of excellence, literary and otherwise, were heeded by many a man and woman. He helped them to free themselves from the trammels of orthodoxy. He at length became respectable as well as prosperous, received an honorary degree from Harvard, and became a Brahmin before he died. His animating spirit survived his body.

Henry David Thoreau, the "best friend" that Emerson ever had, never was a Brahmin. A graduate of Harvard in 1837, he settled in his native Concord. He never made much money. He did not succeed as a teacher or a lecturer; for a time he earned his living by making pencils in his father's little factory; later he was a surveyor. A devout Transcendentalist—even before he met Emerson—he determined to live freely, independently, and morally. He declared pretentiously, "He is blessed who is assured that the animal is dying out in him day by day, and the divine being established." Nevertheless, Thoreau reached his goal. He successfully set aside material things to achieve personal liberation, managed to combine "plain living and high thinking." He sojourned cheaply and happily from 1844 to 1846 in a cabin near Concord. There he was healthy and as free as might be. The record of his experiences there, *Walden*, published in 1854, has inspired countless readers and has become a classic. Pointing out that "The mass of men lead lives of quiet desperation," Thoreau did not urge that they flee to Nature, that they seek refuge on Polynesian islands. They must live simply in society. They must not yield to political or institutional tyranny. To protest against the Mexican War he refused to pay his poll tax in Concord, and he was put in jail for a night. He was quickly released, because someone paid the tax for him, thus saving him from a test of his principles. Very likely he would have passed that test. Nevertheless, he did not supply an easy answer to all the difficulties encountered by a married man in a complex society. He was too proud of his modest wants. Was Thoreau free and happy principally because Nature, or Chance, permitted him to be a bachelor? Certainly his doctrine of civil disobedience, if carried to an extreme by men, women, or children less responsible and less enlightened than Thoreau, must threaten human order, so difficult to establish and maintain.

Emerson and Thoreau went through life with a confidence

that transcends reason. Not so Nathaniel Hawthorne, who was beset by melancholy, by loneliness of the spirit. Not unaffected by Transcendentalism, he had no share in the optimism of its devotees. After graduating from Bowdoin, he was supported for some years by his family while he tried to establish himself as a writer. Eventually, a happy marriage, appointments to political office, and literary success made his lot comfortable. He became famous with the publication of his novel *The Scarlet Letter* in 1850. His short stories, which he called "tales," and his novels, to which he gave the name "romances," brought him a solid durable fame. His long dependence on others and his slow progress as an author led him into pessimism and a feeling of isolation. His novels, except for *The House of the Seven Gables*, indited during a period of euphoria, are not sunny. Often cast against a Puritan background, his narratives also frequently portray emotional and moral clash in and between individuals. He pursued themes of sin, remorse, and personal isolation. What he was trying to say, in symbol or allegory, is not always entirely clear; but he had passion and a haunting power.

The Renaissance of the two decades after 1830 was not confined to New England, or even to the Northern states. One of its most brilliant authors was Edgar Allan Poe, who was born the son of actors in Boston but reared by foster parents in Virginia. If he belonged to any region, he was a Southerner. More accurately, he was an American whose literary standards were not regional, not national, but universal. Twenty-four days older than Abraham Lincoln, Poe was only forty when he died in 1849. He never achieved financial success. He drifted from the University of Virginia to the American army, to this post and that on magazines in cities along the Atlantic seaboard. Rootless and poor, he found solace in alcohol. He is a superb example of the writer who sacrifices nearly all for his art. During his brief and troubled life he composed a number of poems, such as "The Raven," "The Bells," and "Annabel Lee," whose cadences and rhymes are remarkably seductive to the young. They have invited parody. On occasion Poe wrote truly glorious lines, as he did in "A Dream within a Dream":

> I stand amid the roar
> Of a surf-tormented shore,

And I hold within my hand
Grains of the golden sand—
How few! yet how they creep
Through my fingers to the deep,
While I weep—while I weep!

Poe also published many macabre tales, filled with terror, horror, and corpses, and written in a sumptuous prose. Possessing a penetrating intellect, a gift for logical analysis, he invented the "detective story." He also excelled as a literary critic; his assessments in magazines of the work of other authors, if often unflattering, were just as often acute. He was carried from a Baltimore barroom to his deathbed.

The pathetic personal history of the exotic Poe, and estimates of his work offered by Americans during his lifetime and afterward, throw light upon the state of American literature. Emerson, who composed no lovely cadences, spoke of Poe as "the jingle man." Longfellow did not harbor unstinted admiration for the critic who pointed out that he was an imitator, who even accused him of plagiarism—did not Poe derive inspiration from transatlantic sources? The Bostonian James Russell Lowell, himself a poet of less than magnificent reputation but a competent critic, arithmetically and more generously weighed Poe. He was "three-fifths of him genius, and two-fifths sheer fudge." If the fractions were reversed, Poe would still tower above nearly all of his literary contemporaries in America. Begrudged praise by writers whose efforts he quite properly condemned, Poe also suffered in reputation because he was vilified by the Philistines, of whom there have been enough in the American Canaan. He was idolized in Europe before he was properly recognized in America. Nevertheless, the fact that a literary genius was long neglected in his own country does not prove that the state of American letters was unhealthy at the death of Poe. On the contrary, the American Renaissance had not spent its force. Herman Melville and Walt Whitman were joining the galaxy of American writers that could survive even the searching analysis of an Edgar Allan Poe.

The American Renaissance was real enough, and its influence continued, but it was largely limited to literature. It produced no profound systematic philosopher; no great playwright; no earth-shaking scientist; no brilliant composer of music; no supremely gifted painter, sculptor, or architect. Boston toward the middle of the nineteenth century was not a modern Athens, or an equivalent of Florence in the fifteenth century. The arts were looked upon as effete by most Americans. The talented sculptor William Wetmore Story, himself of Massachusetts stock, found even Boston to be most uncongenial after long years of residence and study in Italy. He noted in 1855 that "we criticize everything . . . The sky itself is hard and distant . . . The heart grows into stone . . . We love unhappiness." He returned to Italy. At that time, when most Americans were "Victorian," when they believed that much clothing signified a high level of civilization, when neither ladies nor chickens had breasts or legs, painters and sculptors, with their representations of nudes and near-nudes, were commonly considered to be immoral and decadent. Even educated men and women did not go together to art exhibits. Certain hours were set aside for the gentlemen and others for the ladies. American artists, and writers too, felt that they were cramped in their own country. Many of them would seek freedom and inspiration in Europe for several generations to come.

CHAPTER 15

The Offensive Against Slavery

꽃꽃꽃

ALTHOUGH HE CONDEMNED HIS countrymen because they were too fond of the dollar, Edgar Allan Poe did not use his pen constantly to cleanse his world of all its evils. Nor did he lecture about them; he privately read poetry in a melodious voice and with appealing charm to his friends. Nor did Hawthorne strive to put an end to all the abuses of an imperfect society. It was otherwise with many of those who embraced Transcendentalism. From its ferment came fundamental discontent with American life, and efforts to alter it. Revivalist Christianity also stimulated a demand for basic reformation. In fact, religious converts, reconverts, and disturbed American intellectuals carried on campaigns against many specific ills, such as the eating of flesh, the imbibing of alcohol, the tyranny of the male over the female, cramping clothing, the chains of matrimony, and defective schools. They also established idealistic and communist communities devoted to the wholesale renovation of society. With William Lloyd Garrison taking the lead on the eastern seaboard, and Theodore Dwight Weld supplying guidance in the Old Northwest, they opened an impassioned assault against Negro bondage. When slavery was denounced from the North, Southerners rallied to its defense. The abolitionists won a war of words, but not in the South. They drove Northerners and Southerners apart, goading them to settle their disputes by means of a great Civil War; and they played an important part in the extinction of Negro servitude.

As ancient as Christianity itself is the belief among many of its followers that discomfort in this world leads to perpetual joy in eternity. Other Christians, convinced that this life is of some consequence, have thought that the spread of the true faith must in itself remove every difficulty, temporal or eternal. Between 1830 and 1850 the American churches gained and regained members by the tens of thousands. They also sent missionaries abroad—to Asia, to the South Seas, even to Europe—to convert the heathen. However, Christian fervor did not inexorably lead to Christian behavior, and human suffering survived in regions heavily populated by the devout. Many Christians who would improve the world decided to apply the Gospel, to offer specific remedies for social sicknesses. They found allies among the Transcendentalists and other intellectuals, among men and women whose soul-searching was not confined to religion. Emerson conceived that every person should separately seek his own path to perfection, but his associates and admirers generally fought for social reform.

Not that orthodox preachers and heterodox lecturers spent their energies in the cause of the American proletariat. They disliked the labor union, the device through which the workers would gain power to assert their interests as against capital and government. Without their help, the unions grew slowly. Nor did they flock into the Workingmen's party founded in 1838 to advance the cause of labor at the polls. Its principal aims, the ten-hour day for laborers and educational opportunity for their children, were modest. It was dead within six years. Did reformers desire to avoid intimacy with the muscular and the unpolished? They made no great outcry when President Jackson used troops to break a strike—a "riotous assembly"—by Irish laborers engaged in canal-building in Maryland in 1834.

Much more attractive, indeed enticing, to reformers was a holy assault against the demon rum. English travelers declare in their writings that the Americans were then intemperate as well as illiterate and indelicate. Whether they drank more beer, rum, and whisky than their European contemporaries is doubtful. Too many Americans drank too freely. It was obvious that something ought to be done to keep the unhappy farmer from squandering his substance and ruining his body in the village tavern on Saturday night, to prevent the city worker from ruining himself and his family in the saloon. Christ had found no sin in the drinking of wine; reformers, concerned lest they violate Biblical precepts, convinced themselves that He was not displeased by "unfermented" wine. They, and their high-minded fellows who were not believers in literal interpretation of the Scriptures, moved against the consequences rather than the causes of human misery. Who could defend the drunkard—or the man who might become one? It was clear to preachers and lecturers that the substitution of innocent beverages for alcohol would put an end to a host of troubles and bring happiness to all. Through the American Temperance Union, founded in 1826, and thousands of similar smaller machines, they recruited a "Cold Water Army." Its intemperate officers and soldiers did not strive for moderation in the use of alcohol. Some of them sought to persuade individuals to abstain, to "take the pledge." Others tried to secure the passage of laws limiting or stopping the sale of liquor. The pledge was taken by hundreds of thousands and was at least sometimes kept. Moreover, with Maine leading the way in 1846, several Northern states and many Northern counties and cities restricted or prohibited the sale of the most comforting and enlivening beverages. Rather strangely, the Old South, which had its full share of drinkers and preachers, was not attracted to prohibition until a later time. The drive against drink did not destroy every evil in the North.

The thoughts of men and women not heavily weighed down by the learning of the past may leap to novel notions, to bizarre conclusions, even to new insights. Hence the rise in the United States of the "science" of phrenology, that curious belief that the contours of the human head indicate precisely what is to be found within it. It became fashionable to have one's cerebral bumps "read" by the phrenologist. Hence came also the remarkable career of the Reverend Sylvester Graham, a contentious crank who became convinced that the eating of flesh rather than the drinking of alcohol was the principal bane of mankind. He was ultimately responsible for a basic correction in American—and foreign—diets. A Presbyterian clergyman, Graham after 1830 served as an agent of the Pennsylvania State Society for the Suppression of the Use of Ardent Spirits. Seeking in the Scriptures for arguments against strong drink, he found in the book of Genesis a passage which seemed to him to say that God enjoined the eating of herbs, seeds, fruit, and nuts instead of meat. He soon emerged as the high priest of vegetarianism. Thoreau, Joseph Smith, the revivalist Charles Grandison Finney, and others solicitous for the betterment of the race accepted Graham's teaching, at least in part. Thoreau believed that flesh is "essentially unclean," that "every man who has ever been earnest to preserve his higher or poetic faculties in the best condition has been particularly inclined to abstain from animal food, or from much food of any kind." But Graham was sillier than Thoreau. He insisted that water and bread made from whole-wheat flour, well chewed, would supply nearly all of the basic needs of the body. Moreover, said he, men who substituted cereals for animal food would be better able to avoid committing sexual sins. Toward achieving the same end he forbade the use of salt. He once apologized in a newspaper because he had been ill. But Graham's eccentricities were matched by his contributions. Graham is hardly to be censured because he refused to eat his distant relatives. His bread was decidedly superior to the poor white stuff that so many Americans ate and would eat. In his time his countrymen prepared much of their food in greasy frying pans. If Graham and his disciples made too much of the virtues of rice and beans, they led the way toward a more balanced diet in America and in other nations. The *Graham Journal of Health and Longevity* is no longer published, and Graham Hotels, once prominent in America cities, have vanished. Ought not the preserver of the alimentary canal be gratefully remembered along with the builders of the passageways at Panama and Suez?

Sylvester Graham devoted himself to physical needs, Horace Mann to intellectual advancement. Mann was nevertheless the more conventional of the two. He also labored for several reforms. He is chiefly remembered, however, as the man who successfully insisted that teachers ought to be more than ignorant amateurs. Practical and brave, Mann forthrightly pointed out that the elementary schools in America were inferior to the best ones abroad; as secretary of the Massachusetts State Board of Education he campaigned for more, better, and public schools; and he was the principal founder of the first institution for the professional training of teachers. Mann's ideas were sensible, and eventually they were widely adopted. Tens of millions of American children were better taught as the result of Mann's preaching. It ought not to be held against him that his disciples afterward severely injured American high schools and colleges by training teachers skilled in classroom technique but otherwise ignorant.

Horace Mann desired to send children to good schools; Margaret Fuller wished to get their mothers out of the bedroom, the nursery, and the kitchen—and out of the house. She and other feminists protested bitterly against a society in which women were denied equality with men in education, law, politics, and economic opportunity. Able and learned, Miss Fuller would not concede that she was an inferior copy of a male. The feminists had grievances enough. American men then desired wives who would be saints and slaveys. They did not expect to secure love goddesses for partners, but they firmly believed that the female possessed intuition and that the male had reasoning power. Accordingly, women should be shielded against the sordid, should not be burdened with public affairs beyond their ken, and should devote their talents to the attainment of religious and domestic bliss. Women could not vote; colleges were closed to them; and they were legally subject to the will of father and husband. The clamor of the feminists for their rights had little immediate effect. Most men, and most women, continued to believe that the place of the female was principally in the home under the tender care and guidance of a male. The superior males would have smirked had they known that Miss Fuller at the age of thirty-eight bore a son and then married his father in Italy. Nevertheless, sexual barriers began slowly to weaken. Truly important was the decision of Oberlin College, founded in 1833, to admit young ladies together with young men. And Miss Dorothea Lynde Dix offered, without fanfare, splendid evidence of feminine ability. Beginning her career as a teacher, she carried on after 1838 a great campaign to secure better treatment for the insane, who were usually imprisoned, often in shackles, as if they were criminals. A Woman's Rights Convention held at Seneca Falls, New York, in 1848 aroused some masculine amusement; the hospitals then springing up in several states at the behest of Dorothea Dix were sufficient testimony of the importance of contributions freed females could make.

So many evils did the reformers find, so many societies did they create to strike at those evils, so interwoven were the memberships of those societies, that the "do-gooders" formed a "benevolent empire." They founded an Anti-Tobaccco Society, the Anti-Vivisection Society, and the American Society for Promoting Observance of the Seventh Commandment. They established other societies to guard the morals of sailors in port, to work for peace, and to help "fallen women." Some reformers fancied that females would gain in health and comfort by exchanging their tight corsets and long dresses for the "Bloomer" costumes, which included a flowing jacket and Turkish pantaloons. Others urged that both sexes would improve their health by abandoning their clothing, that it was unwise to try to hide anything from man or God. Some advocated celibacy; others liked "free love."

The most venturesome, the most discontented, the most idealistic, and the most impractical improvers sought to escape from a sorry world, to provide a model for its renovation, by forming communist communities. Such utopias had earlier been formed in America by exotic Christian sects, including the Shakers and the Rappites. Shaker and Rappite communities persisted for decades, even though their members were pledged to celibacy. Other tiny Christian commonwealths failed to flourish because they permitted polygamy. The utopias founded by the more sophisticated and less Christian reformers, alas, did not long endure. The inspiration for them came from Europe, especially from Robert Owen, Etienne Cabet, and Charles Fourier. All three men were idealists who believed that the competitive society of their time grossly injured humanity, that it was beyond repair, that it must be replaced by a noncompetitive socialist society. Toward achieving that end they proposed "pilot" communities. Owen, a rich industrialist, practiced what he preached. He created an ideal "company" village at New Lanark in Scotland, then tried to establish a true utopia at New Harmony, Indiana, after 1825. He ultimately failed, in part because he was hostile to Christianity and held an unorthodox view of marriage, in part because his colony became a Mecca to perverse and contentious seekers of social perfection. However, before the New Harmony experiment collapsed, it inspired the foundation of no fewer than ten other small and short-lived communities.

Cabet, who absorbed some of his notions from the Owenites, was responsible for several "villages of holiness" in the Mississippi Valley and for one in California. They died quickly. Much more successful was John Humphrey Noyes, a Yankee who was "converted" after graduating from Dartmouth College. With a few New England farmers and mechanics he developed a utopia at Putney, Vermont, in 1842, moving it five years later to Oneida, New York. His Oneida Community prospered for several decades, even continuing after 1880 in Canada. The Oneida people not only pooled their property, but also wives and husbands, in order to produce a better breed of mankind. Noyes preached that monogamy was mean and exclusive; that worthy men and women desiring each other should not be kept apart; that the best of men and women should be encouraged to procreate without respect for marriage laws. The Oneida residents held no religious services; Noyes was their high priest.

Most important of the utopians were the followers of Fourier, who called themselves "Associationists." Among them were Horace Greeley of the *New York Tribune*, Charles A. Dana, George Ripley, and other distinguished men and women. They began about three dozen "phalansteries," as Fourier called his utopias, between 1840 and 1850. The most interesting of these was Brook Farm, established near Boston in 1841 by some twenty intellectuals under the leadership of Ripley, a Harvard graduate, clergyman, and Transcendentalist. For a time it ran quite smoothly, partly because the Fourier people were not disturbed by domestic or clerical tyranny. Nathaniel Hawthorne went to Brook Farm in the hope that he would be able to write well there. Its first members were well educated and homogeneous. They shared physical tasks with some cheerfulness, although Ripley discovered that no one was eager to deal with manure, and Hawthorne that physical toil and literary composition were not easy to combine. They ran an excellent school which brought in funds. However, they were joined by Associationist cranks, who brought dissension along with their few belongings. When the main building of the phalanstery burned in 1846, the colonists dispersed. Were the utopian communities all in vain? Some intelligent and useful citizens sprang from the illegal unions of the Oneida colony. Some of the intellectuals who sojourned in the precincts of that and other similar communities learned that it is not easy to create a new society, that it is no small task to maintain any sort of decent order. Some concluded that it was more prudent to try to patch existing fabric than to attempt to find and cut new cloth.

Seeking to perfect, at least to improve, mankind, the reforming intellectuals could not ignore slavery. Indeed, the Southern institution provided an almost ideal abuse to assail—for perfectionists who were Yankee—of either New England birth or ancestry. On January 1, 1831, William Lloyd Garrison, calling for "immediate, not gradual emancipation," published the first issue of the *Liberator* in Boston and opened a determined and almost savage campaign against slavery and slaveholders. Shortly afterward Theodore Dwight Weld began a crusade against Negro servitude in the Old Northwest. He sought "immediate emancipation, gradually accomplished." Garrison and Weld quickly won converts. They and their followers and their allies, including the merchants Arthur and Lewis Tappan of New York City and the plantation owner James G. Birney of Alabama, provoked a great debate over slavery. The abolitionists were not statesmen. They did not offer an acceptable plan for the extinction of Negro servitude; they aroused sectional passions that flamed into a vast armed contest.

It will be recalled that the Founding Fathers, although they condemned slavery, did not forcefully attack it in the South, that it continued there and actually spread across the Mississippi. At the end of the year 1845 slaves were to be found in fifteen states, including the new commonwealths of Texas and Florida. The expansion of Negro bondage in the South does not indicate that the institution escaped censure during the period between the Revolution and the emergence of Garrison as a propagandist extraordinary. On the contrary, efforts to prevent its spread were accompanied by attempts to put an end to it where it already existed. However, very few of the many persons who denounced slavery before 1831 demanded that it be destroyed forthwith in the South. Almost all of them believed that complete emancipation would come very slowly. Many of them desired that the Negroes be free and far away. There were dozens of local societies, chiefly in the Upper South, that opposed slav-

ery before Garrison sounded his trumpet. Cherished by many
foes of slavery, including whites who were not remarkably fond
of Negroes, were plans to free the slaves and to send them to the
island of Haiti or to their ancestral Africa. Enemies of the institution founded the American Colonization Society in 1817. Presidents Madison and Monroe joined it, as did John Marshall and
Henry Clay; and Congress gave it $100,000. A branch of it was
founded in every state except South Carolina. The society,
active for about twenty-five years, collected sufficient funds to
buy and export to Africa several thousand slaves. It played a
large part in the making of the Negro republic of Liberia; the
name of the capital of that country, Monrovia, serves as a re-
minder that an American President gave exportation his blessing.
Another Negro colony in Africa was established by the Mississippi Colonization Society.

Even defenders of slavery could support a scheme that combined Negro freedom with Negro exodus. But most of the
blacks were not eager to go to Haiti or to Africa; free Negroes
preferred to stay in their own country; and the colonizationists
could not get enough money to buy liberty and transport for
Negroes in large numbers. It is clear enough that the most pleasing way to put an end to slavery, so far as the Southerners were
concerned, was to pay the owners for their Negroes and to send
the blacks beyond the sea. Deportation would prevent struggles
between whites and free Negroes in the future. However, neither Northerners nor Southerners were willing to make the necessary, immediate, and vast financial sacrifice required. Quite
conceivably, the Southerners would have consented to compensated emancipation without exportation. In 1833, Parliament,
supplying £20 million to pay the owners, liberated the slaves in
the British West Indies. Had the Americans followed the example of the British at that time, they would have been forced
to pay something like $300 million, then an immense sum, to the
slaveholders. Even so, had they known how much it would later
cost them in treasure and blood to destroy Negro bondage, they
would gladly have burdened themselves with taxes to get the
money. Few men foresaw in 1833, not many foresaw in 1858,
that an extraordinary effort was necessary to prevent civil war.
Garrison, Weld, and other abolitionists made slavery a burning

question in the United States, but they did not proclaim that Northerners must tax themselves as well as Southerners in order to buy the slaves from their owners and to blot out a national evil.

Sober, pious, nearsighted, physically unimpressive, Garrison did not look like a leader of men or women. However, reared in poverty, he was utterly determined to make himself important, and he did. Trained to be a printer, he became an unorthodox publisher. Devoting himself to this good cause and that, he quickly achieved fame when he opened a vehement attack upon slavery in his *Liberator*. In its first issue he condemned the "pernicious doctrine of gradual abolition" and demanded that the Negro slaves be freed immediately. He said nothing about compensating their owners. He declared, "I am in earnest—I will not equivocate—I will not excuse—I will not retreat a single inch—and I will be heard!" In his second number he opened a campaign against the American Colonization Society. The slaves must be relieved of their chains instantly; there was no need to be concerned about their owners; the Negroes must not be sent into exile. Garrison's first supporters were free blacks who had no desire whatever to go to Africa, but he soon became the acknowledged chief of a band of white New Englanders who gave themselves enthusiastically to his cause. Most of his fellow Yankees believed that he was mad. In fact, he was a passionate propagandist, fundamentally more determined to assert himself than to help the slaves. He described the federal Constitution, which did not permit national abolition, at least not without compensation to owners, as a "covenant with hell." He proclaimed slavery to be "a damning crime," and he described the owners of Negroes as "the meanest of thieves" and "the worst of grabbers." He would not admit that they were "within the pale of Christianity, of Republicanism, of humanity." He aroused bitter resentment among Southerners. But did he care for the slaves? After 1835 he urged the Northerners to cleanse their skirts by seceding from the Union. How could they help Negroes in bondage in a foreign country? Some of his followers were even more unbalanced than Garrison. A Quakeress introduced a resolution at a meeting of the New England Anti-Slavery Society in 1842 which proclaimed that the American churches "are combinations of thieves, robbers, adulterers, pirates, and murderers, and as such form the bulwarks of American slavery."

Theodore Dwight Weld stands out among the abolitionists who carried on their labors west of the Hudson River. He and they were somewhat more practical than Garrison and his New England cohorts. A New Yorker converted by the Reverend Charles Grandison Finney, Weld became a vigorous Christian, a professional reformer. At the Lane Theological Seminary in Cincinnati in 1832 he persuaded many of his fellow students, after much soul-searching and debate, that slavery was sinful, that action against it could not wait. Ordered by the president of the seminary, the Reverend Lyman Beecher, to put an end to their extracurricular discussions and to confine themselves to theology, Weld and a body of his converts left Cincinnati and became students at the newly founded Oberlin College in 1833. During the following decade, Weld, humorless, modest, and self-effacing, enlisted and trained dozens of preachers and teachers as abolitionist missionaries. He and his disciples won adherents in the small towns and villages north of the Ohio River. Their demand for "immediate emancipation, gradually accomplished" set them apart from the Garrisonians, but they did not fail to use strong language against slavery and slaveholders. They, too, described slavery as sinful, the slave owner as a sinner. They asserted that Negro bondage violated both the will of God and the Declaration of Independence. It injured both master and man. In 1838, Weld published *Slavery As It Is*, a collection of reports, at least some of them only too true, of frightful cruelties inflicted upon slaves. If the Weldians used less invective than the Garrisonians, they were neither judicious nor cautious.

The abolitionists did not labor in vain. The American Anti-Slavery Society, founded in 1833, had hundreds of chapters and thousands of members five years later, all of them Northerners. To be sure, they remained a small minority in the Northern states. To most Northerners they and their doctrines were fantastic and fanatic. They were often pushed about by mobs, for they were willing to be martyrs. Some of their printing presses were destroyed; and one of their editors, Elijah Lovejoy, who harbored the curious theory that the Roman Catholic Church was responsible for slavery, was murdered by a crowd in Alton, Illinois, in 1837. When the abolitionists went into politics— Garrison would engage in nothing so practical—they won few offices. They founded the Liberty party, and they put forward James G. Birney for the Presidency in 1840 and again in 1844. Birney, who had been forced to leave the South because of his open hostility to slavery, garnered only a few thousand votes. However, the abolitionists forced the Northerners to think about slavery; they gave strength to the many Northern politicians who had long insisted that Negro servitude should not be permitted to spread. They convinced tens of thousands of Northerners that the Southern blacks must ultimately be freed. A few abolitionists made their way as Whigs or Democrats into the halls of Congress, where they compelled discussion about every phase of slavery.

Fostering and fortifying Northern sentiment against the "peculiar institution," the abolitionists also goaded Southerners to defend it. They could not safely hold meetings in the South, and they did not. But they could send their propaganda southward through the mails, and they did. They also bombarded Congress with petitions demanding that this or that step be taken against slavery. Before Garrison began to thunder in his *Liberator*, there were few in the South who extolled the virtues of slavery. There were many who looked upon it as a "necessary evil," not so many willing to sacrifice to put an end to it. The unchristian reproaches heaped upon them by the "holier-than-thou" reformers of the North, beginning in the very era of Nat Turner's rebellion, provoked rage beyond the Mason-Dixon Line. Did the Yankee fanatics, withholding from the Southerners the right hand of fellowship, intend to place weapons in the hands of the blacks? Were many in the North enemies of the South? It became dangerous for a Southerner publicly to condemn slavery. Moreover, Southern extremists took the field against Northern zealots. Professor Thomas R. Dew of the College of William and Mary, James Henry Hammond of South Carolina, and others came forward to proclaim that slavery was a "positive good," and they gained a following. They found warrant for slavery in the Holy Scriptures, for it was mentioned therein without condemnation, along with witchcraft, polygamy, incest, and slaughter of the enemies of the Lord. And was it not sanctioned, even protected, by the federal Constitution? They contended that the Negro was biologically inferior to the white man, that he was fitted for, even happy in, subjection. They would have it that slave families enjoyed security from the cradle to the grave, that their lot was superior to that of the families of Northern laborers. Slavery was beneficent for master and man, and for mistress and maid. They even urged that the slave South was more prosperous than the free North, and that slavery and its benefits ought to be spread. Such extremists did not become a majority among the Southerners. With those who saw the bondage of the blacks as a "necessary evil," they ardently condemned Northern attempts to shatter Southern society.

The bonds between North and South began to break. Southern postmasters declined to deliver abolitionist newspapers and pamphlets and destroyed them. Angry Southerners asserted that those who wrote and circulated the propaganda also ought to be extinguished. Its authors declared that they had been deprived of their legal right to use the mails. The House of Representatives, flooded with abolitionist petitions, decided that they should not be read, that they should be "tabled." The reformers, pointing out that their right of petition had been at least technically denied, clamored lengthily until the House undertook to receive —though not to read—the papers. The abolitionists added economic injury to verbal attack by helping hundreds of Negroes to flee from slavery by "Underground Railroads" to Canada, where they were free. Questions about slavery convulsed the Methodist and Baptist churches, which divided into Northern and Southern units in 1845. The Presbyterians were also torn asunder, although their national assembly continued to meet until 1861. Even before 1840, because of the clash over slavery, there was much talk of Southern secession in Washington. It was offensive to most Southerners and to nearly all Northerners. In time, the majority of Southerners would not only favor but attempt secession.

CHAPTER 16

To the Pacific

✤❋✤

PEERING INTO THE WOMB of time, Jefferson the philosopher President estimated that America, after the Louisiana Purchase, had space and riches enough for her people for long generations to come. And, indeed, the lands east of the "Stony Mountains" were ample for tens of millions of people, even for tens of millions who demanded more living room than Europeans. However, Jefferson's countrymen had not lost their lust for soil, for wealth, for adventure, for freedom from the restraints of society; and the expansion of the republic into the Floridas did not spoil their appetites. Beyond Louisiana, between it and the Pacific Ocean, were wide regions, vast deserts, arid tablelands, and forbidding peaks, but also fertile and thinly peopled places. There were immense metallic treasures in the valleys of the streams that flowed down from the Rockies and the mountains beyond. The Americans poured on westward to the shores of the Pacific, not only to better their personal lot, but also to advance their flag and to forestall other peoples. Fifty years after the purchase of Louisiana they were solidly entrenched on the beaches of Puget Sound, on the lower Rio Grande, and on the northern edges of the deserts of northwestern Mexico. So soon America spread "from sea to shining sea." The Pacific Northwest, part of the Oregon Country, became definitely American territory after much squabbling with England. San Antonio, Santa Fe, and San Diego did not become American without a war against Mexico.

The advance of the Americans to the Pacific was swift, to a

degree because they disdained during several decades to settle in that part of the Louisiana Territory between the Missouri River and the Rockies. Making their way westward, they saw the rich grasslands of eastern Kansas and eastern Nebraska only as so much space that they must traverse, and they looked upon the treeless semi-arid Great Plains as fit for only the buffaloes and the Indians, such as the Sioux, the Pawnee, the Cheyenne, and the Arapaho, who killed those creatures for food, clothing, and shelter. To the westward-moving adventurers and settlers, for several decades, the plains and the Indians who lived upon them were primarily obstacles on the paths to California and the Oregon Country.

If the prairies and plains of the western part of the Missouri Valley long remained a barrier rather than a lure, it was otherwise to the south, for the fertile lowlands of eastern Texas began to entice American pioneers immediately after the War of 1812. Texas was, despite a rather slender American claim to it as part of the Louisiana Purchase, Spanish soil until 1821. Then, when Mexico threw off the Spanish yoke, it became, with all the lands west and south of the Louisiana Territory and the Oregon Country, an outlying part of that new nation. Thrusting across the Sabine River, the Americans could not have been driven back by a feeble Spain; neither could they be restrained by a Mexico that was weak and riven by internal discord. There were in Texas when the Americans entered it about 4,000 Spanish-speaking people, mostly ranchers, together with Comanches and other unsubdued Indians. The rancheros were too few to stand against the Americans, and they could not easily get help from their fellow countrymen. The center of power in Mexico was Mexico City, many hundreds of miles south of the Rio Grande, connected with Texas only by bad roads through rough terrain. In a sense, Texas was a vacuum that sucked in the Americans. They were moving across the Sabine as early as 1815.

Spanish and Mexican governors knew that the Americans would come. Accordingly, like the Roman emperors, they decided to "tame the Goths"—that is, to invite some Americans to come to Texas, to domesticate them, and to convert them into defenders of Texas against their brethren. That policy saved neither Rome nor Texas from the barbarians. When Moses

Austin, a Connecticut Yankee who had settled in Missouri when it was Spanish, asked permission, in 1820, to found a colony of 300 "Goths" in Texas, its governing council quickly consented. Moses Austin died soon afterward, but his son Stephen pursued his scheme. Stephen Austin, a scholar, a performer upon the flute, and an introvert, was also intelligent, generous-minded, and honest. He won the respect and affection of both Latins and rough American frontiersmen, and he was almost astonishingly

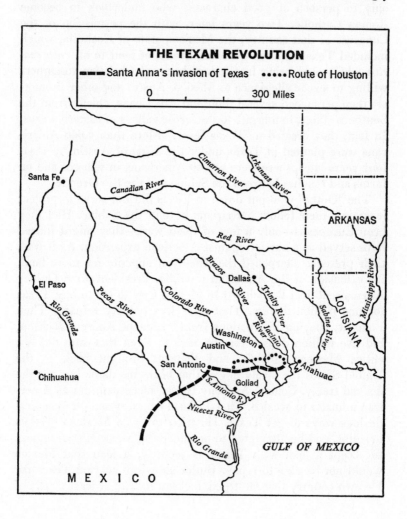

THE TEXAN REVOLUTION

━ ━ ━ Santa Anna's invasion of Texas ••••• Route of Houston

0   300 Miles

successful. In the winter of 1821 he planted 150 settlers from
New Orleans in the valley of the Brazos River. Less than two
years later his "Old Three Hundred" families were firmly established in the town of Austin and its vicinity. Meanwhile, amidst
turbulence, the Spanish flag was lowered in Mexico City, and
Austin had to go there to get final endorsement for his colony.
He secured it from the national government of Mexico in April
1823. He promised to sell lands that he received from Mexico
only to persons of good character who undertook to become
Roman Catholic. Two years later, with the permission of the
Congress of that country, the Mexican state of Coahuila, which
included Texas, offered generous grants of land to all *empresarios* who would bring into it well-behaved Christian foreigners
willing to swear allegiance to Mexico. Austin and other promot-
ers then persuaded several thousand Americans, chiefly from the
Southern states, to migrate to the fertile valleys of eastern Texas.
In fact, they created a "Texas fever." More than 5,600 Americans were planted in Texas under the aegis of Austin by 1831;
four years later, there were 30,000 Americans in villages and on
farms and ranches between the Sabine and the Rio Grande.

The "Goths" who put down in Texas did not serve to protect
it against their fellow barbarians beyond the Sabine. Had they
been Europeans—only a few of them were—they might indeed
have served as a barrier against American expansion. As it was,
their presence sharpened the American appetite for more land,
for extension of the American republic. President John Quincy
Adams sent Joel R. Poinsett to Mexico City to try to buy Texas
for one million dollars. That offer was politely refused. Then
Poinsett, obeying instructions from President Andrew Jackson,
bid five million dollars for the region. Even that sum did not
entice Mexican officials, and Poinsett brought back to the
United States the lovely flower that bears his name but not the
desired treaty. Colonel Anthony Butler succeeded him as American minister to Mexico. That Jackson emissary sought in several
devious ways to get Texas. He tried to bribe Mexican officials
to sell it, and he attempted to persuade the Mexican government
to accept a loan with Texas as security, a loan that Mexico
would not be able to repay. Butler so avidly coveted Texas for
his own country that he urged Jackson to take at least a part of

it by force. His devious maneuvers failed; they aroused suspicion and fear in the Mexican capital. It became only too clear to Mexican politicians that there were those in the United States who lusted for possession of Texas and that Mexican ownership of it was threatened.

A clash between the Anglo-Saxon Texans and the Mexicans could not be avoided. It was exacerbated by the clamor in American newspapers for the annexation of Texas and by the intrigues of Colonel Butler. Stephen Austin and many other settlers sincerely sought to live in peace under the Mexican flag. However, later comers to Texas were often rough frontiersmen who despised Mexico and the Mexicans and who refused to give loyalty to the Mexican regime. Even the settlers who earnestly tried to adjust themselves to Mexican ways and policies failed. There was a cultural gulf between the Americans and the Mexicans that could not easily be bridged. After 1830, both the national government of Mexico and that of Coahuila tardily, feebly, and convulsively undertook to protect Texas and to bring its inhabitants to heel. The Mexicans denied to the Americans more than nominal votes in the legislature of Coahuila. Torn by internal strife, they alternately asserted their authority and retreated in the face of American resistance. They sent garrisons to the coast of Texas, withdrew them, then sent them again. They closed the door to immigrants, then opened it. They angered the Americans—mostly Southerners who desired to import Negro slaves into Texas—by declaring slavery illegal; then they permitted at least temporary subjection of Negroes as servants. The American settlers believed that the creation of a state of Texas within the Mexican republic would put an end to many difficulties. After an armed clash between some settlers and Mexican troops at Anahuac in 1832, Stephen Austin went to Mexico City to urge the formation of such a state. His mission was a failure, and he spent some months in prison at the Mexican capital. Austin had hoped that General Antonio López de Santa Anna, who had assumed power as a presidential dictator, would seek to conciliate the Texans. Instead, Santa Anna, who fancied that he was a Mexican Napoleon, resolved to use force to reduce the Texans to obedience.

Early in 1835, Santa Anna sent small detachments of troops **to** the Texan seacoast and prepared to send larger forces. The news stimulated to action William B. Travis and other hotheaded settlers who deeply resented the combination of anarchy and tyranny imposed upon them by Mexico and who desired nothing less than the destruction of all Mexican authority. Forty of them, on the last day of June, bloodlessly captured a Mexican garrison at Anahuac. More and more of the Americans, including Austin, decided that they must fight for independence. In the following autumn 500 American settlers besieged and captured a Mexican garrison at San Antonio. Most of the Americans were not yet ready to declare their independence. A "Consultation" composed of delegates from the several American communities met at Austin in November and urged an accommodation. But it also created a provisional government and named Sam Houston, an immigrant from Tennessee, commander in chief of an army for defense. In March 1836, another "Consultation" at the village of Washington took the last step. Santa Anna was marching northward at the head of an army and uttering dire menaces. The delegates proclaimed the independent republic of Texas. They could hardly do less than they did, for the Texans were already engaged in a grim war for survival. At San Antonio fewer than 200 of them under Travis were besieged in the Alamo, an abandoned mission, by Santa Anna and 4,000 Mexican troops. The Texans there, including the fabled frontiersmen Davy Crockett and Jim Bowie, resisted desperately, beating off assault after assault. At last, on March 6, four days after the Texan declaration of independence, the Alamo fell, its 187 defenders dying to the last man. They had killed more than 1,500 of their enemies. Three weeks later a body of 350 Texans, after surrendering to another Mexican army, was slaughtered in cold blood at Goliad. It was only too apparent that the Texans could lose little by fighting. They rallied for a decisive struggle.

After the massacre at Goliad the Texans frantically begged Sam Houston to give battle. To do it immediately was to invite defeat, since he could not hope to stand against the armies of Santa Anna with the few hundred undisciplined riflemen he had under his command. He retreated to the east, gathering and drilling men as he went. Dozens of Americans crossed the Sabine to join him. Meanwhile, a pursuing Mexican army under Santa

Anna dwindled as he left garrisons behind him. At last, at San Jacinto on April 21, Houston turned upon his enemies. He chose terrain from which the defeated army could not easily escape. With 783 men he attacked 1,200 under Santa Anna, just as the Mexicans were preparing for their usual siesta. The Texans shouted "Remember the Alamo!" as they charged. They destroyed the Mexican army in fifteen minutes, killing 630 of their enemies and capturing nearly all of the remainder, including its commander, whom they found hiding under a bush. The battle assured Texan independence. Santa Anna acknowledged it in return for his freedom. The Mexican Congress would not so quickly admit that Texas had been lost. However, all the Mexican troops left in Texas after San Jacinto retreated southward, and their generals did not immediately try to retrieve that disaster. Six years later Mexico resumed the struggle, but it was then much too late to destroy the new republic.

Almost to a man, the Texans, in the first flush of freedom, desired to raise the American flag above their settlements. They chose Houston as their first President, instructing him to seek union with the United States. However, they had to wait for nine years. Andrew Jackson would gladly have annexed Texas, but he could do no more than to extend official recognition to the new republic. The addition of Texas would have provoked a war with Mexico. Moreover, northern Whigs, suspecting that Jackson had encouraged, even instigated, the Texan rebellion, insisted that Texas must not immorally become American soil. The abolitionists proclaimed that annexation would be a great and wicked victory for Southern conspirators attempting to spread slavery. The outcry against adding Texas was so widespread and so violent that both Jackson and Martin Van Buren found it prudent to take no action toward that end. But Texas could not, and did not, long remain independent.

The republic of Texas flourished during its brief and troubled existence. Mirabeau Buonaparte Lamar, who succeeded Houston as President in 1838, was too adventurous. Since the United States did not want Texas, he undertook to make of it a nation of imperial proportions. He crushed hostile Indians who threatened its settlements. He secured official recognition from France and England, and he tried to extend the sway of Texas to the

Pacific. Far to the west of Austin and San Antonio was Santa Fe, the capital of New Mexico, which contained about 40,000 inhabitants and some rich mines. Santa Fe was familiar to Texans, for the Americans had opened a commerce with that city by means of the Santa Fe Trail across the Great Plains as early as the 1820s. In 1841, Lamar, informed that New Mexico was torn by intestine quarrels, sent a trading expedition accompanied by a few soldiers to do what might be done at Santa Fe. A Mexican general captured the traders and the troops and sent them upon a "death march" to Mexico City. Moreover, taking the offensive, Mexican troops successfully attacked San Antonio in 1842 and again in 1843. Forced to return the Presidency to Sam Houston, Lamar bequeathed a large public debt to his successor. Houston saw in union with the United States the solution to the basic troubles of the Texans, and he again asked for it. His request was eagerly heard in Washington and was at length approved. The Texas which he led into the United States in 1845 was not the Texas of 1836. It had grown amazingly, for it gave 640 acres of land to every new settler and twice as much to every newcomer who was the head of a family. During the summer of 1837 some 6,000 persons crossed over the Sabine at one ferry. *Empresarios* brought other thousands of settlers from France and Germany. Before the republic vanished, it contained a vigorous and rapidly growing population, a stable society of farmers, widespreading fields of cotton and corn, herds of cattle, schools, newspaper, Methodist and Baptist churches, and Negro slaves. Texas and the Texans were already assuming large dimensions.

Vast as it was, Texas was not the only part of Mexico that lured Americans westward. After the year 1840 far distant California began insistently to beckon to them. They learned about an Eden beside the Pacific, an almost authentic one. California, with its indulgent climate, its fruitful lands, and its enchanting scenery, was tenanted, with its Indians, by fewer than 5,000 Mexicans. Its capital, Monterey, was a charming sleepy village. So was San Francisco. Los Angeles, the largest of the Mexican settlements, was no more than a small town. Most of the Mexicans, together with Christianized and virtually enslaved Indians, lived easily and lazily upon the ranches that studded the seacoast.

A few hundred Mexican troops idly garrisoned that sunny seaside.

California was all the more tempting to Americans because its residents resisted domination from Mexico City. In 1844, in fact, they forced the withdrawal of Mexico's garrison soldiers. By that time scores of Americans had planted themselves in California, and many more were either making their way toward it or preparing to depart for that golden clime. The first intruders from the United States were agents who bought hides and tallow in California harbors for transport around Cape Horn. They came by sea. Soon hardy pioneers came overland, pushing their way westward from Missouri along the Oregon Trail, crossing mountains, deserts, and more mountains into central California. The Americans entered California to improve their personal fortunes, but they also intended to be "benefactors of their race—the founders of a new, enlightened, and powerful state." Nor were they the only Americans who yearned to possess California. There were others in Washington. Daniel Webster, Secretary of State after 1841, twice attempted to purchase San Francisco and its magnificent harbor. In 1842, Commodore Thomas ap Catesby Jones, commanding an American squadron in the Pacific, made an informative mistake. Told that war had broken out between America and Mexico, he seized Monterey. He withdrew in embarrassment when he learned that there was no war.

By 1844 the American republic was ready to embrace, not only Texas, New Mexico, and California, but the Oregon Country, the whole or the bulk of it. The condominium established in that region in 1818 could not endure. Was it to be English, American, or divided? That question could not easily be answered on the basis of prior discovery or settlement. With Presbyterian and Methodist missionaries to the Indians of the Columbia River Valley leading the way, the Americans undertook to win the dispute by massive colonization. The Reverend Jason Lee established himself on the banks of the Willamette River in 1834. He saved very few Indian souls, but he was soon joined by other American missionaries, hunters, and farmers who traversed the long and dangerous Oregon Trail from Missouri. By 1840 there were 500 Americans in the valley of the Willamette, and "Oregon fever" was rising in the United States. The forward thrust of the Americans was temporarily checked at the Columbia River only by the ingenuity of Dr. John McLoughlin of the Hudson's Bay Company. The company for which he toiled sought furs and commerce; he could not persuade settlers to come from eastern Canada, but he managed to convince the Americans that they would be more comfortable on the southern side of the Columbia. He hoped, and so did ministers in the English Cabinet, that all of the Oregon Country north of the Columbia could be gained for England.

The Oregon Country posed only one of several issues that set England and America against each other in the 1830s and early 1840s. There were still Englishmen who saw themselves as the exclusive heirs of the ancient Israelites in religion, the Spartans in fortitude, the Athenians in letters, and the Romans in empire. There were Americans who assumed that they were the specially chosen of God, the most virile of peoples, the sole possessors of liberty, and the only champions of the world's oppressed. A warm dispute about the boundary between Maine and Canada, over territory that was vital to neither country, was settled by the Webster-Ashburton Treaty of 1842. However, British politicians jealous of American expansion did what they could, without recourse to extreme measures, to keep Texas and California out of American hands, and they rejected American offers to divide the Oregon Country at the forty-ninth parallel.

As the Presidential election of 1844 approached, America was not far from armed conflict with both England and Mexico. Nevertheless, the Americans saw their sun through the war clouds. Many of them were suddenly converted to the doctrine of "manifest destiny." Not so named until the following year, "manifest destiny" referred to the obvious intent of the Deity for America to carry the blessings of liberty into Texas, New Mexico, California, and the Oregon Country. The abolitionists did not want Texas and clamored against the spread of slavery. Henry Clay, who once again sought the Presidency as the Whig candidate, cautiously indicated that a war with Mexico might be too high a price to pay for Texas. But the Democrats demanded the "re-occupation of Oregon and the re-annexation of Texas," and they put forward against Clay an able politician and disciple of Andrew Jackson, James K. Polk of Tennessee, who was determined that the Lord's will be done. Polk was victorious, and sentiment for expansion continued to rise after his election. As the year 1844 drew to an end, there was an outcry among the Americans for "All of Oregon or None"; and not a few declared their willingness, their eagerness, to fight the English a third time to carry the Stars and Stripes to the borders of Alaska. There was no war with England. Good sense prevailed in that country. An offer came from London to divide the Oregon Country at the forty-ninth parallel, with Vancouver Island going to England. Good sense also carried the day in Washington. Should the United States fight to get the whole Oregon Country? The Americans, agreeing to the bargain proposed by England, would gain nearly all that they had earlier asked; besides, a clash with Mexico loomed. In 1846, Polk saw to it that the necessary treaty was ratified.

American authority stretched across Texas even before it reached Puget Sound. John Tyler, the outgoing President, would not let Polk have the glory of gaining Texas. He was worried because England and France were trying to make it a permanently independent nation. They had persuaded Mexico to recognize it. Before he left office in March 1845, he secured the passage of a joint resolution by Congress authorizing the President to negotiate a treaty whereby the Texan republic would become American soil. A few months later Texas accordingly entered the Union as a slave state.

The Mexican War followed in 1846. Polk did not desire it, but he did not strive arduously and patiently to avoid it. The boundary between Texas and Mexico was uncertain. Polk insisted that Mexico must not only accept as final the union of Texas with the United States but the lower Rio Grande as a boundary. Mexico contended that the Nueces River was the southern limit of Texas. Polk also demanded compensation for property losses suffered by Americans in Mexico because of the frequent political upheavals in that country. He could get no promise from Mexico City that justified American claims would be paid. Determined to secure California, and as much as possible of the region between Texas and California, he sent John Slidell to the Mexican capital to offer as much as $40 million for those territories. The Mexican President refused even to receive Slidell. Polk then sent word to John O. Larkin, the American consul at Monterey, that if the Californians "should desire to unite their destiny with ours, they would be received as brethren, whenever this can be done, without affording Mexico just cause of complaint." Larkin took the hint. In June 1846 the Americans in California rose in revolt and proclaimed the independent republic of California. They were supported by John C. Frémont, formerly a captain in the American army and a romantic adven-

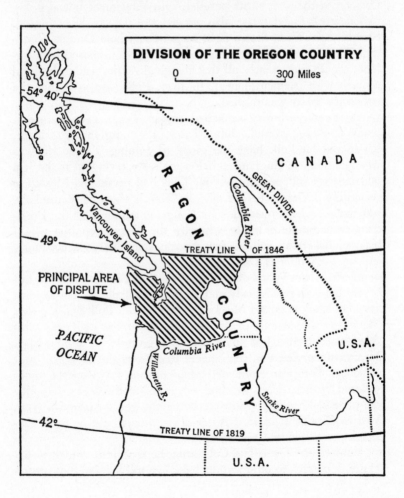

DIVISION OF THE OREGON COUNTRY

0   300 Miles

turer who had marched into California with sixty frontiersmen.
Did Polk arrange to send Frémont to the Pacific coast, or did
that enterprising man independently aspire to be the Sam Houston of California? Certainly Frémont knew that his presence
there would not be utterly distasteful to the President.

If Polk neither directly nor indirectly commissioned Frémont
to take part in the revolt in California, he unquestionably did
order General Zachary Taylor to lead American troops into the
disputed region between the Nueces River and the Rio Grande.
Indeed, on May 9, 1846, he informed his Cabinet that war with
Mexico was inevitable. Mexico had insultingly refused to redress
grievances. Ought not the United States to issue a declaration of
war? The Cabinet, except for one member, agreed in principle
that the President should send a message to Congress asking it
to proclaim the beginning of hostilities. Then came news that
Mexican soldiers had crossed the Rio Grande, had attacked an
American detachment, and had killed some American troops.
Polk then swiftly urged Congress to act. Mentioning earlier
grievances, he said, "After repeated menaces, Mexico has passed
the boundary of the United States, has invaded our territory and
shed American blood on the American soil." There could be no
hesitation. The Congress declared that Mexico had begun an
offensive war against the United States. Later, while it was in
progress, Abraham Lincoln several times asked a most embarrassing question in the House of Representatives. Just where was
the spot of American territory where American blood had been
spilled?

Strange as it may seem, the masters of Mexico deliberately
ordered the shooting. They were moved by pride and pique,
but they believed, unbelievably, that they would be victorious.
They conceived that their army, twice as large as the American
one, could march far to the north, that it would be helped by a
revolt of American slaves, and that it would be able to dictate a
glorious peace. The Mexican troops were brave enough, but
they could not achieve so much. With distance and the deserts
and mountains of their native country as their allies, they could
do no more than make a desperate defense.

Volunteers flocked to the American colors in thousands, especially from the Southern states, and American forces soon took

the offensive. An Army of the West under General Stephen Kearny marched across the southern Great Plains and captured Santa Fe without a struggle. Later, the New Mexicans took up arms but were crushed in battle by Colonel Sterling Price. Meanwhile, Kearny, with a small detachment, hurried on to California. There he encountered defeat by the Mexicans. However, troops put ashore near Los Angeles by the American navy, with a little help from John C. Frémont and the Americans who had earlier entered California, swiftly put an end to Mexican resistance. By February 1847 both New Mexico and California were firmly in American hands. By that time General Zachary

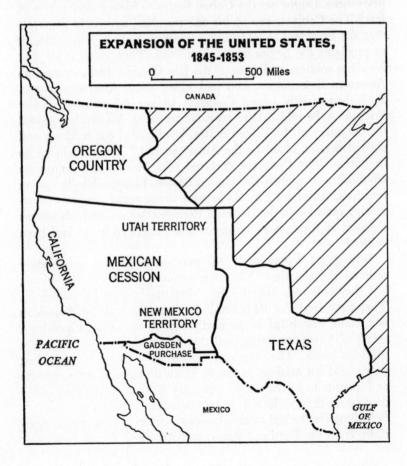

EXPANSION OF THE UNITED STATES, 1845-1853

0 |__|__|__|__|__| 500 Miles

CANADA

OREGON COUNTRY

UTAH TERRITORY

CALIFORNIA

MEXICAN CESSION

NEW MEXICO TERRITORY

PACIFIC OCEAN

GADSDEN PURCHASE

TEXAS

MEXICO

GULF OF MEXICO

Taylor, "Old Rough and Ready," was encamped victoriously at Monterrey in the northern part of Mexico. Driving southward across the Rio Grande, he had decisively defeated Mexican forces opposing him at Palo Alto, Resaca do la Palma, and Monterrey. At Saltillo, Taylor learned that Santa Anna was advancing against him with a large Mexican army—that general had recently returned from exile to power in Mexico. Taylor, with 4,800 men, mostly untrained volunteers, marched to Buena Vista and calmly awaited the onslaught of Santa Anna. In a battle that lasted for two days Taylor inflicted such heavy casualties upon his enemies that Santa Anna's army retreated and collapsed.

A week after Buena Vista, Colonel Alexander Doniphan, leading southward from Santa Fe a contingent of Missouri Mounted Volunteers, captured Chihuahua. The long road southward to Mexico City was then open to Taylor, but he was not allowed to take it. It had already been decided in Washington to pursue a different strategy, to send an army to Vera Cruz and to take the Mexican capital by the shorter land route from the east. It had also been settled in Washington that General Winfield Scott, "Old Fuss and Feathers," abler than Taylor and somewhat more suitable politically, was to lead that army. Scott performed magnificently, and he was assisted by a galaxy of fine young officers who afterward became famous in the Civil War. With 10,000 men he captured Vera Cruz in March, routed a larger Mexican force under Santa Anna at the mountain pass of Cerro Gordo in April, and reached Puebla in May. There Scott rested and gained reinforcements. In August he resumed his advance westward through the mountains, driving larger Mexican forces before him in battle after battle. Badly led and ill-equipped, the Mexican troops fought courageously and suffered extremely heavy losses. At last, during the night of September 13, Scott entered Mexico City with 6,000 men. It became evident soon afterward even to Santa Anna that further resistance was useless. He fled abroad. His successor sued for peace.

At the village of Guadalupe Hidalgo near Mexico City in February 1848 the war was formally ended. In a treaty signed at that place the United States agreed to pay $15 million to Mexico and also to satisfy the claims of American citizens against Mexico. That country accepted the lower Rio Grande as her bound-

ary on the northeast and ceded New Mexico and California to
the United States. The treaty added immense tracts, totaling
nearly 1,200,000 square miles, to the American republic, which
thenceforth stretched across the heartland of North America
from the Atlantic to the Pacific. Five years later, for five million
dollars, in the Gadsden Treaty, Mexico sold the southern parts
of the modern American states of New Mexico and Arizona to
her northern neighbor. Thus the republic acquired empires between the Mississippi Valley and the Pacific. The nation's "manifest destiny" had been attained—or did the Deity, as some of
her people believed, intend that America should extend even
farther?

CHAPTER 17

Toward Tragedy

❧

THE WESTWARD ADVANCE OF the republic to the rim of the Pacific did not put an end to all its woes. It supplied new issues about which the North and the South could and did engage in bitter conflict. The very existence of the nation was sorely threatened only two years after the triumphant end of the war against Mexico. Rising passions between South and North were briefly soothed by the Compromise of 1850. During the following decade the swift occupation of the newly won lands proceeded; the railroads spread and flourished, and with them the iron industry and others; and the Old Immigrants continued to enrich America both physically and intellectually. The poet of democracy, Walt Whitman, free-spirited and exuberant, made his appearance. His fame and influence would grow. Eventually Herman Melville would also become known as a truly distinguished man of letters, as a great novelist. Profound and pessimistic, Melville did not appeal to many readers in the America of the 1850s. Early in that decade the spirit of "Young America" was pervasive; the nation was youthful and glorious, and it would be marvelous in maturity. Who can predict the destiny of man, whether it will be dark or bright? Even as Whitman extolled the virtues and beauties of American democracy, North and South drew further and further apart. It became ever more doubtful that the Union would endure. In 1861 the Americans engaged in bloody civil war.

Not every American subscribed to the principle of "manifest destiny." On the contrary, many Northerners, chiefly abolitionists and members of the Whig party, believed that the war with

Mexico was wanton and unholy, that it arose from the conspiracy directed by Southern planter aristocrats to enlarge the realm of slavery. While their brethren fought against the Mexicans, Northerners and Southerners engaged in political contest at Washington that became ever more alarming. Southerners denied, in the main truthfully, that they had plotted to expand the sway of Negro servitude. They vehemently, stubbornly, and successfully strove to prevent the passage of a national law that would have barred slavery from all the lands acquired from Mexico. On the other hand, angry because the Northern states were not enthusiastically helping to stop fleeing blacks and return them to their masters, they clamored for a law requiring federal officers and courts to assist them in regaining their "property." Another exciting and disturbing issue was posed by the discovery of gold in California early in 1848. The Fortyniners, Northerners, Southerners, and foreigners who went to California in the Gold Rush, were not fond of order or delay. The Californians, rapidly increasing in number, swiftly asked that California be admitted to the Union as a state, without slavery. Were their request granted, the free states would gain a majority, probably a permanent one, in the Senate. Northerners had long been more numerous than Southerners in the House of Representatives. Southerners were exceedingly reluctant to accept numerical inferiority in the Senate. Other questions about slavery exacerbated debate. Should Negro bondage, or at least the auctioning of slaves, be forbidden in the District of Columbia? Ought Congress to close the channels of interstate commerce to the domestic slave trade?

The crisis came in the early months of 1850. Ill and soon to die, John C. Calhoun declared that the nation would be destroyed if Northern assaults against slavery did not cease, if the Constitution was not changed so as to give the South power to protect its interests in Washington. Robert Barnwell Rhett of South Carolina, William L. Yancey of Alabama, and other fiery defenders of "Southern rights" urged that the Southern states secede from the Union. On the other side, Whig Senator William Seward of New York proclaimed that "a higher law" than the Constitution permitted and required the confinement of slavery. Moreover, Zachary Taylor, elected to the Presidency as a Whig in 1848 because of his military prowess, insisted that California be admitted as a free state and that he would resort to force to preserve his country. Taylor was a Louisiana slave-holder but a stout nationalist. Was there no way to avoid an ultimate clash? Henry Clay and Daniel Webster, both old, inter-vened. Clay's fondnesses for whisky, cards, and Kentucky had never seriously interfered with his devotion to his country. He prepared an "Omnibus Bill" containing provisions intended to satisfy both the South and the North and to remove questions about slavery from the public scene. Webster, certain to be castigated in Massachusetts for endorsing Clay's measure, put aside his personal welfare and delivered a magnificent speech in behalf of accommodation. Taylor died, and his successor, Mil-lard Fillmore of New York, endorsed Clay's bargain. Northern Democrats led by Senator Stephen Douglas of Illinois came for-ward to help Clay. Dividing the "Omnibus" into several parts, Douglas secured their passage, one by one, into law. Together they formed the Compromise of 1850. Its more important provi-sions put an end to trading in slaves in the national capital; required federal officials to help with the capture and the return of fugitive Negroes to their owners; made California a free state; and created, between Texas and California, two territories, New Mexico and Utah, in which the inhabitants themselves would decide whether or not they would have slavery. It was most unlikely, as Clay and Webster had pointed out, that either of the territories would become a slave state, since neither of them was suited to the growing of tobacco, cotton, or rice.

So frightened by the crisis were cautious men on both sides of the Mason-Dixon Line that they eagerly welcomed the Com-promise and declared that it marked the end of all dispute be-tween North and South. They prevailed temporarily; the nation relaxed; and talk of secession in the South diminished. But Clay, Webster, and Douglas had secured a truce, not an enduring peace. When tension between South and North revived, Clay and Webster were gone, and there were no magnetic voices among the Northern Whigs that called for conciliation. In fact, by 1852 the Whig party, one of the last bonds between North and South, was falling into sectional parts. In the Presidential campaign of that year it was unable to unite behind the military hero Winfield Scott. A minor Democrat, Franklin Pierce of New Hampshire, gained the highest office in the nation. Before he left it, his party was also dissolving.

There is a great unwillingness among men to face the cruel facts of history, to accept harrowing experiences of the past as sure evidences of more to come. The Americans, more sanguine than other peoples and not well informed about the wretched and wicked history of most of their fellow men, turned their eyes away from the deepening division within their country. It is understandable that many of them wishfully believed what both the Whigs and the Democrats told them in 1852, that the Compromise of 1850 had closed the growing rupture. Even so, their leaders should have known better, should have told them that little more than a respite had been gained, that the solution to the troubles between North and South would not be reached without toil and sacrifice.

There were many Americans in the 1850s who preferred to think of external expansion rather than internal dissension. By 1852 a "Young America" movement was under way. Those who joined it adhered to a special version of "manifest destiny" which called for freedom of international trade; freedom for the European peoples gained with the blessing of youthful and vigorous America; and liberty for the Mexicans, even for all the Latin Americans, under the Stars and Stripes. One of the Young Americans was Senator Stephen Douglas, a man rapidly rising to power in the Democratic party. Did he believe that Mexico or Cuba, regions so suitable for plantation slavery, could be annexed without reviving the desperate clash he had done so much to halt in 1850?

America did not actually spread southward during that decade, except for the Gadsden Purchase. That region was secured so that a railroad might be built from New Orleans to San Diego without crossing the Rocky Mountains. By 1855 it was only too clear that many Southerners who urged expansion into Latin America intended that slavery should follow the flag. They sought to annex Cuba, restive under Spanish rule, and to carve as many as five slave states from it. Northern enemies of slavery again charged that the Southern planter aristocracy was engaged in a conspiracy to drag Negro slavery into areas where freedom prevailed. Protests from the North forced Young Americans and old to abandon their schemes to get Cuba. Complaints from the North also at length compelled the withdrawal of the tacit support given from Washington to William Walker, the filibusterer, who sought to establish himself as a dictator in Nicaragua in 1856 and 1857. It was not Walker's chief purpose to carry slavery into that country; but he was helped and joined by Southerners, and he proclaimed slavery to be legal in Nicaragua. He did not become the Sam Houston of that republic—or of Honduras. Invading Honduras in 1860, he was captured and executed. By that time youthful America was swiftly moving toward an ordeal in which there was no place for adolescent arrogance or bombast.

Whatever may be said about the desire of the Young Americans to impose democracy upon other peoples, it will not be denied that the Americans, young and old, possessed ample living space immediately after the war with Mexico. Certainly they were still hungry for farms, ranches, and mines, for wealth of every sort. However, aggressive as they were, they needed about forty years to fill the commodious domains that lay within their boundaries at the mid-century. The discovery of gold in the Sacramento River Valley stimulated a hectic "rush" to California. Perhaps 25,000 men made their way to the diggings in 1849 by sea, and more than 50,000 by land. More discoveries of gold followed, and more thousands lusting for wealth set off for Eldorado. California yielded more than 81,000,000 ounces of the precious metal in the year 1852. Americans went overland to California; they went by sea to Panama, crossed its isthmus, and continued their journey by water; and they sailed around Cape Horn to San Francisco and other ports in California. In San Francisco they met Frenchmen, Hawaiian Islanders, and Australians. Few of the immigrants became rich by mining, but many of them quickly and successfully turned to farming and commerce. Women came, and helped to create a stable society. Oregon flourished with California and became a state. Moreover, the search for gold led prospectors into Nevada and Colorado, where both gold and silver were found in quantity. So began the settlement of the region of the Rocky Mountains. Meanwhile, farmers moved westward across the Missouri River into eastern

Kansas and Nebraska. By 1860 there were stagecoach and mail service between Missouri and California. The Great Plains were not yet settled, and the Indians who roved across them with the buffalo were not yet conquered. The "West"—the "Wild West"—lasted for another generation, but hunters, prospectors, ranchers, farmers, and railroad builders were preparing to tame it.

Occupying more and more of the wide districts they had gained before the mid-century, the Americans also made rapid economic advance during the decade before the Civil War. To the gold that came from their Far West they added the profits of a lucrative commerce with the Far East. An American naval squadron under Commodore Matthew Perry persuaded the Japanese to open some of their harbors to swift clipper ships and other vessels in 1853. Cotton crops were abundant, and the white stuff brought handsome returns in that decade. Exports of grain grew. Most important of all, however, was the development of the iron industry and the railroads. In 1859 the value of the products of industry, nearly $1.9 billion, for the first time exceeded the proceeds from agriculture. Railroad tracks, engines, and cars came from mills and factories in profusion. By 1860 the American railroads had 30,000 miles of trackage, about three-quarters of it east of the Mississippi River and north of the Ohio River. By that time New York City and Chicago, and Baltimore and St. Louis, were connected by rail. The states north of the Mason-Dixon Line were united by bands of iron as well as by bonds of sentiment and commerce. Railroad building in the South lagged, as did industry. A banking panic that struck the Northern states in 1857 created little distress in the South, persuading some Souherners that they had the sounder economy. Actually, the South was not keeping economic pace with the North. The spreading web of Northern railroads would enable the Union to marshal its forces toward crushing the Confederacy in the Civil War.

The phenomenal American growth in numbers continued as the Civil War approached. In 1860 there were almost 31,450,000 Americans. The population of the United States surpassed that of the British Isles, and it was not far below that of France. It increased more than 35 per cent during the 1850s, in part because the Old Immigration persisted. Nearly 2,600,000 persons, of whom the largest fraction were German, entered the Land of Promise during that decade. Most of them settled in the Northern states. The blood stock of the Americans, outside the South, was becoming less and less English, more and more European.

The mounting flood of Old Immigrants—it reached its peak in 1854—swirled through the streets of the cities of the Eastern seaboard. Was Boston to become a Dublin and New York a Cork? Nativist feeling against the "foreigners," not trifling in the 1840s, rose high in the following decade. Native Americans of English, Dutch, German, French, and Swiss descent declared that the Old Immigrants would destroy the purity of the Anglo-Saxons and undermine the republic that they had created. However, their hostility was directed primarily at the Roman Catholics among the new arrivals, most of them being Irish. In 1850 in New York City sprang up the Supreme Order of the Star-Spangled Banner, also known as the Sons of the Sires of '76, a secret fraternity formed to "preserve America for Americans." Its members were required to prove that they were Americans of the third generation and that neither they, nor their parents, nor their grandparents, were tainted by Roman Catholicism. The society flourished remarkably, for it was obvious that the rapid construction of Roman Catholic churches, convents, and parochial schools portended a Jesuit and Papist revolution. Called Know-Nothings because they always answered, "I don't know," or "I know nothing," to questions about their fraternity, the nativists grew so potent that they were able to elect many men of their prejudices to high state and federal office during the years 1854–56. Their American party, getting the votes of many men who had been Whigs, secured almost a million ballots for the Presidency in 1856. Thereafter it swiftly vanished. Sentiment against the Roman Catholics persisted, but the nation was convulsed by the struggle between South and North.

There were two Americans descended from early English and Dutch immigrants who dedicated themselves, not to the pursuit of priests and nuns, but to that of poetry and prose. They, Walt Whitman and Herman Melville, were new stars in the American literary firmament of the 1850s, suns whose light became brighter after their own time. One of them, Whitman, was extolled before he died by a discerning few on both sides of the Atlantic but was ignored or condemned by the many; the other, Melville, remained an almost unknown genius until the twentieth century. Whitman did not barrenly parrot the English Pope or the English Shelley; he was shockingly original. Melville was also his own man. The year 1851, in which Melville's *Moby Dick* appeared, and the year 1855, in which Whitman's *Leaves of Grass* came from the press, were peculiarly important ones in the history of American literature. Whitman and Melville offered assurance that the American Renaissance was not a passing phenomenon.

Walt Whitman was thirty-six when he published the first edition of *Leaves of Grass*, which he later reprinted with additions. It was a collection of poems that, for many, did not resemble poetry, for he did not usually bother with rhyme or meter. He wrote free verse that looked like prose, and it often was, and bad prose at that. He composed crude, banal, pretentious, preposterous, and even meaningless lines. He himself declared that he emitted a "barbaric yawp." But he also indited magnificent passages of free verse, as he did in his "Song of Myself":

> I am he that walks with the tender and growing night,
> I call to the earth and sea half-held by the night,
> Press close bare-bosom'd night—press close magnetic
>   nourishing night!
> Night of South winds—night of the few large stars!
> Still nodding night—mad naked summer night.

Whitman could, when it pleased him to do so, write splendid conventional poetry, as he did in "O Captain! My Captain!" His message was as remarkable as his manner. Born on New York's Long Island, he was largely self-educated, a teacher, printer, civil servant, bachelor, idler, and roamer. He also served as a nurse to wounded and sick soldiers in the Civil War. In his poetry he chanted melodiously about the American landscape; he called for comradeship; he brazenly urged his readers to cast aside their fears, sexual and otherwise, hidden beneath their "Victorian" behavior, and to live freely and bravely. Above all, Whitman was the inspiring poet of democracy. According to him, it was not dying in America; it would not die. It was the "good old cause" of liberty, for which men had fought in the past, for which they must continue to sacrifice. It would triumph in America, and everywhere. For Whitman, though deeply conscious of the personal agonies of life, was sure that freedom and justice would ultimately prevail in the world.

Even the catastrophe of the Civil War did not shake the conviction of Walt Whitman that mankind was marching upward, but the mature Herman Melville did not believe that all was or would be well in America or elsewhere. Born in New York City in 1819, he was two months younger than Whitman. He left school at fifteen, was clerk, farmer, teacher, and sailor. Fleeing from a whaling vessel in the South Seas in 1842, he spent some months among the natives in the Marquesas Islands and at Tahiti. He returned to America and then swiftly published five novels. They attracted readers, for he chronicled adventures on the seas and described idyllic scenes and friendly maidens of the tropical islands of the Pacific. But Melville turned from romance to speculation about man and his destiny. The appearance of his masterpiece, *Moby Dick*, in which the sailor Ahab struggled with a whale and was conquered, marked the end of his popularity. He wrote more novels, and some poetry, but he spent the last forty years of his life in obscurity. For the Americans of Melville's generation did not read books that offered a tragic view of human existence. Melville saw about him an endless struggle between good and evil, in which a remote God or gods did not intervene. Hence, a man, without comfort from the divine, but in the company of his fellows, could only contend as bravely as he might against evil. Conquered, he could rejoice in having fought the good fight. Melville was much closer to Marcus Aurelius than he was to John Calvin or John Wesley.

The Americans of the 1850s were not a sophisticated people. They liked vivid history better than free verse or symbolic tragedy. *The History of the Conspiracy of Pontiac*, by the Bostonian Francis Parkman, was published in the same year as *Moby Dick* and was received with pleasure. Although written first, it proved to be the sequel to a great series of books in which Parkman related the epic contest between France and England for North American empire. If one considers both form and content, Parkman was the foremost American historian of his time, possibly of any time. Nevertheless, his books, like those of Emerson and Hawthorne, were not truly popular. Shallow sentimental novels by female scribblers had vast appeal in the "Feminine Fifties." Temperance tracts were purchased in huge numbers. Americans much preferred the melodious popular songs of Stephen C. Foster, including "O Susanna" and "Old Black Joe," to classical music. It should not surprise us that they continued to produce composers, architects, and sculptors who were worthy rather than truly great. Their painters, however, were of a higher order. If the landscapes of Asher B. Durand and other men of the "Hudson River School" are rather soft and pretty, they please the eye; and the rustic Rembrandt of New York, William Sidney Mount, self-taught and talented, skillfully and charmingly put on canvas scenes and people of his native Long Island.

Ignoring the deeply thoughtful Herman Melville, the Americans perused through their tears and with gusto the *Uncle Tom's Cabin* of Harriet Beecher Stowe, published in 1852, a pathetic tale that fixed the attention of a multitude of readers upon the evils of Negro slavery. Mrs. Stowe's novel attained its first popularity in England. However, within one year of its appearance as a book in America, 300,000 copies of *Uncle Tom's Cabin* were sold, and the quarrel over slavery revived and flamed.

It is easier to see the shortcomings of past generations than those of one's own, and easier to find ways to prevent the tragedies of times gone by than to ward off those of the future. Before the end of the year 1853 the clash over slavery was angrily resumed; it was not peaceably resolved; and it led at last to secession and Civil War. Was that bloody struggle fated? It may be urged that the American people lacked the wisdom and the magnanimity needed to avert it. It is true enough that most of them did not recognize the necessity for sacrifice to solve a deepening crisis. Nevertheless, there was among them a generosity of spirit. Statesmen might have appealed to it, might have guided the nation to a friendly solution of the issues that divided it. Except for the many questions that arose on account of the existence of slavery, there were no vital quarrels between North and South. Had Northern leaders proclaimed that Negro servitude must cease to spread, that it must gradually be destroyed, that Northerners as well as Southerners must make sacrifices to put an end to it, that the whole nation had to undertake to compensate, at least in part, the slave owners, it may be believed that chivalrous and large-hearted Southerners, like Robert E. Lee, would have responded. No well-known Northerner came forward with such a proposal.

Instead, the gap between South and North was allowed to widen. *Uncle Tom's Cabin* resuscitated the propaganda war over slavery. Attacks upon it and upon slaveholders provoked counterattacks. The execution, and nonexecution, of the Fugitive Slave Law of 1850 exasperated both Southerners and Northerners. Federal officers who sought to enforce it were not very successful. The Underground Railroad, despite their efforts, continued to run and to carry fleeing Negroes, though relatively few, to the North and to Canada. Some Northern states tried to interpose their authority in behalf of the runaway blacks. On the other hand, the law was so phrased that it was possible for slave hunters to seize free Negroes in the North and carry them southward across the Mason-Dixon Line. The abolitionists gained some converts; more important, antislavery sentiment among the Northerners hardened, although many of them remained indifferent to the plight of the Negroes. Meanwhile, Southern backs stiffened, and talk of secession revived.

Among the Northern politicians who did not provide magnificent leadership was Senator Stephen Douglas, the "Little Giant" of Illinois. Born in Vermont, he was a vigorous driving man, a skillful debater, perhaps the ablest of all the Northern Democrats of his time. No one labored more than he to arrange the Compromise of 1850. Nevertheless, while soothing the sectional passions that threatened to tear apart the nation in 1850, he somehow failed to assess their disruptive power. Thinking of slavery as a political nuisance, he drove through Congress in 1853–54 the Kansas-Nebraska Act, a measure that resurrected the question of slavery in the territories. To get Southern support for this measure, which established the territories of Kansas and Nebraska, Douglas put into it the principle of "popular sovereignty." Those who settled in Kansas and Nebraska would

determine whether or not there would be slavery in those
territories—and in those states. The law, also to please Southerners, explicitly repealed that part of the Missouri Compromise
which forbade slavery in the regions included in those territories. Douglas fancied that the change was only theoretical, and
unimportant, since plantation slavery could not actually spread
across the Great Plains. He committed a gross blunder. Abolitionists, Northern Whigs, and some Northern Democrats
swiftly concluded that Douglas intended to allow the expansion
of slavery into areas where it had been forbidden for thirty-four
years. They saw a great moral issue in the Douglas measure. In
the summer of 1854 they joined to found the Republican party,
dedicated to prevention by law of the extension of slavery into
the territories. It speedily became the principal rival of the Democratic party in the Northern states. Rallying behind the glamorous explorer John C. Frémont, it almost captured the Presidency in 1856. Frémont was defeated by James Buchanan of
Pennsylvania, who had been minister to England in 1854 and was
therefore not involved in the controversy over Kansas and Nebraska, who was satisfactory to Southern Democrats, and who
pleased cautious Northerners, especially those of his native
state.

The rapid rise of the Republican party, its adherents being
almost exclusively Northerners, caused anger in the South.
Moreover, it was already apparent in 1856 that "popular sovereignty" was a failure in Kansas. It was not given a fair trial
there. Many Southerners went into the territory to settle—and
to win it for slavery; more Northerners moved into it to settle—
and to keep slavery out. The Southerners brought with them
very few slaves, as Douglas had expected; but both they and the
Northerners carried in guns, to Douglas's dismay. They engaged
at the polls and in murderous affrays, and Kansas was "Bleeding
Kansas" when Buchanan entered the Presidency. By that time
Northerners and Southerners were also exchanging threats and
some blows in the halls of Congress. In his inaugural address
Buchanan expressed the vain hope that the question of slavery in
the territories would shortly be settled by a decision of the
Supreme Court. But the Court could not stifle controversy, in
fact embittered it. It announced its ruling in the Dred Scott case

two days later. A majority of the judges approved of an opinion written by Chief Justice Roger B. Taney which declared that Congress could not constitutionally deprive a slave owner of his right to take his human property into the territories. Two Northern judges asserted that Congress could do so, that, beginning with the Northwest Ordinance of 1787, it had done so many times. The decision was acclaimed in the South. Both the judgment and the judges who made it were furiously condemned by the Republicans. They declared that they would prevent the threat of slavery no matter what the Supreme Court might say.

The crisis grew. In 1858, Republican Abraham Lincoln unsuccessfully tried to take from Stephen Douglas his seat in the Senate. However, in a series of debates between the two men, Lincoln drove a wedge between the Democrats of the North, who were rallying behind Douglas, and those of the South. Lincoln said that slavery must be confined, that it must eventually be destroyed. He asked Douglas again and again how the people of a territory, in view of the Dred Scott decision, could exercise "popular sovereignty." Must not Douglas abandon his doctrine? Again and again Douglas answered that they still could and should exercise it. Reports of those debates were read in the South, and many Southerners realized that Douglas, although no enemy of slavery, was determined not to obey the ruling of the Supreme Court that sanctioned "Southern rights." Northern and Southern Democrats began to separate. In 1859 the mentally unbalanced abolitionist John Brown, who had fought and killed in "Bleeding Kansas," invaded Virginia with a few followers to begin a slave insurrection. He was quickly captured and executed. Many Northerners saw Brown as a fallen hero. To most Southerners he was an incendiary. Passions continued to rise on both sides of the Mason-Dixon Line.

In the year 1860 the Democratic party divided into two parts, and the Southern states began to secede. Southerners of the Democratic persuasion refused allegiance to Douglas, since he would not defend their "rights." They named John C. Breckinridge for the Presidency. The Northern Democrats put Douglas forward. More moderate Southerners, with a few Northerners, formed the Constitutional Union party and named John Bell of

Tennessee for the Presidency. They deplored the rise of sectional parties, called for allegiance to the Constitution, and desired compromise. Under the circumstances the Republicans could hardly fail to secure the Presidency, and they did not. They nominated for it Abraham Lincoln. Renewing their pledge to restrict slavery, they announced that they favored a protective tariff and the giving of homestead farms by the nation to all who would settle upon its public lands. They also censured discrimination against the Old Immigrants. Thus they appealed to Eastern industrialists, Western farmers, and new Americans, especially those who had come from Germany. The votes for Lincoln were concentrated in the Northern states. He carried everyone of them except New Jersey and won an easy victory in the electoral college, even though he did not get a single vote in the South.

The Breckinridge Democrats were victorious in the Deep South. As election day drew near, they declared that if Lincoln was chosen, the Southern states must secede. Aware that he could not win, Douglas, himself utterly committed to the Union, went into the South to urge that no rash step be taken. The Republicans would not dominate Congress, and they would not be able to move against vital Southern interests. Many of the numerous supporters of Bell in the Far South believed that no action should be taken until Lincoln and the Republicans did something definitely injurious to the South. Their pleas went unheeded. On December 20, following the Calhoun formula, a convention in South Carolina announced the secession of that state from the Union. The example of South Carolina was rapidly followed in the Far South. Before the end of February 1861, Georgia and all the states bordering upon the Gulf of Mexico also seceded. Indeed, before the end of that month the Confederate States of America appeared. Delegates from the seven states that had seceded gathered at Montgomery, Alabama, adopted a constitution for the Confederacy, and named Jefferson Davis of Mississippi as provisional President of the Confederacy. They believed that they were founding a great Southern republic. They hoped that it would soon include all of the South.

While the framers of the Confederacy labored, men of the Upper South and conciliatory Northerners strove for an accommodation in Washington; but in vain, for the Republicans would not, could not honorably, retreat from the firm stand they had taken against the extension of slavery into the territories. Sentiment in the Upper South was badly divided. Some of its people were utterly loyal to the Union. Some were for immediate secession. There were many who desired to be neutral. At last they were forced to choose.

In the face of the secession of the states of the Far South, many Northerners were also reluctant to act. Abolitionists urged that the seceders be permitted to separate from the nation—with their slaves. Not a few Northern Democrats opposed the use of force against the emerging Confederacy, although Douglas insisted that the Union must be preserved at all costs. Lincoln did not hesitate. Traveling from Illinois to Washington amidst gloom and threats against his person, he announced his intentions in his First Inaugural Address in magnificent phrases. The United States could not be divided into two friendly nations; secession was illegal; he would not deny the right of revolution to the Southerners; he was bound by his oath of office to do what he could to save the Union. He would not move against slavery where it existed. He made it utterly clear that he would use force, if necessary, to maintain the integrity of the Union.

Lincoln was soon put to the test. President Buchanan had permitted Confederates to take, without resistance, Union military posts located in the Far South. In early April, Lincoln determined to send provisions to a Federal garrison at Fort Sumter in the harbor of Charleston, South Carolina. On the twelfth of that month South Carolina troops bombarded the fort, killing no one but forcing its surrender. Three days later the President proclaimed that an "insurrection" existed in the South and called for 75,000 volunteers to help suppress it. The Civil War had begun. Virginia, North Carolina, Tennessee, and Arkansas rapidly seceded and joined the Confederacy. However, not all of the Old South left the Union. Loyalty to the Old Flag was so strong in Maryland, Kentucky, and Missouri that Unionists in those states, with help from Lincoln, managed to prevent secession. Even so, the Confederacy was formidable. The Americans engaged in a bloody and protracted struggle, with the very existence of the nation at issue.

CHAPTER 18

The Union Against the Confederacy

❦

AT THE BEGINNING OF the Civil War there were those among the Confederates who believed that the Yankees would not fight; that if they did, they would soon be overwhelmed by Southern soldiers. Among those who clung to the Union there were foolish people who assumed that the Stars and Stripes would soon fly again over Richmond and Montgomery. Wrath and courage are more common than wisdom in mankind. The powers that arrayed against each other in 1861 were immense for the time. The Civil War was a long grinding struggle. So much was at stake— a social order, the fate of the republic, and even democracy itself. At first President Lincoln declared that his great purpose was to save the Union. After two campaigns he proclaimed a second purpose, that slavery must be destroyed. During those two campaigns the forces of the Union, encountering formidable resistance, advanced slowly and haltingly. At the end of 1862 it seemed that the Confederacy might endure, might long enough withstand the attacks of the Unionists so that they would from war-weariness concede its independence. Appearances deceived; the vast power of the North had not yet been fully exerted.

There never was any likelihood that Confederate troops would march triumphantly in the streets of New York City or Chicago. But it was not necessary that the South, to become a nation, should overwhelm the Federal armies. The Southerners, like the Patriots in the War of Independence, could achieve their goal by stubborn and successful defense. The forces of the Union had to protect Northern cities and supply lines and simultaneously penetrate into the bowels of the Confederacy in order to destroy it.

On the defensive, the Southerners profited from the magnitude of the Confederacy, which was as large as western Europe. Also to their advantage were its mountains, its extensive forests, its many rivers, and its swamps, these providing barriers against attack. Nor was the Confederacy without men to make use of its natural advantages. It contained about nine million people, of whom nearly 40 per cent were slaves. It could and did raise formidable armies of men accustomed to the use of weapons. Moreover, it did not lack gifted professional officers, for many of its commanders were trained veterans who had served in the United States Army. The slaves were an asset, especially during the early years of the war. With their help Confederate civilians were able to supply the Southern soldiers with food, clothing, and arms. Another asset of the Confederacy, the value of which only time would reveal, was the good will extended to it by England and France. The masters of those nations desired the collapse of American democracy. Intervention by them might assure Southern independence.

The Confederacy also had its weaknesses. The Southerners were able quickly to form a "permanent" central government at Richmond. Their President, Jefferson Davis, and their Congress performed respectably. However, they were cramped by assertions of states' rights, especially from North Carolina and Georgia. The Confederacy was poor in money and was able to borrow only a little abroad. It could and did float internal loans. It put forth a paper currency, but its paper money bought less and less as the war continued. The Southern railroads were sadly deficient when the conflict began, and they deteriorated as it proceeded. Southern industry was not sufficiently developed or productive to supply arms plentifully for the Confederate troops, or to repair railroads. Nor could Southern shipyards soon provide a navy. Nor was every Southerner, even in the states that seceded, utterly devoted to the Confederacy. In the Appalachian highlands of Virginia, North Carolina, and Tenessee tens of thousands of men remained faithful to the Union.

These were so numerous in the interior of Virginia that they were able to form a new state of West Virginia, which was admitted to the Union in 1863.

If Jefferson Davis in Richmond was plagued by internal divisions, Lincoln, only a hundred miles to the north in Washington, was profoundly embarrassed by discord within the states that stayed in the Union. There were tens of thousands in Delaware, Maryland, West Virginia, Kentucky, and Missouri who gave their hearts to the Confederacy. It received many regiments of recruits from those Border States. Nor was it without friends above the Mason-Dixon Line. In those parts of Ohio, Indiana, and Illinois lying immediately north of the Ohio River resided folk of Southern ancestry who cared little for the Union. Everywhere in the North there were men who did not hate slavery, not a few who approved of it. On the other hand, there were those in the North who contended that the destruction of Negro servitude must be the chief purpose of the Union forces. Democrats who were loyal to the Union made difficulties for Lincoln because he was a Republican; and Republicans distrusted Democrats generally. It was not so obviously important to Northerners that they must win the war as it was to Southerners that they must not lose it. The way of life of the Northerner was not immediately menaced as was that of the Southerner.

Even so, the Union had vast resources in spirit, flesh, food, and machines. Among the 22 million people who remained under the Stars and Stripes a large majority was consecrated to the American republic. It included Virginians like General George Thomas and Tennesseans like Admiral David Farragut, as well as lumbermen of Michigan and farm boys of New Hampshire. Those devoted Unionists were virile, brave, and willing to make every sacrifice for their country. With machines the older men, the boys, and the women of the North could produce food from fertile fields to nourish themselves, their soldiers, and their sailors. The cultivated lands of the North were actually increased during the war, though not because the Republicans, keeping their campaign promise of 1860, secured the passage of the Homestead Act in 1862, which offered a farm to anyone who would settle on national lands.

The Homestead Act had little immediate effect. Northern factories could supply guns, ammunition, ships, clothing, nearly everything needed by the Union armies and fleets. What could not be produced at home could be bought abroad, for there was money enough in the North to support a great and continuing war effort. The Union possessed a long established government at Washington to direct that effort. Not the least of its resources was the navy. Many officers of the United States Army entered Confederate service; but Southerners in the navy, accustomed to defending the American flag in remote places and little informed about Southern grievances, usually declared and manifested their loyalty to the Union.

Of first value to the imperiled republic was Abraham Lincoln. Jefferson Davis, an experienced civil and military officer, was merely competent. A Kentuckian by birth, like Davis, Lincoln, when he entered the Presidency, seemed unfit to carry an enormous burden. There were several men in his Cabinet, including Secretary of State William Seward and Secretary of the Treasury Salmon P. Chase, who fancied themselves his superiors during his first months in office. Born in a log cabin, he was of humble origins, his parents being plain farmer folk, as much Southern as Northern. Removing with his family to Indiana, and then to Illinois, he did not achieve early fame. The most important post he had held before he became President was that of member of the House of Representatives, in which he had served as a Whig for only two years. Tall, lanky, ungraceful, with a face brown and seamed by care, he looked like a backwoods politician. It was known that he possessed a gift for debate. His appearance was deceptive. With very little formal education, he had risen in the world by exerting remarkable talents, by displaying honesty and a sober courage. Not widely read, he had become a master of English and a successful lawyer. He had married a good and cultivated Southern woman. His eloquence, his noble spirit, his fits of melancholy, his fondness for jokes are well remembered. But he was also intelligent, shrewd, industrious, patient, and confident of his own powers. It is not doubted that he was superbly qualified to make peace; it is sometimes forgotten that he was a magnificent leader in war. It should be added that he did not think he was a heaven-sent man of mission; he modestly saw himself as a defective human being engaged in a tragic struggle.

After the surrender of Fort Sumter, Lincoln undertook to move against the Confederacy by both land and sea. He enlarged the regular army, which was small at the beginning of the war, called more and more volunteers and militia into service, and sent them southward. The hastily raised Federal troops were confronted by Confederates equally inexperienced. By the summer of 1861 armies were engaged from Virginia to Missouri. Before the close of the year the Unionists gained superiority in Missouri, Kentucky, and West Virginia. However, their triumphs in those states, important as they were because they limited the Confederacy, did not grievously injure it. Moreover, in the first great battle of the war, fought at Bull Run, Virginia, in July of that year, the Union army suffered a humiliating defeat. "On to Richmond," too confident Northerners had cried in the early summer. General Irwin McDowell, encamped immediately south of the Potomac River with 30,000 men, advanced toward the Confederate capital. Members of Congress and other civilians followed McDowell so that they might watch his triumphal progress. He successfully attacked a somewhat smaller Confederate army under General Pierre Beauregard at Bull Run. Then Beauregard was joined by fresh troops, counterattacked, and drove McDowell's troops backward. Retreating, McDowell's men fell into utter confusion. Mingled with panic-stricken civilians, they fled toward Washington. Fortunately for the Union, the Confederate forces were too weary to pursue them. The defeat at Bull Run taught Lincoln and the Unionists a stern lesson. They prepared in grim earnest to send forward larger and more formidable armies in 1862.

The navy of the Union encountered fewer difficulties than did its armies in 1861 and quickly began to strike at the Confederacy from the sea. Six days after the fall of Fort Sumter, Lincoln declared that it was under naval blockade. At the moment the navy was small, both in men and ships, and all of its vessels were wooden. The blockade was therefore not immediately enforced. However, the Union possessed everything necessary to build powerful forces on the water. The efficient Secretary of the Navy, Gideon Welles, enlisted sailors, converted merchant vessels into war craft, stimulated the making of marine engines, and hastened the manufacture of small ironclad ships. Before the end of the first year of the war the navy was turning Lincoln's paper blockade into a real one maintained by armed vessels. It had also begun, with the help of Union troops, to seize and to close harbors along the seaboard of the Confederacy. In 1860 merchant vessels numbering 6,000 entered ports of the states that formed the Confederacy; only 800 such ships made their way into those ports the following year. The South could not, because of poor and disconnected railroads, import large quantities of supplies by way of Mexico; on the north and west it was cut off by the Union armies; it was increasingly deprived both of markets for its cotton and of access to foreign arms, machines, medicines, and other military paraphernalia.

Mobilizing after the defeat at Bull Run for onslaughts against the Confederacy, Lincoln and the Unionists were confronted by the threat of British intervention; and the President was plagued by a faction in his Republican party. Leaders of the Confederacy hoped that it would soon be officially recognized by England, and that it would receive both moral and material aid from that country. Some of them believed that Southern cotton, made into cloth in numerous English factories, was indispensable to English prosperity, and that England would be forced to use the Royal Navy to break the Union blockade in order to get the fluffy stuff. They were mistaken; English manufacturers were able to feed their machines with the supply of cotton they had on hand, increased by imports from India and elsewhere. Nevertheless, the Confederates could reasonably hope for help from England. The aristocrats, industrialists, and merchants of that country did not admire political democracy. They were faced by a demand for extension of the suffrage in England. They would have been pleased to see American democracy collapse. Moreover, the Republicans had committed themselves to the protection of American industry by means of tariffs. To achieve this end and to get money, they raised tariff rates soon after they gained power in Washington. On the other hand, the Confederacy eagerly sought to exchange its raw materials for British finished goods. Early in May 1861, Lord John Russell, the British Foreign Secretary, received two Confederate agents, and

England recognized the Confederacy as a belligerent on the thirteenth of that month. A protest from Washington persuaded Russell to say that he would meet no more Southern emissaries. But it was only too evident that he preferred Southern aristocrats to Northern democrats. In November, Captain Charles Wilkes, commanding the U.S.S. *San Jacinto*, forcibly took from the *Trent*, a British merchant vessel en route from Cuba to England, two Confederate commissioners, James M. Mason and John Slidell. Russell swiftly demanded the release of the two men, amidst passionate denunciations in England of Yankee arrogance. The British chose to forget that they had many times similarly insulted the American flag a half-century earlier. War between the Union and England loomed. There were those in Washington who would concede nothing to avoid it. Lincoln prudently concluded that one war at a time was enough. Mason and Slidell were of no consequence; he ordered their release. So the *Trent* affair became only an awkward incident, but concern remained in Washington lest England should intervene in behalf of the South.

The patience and prudence of the President were also tried by disunity among the Unionists. It was sufficiently embarrassing to him that many Northern Democrats opposed the prosecution of the war. He also suffered because the followers of Stephen Douglas who rallied to the cause of the Union were left leaderless when Douglas died not long after Lincoln's inauguration. The "War Democrats" did not give him their utter political loyalty. What was worse, a Republican faction—the Radicals—began to assail the President because he did not immediately undertake to free the slaves of the Confederates, because he did not quickly force the Southern aristocrats to their knees. They insisted that he employ generals of the Radical persuasion rather than more skillful commanders. In the summer of 1861, Lincoln had to restrain some Radical officers who tried to emancipate slaves by virtue of their military authority. He was alarmed lest precipitate action against Negro servitude should drive the many Unionists of the Border States who did not hate slavery into neutrality or even into the camp of the Confederacy. He insisted that it was all-important to preserve the nation, with or without slavery. Nevertheless, he was prepared to take steps against slavery that would not injure the cause of the Union. In August 1861, he signed the First Confiscation Act, which declared that slaves fighting in or working for the Confederate forces were free. The Radicals in Congress were not satisfied. They demanded that he move decisively and harshly against slavery and the Confederacy. To push him on, they formed a joint Congressional committee on the conduct of the war, which they dominated. The committee threatened to usurp the authority of the President. But to avoid damaging discord, he cheerfully sought to work with the committee in particular and with the Radicals in general. Both would continue to vex him.

There was much more of preparing for war in 1861 than there was of war itself, but the conflict was waged in deadly earnest the following year. Nearly 600,000 men served under the Stars and Stripes, about 350,000 under the Confederate Stars and Bars. Although most of the men on both sides were volunteers, the Confederacy resorted to conscription in the spring of the year, a measure which the Union was compelled to adopt in 1863. The Union navy continued to tighten its sea blockade. Meanwhile, a formidable Army of the Potomac tried to take Richmond; a second Federal drive was mounted against Chattanooga and Atlanta, in the hope of severing the Confederacy in general and its most important railroads in particular; and other Union contingents on land and sea undertook to divide the Confederacy by securing control of the Mississippi River. At the end of the campaigns of 1862 the prospects of the Confederacy seemed bright to optimistic Southerners, also to pessimistic Northerners. The outlook for the Southern republic would indeed have been splendid had all the Union forces accomplished no more than did the Army of the Potomac. Its troops were confronted by the potent Army of Northern Virginia; its commanders could not match the military genius of the Confederate Generals Robert E. Lee and Thomas J. "Stonewall" Jackson; and it won no spectacular victories. However, the Confederacy suffered heavy blows west of the Appalachians; it did not secure vital foreign assistance; and the Union had as yet to exert fully its massive power.

The Army of the Potomac marched back and forth, served under three different commanders, fought battle after battle,

and was as far from Richmond in December 1862 as it had been
the preceding January. It was a powerful, disciplined, well-
equipped army, and its commanders were and have been censured because its soldiers did not soon pour through the streets
of the Confederate capital. To be sure, no one of their leaders
was a Caesar or a Napoleon. However, their task was extraordinarily difficult. The Army of Northern Virginia was nearly as
formidable as the Army of the Potomac. It is doubtful that the
forces of the Union were sufficient to move against Richmond
and at the same time to protect Washington against attack from
the south and from the Shenandoah Valley. General George
B. McClellan, a splendid drillmaster, opened the campaign by
advancing against Richmond from the east. Unfortunately for
him, Stonewall Jackson, a brilliant corps commander, defeated in
turn several small Federal forces in the Shenandoah and then
joined the defenders of Richmond. The combined Confederate
forces, after bitter fighting, drove McClellan back. He was replaced by General John Pope, who was instructed to move
against Richmond from the north.

Meanwhile, the great Robert E. Lee had been placed at the
head of the Army of Northern Virginia. A Virginian who had
freed his own slaves, Lee was a graduate of West Point, so
splendid an officer that General Winfield Scott described him at
the end of the Mexican War as "the greatest living soldier in
America." Dignified, magnanimous, and resourceful, he had
regretfully cast his lot with his native state against the Union.
Once committed to the Southern cause, he spent himself utterly
in its behalf. Lee marched northward in the late summer of
1862; with the help of the redoubtable Jackson, he defeated
Pope in the Second Battle of Bull Run; then he drove forward
into Maryland. Lincoln hastily replaced Pope with the experienced McClellan, who checked Lee in the bloody battle of
Antietam in September. With a weakened army Lee was compelled to retreat into Virginia. When McClellan neglected to use
his superior forces to interrupt Lee's withdrawal, Lincoln replaced him with General Ambrose Burnside. In December,
Burnside fruitlessly and expensively assailed a strongly entrenched Lee at Fredericksburg. Disgusted, Lincoln entrusted
the Army of the Potomac to General Joseph Hooker to make

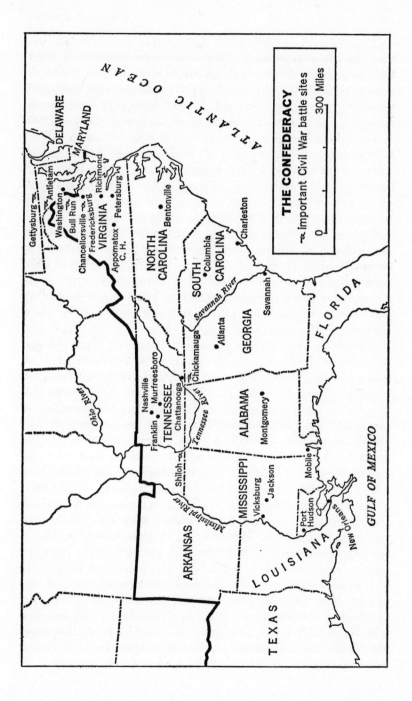

ATLANTIC OCEAN

DELAWARE

MARYLAND

Gettysburg

Antietam

Washington

Bull Run

Chancellorsville

Fredericksburg

Richmond

Petersburg

VIRGINIA

Appomattox
C. H.

NORTH
CAROLINA

Bentonville

SOUTH
CAROLINA

Columbia

Charleston

Savannah River

GEORGIA

Savannah

FLORIDA

Atlanta

Chickamauga

Nashville

Murfreesboro

Franklin

TENNESSEE

Chattanooga

Tennessee River

ALABAMA

Montgomery

Ohio River

Shiloh

MISSISSIPPI

Vicksburg

Jackson

Mobile

Port
Hudson

Mississippi River

ARKANSAS

GULF OF MEXICO

New Orleans

LOUISIANA

TEXAS

THE CONFEDERACY

⌒ important Civil War battle sites

0   300 Miles

ready for the next campaign. The army had accomplished more
than was readily apparent. It had stopped the aggressive Lee at
Antietam. Suffering heavy losses, it had killed, wounded, and
captured many thousands of Confederates. The Army of
Northern Virginia was beginning to suffer from attrition.

With the help of naval vessels traversing the Mississippi River
and its tributaries, the troops of the Union who fought in the
valley of the great river accomplished more in 1862 than their
comrades of the Army of the Potomac. The Confederates west
of the Appalachians resisted as fiercely as those who defended
Richmond. But their generals were not equal to Robert E. Lee
and Stonewall Jackson, while the forces of the Union beyond the
mountains had commanders, including General Ulysses S.
Grant, General George H. Thomas, and Admiral David Farragut, who were superior to McClellan, Pope, and Burnside. The
Union forces did not reach Chattanooga, but they moved against
Nashville from the northwest, captured it, and held it. They
checked Confederate advances into Kentucky. In Tennessee
they repelled one massive attack by General Albert Sidney
Johnston at Shiloh and another by General Braxton Bragg at
Murfreesboro. West of the Mississippi they drove back the Confederate troops in Arkansas. Moreover, advancing from the
South, Admiral Farragut captured New Orleans as other Union
commanders moved down the Mississippi from the north. By the
end of the year the Confederacy was almost split apart by Federal land and naval contingents which controlled the lower and
upper reaches of the Mississippi. Besides, it was suffering from
attrition west as well as east of the Appalachians.

Assisting the armies of the Union, its navy steadily gained
power; captured more and more Confederate ports; and steadily
tightened its blockade. Momentarily, in March 1862, the Union
navy was threatened by the *Virginia*, a warship the Confederates
had ingeniously covered with iron armor. Almost all of the
Union warships were still wooden. The *Virginia* destroyed two
of them near Norfolk and was preparing to finish the career of a
third when it was challenged by the *Monitor*, a small, raft-like
iron vessel with a revolving turret that had been put into commission by the Federal navy a short time before. The duel that
followed, the first between ironclads, went on for five hours, at

the end of which the *Virginia* had to go into port for repairs. Before they could be completed, the Confederates had to destroy their ship in order to prevent its capture by Union troops. Since the Confederates failed in other, later attempts to get an ironclad to sea, the Union could continue to use its many wooden vessels. The Confederates were able to send out swift cargo ships to run the blockade. These often managed to elude the Union war craft hovering along the Southern coasts, to carry out cotton for sale, and to bring back military and other supplies. However, their exploits were glamorous but not truly valuable to the Southern cause. As the war proceeded, more and more of the blockade runners were captured, and it became increasingly difficult to get new ones. Before the war ended, all the principal harbors of the Confederacy had been captured by Union forces, and it was almost cut off from the outside world.

Unable to break through the barricades formed along its shores, the Confederacy managed during and after 1862 to strike heavily at the Union merchant marine—and so to embarrass the Union navy. Confederate agents, welcomed in many private quarters in England and France, tried feverishly to get an ironclad from a French shipyard. They finally secured one but too late in the war to make use of it. However, they soon persuaded English shipbuilders to construct wooden cruisers for the Confederacy, and they managed to put cannon and crews aboard those vessels. Of such was the *Florida*, which went to sea in the spring of 1862, and the *Alabama*, which slipped out of Liverpool the following summer. The *Florida*, the *Alabama*, and other Southern cruisers, dodging Union war craft quite successfully, virtually ruined the American merchant marine before the end of the war. They destroyed more than 250 cargo vessels, and the owners of 700 others transferred them to foreign registry. The U.S.S. *Kearsarge* finally caught and sank the *Alabama* off the coast of France in 1864, but one of the sister ships of the Confederate raider was hunting down American whalers as late as the spring of 1865.

The Union did not desperately need military supplies from abroad in order to carry on the war, and the destruction of its merchant shipping injured its pride rather than its power. But

Lincoln and his advisers had reason to fear not only that England
and France would permit the Confederates to procure ships intended for military use from their harbors, in violation of international law, but that those two nations would do much more
for the Southerners. When Charles Francis Adams, the American minister in London, complained in London that England, by
permitting the Confederates to secure the cruisers in her ports,
was not behaving as a neutral should, he received evasive answers for many months. Indeed, it seemed likely in the summer
of 1862 that both England and France would recognize the independence of the Confederacy. The Emperor Napoleon III of
France wished to do so. Taking advantage of the struggle in the
United States, he was trying to impose his puppet emperor,
Maximilian, upon Mexico, despite warnings—prudently soft—
from Secretary of State William Seward that he was violating
the Monroe Doctrine. There were those in the English Cabinet,
including Lord Palmerston and William E. Gladstone, who were
willing to recognize the Confederacy. Palmerston hoped that
Confederate victories would permit the Cabinet to act, on the
ground that the Southerners could not be defeated. The news
that Lee had been checked at Antietam persuaded the Cabinet to
delay its decision. To sanction the Confederacy was to invite a
declaration of war from Washington. Napoleon III continued to
press for open intervention but without success. Gradually, as
the tide of war ran faster in favor of the Union, the threat of
foreign interference began to fade.

After Antietam, Lincoln made it difficult for the English
Cabinet to meddle in the American conflict by appealing to the
conscience of the English people. In the spring and summer of
1862 he signed laws that forbade slavery in the District of Columbia and the national territories, and that called upon the loyal
Border States to provide for compensated emancipation. He also
put his name to the Second Confiscation Act, which proclaimed
the freedom of the slaves of all those persons who were guilty of
treason or rebellion. He became convinced that the servitude of
the Negroes must be obliterated, that the United States should
announce its intent to crush both the Confederacy and slavery.
The Border States had been saved and soothed. He resolved to
notify the world as soon as a Union victory permitted him to do

so; he did not wish his announcement to be thought an act of desperation. Deciding that Antietam could be called a victory, he let it be known on September 22 that he would issue an Emancipation Proclamation on January 1, 1863, and he did. That famous document did not put an end to Negro bondage everywhere in America. It did not go much beyond the two Confiscation Acts. It declared that all slaves within the Confederate lines were "thenceforward, and forever free." The Proclamation was constitutionally doubtful, for the right of the President to issue it rested only upon his authority as commander in chief of the armed forces. It did not immediately free even one slave. However, Lincoln left no doubt that the triumph of those forces would be accompanied by the blotting out of slavery, not merely in the area held by the Confederates on January 1, 1863, but everywhere in America. His intention was obvious enough, and his Proclamation dramatically announced that the cause of the Union was that of humanity.

Although the Confederacy gained the sympathy of aristocrats, industrialists, and merchants in England, the laborers in English factories, denied the right to vote and seeking it, became increasingly friendly to the Union. They saw it as the great champion of democracy; they felt no affection for Southern aristocratic planters. It became evident to the English Cabinet that a war against the United States would not be heartily supported by the English common folk. When Lincoln made it clear that the Union would put an end to slavery, English humanitarians demanded that their country refrain from helping the Southern republic. The Cabinet could find other reasons for avoiding war. Relations between England and imperial Russia were uneasy in 1863, and there were storm clouds in central Europe. It was to be expected, in the event of such a war, that the Union navy would severely damage the English merchant marine. If the English fleet broke the blockade of the Confederacy and thus assured Southern independence, might not the Union use part of its ever growing forces to seize Canada in compensation? By the spring of 1863 English—and French—intervention had become unlikely. In April, conceding that the building of Confederate raiders in English shipyards was dubious business, English officials seized the cruiser *Alexandria*, then making ready to go to sea as a Confederate raider. An English court declared that they had no right to detain the vessel, since Confederate ownership could not be established, and they felt forced to let it proceed. Confederate agents arranged for the building of ironclads, the so-called "Laird rams," in Liverpool. Charles Francis Adams had protested long and in vain. At last, after the great Union victory at Gettysburg in the summer of 1863, Adams informed the British Foreign Office that the "escape" of the ironclads to sea must be followed by a declaration of war from Washington. His warning proved to be unnecessary. An order to prevent the departure of the vessels had already been issued, and they were kept in Liverpool. The Confederates could now gain independence only by their own efforts.

CHAPTER 19

The Overthrow of
the Confederacy

❈

THE ORDEAL OF THE Civil War proceeded. Its toll of destruction, of death, of wounds, of sorrows, grew ever larger. Resorting to conscription, the Union put ever more powerful forces in motion against the Confederacy. War-weariness and disaffection increased in the North. Vexed by the Radical Republicans, assailed by those who desired peace at any price, Lincoln resolutely demanded every sacrifice necessary for victory. He was censured by legalists because he sometimes stretched his constitutional authority to suppress defeatism and disloyalty behind the Federal lines. Gentle but firm, he was denounced for his weakness and reviled for his tyranny. It long seemed likely that he would be deprived of the Presidency in the election of 1864. But the Confederacy also suffered from lack of faith, from internal divisions, from the naval blockade, and above all from battering by the Union armies. The military outlook brightened for the Union in 1863; at the end of the following year the Confederacy was collapsing; it fell in the spring of 1865. Lincoln did not survive it. The power that he had wielded abruptly passed to men with weaker heads, less generous hearts, and harsher hands. He was not permitted to reap the fruits of victory, or to heal the wounds of defeat.

Lincoln was a superb politician. Bringing into his Cabinet the able, aggressive, and irascible Edwin M. Stanton as Secretary of War early in 1862, the President kept him in office, despite

Stanton's outbreaks of temper, because Stanton was efficient. At length the Secretary of War acknowledged that his talents were somewhat less than those of the President. Salmon P. Chase, Secretary of the Treasury, was also competent and excessively pleased with himself. He yearned for the Presidency. At last, in 1864, Lincoln disposed of the ambitious Chase by appointing him Chief Justice of the Supreme Court. Had the Radical Republicans had their way, Lincoln would not have been master of his official household. They, including such men as Senator Charles Sumner of Massachusetts, continued to worry Lincoln as long as he lived. Passionately loyal to the Union, they hated Southerners, disliked Democrats of all sorts, and constantly urged extreme measures. At first they sought to dominate Lincoln; later they strove to remove him from the Presidency. In the election of 1862 the Democrats gained several seats in Congress and control of Lincoln's own state of Illinois. The response of the Radical Republicans was to demand the discharge of Secretary of State Seward, who had learned that it was prudent to follow Lincoln. They hoped to force the President to fill his Cabinet with Radical Republicans. Lincoln was then preparing to issue his Emancipation Proclamation. He might declare that the Negroes behind the Southern lines were free; but he could not gain freedom for himself from the importunities of the Radical Republicans. He was able, however, by clever maneuvering and soft words, to defend Seward and to retain control of his Cabinet. He managed to put off an open clash with the hotheads in his party until the summer of 1864.

Refusing to yield to the Radical Republicans, Lincoln managed to retain their support and that of moderate Republicans and War Democrats for an ever greater effort to crush the Confederacy. Partly by conscription, used after 1863, the Union armed about 1,500,000 men during the Civil War. It spent vast sums of money, getting it from tariff duties, excise and income taxes, the sale of bonds through a newly created system of national banks, and the issuance of unsupported "greenback" paper currency. It expended, altogether, about $5 billion. Using machines, its older men, women, boys, and girls produced food and weapons in almost amazing quantities. The Union was even able to send grain abroad. It bought military supplies in England. The Union became a formidable engine for waging war.

To many in the North, the costs of victory—if it came—were excessive in toil, treasure, and above all in blood. The lists of the dead, the wounded, and the sick grew by the tens of thousands. Industrialists became rich and richer, sometimes by making shoddy clothing and shoes for soldiers and sailors. They profited from rising prices. However, wages did not keep pace with prices, and poorer folk suffered under the combined burden of inflation and higher taxation. Conscription created furious resentment. Its enemies said that it was unconstitutional, that it was a device of "military despotism," even though the American colonies had commonly exacted military service, even though the federal government was clearly authorized by the Constitution to wage war. In the summer of 1863 rioters protesting against conscription in New York City raged and ravaged through its streets for four days, killing and wounding perhaps a thousand Negroes and devoted Unionists. Regiments of troops had to be sent to the city to restore order. Elsewhere, several men who executed the Conscription Act were murdered. The law was disliked even by the most loyal Unionists, partly because it contained exemptions, but especially because it permitted a wealthy man to escape being drafted by paying $300 for a substitute. Many of the less prosperous began to suspect that they were engaged in "a rich man's war and a poor man's fight."

The miseries of war weighed so heavily upon the Northern people that a large minority among them came to wish for peace at any price. Why make sacrifices to free the Negroes? Behind the Union lines "Copperheads," men who urged peace without victory, who were often secret friends of the Confederacy, openly spoke and wrote against continuing the war. The Knights of the Golden Circle, a Copperhead clandestine society, enlisted many thousands in the Southern parts of the Old Northwest. Lincoln, the Congress, and Union army officers moved vigorously against the seditious. They did not scruple to suspend the writ of *habeas corpus*, or to impose martial law upon civilians in areas behind the Union lines. Disaffection was repressed. Hundreds of men were arrested; some were kept in prison for months without trial; others were tried by military tribunals and locked up. A few innocents suffered with the many who were guilty of aiding the Confederacy. Lincoln was savagely condemned because he violated the "rights" of citizens. Typical of Lincoln's conduct was his behavior in the Vallandigham affair. A good-looking, bland Ohio politician and Democrat, Clement Vallandigham campaigned for "peace and reunion," a program unacceptable to both the Confederacy and the Union. He was sent to prison by a military court. However, Lincoln ordered that he be released and escorted to the Confederate lines. The Southerners helped Vallandigham to reach Canada. He returned to Ohio, but he was not again molested by Union officers. Judges and scholars afterward said that Lincoln and many Union commanders and officials had exceeded their constitutional authority in this affair and others. Lincoln ordered no wholesale executions. Nor did he go far beyond his legal powers; it was his duty to save the American republic; were it dismembered, the Constitution must lose value.

If the contributions of the Northerners to the cause of the American republic were enormous, they did not proportionately match those of the Southerners to the Confederacy. At no time during the Civil War was there a serious lack of food, clothing, or medicines in the Northern states. Their schools and colleges remained open; in fact, many new ones were established. Immigrants continued to display their faith in the republic and to enter Northern ports, fewer than 100,000 of them in 1862 but almost 200,000 in 1864. It was otherwise with the Confederacy. Virtually surrounded by the Union navy and armies, the Southerners fought on amidst mounting losses. Perhaps one million men, a large fraction of the white men of the South, served in its armed forces. The casualties suffered by the Confederate armies were numerically fewer than those of the Union forces, but they were relatively much larger. Toward the end of the war many of the Southern soldiers were old men and boys. Securing some arms through the blockade, making others, and using weapons captured from its opponents, the Confederacy was barely able to supply its troops with guns and ammunition. Occasionally, for want of their customary gray uniforms, they wore blue ones captured from their foes. Even with the help of the slaves, most of whom faithfully plowed and reaped so that their masters might carry arms, the South could not properly feed both its fighting men and its civilians. After 1863 the

Southern railroads could not be efficiently maintained, and it became more and more difficult to move stores of arms, food, and clothing. Morale and the value of Confederate paper currency sank. Conscription was almost as bitterly opposed in the South as it was in the North. Exemption from military service of men who owned many slaves exasperated those who had few or none. North Carolinians as well as New Yorkers asked whether they were engaged in a "rich man's war and a poor man's fight." Speculators and blockade runners who profited from shortages angered the many who sacrificed everything in behalf of the Confederacy. The ravages of the armies, seldom felt in the North, deeply injured the South. As the Union troops advanced ever deeper into the South, the Negroes, learning that they would be free behind the Northern lines, at length began to flee in numbers from their tasks. One difficulty exacerbated another. Jefferson Davis, like Lincoln, was attacked as both an incompetent and a tyrant. The governors of North Carolina and Georgia denounced him for violating states' rights. As the war went on and on, gloom spread over the Confederacy.

Moving against Richmond from the north in 1863, the Army of the Potomac again failed to reach that place. Believing that its last commander of 1862, Ambrose Burnside, was less than superb, Lincoln had put it under General Joseph "Fighting Joe" Hooker, an officer who eagerly sought battle. General Lee gave it to him. With 60,000 men Lee checked Hooker with 100,000 at Chancellorsville early in May, drove back the Union right flank, and forced Hooker to retreat. Hooker's army suffered more than 10,000 casualties. Lee's losses were as great, and they included "Stonewall" Jackson, accidentally slain by his own troops. Nevertheless, Lee took the offensive. He marched northward into Pennsylvania with 90,000 men. Hooker collected an even larger army, more than 100,000, and followed Lee, keeping Washington behind him. Lee spread panic before him, but neither Lincoln nor the Army of the Potomac faltered. Lincoln called for and secured 100,000 volunteers to serve for six months. When Hooker resigned his command at an awkward moment, on June 27, Lincoln put General George G. Meade in his place. The two great armies converged at Gettysburg. Minor clashes between them grew into a battle that raged during the

first three days of July. The advantage swayed back and forth
until the third day, when Lee sent forward 15,000 infantry to
take a strong Union position on Cemetery Ridge. "Pickett's
Charge" failed disastrously. The advancing Confederates suffered terribly from artillery and rifle fire; only a handful reached
the Union lines, and they were killed or captured. Nearly 4,000
of Lee's troops were slain at Gettysburg; perhaps 24,000 of them
were wounded or missing. Meade's losses were almost as great,
but Lee had to retreat. Had he hoped to break the Northern will
to fight, to persuade England that it was not too risky to intervene? As it was, he turned back toward Virginia on July 4, a
black day for the Confederacy. He was not closely pursued by
Meade. The Union general, indeed, undertook no adventures
during the remainder of 1863. Lee was able to rest his troops in
Virginia, and even to send a contingent to help hard-pressed
Confederate forces in Tennessee. But Lee knew that the Army
of the Potomac was becoming ever more powerful. He would
win no more brilliant and profitable victories.

On that same Independence Day on which Lee fell back from
Gettysburg, far to the west, upon bluffs overlooking the Mississippi, another Confederate commander acknowledged defeat and
surrendered an army. Moreover, it became evident to Lincoln
that he had found, in Ulysses S. Grant, the skillful and resolute
general who could deal with the resourceful Lee. In the spring
of 1863 the fortress of Vicksburg was held by a Confederate
army under General John C. Pemberton. Not far away was a
second Southern army under General Joseph E. Johnston that
could support Pemberton. In a brilliant campaign Grant slipped
between the two Southern forces, drove Johnston's troops back
in a series of engagements, then besieged Pemberton in Vicksburg. At last, unable to resist longer, that officer had to yield
himself and more than 20,000 soldiers. Five days later the Confederates also had to give up Port Hudson in Louisiana, their
only remaining post on the Mississippi. Thus, the river became a
completely Federal waterway, and the Confederacy was cut
apart.

The military genius of Ulysses S. Grant has not always been
fully recognized. He lacked the patrician dignity of Robert E.
Lee. A plain, cigar-smoking, whisky-drinking man, he was, like

Lee, a graduate of the Military Academy at West Point, a veteran of the Mexican War. He knew how to manage large forces, usually chose the ablest officers available to help him, and efficiently sent officers and men to do the right tasks. Not to the manor born, he was businesslike, cool, and determined. Before the end of 1863 he added achievements in the mountains of Tennessee and northern Georgia to his exploits on the Mississippi. In September of that year, General William S. Rosecrans led the Union Army of the Tennessee into Chattanooga. However, with help sent by Lee, the Confederate General Braxton Bragg attacked Rosecrans at Chickamauga, drove him back after a bloody battle, and invested his army in Chattanooga. Grant was sent to the scene. With aid from the Army of the Potomac, he swiftly opened a supply line into Chattanooga, drove Bragg back through the mountains south of that city, and opened the way for an advance to Atlanta—and beyond.

At last, in 1864, the Union was able to mobilize armies sufficient to crush the Confederacy. And Lincoln, after much testing, had found a commander in chief who knew how to lead those forces—General Ulysses S. Grant. Once in command, Grant sent General William Tecumseh Sherman with the Army of the Tennessee against Atlanta. He himself moved southward against Lee. In the Battle of the Wilderness early in May, Lee, displaying his customary skill, attacked and inflicted heavy losses upon Grant's army. Grant would not be discouraged. He drove on. He was checked with heavy losses by Lee at Spotsylvania Courthouse and again at Cold Harbor. By mid-June he had lost as many men as Lee had had at the beginning of the campaign, 60,000. But Lee had also suffered heavy casualties, at least 25,000, and they were almost irreplaceable. Grant adroitly slipped southward across the James River and advanced against Richmond and Petersburg from the east. He was stopped again by Lee. Entrenched Confederates at Petersburg successfully withstood attacks by Grant for nine months. But Grant permitted Lee no rest. Nor did he lose his composure when the Confederate General Jubal Early, sallying from the Shenandoah Valley, moved against Washington. He sent back two divisions to help defend the capital, but he did not relax his efforts at Petersburg. Early was forced to retreat, and Grant ordered General Philip

Sheridan to drive him back through the Shenandoah. In a series
of battles the aggressive Sheridan crushed Early's army and assured the safety of Washington. Lee held on desperately in his
lines into 1865 but with a dwindling army.

While Grant battered away in Virginia, General Sherman
with an army of 100,000 men, moved steadily forward from
Chattanooga, driving before him the Confederate defenders of
Atlanta. He captured that town on September 2. Then, with
60,000 troops, marching through the heart of the Confederacy,
he pushed on to Savannah. He encountered almost no resistance,
for the Confederate General John B. Hood, after evacuating
Atlanta, desperately attempted to bring Sherman to a halt by
invading Tennessee. Sherman did not turn back, for he had faith
in General George Thomas, who commanded the Union troops
in that state. His trust in Thomas was well placed. Hood attacked a part of Thomas's forces at Franklin, Tennessee, and
was repulsed with frightful slaughter. He nevertheless went on
to Nashville, where Thomas, gathering all available men, waited
for him. In mid-December Thomas attacked Hood, routed his
army, and all but destroyed it. A week later Sherman entered
Savannah. By the end of 1864 the Confederacy was collapsing
behind Lee's army.

Even in the summer of 1864, when the Confederacy was beginning to totter, the long lists of the dead and wounded sent
back by Grant from Virginia convinced all those Northerners
who believed the fighting to be useless that it ought to be ended
at any price. Many others who had steadily offered their loyalty
to the Union were appalled. Lincoln was attacked by the Peace
Democrats as a tyrant who insisted upon useless bloodshed. On
the other hand, Radical Republicans, as of yore, denounced him
for lack of vigor. He did not falter. For a time it seemed that he
would lose the Presidency in the election of that year, required
by the Constitution, war or no war. The Radical Republicans
made ready to propose their own candidate, and the Democrats
looked forward to triumph at the polls. But the divisions among
Lincoln's political enemies and the victories of the Union armies
over his military foes brought victory to the President. The
majority of the Democrats in their national convention called
for peace, but inconsistently named for the Presidency General

George McClellan, who declared that the war must proceed. Republicans, Democrats, and others whose first loyalty was to the nation rallied behind Lincoln, forming a Union party. They put forward for the Vice-Presidency Andrew Johnson of Tennessee, formerly a Democrat. The capture of Atlanta by Sherman made it clear that the Confederacy could not long endure. It temporarily silenced the Radical Republicans, and Lincoln and Johnson were elected by an overwhelming majority in the electoral college. Lincoln lived long enough into his second term in the Presidency to see the Confederacy in dissolution.

It was evident to Southern leaders before the end of 1864 that their situation was desperate. The Confederate Congress urged that slaves be promised freedom in exchange for service in the weakening Southern armies. Southern soldiers were deserting in large numbers. There were food riots in cities still in Confederate hands. In the early weeks of 1865 several Union armies converged upon those parts of Virginia and the Carolinas still held by the Confederates. Too late, Jefferson Davis called slaves to the Southern colors. General Sherman pushed northward from Savannah, his troops wrecking and burning as they went. General Joseph E. Johnston, gathering scattered Confederates, was able to check Sherman only momentarily in North Carolina. Then, at last, Lee and his army could no longer withstand the attacks of Grant. Failing in desperate attempts to break through Grant's lines, Lee evacuated Richmond and Petersburg early in April. He moved southwestward in the hope of joining Johnston. His army shrank as it retreated. Virtually surrounded, Lee surrendered with fewer than 30,000 men at Appomattox Courthouse on April 9. Seventeen days later, perceiving the uselessness of further resistance, Johnston ordered his army of 37,000 to lay down its arms. Jefferson Davis, fleeing southward, was captured in Georgia. Other Confederate commanders of smaller forces soon followed the example of Lee and Johnston. Paroled, many of the Southern soldiers reached home in time to do the spring plowing. The Confederacy vanished. The American nation had survived a great test.

The republic was not what it had been. The costs of the war were enormous, even to the victorious North. Sad statistics related that more than 350,000 men gave their lives for the cause of the Union. How many of its soldiers and sailors survived with broken bodies and injured morale one may not estimate. Nor is it possible to weigh the losses of families deprived of healthy vigorous men. It is apparent that the Union, to win the war, spent money lavishly. At the end of the conflict the national debt was not far from one billion dollars. If the Confederates did little damage to Northern property, inflation and profiteering hurt many of the poor in goods and in spirit. Too often the unscrupulous profited richly from the war. It grievously injured public and private morals. It left among the Northerners a legacy of hatred against Southerners that shallow and self-seeking politicians could manipulate to their own advantage. The woes that came to the Northerners from the Civil War were softened by the joy of victory. They might believe that the preservation of the Union was worth the sacrifices they had made. They had not exhausted their resources; their farms, shops, and factories had not been destroyed; and they were able to bear, without great strain, the economic burdens that proceeded from the conflict.

It was otherwise for the Southerners, defeated, impoverished, confronted by a racial problem changed but not solved. The Confederate lists of killed, wounded, and sick were shorter than those of the North, but Southern losses in men were comparatively far greater. The Southern dead numbered more than 250,-000. The maimed and exhausted were also numerous. The generation of Southerners who fought in the war was appallingly reduced. That generation, with its thinned ranks, could not supply the vigor and leadership that the defeated South so badly needed. Never truly as rich as the Northerners, the Southerners, with few exceptions, became poor as the result of the war. Those who had owned slaves, of course, lost them. Those who possessed Confederate currency and bonds held worthless paper at the end of the struggle. Many Southern banks died with the Confederacy. Southern towns and cities, such as Richmond, Atlanta, and Columbia, South Carolina, had been burned, and wide stretches of the Southern countryside had been ravaged. The valley of the Shenandoah was a scene of desolation. Even in those districts where there had been little fighting, factories, shops, and homes, neglected during the war, were in sad disrepair. The destruction of bridges, tracks, engines, and cars had left the Southern railroads in miserable condition. Cattle, horses, and mules in large numbers had been carried off or consumed. Even fields and orchards had deteriorated for lack of care. In sum, the South was an economic shambles after Appomattox. If the economic plight of the Southern whites was almost desperate, it must be said that the lot of the Negroes—whose freedom was established beyond cavil by the passage of the Thirteenth Amendment to the Constitution in 1865—was far worse. Most of them clung loyally to their masters and mistresses until the end of the war. Then, suddenly liberated, uneducated, usually unskilled, lacking money or land, they had to learn to care for themselves. To whom could they go for help?

The economic outlook for the South was dark, and its racial difficulties were not resolved by the emancipation of the blacks. Were they to vote? To hold office? Could freed Negroes and whites create a social order that was just, peaceful, and congenial? Both the hereditary and the cultural differences between the races were large. Could the freed Negroes forget their sufferings as slaves? Could the whites accept the blacks as their full equals in a democratic society? Or would the Negroes, though legally free, be otherwise kept in subjection? It was too much to ask of the blacks that they should quickly pardon the wrongs inflicted upon them and their ancestors. It was too much to demand that the Southern whites should immediately acknowledge and treat the Negroes as their equals in every respect. All the political and social difficulties of the South were compounded by economic distress. And Southern schools, never of superior quality, were grievously hurt by the war. The reconstruction of Southern society would be long and painful.

So devoted to the Southern cause were a few Confederates that they chose to flee to foreign lands, to Brazil, to Mexico, to England, rather than to accept defeat. Others who hated the Yankees remained at home. Most of the Southerners, following the example of Robert E. Lee, accepted the triumph of the Union as final and turned toward the future, dark though it might be.

That future was all the more somber because Abraham Lincoln lay dead six days after Appomattox. Six weeks earlier, in his

Second Inaugural Address, Lincoln had declared in noble
poignant phrases his merciful intent to do all that he could to
heal the wounds of the nation. He would not impose all blame
for the war upon the South; he would not try to punish the
defeated Southerners. But he had come to believe that American
democracy must be widened to include the Negroes, even that
the suffrage should be promptly extended to those blacks who
could vote intelligently. Matured and ennobled by the agonies of
war, Lincoln was superbly qualified to lead the republic in
peace, to soften hatreds, to point the way toward a better society. Attending a Washington theater, he was shot and mortally
wounded by John Wilkes Booth on the evening of April 14,
1865. He died the following morning. Booth was a Marylander,
a mentally unbalanced young actor, and a partisan of the Confederacy. Madly seeking revenge, he had enlisted other disappointed supporters of the Confederacy in a conspiracy to kill the
President, Secretary of State Seward, and Vice-President Johnson. Andrew Johnson was not actually attacked; Seward was
only wounded; but Booth fired a pistol at Lincoln with tragic
accuracy. He was hunted down to his death in Virginia, and
several of his fellow conspirators were executed amidst wild
excitement. Robert E. Lee and all thoughtful Southerners
mourned the loss of Lincoln. They knew that the South must
suffer for Booth's deed. Without Lincoln to guide it, the nation
entered upon a period of punishment for the South, of savage
party warfare, of corruption in public life. Many of the scars
left upon America by the Civil War did not diminish but deep-
ened during the years immediately after that conflict. Walt
Whitman expressed his own grief and that of bewildered millions of people at the death of Lincoln:

> When lilacs last in the dooryard bloom'd
> And the great star early droop'd in the western sky in the night,
> I mourned, and yet shall mourn with ever-returning spring.
>
> Ever-returning spring, trinity sure to me you bring,
> Lilac blooming perennial and drooping star in the west,
> And thought of him I love.

CHAPTER 20

Changing America

❧

AMERICA WAS NEVER A mere excrescence of England, or of Europe. Her proportions were continental, dwarfing those of the homelands from which most of the Americans migrated. Her natural resources, including fertile soil, waters teeming with fish, abundant forests, and vast stores of precious minerals and metals, were immense and almost untouched when the English gained their first footholds on the western side of the Atlantic. They brought to it the language, the literature, the modes of thought, the ways of life, the institutions of their islands. Europeans and Africans who joined them in the New World had to fit themselves, at least ultimately, into the molds shaped by the English settlers. The first inhabitants of America, the Indians, were similarly constrained.

However, the English in North America did not precisely copy Old England. Divergence between the English in America and those who remained at home inevitably began with the planting of Jamestown. Moreover, the English settlers felt the influence of non-English residents and immigrants. America and the Americans began to emerge at the very founding of the colonies that later became parts of the United States.

The largest element among the settlers in the North Temperate Zone of the New World was and remained English for many generations. The English language, dominant from the beginnings of the colonies, was never seriously threatened by any other. In time, the English of the Americans and the English of the English became slightly different, but the Americans did not develop a new language. Their parliaments, their courts, their laws, their churches, their schools, their economic order, and their intellectual and artistic endeavors were imported from the British Isles. Moreover, English men, things, and thought continued to exert influence, an influence that endured, somewhat diminished, long after the colonists cut their political ties with Britain.

However, the colonies along the Atlantic seaboard from Maine to Georgia were never mere crude replicas of England. Her nobility, sufficiently content at home, did not migrate across the ocean; nor did many untitled English aristocrats seek to improve their fortunes in Connecticut or Pennsylvania or South Carolina. No English monarch even visited the colonies. No Anglican bishop ever established himself in a colonial diocese, and the Anglican Church never became entrenched in America as it was in England. Not all of Old England was reproduced in the Thirteen Colonies—and everything English changed, sometimes remarkably, on the western side of the Atlantic. Besides, the English were joined there by many Europeans and Africans. Society there was much more fluid that it was in the Old World. The settlers, except for the Negroes, gained in both goods and social standing. Their ancestors were largely tenant farmers, artisans, and clerks. Not a few of them were convicts; an imposing minority of them can be described, technically, as servants. It would be a mistake to think of them as clodhoppers. The humble and the downtrodden commonly became prosperous and confident in America. There it was not difficult to get a homestead farm. Gentry and tenants, and slaves, could be found in America, but attempts to transplant orders of nobility, feudal manors, feudal courts, and rigid class distinctions —at least so far as the white man was concerned—ultimately failed. Most of the colonists, farmers and landholders, moved toward economic independence and, in consequence, toward social and political equality. Of diverse religious beliefs, but very largely Protestant when they entered American harbors, they also advanced toward religious liberty.

It is apparent that a new people and a new pioneer society were emerging in America before the Revolution. The colonists —English, Dutch, Scotch-Irish, German, and French, with other breeds from the Old World—were coalescing into the Americans. There was mingling even of white and Negro blood. The Americans acquired their name before they sought independence from England. Possessing political freedom in large measure during their colonial time, they would not let George Grenville, Charles Townshend, Lord North, or George III take any of it from them. Rebelling against Parliament and King, they began to define their rights within the British Empire more generously. Then, in the War of Independence, they announced their separation from England and achieved it. During and immediately after that struggle the Patriots founded the American republic; they moved rapidly toward political and social equality —for whites; and they largely achieved religious liberty. Facing a common and dangerous enemy, they drew together in sentiment. They erected Thirteen States. Reconciling North and South, and overcoming other internal jealousies, they also formed a strong central government under the Constitution of 1787. That generation of Americans failed to strike hard against Negro slavery, and it bequeathed a perplexing racial problem to its descendants.

Separating from England, the Americans, much as many of them wished to do it, were unable to turn their backs to Europe. During the quarter-century after Washington assumed the Presidency, they were emotionally and commercially entangled in the great struggle waged by England and her allies against the First French Republic and Napoleon. At length, indeed, the new nation slipped into a second and militarily inconclusive war, in 1812, with England. But tumult beyond the Atlantic also enabled the republic to buy Louisiana, and so to get lands far beyond the Mississippi River. Also vital to the Americans were their growing numbers, their increasing wealth, and the advance of their settlements to and across the Mississippi. They were firmly established beyond the Appalachians at the close of the War of Independence. During the generation that followed, they founded the commonwealths of Tennessee, Kentucky, Ohio, and Louisiana. At the close of the second war with England, they firmly occupied the eastern part of the valley of the Mississippi. They were pushing far into the Old Northwest, across the Mississippi into Missouri, and even into Texas. Their westward march, unimpressive in detail, was awesome.

Nor was it of little moment that the principle of self-government announced in the Northwest Ordinance of 1787 was steadily applied everywhere beyond the Appalachians. The pioneers who led the van toward the Pacific were not treated as colonials. In fact, every advance toward the setting sun brought with it progress toward political and social democracy. In the new settlements class distinctions almost vanished, and one white man was considered to be as good as another. It was in the regions beyond the Atlantic Tidewater that the suffrage for free males was first and firmly established. Moreover, the democracy of the West influenced the East. It helped to bring the Jeffersonians into power at the nation's capital. The Federalists, led by Washington, Hamilton, and John Adams, rendered great and lasting service to their country in the last decade of the eighteenth century. During that brief period, the new national government became solvent, vigorous, and dignified. However, the Federalists were afflicted by notions of hereditary and cultural superiority. The coming of Jefferson to the Presidency in 1801 was a triumph for moderate, liberal republicanism.

During the half-century after the War of 1812, the Americans, continuing to increase rapidly in numbers, also gained access to the rich natural resources of the lands between the Louisiana Purchase and the Pacific. Homestead farms spread to the West Coast. Most white Americans continued to enjoy economic independence and opportunity. They substantially achieved social and political equality. Nearly all white males gained the right to vote. At state capitals and in Washington power passed from Jeffersonian gentlemen to new men who were more pleasing to the masses of voters, men who were eager to cater to those masses. The voters usually elected to the Presidency military heroes or civilian nonentities. The new democracy had much more serious defects. It did not extend to the Negroes, almost all of whom remained slaves in the South; nor were females permitted to enter the rough world of politics.

Even as Jacksonian democracy prevailed, the economic order underlying it was altering. For the Industrial Revolution had begun in America. It was making rapid progress in New England when Andrew Jackson was in the White House. The inventor and the entrepreneur became ever more important.

The building of railroads during the decade before the Civil War powerfully stimulated the American iron industry. The growth of manufacturing and commerce created new men of wealth, greatly enlarged the number of laborers and clerks, and contributed to the rise of cities. Even in a land of plenty, if a large part of the American people lost economic independence, could social and political equality survive? Some Americans saw in the Old Immigration an even more formidable threat to their democracy. Certainly the coming to America during the three decades before the Civil War of nearly four million persons, chiefly German and Irish, was no small matter. Would not the nation suffer from the introduction of so many poor, of so many followers of the Pope? The Roman Church did acquire strength in America. The Americans became less English and more European. They did not consequently become less devoted to democracy.

Less and less English as the nineteenth century proceeded, the American society nevertheless retained solid links with that of England. Their joint tongue assured easy intellectual intercourse, even, to a degree, a common cultural isolation, for neither the English nor the Americans yearned to speak or read "foreign" languages. However, their "special relationship" altered as the American society matured. Until the nineteenth century was well under way, it gave little to, but received much from, the society of England. Then, the English began seriously to import American political and social thought. Besides, the Americans commenced to add substantially to the common stock of learning and letters. The American Renaissance was not ignored in England. American poets and writers of fiction, Edgar Allan Poe, Walt Whitman, and Nathaniel Hawthorne, were read there. Longfellow gained a great popularity in England.

With all its bright facets, the American democratic society had its grave flaws, of which the deepest and widest was, by far, slavery. One-eighth of its population, black, was owned by whites in the land of liberty until the seventh decade of the civilized nineteenth century. Nor did the white Americans manage peaceably to put an end to slavery. Neither Andrew Jackson, nor Henry Clay, nor Abraham Lincoln, nor any other political leader, nor any abolitionist reformer, devised a suitable formula for its orderly extinction. In 1859 that brilliant French student of American democracy, Alexis de Tocqueville, marveled because the republic had never been torn by internal strife. Less than two years later, North and South, estranged primarily because of slavery, engaged in the Civil War. It expensively destroyed more than the bondage of the blacks.

The republic, except for the South, was not impoverished by the Civil War. Indeed, with the South lagging behind, it became ever richer, except for the years of the Great Depression, during the century after Appomattox. The fabled Great West—that of the Great Plains and the Rocky Mountains—was overrun by ranchers, miners, farmers, and railroads before 1900. New wealth came from that region. With the passing of that West, America could no longer offer free or cheap land, except in Alaska, to the homesteader. But American industry began to grow massively soon after the Civil War. Exploiting the vast natural resources at their easy command, the Americans became the richest people on the globe in the twentieth century. New York City replaced London as the world's greatest banking center. The average income of the American doubled in terms of buying power between 1940 and 1965. The collective personal income of the Americans reached $500 billion per annum. They also multiplied in numbers during the century after the Civil War. There were in 1965 more than 190 millions of them. Their prosperity and their standard of living were the envy of the world. With fifty states, including Alaska and Hawaii, and a few extracontinental possessions, America also then had the most powerful military machine upon the globe.

The progress of the Americans during that century was not confined to things physical, economic, and military. They provided ever more generously for the education of their children. By 1965 they were extending to nearly half of their young people the opportunity to secure collegiate and professional instruction. At length their schools excelled in quality as well as quantity. The Americans were creative and productive in medicine, science, literature, the arts, and music. They were giving to a Europe battered by two World Wars perhaps as much as they received. Many Europeans then feared that they would be "Americanized."

The American society underwent other remarkable changes. It became urban and suburban. Less than one-tenth of the Americans, using complicated and subtle machines, lived on the land in 1965. These easily fed themselves, the dwellers in American towns and cities, and millions of people in other nations. The skyscraper appeared in Chicago and New York, later in Detroit, Dallas, and Far Western cities. The center of population moved steadily—in the middle of the twentieth century rapidly—toward the Pacific. Constantly more numerous, constantly more urban, the Americans also acquired new recruits, some from China and Japan, many more from southern and eastern Europe. During the generation before World War I millions of Italians, Greeks, Jews, Czechs, Poles, Russians, and other Slavic breeds made their way across the Atlantic. The flood of these "New Immigrants" was at least temporarily reduced by law after World War I, but it had already fundamentally altered the Americans. In 1965 they were a remarkable mixture—or at least medley—of people from many parts of the world.

The astonishing prosperity of the Americans did not indicate that they had found the solution to every human difficulty. It was not at all certain that it would endure. They had exhausted many of their natural resources; they had wastefully used others. By 1960, having depleted the generous supplies of iron ore in their own country, they were seeking it in Labrador. Were they merely enjoying a "boom" that had lasted for centuries, that was based upon those dwindling riches, that must soon end? It seemed not unlikely that the Americans could, by employing the discoveries of science, artificially replace the resources they had so extravagantly exploited. It could be hoped, indeed, that science and technology would at length care for all the physical wants of all mankind. There was no assurance that the Americans had learned how to divide fairly among themselves the products of their fields and machines. They had found it necessary to employ governmental power extensively to spread the benefits of their economy, to provide for their poor, their sick, and their unemployed. So doing, they inevitably restricted personal liberty. The "New Nationalism" of Theodore Roosevelt, the "New Freedom" of Woodrow Wilson, the "New Deal" of Franklin D. Roosevelt, the "Fair Deal" of Harry S Truman, and the "New Frontier" of John F. Kennedy led to and maintained a regulated capitalistic economy. This change came during a period when England was converted into a socialistic monarchy, when western Europe turned toward socialism, when Communism took root in Russia and elsewhere. America was able to raise the living standard of her poor and unfortunate, to give them a measure of security, without despoiling the rich. However, serious economic inequities remained. In 1964, President Lyndon B. Johnson declared that all poverty could and must be ended in America, that it could be done without serious disturbance of the affluent. He proposed to create a "Great Society." Older and less confident Americans recalled that President Herbert Hoover had spoken in the same vein in 1929, immediately before the onset of the Great Depression.

Could there be a "Great Society" in which the American blacks were treated as inferiors by American whites? The Negroes, after a century of freedom, still suffered from political, economic, and social discrimination. After the Civil War, lacking the wisdom of Lincoln, the Republicans had done no more for the Negroes than to engage in a brief and largely fruitless effort to give them the right to vote. The Southern whites regained and retained dominance below the Mason-Dixon Line. With the consent, if not the approval, of Northerners, they imposed social segregation upon the blacks. The South, so much injured by the Civil War, remained poorer than other parts of America; and its Negroes remained the poorest folk in the South. Educational opportunity in that region was long limited by lack of money; and the Negroes in the South, attending separate and inferior schools, if any, were given less of that opportunity than the whites. Their economic and social advance was very slow. In the twentieth century they migrated in large numbers to Northern and Western cities. The problem of relations between the races then became truly national. It was not swiftly solved. In ghettos of New York City, Chicago, and Los Angeles, the Negroes learned that race prejudice was not confined to Southern whites. If those who left the South fared better than those who remained there, they suffered nevertheless. After World War II, the Negroes, with the support of conscious-stricken whites, made rapid progress, but they continued to feel the indifference and the hostility of many whites.

If their economic and social condition was superior to that of many persons of all colors in many parts of the world, they had by no means reached full equality in America a hundred years after the Civil War.

That war firmly established the superiority over the states of the American central government at Washington. In the twentieth century authority was increasingly concentrated in that city, in part because domestic questions became national, in part because international tensions and foreign wars compelled it. Constitutionally, that massing of power was largely justified by resort to the doctrine of implied powers; the Constitution, little changed in form, was much altered in reality. The threat that government has always posed to liberty became a serious one in America. The danger arose that the President might become a democratic Caesar. The Congress, the federal courts, and, above all, the devotion of the Americans to true democracy continued to check the authority of the President. Their freedom was also menaced, but less seriously, by the rise of a vast bureaucracy, by the rapid growth of federal police forces, and by a burgeoning military machine. However, there was reason to fear that the ancient tyrannies of magicians, monarchs, aristocrats, and bishops would be revived by elected dictators, republican generals, arrogant and unchecked civil servants, and uncivilized technicians.

The world shrank swiftly in the twentieth century, and the Americans, with other peoples, were confronted by new and awesome dangers, and by novel and amazing opportunities. The oceans continued to defend America until that century was well begun. However, it became impossible for her citizens to live in peace, safety, and isolation in the New World. They acquired an overseas empire of sorts during their war with Spain in 1898, and then sensibly undertook to dispose of most of it. But they did not escape the convulsion of World War I. A generation later in World War II, huge American armed forces, with allies, fought almost everywhere outside the New World against the Berlin-Rome-Tokyo Axis. That conflict ended suddenly and ominously in 1945 after American fliers dropped atomic bombs upon two Japanese cities, Hiroshima and Nagasaki. Thereafter American garrisons remained on guard in various parts of the world, in

large part because the Americans, and other peoples, were menaced by a rising tide of Communist despotism. They spent blood
and enormous treasure to check it—they gave in "foreign aid,"
to strengthen the nation's friends abroad, more than $100 billion
during the twenty years after the end of World War II. The
peril of a third, and perhaps a fatal, world conflict began to loom
soon after the second one. Europe, Asia, Africa, and Latin
America were in ferment, in upheaval. That the newly formed
United Nations could preserve peace and a measure of order
upon the globe was uncertain. The American homeland was still
relatively safe from attack in World War II. It did not remain
so. The airplane, the submarine, the rocket, the nuclear bomb—
these and other inventions and weapons put the Americans, and
all mankind, in direst jeopardy. The ingenuity of the human
race had at last made possible its own destruction. That defenses
could be found against nuclear attack, that man would refuse to
make massive resort to it, remained doubtful.

The rise of nuclear science, the rise of science in general, also
offered almost unlimited opportunity for improving the lot of
mankind. It became possible to prevent and to cure diseases from
which men had suffered since time beyond memory; to feed,
clothe, and house all men, if they did not too freely reproduce
themselves; even to journey far into the solar system. It seemed
likely that men would land upon the moon by the year 1970, and
not utterly impossible that the human race would ultimately be
able to communicate with other intelligent beings in the distant
universe. But to the Americans, and to the other peoples of the
earth, a question that had long worried every thoughtful man
was immediately posed. Could the human race, so clever, learn
to control its savage impulses and to live in peace? The traditional easy optimism of the Americans faded; sobered, they remained venturesome and hopeful.

Essay Upon Authorities

The writings of the scholars about America are, of course, immense in quantity. Because of lack of space it is possible here to recommend only a few dozen books that describe important facets of American society as it was before the United States became an industrial giant. Inevitably many other books and scholarly articles of equal or greater value will be omitted. For a generous bibliography the reader may consult Oscar Handlin and others (eds.), *The Harvard Guide to American History* (1954).

Three general works about the red men are: J. C. Collier, *Indians of the Americas* (1940); Paul Radin, *The Story of the American Indian* (third ed., 1944); and W. T. Hagan, *American Indians* (1961). The background of European colonization is described in an excellent synthesis by W. K. Ferguson, *Europe in Transition, 1300–1520* (1962). The best biography of Columbus is S. E. Morison's fluent *Admiral of the Ocean Sea* (2 vols., 1942). Wallace Notestein has limned with accuracy and in fine prose *The English People on the Eve of Colonization, 1603–1630* (1954). The beginnings of that colonization are pungently narrated by A. L. Rowse in *The Expansion of Elizabethan England* (1955) and *The Elizabethans and America* (1959). D. B. Quinn's *Raleigh and the British Empire* (1947) is the work of a careful scholar.

The books about the American colonial period are numerous. Louis B. Wright has provided an excellent brief introduction to it in *The Atlantic Frontier: Colonial American Civilization (1607–1763)* (1947). The magisterial work by C. M. Andrews, *The Colonial Period of American History* (4 vols., 1934–38), deals with the seventeenth century and English commercial policy. It is solid rather than exciting. An earlier overview of the entire era by Andrews, *The Colonial Background of the American Revolution* (rev. ed., 1931), is brief, smoothly written, and illuminating. J. T. Adams offers the best brief coverage of the eighteenth century in his vivid *Provincial Society, 1690–1763* (1927). The Anglo-French struggle for empire is brilliantly chronicled in Francis Parkman's classic *France and England in North America* (9 vols., 1895–1912). Parkman did not love the Roman Catholic Church

or the French. He had little to say about rivalry between the
English, French, and Spanish involving Carolina, Louisiana, and
Florida, which is partly covered in V. W. Crane, *The Southern
Frontier, 1670–1732* (1929). Good on regional development are
the first two volumes of J. T. Adams, *The History of New England*
(3 vols., 1921–26), which is anti-Puritan; W. F. Craven, *The
Southern Colonies in the Seventeenth Century, 1607–1689* (1949),
a sober and careful study; and R. L. Morton, *Colonial Virginia*
(2 vols., 1960). For Plymouth colony one can happily go to William
Bradford, *Of Plymouth Plantation* (ed. S. E. Morison, 1952). Some
economic aspects of colonial life are incisively covered in Joseph
Dorfman, *The Economic Mind in American Civilization, 1606–1865*
(2 vols., 1946).

The social and intellectual history of the colonies has not been
neglected. M. L. Hansen has covered *The Atlantic Migration,
1607–1860* . . . (1940). Alan Simpson's *Puritanism in Old and
New England* (1955) helps to explain the Puritan transplanting.
Perry Miller, in *Orthodoxy in Massachusetts, 1630–1650* (1933),
Roger Williams (1953), *The New England Mind* (2 vols., 1939–
53), and other splendid works, has thrown much light upon the
religious and intellectual history of colonial New England. *Jonathan Edwards* (1940), by O. E. Winslow, is a good biography of
that Puritan divine. The first volume of Vernon Parrington's classic *Main Currents in American Thought* . . . (3 vols., 1927–30),
not satisfactory in detail, continues to offer stimulating discussion
of colonial writings. Two excellent studies of intellectual advance
in early America are: L. B. Wright, *The Cultural Life of the
American Colonies, 1607–1763* (1957), a well-rounded survey;
and H. M. Jones, *O Strange New World* . . . (1964). Michael
Kraus, *The Atlantic Civilization: Eighteenth Century Origins*
(1949), is valuable. Two different views of the intellectual and
artistic achievements of the Southern colonists are to be found in
L. B. Wright, *The First Gentlemen of Virginia* . . . (1940), and
Carl Bridenbaugh, *Myths and Realities: Societies of the Colonial
South* (1952). I. B. Cohen, in *Franklin and Newton* . . . (1956),
has contributed a major study in the history of science. The best
long biography of the great Philadelphian is Carl Van Doren, *Benjamin Franklin* (1938); the best shorter one is that by V. W.
Crane, *Benjamin Franklin and a Rising People* (1954). Franklin's
own autobiography, available in many editions, remains a classic
of its kind. R. H. Shryock has written authoritatively about *Medicine and Society in America, 1660–1860* (1960). Louis Hartz, in

The Liberal Tradition in America (1955), has written learnedly
and provocatively about early—and later—American political
thought. S. E. Morison's *Three Centuries of Harvard, 1636–1936*
(3 vols., 1936) is of value to readers who are not among graduates of that institution. *Government and Labor in Colonial America* (1946), by R. B. Morris, is a special and thoughtful study.
Two volumes by Carl Bridenbaugh, *Cities in the Wilderness* . . .
(second ed., 1955) and *Cities in Revolt* . . . (1955), exhaustively
describe urban life in colonial and Revolutionary America. A
smaller New England community has been splendidly described in
C. G. Grant, *Democracy in the Connecticut Frontier Town of
Kent* (1961). An interesting study is S. F. Kimball's *Domestic
Architecture of the American Colonies and of the Early Republic*
(1922).

One could fill a substantial library with books about the era of
the Revolution. J. C. Miller, *Origins of the American Revolution*
(second ed., 1957), is a readable account of the events leading to
the War of Independence. The same ground is covered by an older
and still valuable study, C. H. Van Tyne's *The Causes of the War
of Independence* (1922). Van Tyne strove to set aside the bias of
an American, and succeeded. In *The Coming of the Revolution,
1763–1775* (1954), L. H. Gipson, an American, looks at the
onset of the Revolution from an "imperial" point of view. The best
analysis of its beginnings is that of Bernhard Knollenberg, *Origin
of the American Revolution, 1759–1766* (1960), which coolly
reminds us that the colonists had real and substantial grievances.
In *Mitre and Sceptre* . . . (1962) Carl Bridenbaugh provocatively
urges that dispute over religion primarily divided the colonists
from England. His evidence is not fully persuasive. *The Stamp Act
Crisis* . . . (1953) of E. S. and H. M. Morgan is important. O. M.
Dickerson, in *The Navigation Acts and the American Revolution*
(1951), not entirely free of American bias, argues that misconduct of British officials vitally aroused colonial discontent. R. C.
Adams, *Political Ideas of the American Revolution* (1922), retains value. It has been said by some that J. R. Alden, *The American Revolution, 1775–1783* (1954), is the best and most readable
account covering the years of the War of Independence. C. L.
Becker's *The Declaration of Independence* . . . (1922) is a classic
study of that document and its ideas by a great historian. There is
no full and impeccable military history of the War of Independence. Christopher Ward, *The War of the Revolution* . . . (2 vols.,
1952, ed. J. R. Alden), crisply and fluently narrates the cam-

paigns on land. W. M. Wallace, *Appeal to Arms* (1951), offers a
readable brief account. W. B. Willcox, *Portrait of a General . . .*
(1964), definitively relates the role in the war of one British
commander in chief, Sir Henry Clinton. S. F. Bemis, *The Diplomacy of the American Revolution* (1935), remains standard.
Those who clung to the British Empire are sympathetically described in C. H. Van Tyne, *The Loyalists in the American Revolution* (1902), and in W. H. Nelson, *The American Tory* (1961).
For the social side of the Revolution one must go to J. F. Jameson,
The American Revolution Considered as a Social Movement
(1926), a very interesting, pioneer, and now somewhat outdated
work. A. P. Stokes, *Church and State in the United States* (3 vols.,
1950), deals in detail with its subject, a most important one in the
Revolutionary period. J. R. Alden, *The South in the Revolution,
1763–1789* (1957), among other things, analyzes divisions
among the Patriots and internal changes. A. C. McLaughlin, *The
Confederation and the Constitution, 1783–1789* (1905), still
offers the clearest description of the postwar years. C. A. Beard, in
*An Economic Interpretation of the Constitution of the United
States* (second ed., 1935), created a sensation by contending that
the framers of the Constitution primarily sought their personal
economic advantage. Carl Van Doren, *The Great Rehearsal . . .*
(1948), offers a better balanced and readable account of the making and ratification of the Constitution.

Biographies of the great Americans—and some not so great—of
the Revolutionary generation are numerous, and they throw light
upon the early part of the nineteenth century as well as the second
half of the eighteenth. More of such personal studies, and doubtless better ones, will appear in the future, for several scholars are
extremely busy with the editing and publishing in many volumes of
the papers of those men. There are presently many books about
Washington and very few good ones. He defies the writers as he
did the redcoats. The massive D. S. Freeman, *George Washington
. . .* (7 vols., 1948–57), is weighty rather than powerful. J. C.
Fitzpatrick's *George Washington Himself . . .* (1933), like many
books about the towering Virginian, is afflicted by a desire to gild
the lily. Bernhard Knollenberg, *George Washington: The Virginia
Period, 1732–1775* (1964), so far as it goes, is healthily realistic.
The biography by the English scholar Marcus Cunliffe, *George
Washington: Man and Monument* (1960), is readable. The as yet
unfinished biography by Dumas Malone, *Jefferson and His Time*
(3 vols. to date, 1948–), is friendly to its subject and good on

political history. Marie Kimball, *Jefferson* . . . (3 vols., 1943–50), emphasizes Jefferson's intellectual and artistic interests. The best short life is Gilbert Chinard, *Thomas Jefferson, the Apostle of Americanism* (second ed., 1939). Chinard has also written the best one-volume life of *Honest John Adams* (1933). Of the many lives of Alexander Hamilton two recent ones stand out: Broadus Mitchell, *Alexander Hamilton* (2 vols., 1957–62), which makes somewhat excessive claims for its subject; and J. C. Miller, *Alexander Hamilton, Portrait in Paradox* (1959). Irving Brant has exhaustively related the career of *James Madison* . . . (6 vols., 1941–61). A fine study of a Virginia Conservative is D. J. Mays, *Edmund Pendleton, 1721–1803* (2 vols., 1952).

Also helpful to an understanding of the early national period (1789–1815) are J. S. Bassett, *The Federalist System, 1789–1801* (1906), and J. C. Miller, *The Federalist Era, 1789–1801* (1960). Henry Adams, *History of the United States of America during the Administration of Thomas Jefferson and James Madison* (9 vols., 1891–98), retains its splendid reputation. For the history of the First Bank of the United States, and later national and state banks, Bray Hammond, *Banks and Politics in America, from the Revolution to the Civil War* (1957), is indispensable. For the development of the American army and navy, O. L. Spaulding, *The United States Army in War and Peace* (1937), and D. W. Knox, *A History of the United States Navy* (rev. ed., 1948), may be consulted. Leonard D. White, *The Federalists: A Study in Administrative History* (1948), ought not to be ignored. W. W. Binkley, *American Political Parties: Their Natural History* (fourth ed., 1962) chronicles the rise and development of parties in the United States. H. C. Allen, *Great Britain and the United States* . . . (1955), describes relations between England and the American republic. J. M. Smith tells about the commotion over the Sedition Act in *Freedom's Fetters* . . . (1956). A. J. Beveridge, *The Life of John Marshall* (4 vols., 1916–19), has not been replaced. C. G. Haines, *The Role of the Supreme Court in American Government and Politics* (2 vols., 1944–57), is enlightening regarding the American practice of judicial review. T. P. Abernethy, *The Burr Conspiracy* (1954), serves as a recent introduction to a mystery that is probably insoluble. R. B. Nye has covered *The Cultural Life of the New Nation, 1776–1830* (1960). For technological advance, see Jeannette Mirsky and Allan Nevins, *The World of Eli Whitney* (1952), and Constance Green, *Eli Whitney and the Birth of American Technology* (1956). J. T. Flexner,

America's Old Masters (1939), may be consulted for the development of American painting.

The expansion of American settlements across the Mississippi and its effect upon the nation as a whole have stimulated much writing and dispute. The reader ought not to ignore *The Rise of the New West, 1819–1829* (1906), by F. J. Turner, the only book written by that thoughtful and inspiring historian. Turner's profoundly stimulating essay of 1893, "The Significance of the Frontier in American History," and other pieces are conveniently available in F. J. Turner, *The Frontier in American History* (1920). H. M. Smith, *Virgin Land: The American West as Symbol and Myth* (1950), is also very interesting. Exponents and critics of Turner are innumerable, among them W. P. Webb, *The Great Frontier* (1952), and D. M. Potter, *People of Plenty* . . . (1954), who suggest that American wealth helps to explain many things American. R. C. Buley, *The Old Northwest* . . . *1815–1840* (2 vols., 1950), is a storehouse of information about that region. R. L. Power, *Planting Corn Belt Culture* (1953), contains suggestive data about the adjustment of Yankees and Southerners to a new life in the same area. B. A. Weisberger, *They Gathered at the River* (1958), is amusing and informative about evangelists of the frontier and other parts of America. The nation was not merely Western during the years following the War of 1812. A. de Tocqueville, *Democracy in America* (2 vols., 1945, ed. Phillips Bradley), is a classic examination by a Frenchman of America as it was about 1830. Cushing Strout, *The American Image of the Old World* (1963), analyzes American views of Europe. V. L. Parrington covers intellectual and cultural advance in the second volume of his stimulating trilogy, *The Romantic Revolution in America* . . . (1930). V. W. Brooks offers excellent and truly readable literary history in *The World of Washington Irving* (1944).

For politicians and politicking during the generation after the War of 1812, one may begin with George Dangerfield, *The Era of Good Feelings* (1952), and G. C. Van Deusen, *The Jacksonian Era, 1828–1848* (1959). A. P. Whittaker has covered *The United States and the Independence of Latin America* . . . (1941). Dexter Perkins, offering *A History of the Monroe Doctrine* (rev. ed., 1955) and other works about that subject, is the authority upon it. S. F. Bemis, *John Quincy Adams and the Union* (1956), is a solid contribution to learning. Marquis James wrote two readable books about "Old Hickory," *Andrew Jackson, the Border Captain*

(1933) and *Andrew Jackson, Portrait of a President* (1937). A. M. Schlesinger, Jr., *The Age of Jackson* (1945), is stimulating. The three outstanding Senators of that period have inspired many biographies, including G. C. Van Deusen, *The Life of Henry Clay* (1937), Charles Wiltse, *John C. Calhoun . . .* (3 vols., 1944–51), and R. N. Current, *Daniel Webster and the Rise of National Conservatism* (1955).

The Old South has been the subject of much controversy. Less attention has been paid to a New North. F. B. Simkins, *A History of the South* (third ed., 1964), is a brilliant survey by a Southerner. Clement Eaton, *The Growth of Southern Civilization, 1790–1860* (1961), is also helpful. J. H. Franklin has contributed *From Slavery to Freedom: a History of American Negroes* (second ed., 1956). U. B. Phillips, a Southerner, wrote extensively and rather gently about slavery in *American Negro Slavery . . .* (1918), *Life and Labor in the Old South* (1929), and other works. K. M. Stampp is much more critical of it in *The Peculiar Institution . . .* (1956). Frederic Bancroft, *Slave-Trading in the Old South* (1931), covers an ugly business. F. L. Owsley, *Plain Folk of the Old South* (1949), deserves more attention than it has received. Indispensable to an understanding of the South is J. B. Hubbell, *The South in American Literature, 1607–1900* (1954). For the New North, T. C. Cochran and William Miller, *The Age of Enterprise . . .* (second ed., 1961), P. W. Gates, *The Farmer's Age . . . 1815–1860* (1960), and G. R. Taylor, *The Transportation Revolution, 1815–1860* (1951), are very useful. V. S. Clark, *History of Manufactures in the United States* (rev. ed., 1929), may be consulted, along with W. B. Kaempffert (ed.), *Popular History of American Invention* (2 vols., 1924). For the Old Immigration see M. L. Hansen, *The Immigrant in American History* (1940), and other books listed on p. 308.

The American Renaissance is chronicled in V. W. Brooks, *The Flowering of New England, 1815–1865* (second ed., 1940), and analyzed by F. O. Matthiessen in *American Renaissance: Art and Expression in the Age of Emerson and Whitman* (1941). For Emerson the reader may go to R. L. Rusk, *The Life of Ralph Waldo Emerson* (1949), and S. F. Whicher, *Freedom and Fate: An Inner Life of Ralph Waldo Emerson* (1953). J. W. Krutch has written about *Henry David Thoreau* (1949). For Hawthorne, see Mark Van Doren, *Nathaniel Hawthorne* (1949), and H. H. Waggoner, *Hawthorne: A Critical Study* (1955). E. H. Davidson has written *Poe: A Critical Study* (1957), and Perry Miller, *The*

Raven and the Whale: The War of Words and Wits in the Era of Poe and Melville (1956). Reference must again be made to J. B. Hubbell, *The South in American Literature, 1607–1900* (1954). A. H. Quinn, *A History of the American Drama: from the Beginning to the Civil War* (second ed., 1943), is standard. M. E. Curti may be consulted for *The Growth of American Thought* (second ed., 1951) and H. W. Schneider for *A History of American Philosophy* (second ed., 1963). For magazines and newspapers reference must be made to works by F. L. Mott, *A History of American Magazines* (4 vols., 1938–57), and *American Journalism: a History* (third ed., 1962). American painting, sculpture, and architecture may be studied in O. W. Larkin, *Art and Life in America* (rev. ed., 1960); Virgil Barker, *American Painting* (1950); J. T. Flexner, *That Wilder Image* (1962); M. F. Thorp, *The Literary Sculptors* (1965); S. F. Kimball, *American Architecture* (1928); and John Burchard and Albert Bush-Brown, *The Architecture of America* (1961). J. T. Howard has written authoritatively about *Our American Music* . . . (third ed., 1954). D. J. Struik has contributed *Yankee Science in the Making* (1948). Two of the few mature studies of American education are: R. F. Butts and L. A. Cremin, *A History of Education in American Culture* (1953), and Richard Hofstadter and Walter Metzger, *The Development of Academic Freedom in the United States* (1955).

A. F. Tyler, *Freedom's Ferment* (1944), and E. D. Branch, *The Sentimental Years, 1830–1860* (1934), serve as introductions to the reform movements of the generation before the Civil War. A. W. Calhoun, *A Social History of the American Family* . . . (3 vols., 1917–19), the standard study, describes the status of women. The feminist crusade is limned in Eleanor Flexner, *Century of Struggle* . . . (1959). H. E. Marshall, *Dorothea Dix* . . . (1937), is a biographical study of a Samaritan. Merle Curti has written about *The American Peace Crusade, 1815–1860* (1929) and J. A. Krout concerning *The Origins of Prohibition* (1925). Arthur Bestor has described the *Backwoods Utopias* (1950). An interesting estimate of the importance of those communities is given in A. E. Morgan, *Nowhere Was Somewhere* (1946). The abolitionist movement is chronicled in G. H. Barnes, *The Anti-Slavery Impulse, 1830–1844* (1933), which emphasizes the importance of Theodore Dwight Weld as against William Lloyd Garrison; Louis Filler, *The Crusade Against Slavery, 1830–1860* (1960); and D. L. Dumond, *Antislavery: The Crusade for Freedom in America* (1961), which warmly defends the abolitionists.

Two studies of Garrison appeared in 1963: J. L. Thomas, *William Lloyd Garrison;* and W. M. Merrill, *Against Wind and Tide: a Biography of William Lloyd Garrison.* B. P. Thomas has published a life of *Theodore Weld* (1950), and Betty Fladeland one of *James Gillespie Birney* (1955).

The American advance to the Pacific is narrated in R. A. Billington, *The Far Western Frontier, 1830–1860* (1956), a book that is both scholarly and sprightly. Motives for expansion are considered in A. K. Weinberg, *Manifest Destiny* . . . (1935); N. A. Graebner, *Empire on the Pacific* . . . (1955); Frederick Merk, *Manifest Destiny and Mission in American History* (1963); and Bernard de Voto, *Year of Decision, 1846* (1943). Among the good studies of the American settlement of Texas and of the Texan republic are: E. C. Barker, *The Life of Stephen F. Austin* (1925); W. C. Binkley, *The Texas Revolution* (1952); Marquis James, *The Raven* . . . (1929), a biography of Sam Houston; and W. R. Hogan, *The Texas Republic* (1946). The advance of the fur traders into the Rocky Mountain region has been colorfully described in Bernard de Voto, *Across the Wide Missouri* (1947). Josiah Gregg, *Commerce of the Prairies* . . . (1844), is a classic account of trading on the Santa Fe trail. Francis Parkman covered *The California and Oregon Trail* in person and in print (1849). For the Oregon Country see O. O. Winther, *The Great Northwest* (second ed., 1950), and D. O. Johansen and C. M. Gates, *Empire of the Columbia* (1957). Concerning Joseph Smith and the Mormon settlements, F. M. Brodie, *No Man Knows My History* . . . (1945), a biography of Smith, and L. H. Creer, *The Founding of an Empire* (1947), may be consulted. C. E. Chapman has written about pre-American California in *A History of California: The Spanish Period* (1921). Josiah Royce, *California* (1886), narrates the American invasion and conquest of California. Allan Nevins has related the history of *Frémont, Pathmarker of the West* (1939). O. A. Singletary, *The Mexican War* (1960), is a brief and good military history.

The approach of the Civil War overshadows the 1850s, and it has been studied by many historians. Among the more recent writings about it are Allan Nevins, *Ordeal of the Union* (2 vols., 1947), *The Emergence of Lincoln* (2 vols., 1950), and *The War for the Union* (2 vols., 1959), which are dispassionate. A. O. Craven has described it from the viewpoint of a Southerner and a scholar in several books, including *The Growth of Southern Sectionalism, 1848–1861* (1953), and *The Coming of the Civil War* (second ed., 1957). Holman Hamilton has dealt with the complexities of *The Compromise of 1850* (1963). G. F. Milton has limned Stephen A. Douglas in *The Eve of Conflict* (1934). A. J. Beveridge, *Abraham Lincoln, 1809–1858* (2 vols., 1928), objectively covers in detail the early career and rise of Lincoln. For the Old Immigrants and the nativist reaction of the 1850s reference may be made to Carl Wittke, *We Who Built America* (1939); Oscar Handlin, *The Uprooted* (1951); and R. A. Billington, *The Protestant Crusade, 1800–1860* . . . (1938). The literary scene has been described in V. W. Brooks, *The Times of Melville and Whitman* (1947). Two studies of Walt Whitman are: Richard Chase, *Walt Whitman Reconsidered* (1955); and G. W. Allen, *The Solitary Singer* . . . (1961). Two good biographies are: Lewis Mumford, *Herman Melville* (1929); and Newton Arvin, *Herman Melville* (1950). For things economic, reference should be made to works cited above, by T. C. Cochran and William Miller, P. W. Gates, G. R. Taylor, and V. S. Clark.

Writings about the Civil War and its leaders are, to say the least, copious. J. G. Randall, *Lincoln the President* (4 vols., 1945–55), completed by R. N. Current, is an impressive work. B. P. Thomas, *Abraham Lincoln* (1952), and R. H. Luthin, *The Real Abraham Lincoln* (1960), are the best short biographies of that remarkable man. Lord Charnwood, *Abraham Lincoln* (1916), and K. C. Wheare, *Abraham Lincoln and the United States* (1948), are interesting studies by an Englishman and an Australian. T. H. Williams, *Lincoln and His Generals* (1952), is most instructive concerning Lincoln as a military leader. The same author has thrown light upon *Lincoln and the Radicals* (1941). D. S. Freeman has written exhaustively about *R. E. Lee* . . . (4 vols., 1934–45), and *Lee's Lieutenants* (3 vols., 1942–44). F. E. Vandiver has contributed a modern biography of Thomas J. Jackson in *Mighty Stonewall* (1957). Among many well-written books about the Civil War by Bruce Catton is *U. S. Grant and the American Military Tradition* (1954). Lloyd Lewis has written a good biography of William Tecumseh Sherman in *Sherman, Fighting Prophet* (1932). A short sound military history is Fletcher Pratt, *Ordeal by Fire* (1948). Allan Nevins, *The War for the Union* (2 vols. to date, 1959–), will soon be completed. Two good books about the short-lived Southern republic are: E. M. Coulter, *The Confederate States of America, 1861–1865* (1950), and Clement Eaton, *A History of the Southern Confederacy* (1954). E. D. Adams, *Great Britain and the American Civil War* (2 vols., 1925), is nearly a classic. Donaldson Jordan and E. J. Pratt, *Europe and the American Civil War* (1931), and H. C. Owsley, *King Cotton Diplomacy* (second ed., 1959), are also instructive concerning the diplomatic side of the war. Two special studies by B. I. Wiley deserve mention, *Southern Negroes, 1861–1865* (1938), and *The Plain People of the Confederacy* (1943).

Index

ABOLITIONISTS, 217, 225-9, 240, 257, 261
Adams, Charles Francis, 274, 276
Adams, John, 47, 78, 88, 89, 94, 105,
    108, 114, 126, 127, 130, 141, 142,
    144, 292; Presidency of, 138-40
Adams, John Quincy, 144, 178, 179,
    186, 234; in Presidency, 180-2
Adams, Samuel, 76, 77, 114
Alabama, the, 273
Alamance, Battle of the, 59
Alamo, Battle of the, 236, 237
Alexandria, the, 275-6
Allston, Washington, 170
America, and Americans, use of the
    names, 48, 60-1
American Anti-Slavery Society, 228
American Colonization Society, 226,
    227
American party, 253
American Renaissance, 202, 212-17,
    293
American Revolution, results of, 62-3,
    95-110; causes of, 66-78; *see also*
    War of Independence
American Society for Promoting Ob-
    servance of the Seventh Com-
    mandment, 223
American Temperance Union, 220
Amherst, General Jeffrey, 68
Anahuac, 236
Anglicans, 17, 21, 24-5, 27, 31, 43, 54,
    55, 57, 66, 82, 290; in Southern
    colonies, 50
"Annabel Lee," 215
Annapolis Convention, 114
Antietam, Battle of, 270, 274
Antifederalists, 122-5
Anti-Tobacco Society, 223
Anti-Vivisection Society, 223
Appleton, Nathan, 203
Appomattox, 285, 287
Arapaho, the, 232
Araucanian Indians, 12
Aristocracy in America, 48-52, 57, 103-
    105, 192, 194, 207, 289, 290
Arizona, 17
Armada, Great, 19
Army of Northern Virginia, 269-70,
    272, 281-2, 283-4, 285
Army of the Potomac, 269-70, 272,
    281-2, 283-4, 285

Arnold, General Benedict, 84, 93
Articles of Confederation, 97-8, 104,
    114, 115, 118, 121, 123; defects of,
    112-13
Assemblies, powers of colonial, 43-4
Associationists, 224
Assumption of state debts, 132-3
Atlanta, 193, 269, 283, 284
Atlantis, 4
Austin, Moses, 232-3
Austin, Stephen, 233-4, 235, 236
Austria, 64
Aztec confederacy, 10, 13

BACON'S REBELLION, 59
Bancroft, George, 80-1
Bank of the United States, First, 133-
    134, 147, 154; Second, 175-6, 177,
    184, 185-7, 188
Baptists, 28, 106, 169, 195, 208, 209,
    211, 230, 238
Barbary States, 145
Barron, Commodore James, 152-3
Bartram, John, 58
Bartram, William, 58
Beauregard, General Pierre, 266
Bedford, Gunning, 116, 117
Beecher, Reverend Lyman, 228
Beggars, 37
Bell, John, 259-60
"Bells, The," 215
Bewick, Thomas, quoted, 173
Biddle, Nicholas, 175, 184, 186
Bill of rights, 44; state, 100; federal,
    121, 122, 123, 124, 128
Bingham, William, 102
Birney, James G., 225, 229
Black Belt, 159
Blockade runners, 273
Bloomer costume, 223
Bondservants, 38-9, 49, 51
Book of Mormon, The, 209
Booth, John Wilkes, 288
Border States, 264, 268, 274
Boston, 26, 52, 55, 56, 160, 161, 162,
    169, 172; Tea Party, 77; as cultural
    center, 212-15, 217
Bowie, Jim, 236
Bradstreet, Mrs. Anne, quoted, 56
Bragg, General Braxton, 272, 283
Brahmins, the, 212, 213, 214

Brandywine, Battle of, 91
Brazil, 17
Breckinridge, John C., 259, 260
Britain, 99, 146, 147, 162; legacy from,
    3, 49, 57–8, 59–61, 171, 191, 211–
    212, 253–4, 289–91, 293; and In-
    dians, 13, 34, 109; colonization
    from, 16–31, 36–41; colonial pol-
    icy of, 42–5; and American Revo-
    lution, 62–95; empire of, in 1763,
    63–6; trade restrictions and im-
    pressment, 136–7, 144–5, 151–54;
    War of 1812, 154–5; first rap-
    prochement with America, 155–6;
    and Latin America, 179–80; quar-
    rels with United States over Ca-
    nadian boundaries, 240–1; and
    Civil War, 263, 267–8, 273–6
Brook Farm community, 224
Brown, John, 259
Brown University, 53
Bryant, William Cullen, 171
Buchanan, James, 258, 261
Buena Vista, Battle of, 244
Bull Run, first Battle of, 266, 267;
    second Battle of, 270
Bumppo, Natty, 171
Bunker Hill, Battle of, 84
Burgoyne, General John, 91
Burke, Edmund, 78
Burnside, General Ambrose, 270, 281
Burr, Aaron, 131, 140, 141; conspiracy,
    150–1; duel with Hamilton, 150–1
Bushido, code, 56
Bute, Earl of, and American colonies,
    67–71
Butler, Colonel Anthony, 234, 235
Byrd, William, II, 53
Byron, Lord, 195

CABET, ETIENNE, 223, 224
Cabot, John, 17
Calhoun, John C., 175, 176, 182, 184,
    185, 188, 248, 260
California, 17, 46, 47, 239, 240, 241,
    245; Spanish, 238–9; revolt in,
    243; becomes a state, 248–9;
    growth of, 251
Calvinists, German, 37
Calvert family, and Maryland, 23–4
Cambridge University, 25
Canada, 95; French, 31, 44–6; Patriot
    invasion of, 84–5; and War of
    1812, 153–5; boundaries of, with
    United States, 156, 239–40
Canning, George, 179, 180
Carleton, General Guy, 84, 86, 90
Carlisle, Earl of, 92
Carlisle Commission, 92

Carters, the, 52, 70
Carthage, 5, 6
Cartwright, Peter, 170
Catawba Indians, 12
Cavaliers, of Virginia, 21, 191, 195
Cellini, Benvenuto, 195
Celts, 9
Cerro Gordo, Battle of, 245
Certificates of indebtedness, 132
Chancellorsville, Battle of, 281
Charles I, 21, 25, 27
Charles II, 30
Charles III, 92
Charleston, South Carolina, 31, 48, 50,
    94
Chase, Salmon P., 265, 277
Chase, Samuel, 143
Chattanooga, 269, 272, 283
Cherokee, 8, 11, 12, 14, 90, 91, 135, 187
Chesapeake affair, the, 152–3
Cheyenne, the, 232
Chickamauga, Battle of, 283
Chickasaw, 12
Chinese in America, 9, 295
Choctaw, 8, 11, 12, 187
Cincinnati, 160
"City of Raleigh," 19
Civil War, 261–87, 294, 296; causes of,
    217, 256–7; results of, 285–7
Clark, William, 149–50
Clay, Henry, 175, 176, 181, 186, 187,
    188, 226, 240, 249, 293
Clermont, the, 161
Clinton, George, 131
Clinton, General Sir Henry, 92, 93–4
Coercive Acts. *See* Intolerable Acts
Cohens v. Virginia, 177
Cold Harbor, Battle of, 283
Colden, Cadwalader, 38
Coleridge, Samuel, 58
College of William and Mary, 50, 108,
    131
Colleges, 50, 52–3, 58, 108, 166, 172,
    210–11
Colonies, American, development of,
    32–46; religious toleration in, 43;
    government of, 43–4; education
    in, 52–4, 57–8; Middle, 56–8. *See*
    Colonists
Colonists, hardships experienced by,
    33–6; struggles with Indians, 34–5;
    homes of, 36; diet of, 37; numbers
    of, 37; divisions among, 47–8; an-
    cestors of, 59–60; fusing among,
    60–1
Colorado, 251
Colt, Samuel, 202–3
Columbia University, 58
Columbus, 5, 6, 7, 8, 10, 15

"Common School Revolution," 210
Common Sense, 87
Compromise of 1833, 185, 190
Compromise of 1850, 247–50, 257
Conciliatory Resolution, 78–9, 83
Concord, Battle of, 79
"Concord Hymn," 213
Confederacy, the, 260–87
Confiscation Act, First, 269; Second, 274
Congregational Church, 25, 26, 66, 166, 169; established, 43; weakening of, 54–7; disestablished, 105–6
Connecticut, 52, 86; founding of, 27
Connecticut Compromise, 117
Connecticut River valley, 32
Conscription, 279, 281
Conservatives, Revolutionary, 101–2, 111–12, 113–14, 122, 125
Constitution, federal, 97, 98, 99, 100, 104, 227, 230, 291, 297; ratification of, 122–4
Constitutional Convention, device of, 91–100
Constitutional referendum, device of, 100
Constitutional Union party, 259–60
Continental blockade, 152
Continental Congress, First, 78; Second, 78, 83, 87–8, 92
Convicts, sent to America, 39–40
Cooper, James Fenimore, 171
Copley, John Singleton, 54
Copperheads, 279
Cornwallis, General Lord Charles, 90, 94
Cortes, Hernando, 10
Cotton Kingdom, 159
Cotton raising, 159, 191–2
Council for New England, 24, 26, 28
Creek Indians, 11, 12, 14, 135, 187
Crèvecoeur, J. Hector St. John de, quoted, 61
Crockett, Davy, 236
Crown Point, 84
Cuba, 250
Cumberland Road, 161
Currency Act of 1764, 72
Customs Commissioners, at Boston, 75
Czechs in America, 295

DANA, CHARLES A., 224
Dartmouth College, 53
Davis, Jefferson, 260, 263, 264, 265, 281, 285
Declaration of Independence, 63, 105; background of, 86–8; analysis of, 88–9
Declaratory Act, 74

Deerslayer, The, 171
De Grasse, Admiral, 94
Deists, 55
Delaware, founding of, 30
Democratic party, 186, 187–8, 193, 240, 249, 250, 257, 258, 259, 260, 261, 268, 277, 284–5
Democratic-Republican party, 128, 130–1, 138, 139, 140, 142, 148, 152, 157, 174, 175, 180, 292
D'Estaing, Comte, 93
Detroit, capture of, 154
Dew, Thomas R., 229
Dickens, Charles, 211
Dickinson, John, 88, 115
Diggers (Indians), 9, 10
Directory, French, 139
Dix, Dorothea Lynde, 222
Domestic Manners of the Americans, 173
Dominion of New England, 43
Doniphan, Colonel Alexander, 244
Dorchester Heights, 84
Douglas, Stephen, 249, 250, 257–8, 259, 260, 261, 268
"Dream within a Dream, A," quoted, 215
Dred Scott case, 258–9
Dryden, John, quoted, 170
Dunmore, Earl of, 84, 87
Dutch, empire of, in America, 13, 16, 29–30, 31; people in America, 51, 57, 58, 158, 206, 253, 254, 290
Dutch West India Company, 29
Durand, Asher B., 256

EARLY, GENERAL JUBAL, 283–4
East India Company, 19, 76, 77
Edinburgh, 50
Education, 50, 52–4, 57–8, 166, 172, 210–11, 221–2, 280, 294
Edwards, Jonathan, 54, 55
Elizabeth I, 17, 18, 19
Ellsworth, Oliver, 115
Emancipation Proclamation, 274–5, 277
Emerson, Ralph Waldo, 170, 202, 203, 211, 213, 214, 219, 256
Empresarios, 234, 238
England. *See* Britain
Entail, abolition of, 103
Episcopal Church, 195; disestablished, 105–6. *See* Anglican Church
"Era of Good Feelings, The," 174
Ericson, Leif, 7
Ericsson, John, 202–3
Erie Canal, 160
Eskimos, 7
"Exposition and Protest," 184

"Fair Deal," 295
Fairfax, Mrs. Sally, 126, 138
Fallen Timbers, Battle of, 135
"Farewell Address," 137–8
Farragut, Admiral David, 264, 272
Federal Convention, 114–21
Federal government, described in Constitution, 120–1
Federalist, The, 122
Federalist party, 127, 130, 136, 138, 139, 140, 141, 142, 143, 144, 147, 152, 153–4, 157, 174, 175, 292
Federalists, for Constitution, 122–4
"Feminine Fifties," 256
Feminists, 222
Ferdinand VII, 179
Fillmore, Millard, 249
Finney, Reverend Charles Grandison, 170, 221, 228
First Families of Virginia, 131
Fishing, 51
Florida, and Floridas, 17, 45, 95, 139, 179. *See* West Florida
Florida, the, 273
Force Bill, 185
Forty-niners, 248
Foster, Stephen C., 256
Fourier, Charles, 223, 224
France, 32, 63, 64; loses North American empire, 44-6, 47; and American Revolution, 79, 81, 85, 87, 91, 92–5. *See* French
Franklin, Battle of, 284
Franklin, Benjamin, 36, 47, 67, 83, 88, 115, 131; sketch of, 58; in France, 92, 94
Franklin, Governor William, 83
Frederick the Great, 45, 63, 65
Fredericksburg, Battle of, 270
Frémont, John C., 243, 244, 258
French, empire of, in America, 6, 11, 12, 13; people in United States, 60, 253, 290; Canadians, 64–6, 68, 77, 85; Revolution, 127, 136–7. *See* France
Freneau, Philip, 171
Fugitive Slave Law, 249, 257
Fuller, Margaret, 222
Fulton, Robert, 161, 202
Furs, 42

Gadsden Treaty, 245, 250
Gage, General Thomas, 68, 77, 79, 83, 84
Gainsborough, Thomas, 54
Gallatin, Alexander, 144
Garrison, William Lloyd, 217, 225–6, 227, 228, 229
Gates, General Horatio, 91

"General assessment" scheme, 106
George III, 46, 67, 74, 78, 81, 85, 86, 98, 99, 127, 291; denounced in Declaration of Independence, 88–9
Georgia, 32; founding of, 44–5
Germans in America, 9, 45, 49, 57, 58, 158, 206–7, 253, 290, 293
Germantown, Battle of, 91
Gettysburg, Battle of, 281–2
Ghent, Treaty of, 155–6
Gibbon, Edward, 157, 168
Gibbons v. Ogden, 177
Gibraltar, 63, 93, 95
Gilbert, Sir Humphrey, 17–18, 19
Gladstone, William E., 274
Glover, General John, 56
Glover, Mrs. John, 56
Gold Rush, 248, 251
Goliad, 236
Goodyear, Charles, 203
Gorges, Sir Ferdinando, 20
Gorges family, 28
Graham, Reverend Sylvester, 220–1
Graham bread, 221
Graham Hotels, 221
Graham Journal of Health and Longevity, 221
Greeley, Horace, 224
Grenville, George, 291
Grafton, Duke of, 75
Grand Banks of Newfoundland, 6
Grant, General Ulysses S., 272, 283–4, 285; sketch of, 282–3
Great Awakening, the, 55–6, 57–8
"Great Migration," 25
Great Plains, 252
"Great Society, the," 296
Greeks in America, 295
Greene, General Nathanael, 94
Greenland, 7, 8
Grenville, George, and American colonies, 67–74
Griswold family, 52
Guadalupe Hidalgo, Treaty of, 245

Habeas Corpus, Writ of, suspended, 279
Habsburgs, 63
Haiti, 146
Hamilton, Alexander, 99, 106, 115, 122, 124, 131, 138, 139, 140, 144, 292; as Secretary of the Treasury, 126, 128, 132–5, 136; sketch of, 129–30; killed, 150–1
Hamilton, Elizabeth Schuyler, 129
Hammond, James Henry, 229
Hanover, 64
Harrison, William Henry, 155, 188–9
Hartford Convention, 174

Harvard College, 52, 172, 212, 213, 214
Hawkins, John, 17–18
Hawthorne, Nathaniel, 203, 214–15, 218, 224, 256, 293
Hayne, Robert Y., 185
Henrietta Maria, Queen, 21
Henry VIII, 17
Henry, Patrick, 37, 73, 78, 88, 106, 114–115, 124, 189
Hessian troops, 85–6, 87, 89–90, 91
Hiroshima, 297
History of the Conspiracy of Pontiac, The, 255
Holland, 93; Pilgrims in, 25–6; and American Revolution, 79, 81. *See* Dutch
Holmes, Dr. Oliver Wendell, 212
Homer, 157
Homestead Act, 102–3, 166, 260, 264–5
Honduras, 251
Hood, General John B., 284
Hooker, General Joseph, 270, 281
Hooker, Reverend Thomas, 28
Hoover, Herbert, 296
Horseshoe Bend, Battle of, 155
House of Burgesses, 21, 23–4, 44
House of Seven Gables, The, 215
Houston, Sam, 236, 237, 238, 239
Howe, Elias, 203
Howe, Admiral Lord Richard, 85
Howe, General Sir William, 84, 86, 90, 91, 92
Hudson Bay country, 31
"Hudson River School," 256
Hudson's Bay Company, 240
Huguenots, 37
Hunt, Walter, 203
Hussey, Obed, 203
Hutchinson, Mrs. Ann, 27
Hutchinson family, 52

Iceland, 7
Immigration, 37–41, 202, 205–7, 247, 252–3, 289, 290
Impressment, 137, 152, 153
Incas, 9–10, 11, 13
India, 63
Indians, 3, 19, 26, 47, 60, 87, 109, 149, 153, 237, 289; origins of, 4–12; religion of, 10–11; feuds of, 12; clash between whites and, 13–15; influence upon whites, 15; and Jamestown, 20; forced back by colonists, 34–5; British policy regarding, 68–71, 75; in War of Independence, 90–1; federal power over, 98. *See* names of tribes
"Indian Burying Ground, The," 171
Indian superintendents, British, 70

Indigo growing, 48, 159
Industrial Revolution, 63, 159, 161–2, 203–5, 293
Innes, George, 124
Inns of Court, 50
"Internal Revolution," 96–7, 102, 110
Intolerable Acts, 77, 78
Irish in America, 39, 59, 206–7, 293
Iron manufacturing, 56
Iroquois, 14, 29, 58, 90, 91. *See* Six Nations
Irving, Washington, 171
Ishtar, 170
Israel, 5
Italians in America, 295

Jackson, Andrew, 155, 168, 178–9, 181, 195, 201, 211, 219, 234, 237, 241, 293; sketch of, 182–3; Presidency of, 183–7
Jackson, Patrick Tracy, 203
Jackson, Mrs. Rachel, 181, 183
Jackson, General Thomas J. "Stonewall," 269, 270, 272, 281
Jacksonian democracy, 157, 168, 183–4, 292
Jamaica, 63
James I, 19, 22, 25
James II (Duke of York), 29–30, 43
Jamestown, 16, 20, 36
Japan, 252
Japanese in America, 9, 295
Jay, John, 94, 122, 137
Jay's Treaty, 137
Jefferson, Isaac, 197
Jefferson, Thomas, 50, 83, 101, 103, 104, 105, 106, 107, 114, 138, 160, 164, 195, 197, 231, 292; and Declaration of Independence, 88–9; in Washington's Cabinet, 127, 128, 130; sketch of, 131–2; Presidency of, 140–53
Jefferson, Mrs. Thomas, 197
Jesuits, 24
Jews in America, 29, 37, 57, 106, 295
Johnson, President Andrew, 182, 285, 288
Johnson, Lyndon B., 296
Johnson, Dr. Samuel, 40
Johnston, General Albert Sidney, 272
Johnston, General Joseph E., 282, 285
Jones, Commodore Thomas ap Catesby, 239
Judiciary Act of 1789, 128, 142

Kansas, 252, 257–8, 259
Kansas-Nebraska Act, 257–8
Kearny, General Stephen, 244
Kearsarge, U.S.S., 273

Kennedy, John F., 295
Kensington Stone, 7
Knights of the Golden Circle, 279
Know-nothings, 253
Knox, General Henry, 104, 139
"Kubla Khan," 58

Labrador, 7
La Hogue, 31
Laird rams, 276
Lamar, Mirabeau Buonaparte, 237–8
Lane Theological Seminary, 228
Larkin, John O., 242–3
Laurens, Henry, 94, 107
League of Armed Neutrality, 93
Leaves of Grass, 254
Lee, General Henry, 124, 135
Lee, Reverend Jason, 239
Lee, Richard Henry, 88, 124
Lee, Robert E., 257, 269, 270, 272, 281,
    282, 283, 284, 285, 287, 288
Lee family, 52, 70
"Legend of Sleepy Hollow, The," 171
Leopard, the, 152, 153
Lewis and Clark expedition, 149–50
Lewis, Meriwether, 149–50
Lexington, Battle of, 79
Lexington, Mass., 60
Leyden, 25, 50
Liberals, Revolutionary, 101–2, 113,
    122
Liberator, the 225, 227
Liberia, 226
Liberty party, 229
Lincoln, Abraham, 191, 215, 243, 259,
    260, 261, 293; and the Civil War,
    260–1, 264, 267, 268, 269, 270, 275–
    286; sketch of, 265–6
Livingston, Robert R., 88, 146
Livingston, William, 58
Livingstons, the, 30, 57
Locke, John, 53, 89
London Company, 19–20, 21, 23, 25
Longfellow, Henry Wadsworth, 212–
    213, 216
Louis XIV, 31
Louis XV, 64
Louis XVI, 92, 136
Louisiana, 31, 45–6, 139; Purchase,
    145–9, 179, 231; Territory, 231–2
Lovejoy, Elijah, 229
Low Country, 48
Lowell, James Russell, 216
Lowell, Massachusetts, as manufactur-
    ing center, 163
Loyalists, American, 85, 91, 95, 96, 99,
    118; description of, 81–2; lands of,
    confiscated, 102

Lutherans, 37, 57
Lyceums, 211

Madison, James, 50, 101, 104, 106, 122,
    124, 130, 132, 142, 143, 153, 154,
    155 175, 176, 226; in Federal Con-
    vention, 115–17, 119
Madoc, Prince, 6
Magazines, 211
Magyars, 9
Maine, early history of, 27–8
Malaria, 35
"Manifest destiny," 244, 245, 250
Mann, Horace, 221–2
Manufacturing, 252, 265, 293. *See* In-
    dustrial Revolution
Marbury, William, 142
Marbury v. Madison, 142–3
Marie Antoinette, Queen, 136
Marshall, John, 106, 124, 151, 226; as
    chief justice, 141–4, 177
Mary I, 17
Mary, Queen of Scots, 17
Maryland, 49, 101; early history of,
    21–4
Mason, George, 115, 119, 120
Mason, James M., 268.
Mason family, 28
Massachusetts Bay, 51–2; early history
    of, 26–8
Massachusetts Bay Company, 26
Mather, Cotton, 53–4
Maximilian, Emperor, of Mexico, 274
Maya, civilization of, 8, 9–10, 11
Mayflower, the 26
Mayflower Compact, 26
Mazzini, Giuseppe, 99
McClellan, General George B., 270,
    284–5
McCormick, Cyrus, 202–3
McCulloch v. Maryland, 177
McDowell, General Irwin, 266
McGillivray, Alexander, "King of the
    Creeks," 135
McLoughlin, Dr. John, 240
Meade, General George G., 281–2
Melville, Herman, 216, 247, 253–5, 256
Mennonites, 30, 37
Methodists, 169, 195, 211, 230, 238, 239
Mexican War, 241–5
Mexico, 17; valley of, 9, 10; and Texas,
    230–8, 241–2; war with United
    States, 241–5
Miller, William, 209
Milton, John, 53
Minorca, 63
Mississippi Colonization Society, 226
Missouri controversy, 177–8
Mobile, 68, 95

Moby Dick, 254, 255
Molasses Act, 42, 71
Mongols, 9
Monitor, U.S.S., 203, 272–3
Monroe Doctrine, 174, 179–80
Monroe, James, 146, 174, 175, 176, 178, 179, 226
Montgomery, General Richard, 84
Moore's Creek Bridge, Battle of, 84
Moravians, 30, 37, 57
Mormons, 209–10
Morris, Gouverneur, 115
Morris, Robert, 102
Morse, Samuel F. B., 203
Mount, William Sidney, 256
Mu, 5

NAGASAKI, 297
Napoleon I, 31, 139, 144, 145–7, 151–2, 154, 291
Napoleon III, 274
Nariño, Antonio de, 99
Nashville, Battle of, 284
National Republicans, 182, 186
Nat Turner insurrection, 201, 229
Nauvoo, Illinois, 209–10
Naval stores, 42
Naval war with France, 139
Navigation Acts, 42, 71–2, 112
Nebraska, 252, 257–8
Negro slavery, 23, 51, 87, 103, 109, 183, 189–94, 197–201, 248, 249, 250, 256, 257, 261, 262, 264, 268–9, 285, 293–4; condemned by Revolutionary leaders, 106–7; abolitionist attacks upon, 217, 225–9; Southern defense of, 229–30; in Texas, 235; in Kansas and Nebraska, 257–9; abolition of, 226, 274–5, 277, 287. *See* Slave trade, Negroes
Negroes, 21, 33, 48–9, 82, 96, 158, 167, 279, 287, 288, 290, 291, 296
Nevada, 9, 251
New Amsterdam, 29
New Deal, 295
New England, colonial, 51–6
New England Anti-Slavery Society, 227
Newfoundland, 31
"New Freedom," 295
"New Frontier," 295
New Hampshire, early history of, 27–8
New Haven colony, 28
New Harmony community, 223–4
New Immigration, 295
New Jersey, 43; founding of, 29–31
New Jersey Plan, 116
New Mexico, 17, 238, 240, 241, 245
"New Nationalism," 175–7

"New Nationalism" of Theodore Roosevelt, 25
New Netherland, 29–30
New Orleans, 45, 160
Newspapers, 211
Newton, Isaac, 55, 58
New York, 43, 101; early history of, 29–30
New York City, 56, 160, 161, 205, 208, 294, 295
Nicaragua, 25
North Carolina, early history of, 30–1, 50–1
North, Frederick, Lord, 92, 291; American policy of, 75, 76–7, 78, 85–6
North, Simeon, 162
Northmen in America, 6–9
Northwest Ordinance, 107, 109, 259, 292
Nova Scotia, 31
Noyes, John Humphrey, 224
Nueces River, 241, 242
Nullification controversy, 184–5

OAXACA, 10
Oberlin College, 222, 228
Oglethorpe, General James, 44–5
"Old Black Joe," 256
Old Immigrants, 202, 205–7, 247, 252–3, 260, 293
Old Northwest, 109
"Old Three Hundred," the, 234
Old West, 59
Olive Branch Petition, 83
Omnibus Bill, 249
Oneida community, 224–5
Oregon Country, 156, 231, 239; division of, 240, 41
Oregon Trail, 239
"O Susanna," 256
Owen, Robert, 223

PACIFIC NORTHWEST, 231
Paine, Thomas, 87, 105
Painting, 54, 170–1, 203, 217, 256
Pakenham, General Edward, 155
Palmerston, Lord, 274
Palo Alto, Battle of, 244
Paris, Treaty of, 45–7, 63
Parkman, Francis, 255–6
Patagonia, 9
Paterson, William, 116, 117
Pawnee, the, 232
Peace of Paris, 94–5, 109, 112
Pemberton, Israel, 57
Pemberton, General John C., 282
Pendleton, Edmund, 49
Penn, William, 30, 34

Pennsylvania State Society for the Suppression of the Use of Ardent Spirits, 220
Pennsylvania, University of, 58
Pensacola, 68, 95
Perry, Commodore Matthew, 252
Perry, Commodore, Oliver Hazard, 155
Persians, 9
Petersburg, investment of, 283–4, 285
Philadelphia, 56, 160, 205
Philip II, 17, 18
Philipses, the, 57
Phrenology, 220
Pickering, Timothy, 150
Piedmont, the, 32, 101, 102, 196
Pierce, Franklin, 250
Pike, Zebulon, 150
Pilgrims, the, 25–6
Pinckney, Charles, 115
Pinckney, Charles Cotesworth, 115, 119, 120, 130
Pinckney, Thomas, 130
Pinckneys, the, 52
Pinckney's Treaty, 137
Pitt, William, Earl of Chatham, 74, 78
Plummer, William, 178
Plymouth Company, 19–20, 24–6
Poe, Edgar Allan, 202, 203, 215–16, 218, 293
Poinsett, Joel R., 234
Poles in America, 295
Polk, James K., 241–3
Polynesians, 6
Pontiac's War, 68, 70
"Poor white trash," 49, 51, 165, 194, 195–6
Pope, General John, 270
"Popular sovereignty," 257–8, 259
Port Hudson, capture of, 282
Portugal, 17, 64
Powell, Benjamin, 49
Prairie, The, 171
Presbyterians, 66, 169, 195, 211, 230, 239
Price, Colonel Sterling, 244
Primogeniture, abolition of, 103
Princeton, Battle of, 90
Princeton University, 58
Proclamation of 1763, 70
Prohibitionists, 219–20
Proletariat, American, 207–8
Protestants, foreign, welcomed in colonies, 39. *See* Religion, names of sects
Puritans, 37; in New England, 24–9, 54–7
Pyramids, 10

QUADRUPLE ALLIANCE, 179, 180
Quakers, 28, 34, 57; in New Jersey and Pennsylvania, 30
Quartering Acts, 71, 76
Quebec, city of, 45, 65
Quebec Act, 77

RADICAL REPUBLICANS, 268, 269, 277, 278, 284, 285
Radicals, Revolutionary, 101–2, 112, 113, 122
Railroads, 204–5, 263, 267, 281, 287, 293
Raleigh, Sir Walter, 19
Randolphs, the, 131
Rappites, 223
"Raven, The," 215
Regulators, 59
Religion, 168–70, 196, 205, 208–11, 217–218, 252, 290, 291; freedom of, 105–106; First Amendment, and, 106. *See* names of sects
Republicanism of Americans, 98–9
Republican party, 258, 260, 261, 264, 267, 268, 277, 278, 296
Resaca de la Palma, Battle of, 244
"Revolution of 1800," 141, 142
Reynolds, Sir Joshua, 54
Rhett, Robert Barnwell, 248
Rhode Island, 86; founding of, 27–9
Ripley, George, 224
Rice growing, 42, 48, 191
"Rip Van Winkle," 171
Roanoke Island, 19
Rockingham, Marquis of, 74
Romanovs, the, 63
Roman Catholics, 21–4, 37, 39, 105, 106, 206–7, 208, 228, 234, 253, 293
Roosevelt, Franklin D., 295
Roosevelt, Theodore, 295
Roosevelts, the, 30
Rosecrans, General William, 283
Rush, Dr. Benjamin, 108
Russell, Lord John, 267, 268
Russia, 64, 179–80
Russians in America, 295
Rutgers University, 58
Rutledge, John, 78, 115, 119, 120, 130

ST. AUGUSTINE, FLORIDA, 30
St. Brendan, 6
St. Clair, General Arthur, 135
St. Leger, Colonel Barry, 91
St. Mary's, 23
Salem, Massachusetts, 55
Saltonstall family, 52
Samurai, the, 56
Sandys, Sir Edwin, 21
San Ildefonso, Treaty of, 145

San Jacinto, Battle of, 237
San Jacinto, U.S.S., 268
Santa Anna, Antonio López de, 235, 236, 237, 244, 245
Santa Fe Trail, 238
Saratoga, convention of, 91
Savannah, 45, 93
Savannah, the, 161
Scandinavians, 206
Scarlet Letter, The, 214
Schuylers, the, 30
Scrooby, 25
Scotch-Irish in America, 39, 49, 57, 58, 290
Scots in America, 39, 45, 49, 58, 82, 84
Scott, Sir Walter, 195, 211
Scott, General Winfield, 244-5, 250, 270
Sculptors, 216-17, 256
Sedition Act of 1798, 139-40
Separatists, 25-6
Seventh Day Adventists, 209
Seven Years' War, 32, 66, 70
Seward, William, 248, 264, 274, 277, 288
Shakers, 223
Shawnee, the, 91
Shays, Daniel, rebellion of, 113, 114
Sheridan, General Philip, 283-4
Sherman, Roger, 88, 115
Sherman, General William Tecumseh, 283, 284, 285
Shiloh, Battle of, 272
Sidney, Algernon, 89
Simms, William Gilmore, 195
Sioux, the, 232
Six Nations, 11
Slater, Samuel, 162
Slavery As It Is, 228
Slave trade, 17-18, 40-1, 107-8, 200, 248, 249
Slidell, John, 241-2, 268
Smallpox, 15, 35
Smith, Hyrum, 210
Smith, Joseph, 209-10, 221
Social Registers, 105
"Song of Myself," quoted, 254
Sons of the Sires of '76, 253
South, colonial, described, 48-51, 59; Old, 189-201
South Carolina, founding of, 30-1
Spain, and the Americas, 8, 12, 17, 30-32, 34, 45-6, 60, 63, 64, 109, 112, 139, 149, 153; loses Floridas, 44-6; acquires Louisiana, 45-6; American Revolution, 79, 81, 85, 87, 91, 92-3, 95; cedes Louisiana to France, 145-6; loss of empire, 179-180
Spartans, the, 56

"Spoils system," 183
Spotsylvania Courthouse, Battle of, 283
Stamp Act, 67; crisis, 72-5, 81
Stanton, Edwin M., 277
Statute of Religious Liberty, 106, 149
Steuben, Baron von, 104
Story, William Wetmore, 216
Stowe, Harriet Beecher, 256
Stuart, John, Indian superintendent, 83
Suffrage. 26, 27, 101, 167-8, 183, 287, 288, 292
Sugar Act, 71-2, 75
Sugar raising, 159, 191
Sullivan's Island, Battle of, 84
Sumner, Senator Charles, 277
Sumter, Fort, 261
Supreme Court of the United States, 121, 128-9, 141-4, 147, 177, 258-9
Supreme Order of the Star Spangled Banner, 253
Swedes, on the Delaware, 29
Swiss, the, in America, 51, 253
Syphilis, 15, 35

Taney, Roger B., 186, 258-9
Tappan, Arthur, 225
Tappan, Lewis, 225
Tariff protection, 134, 175, 176, 181, 184-5, 190, 260, 267
Taylor, Edward, 53
Taylor, General Zachary, 243, 244, 248-249
Tecumseh, 154
Texas, 147, 150, 179, 239, 240; settlement of, 232-5, 238; revolution in, 234-7; republic of, 236, 237-8; annexed to United States, 241
Thermidorean reaction, 111
Thirteenth Amendment, 287
Thomas, General George H., 264, 272, 284
Thoreau, Henry David, 213-14, 221
Ticknor, George, 212
Ticonderoga, Fort, 84, 85, 90, 91
Tidewater, 32, 48, 59, 101, 102
Titles, hereditary, 103-5
"To a Water Fowl," 171
Tobacco, 20, 23, 41, 42, 48, 159, 191
Tocqueville, Alexis de, 162, 294
Toleration Act of Maryland, 24
Townshend, Charles, 291; American policy of, 75-6
"Trail of Tears," 187
Transcendentalism, 213, 214, 217, 219, 224
Travis, William B., 236
Trent affair, 268

Trenton, Battle of, 90
Tripolitan War, 145
Trollope, Mrs. Frances, 173
Truman, Harry S, 295
Trumbull family, 52
Tryon, Governor William, 59
Tuberculosis, 15
Turnpikes, 161
Twelfth Amendment, 140
Tyler, John, 188, 211, 241

Uncle Tom's Cabin, 256, 257
Underground Railroad, 230, 257
Underhill, Captain John, 54
Union party, 285
Unitarians, 55, 105, 169, 208, 213
United Nations, 298
University of North Carolina, 108
University of Virginia, 149, 172
Utopias, American, 223–5
Utrecht, Treaty of, 31, 32, 44

VALLANDIGHAM, CLEMENT, 280
Valley Forge, 92
Van Buren, Martin, 183, 187–8, 211, 237
Vanderlyn, John, 170
Van Rensselaers, the, 57
Vergennes, Comte de, 92
Vermont, 101
Vesey, Denmark, 200–1
Vicksburg, surrender of, 282
Vikings. *See* Northmen
Vinland, 7, 8
Virginia, planting of, 16, 19–21
Virginia, the, 272–3
Virginia and Kentucky Resolutions, 139–40
Virginia Plan, 116

WALDEN, 214
Walker, William, 251
Waltham, Massachusetts, as manufacturing center, 163
Wampum, 9
"War Democrats," 268, 277, 285
War Hawks, 153
War of 1812, 153–6
War of Independence, 80–95, 101, 291; destruction in, 96
War of Jenkins' Ear, 45
Washington, D.C., made capital, 133
Washington, George, 49, 51, 56, 78, 87, 104, 105, 106, 108, 113, 118, 138, 144, 292; appointed commander in

chief, 83; in War of Independence, 90, 91, 93, 94; rejects crown, 98; and making of Constitution, 115; and ratification of Constitution, 123–4; sketch of, 126–8; Presidency of, 128–37; death of, 137–8
Washington, Mrs. Martha Custis, 126, 198
Washington, the, 161
Washingtons, 70
Watts, John, 37
Wayne, General Anthony, 135
Webster, Daniel, 176, 184–5, 186, 239, 249
Webster-Ashburton Treaty, 240
Weld, Theodore Dwight, 217, 225, 226, 228
Welles, Gideon, 266
West Florida, 146, 147, 155, 156. *See* Floridas
Westminster School, 50
West Virginia, 264
"West, Wild," 252, 294
Whig party, 182, 187–8, 193, 237, 240, 249–50, 253, 258
Whisky Rebellion, 134–5
Whitman, Walt, 216, 247, 253–5, 293; quoted, 254, 288
Whitney, Eli, 159, 162, 164, 203
Wilderness, Battle of the, 283
"Wild Honey Suckle, The," quoted from, 171
Wilkes, Captain Charles, 268
Wilkes, John, 78
Williams, Roger, 27–8
Wilson, James, 115
Wilson, Woodrow, 182, 245
Winthrop, John, 27
Witherspoon, Dr. John, 82
Witchcraft mania, 55
Woman's Rights Convention, 222
Workingmen's party, 219
World War I, 294, 295, 297
World War II, 294, 295, 297, 298

YALE COLLEGE, 53
Yamassee Indians, 12
Yancey, William L., 248
Yankees, 48, 51; in Old Northwest, 158, 159, 166
Yorktown, siege of, 94
"Young America," 247, 250–1
Young, Brigham, 210

ZENO NARRATIVES, 6

A Note about the Author

JOHN R. ALDEN was born in Michigan in 1908, and attended the University of Michigan, where he received his A.B. (1929), M.A. (1930), and Ph.D. (1939). He taught at the University of Nebraska (1945–55), then transferred to Duke University in 1955, where he has been chairman of the Department of History (1957–60), and was appointed, in 1963, James B. Duke Professor of History. He has also taught at the University of Chicago, the University of Michigan, and Columbia University. Among his many academic honors is the Albert J. Beveridge Prize of the American Historical Association (1945) and a Guggenheim Fellowship (1955–6). Mr. Alden was invited to be Commonwealth Fund Lecturer at University College, London, in 1960, and Donald Fleming Lecturer at Louisiana State University in 1961. His published works include *John Stuart and the Southern Colonial Frontier* (1944), *General Gage in America* (1948), *General Charles Lee* (1951), *The American Revolution, 1775–1783* (1954), *The South in the Revolution, 1763–1789* (1957), and *The Rise of the American Republic* (1963). Mr. Alden makes his home, with his wife and daughter, in Durham, North Carolina.

January 1966

A Note on the Type

The text of this book is set in Monticello, a Linotype revival of the original Binny & Ronaldson Roman No. 1, cut by Archibald Binny and cast in 1796 by that Philadelphia type foundry. The face was named Monticello in honor of its use in the monumental fifty-volume *Papers of Thomas Jefferson*, published by Princeton University Press. Monticello is a transitional type design, embodying certain features of Bulmer and Baskerville, but it is a distinguished face in its own right.

The book was composed, printed, and bound by The Haddon Craftsmen, Inc., Scranton, Pennsylvania. The illustrations were printed by Halliday Lithograph Corporation, West Hanover, Massachusetts.